Martin Luther's Theology of Two Kingdoms in Buddhist and Christian Communities

Martin Luther's Theology of Two Kingdoms in Buddhist and Christian Communities

Transforming Contemporary Myanmar Society

Pa Yaw

LEXINGTON BOOKS/FORTRESS ACADEMIC
Lanham • Boulder • New York • London

Published by Lexington Books/Fortress Academic
Lexington Books is an imprint of The Rowman & Littlefield Publishing Group, Inc.
4501 Forbes Boulevard, Suite 200, Lanham, Maryland 20706
www.rowman.com

86-90 Paul Street, London EC2A 4NE, United Kingdom

Copyright © 2024 by The Rowman & Littlefield Publishing Group, Inc.

All rights reserved. No part of this book may be reproduced in any form or by any electronic or mechanical means, including information storage and retrieval systems, without written permission from the publisher, except by a reviewer who may quote passages in a review.

British Library Cataloguing in Publication Information Available

Library of Congress Cataloging-in-Publication Data

Names: Yaw, Pa, 1968– author. Title: Martin Luther's theology of two kingdoms in Buddhist and Christian communities : transforming contemporary Myanmar society / Pa Yaw.
Description: Lanham : Lexington Books/Fortress Academic, [2024] | Includes bibliographical references and index. | Summary: "Martin Luther's Theology of Two Kingdoms in Buddhist and Christian Communities examines the principle of separation through Martin Luther's model of two distinct but interconnected systems between religion and politics in the context of religious communities to give constructive advice and criticism for the health of all human beings"— Provided by publisher.
Identifiers: LCCN 2024004520 (print) | LCCN 2024004521 (ebook) | ISBN 9781978716681 (cloth) | ISBN 9781978716698 (epub)
Subjects: LCSH: Buddhism and politics—Burma. | Christianity and politics—Burma. | Lutheran Church—Burma—Influence. | Two kingdoms (Lutheran theology) | Burma—Religion—Political aspects.
Classification: LCC BL2051 .Y39 2024 (print) | LCC BL2051 (ebook) | DDC 294.3/37209591--dc23/eng/20240217
LC record available at https://lccn.loc.gov/2024004520
LC ebook record available at https://lccn.loc.gov/2024004521

♾️ The paper used in this publication meets the minimum requirements of American National Standard for Information Sciences—Permanence of Paper for Printed Library Materials, ANSI/NISO Z39.48-1992.

Contents

Acknowledgments	vii
Introduction	1
Chapter 1: Persecution of Ethnic and Religious Minorities in Myanmar: Myanmar as an Ethnically and Religiously Pluralistic Society	7
Chapter 2: Martin Luther's Theology of Two Kingdoms as a Tool for Transformation in Myanmar Society: The Intersection of Religion and Politics in Luther's Reform Movement	59
Chapter 3: Dietrich Bonhoeffer's Theology of Political Resistance in Light of Luther's Theology of Two Kingdoms: Historical Context of Dietrich Bonhoeffer	85
Chapter 4: Social and Religious Engagement in Myanmar Society: Engaged Buddhism in Myanmar Society	115
Chapter 5: The Implications of Luther's Theology of Two Kingdoms in Dialogue with Engaged Religious Communities in Myanmar Today: Reinterpretation of the Myanmar Baptist Understanding of Church and State	159
Conclusion	199
List of Abbreviations	209
Bibliography	211
Index	229
About the Author	243

Acknowledgments

This book is the product of my own lived experiences in Myanmar as a person who is religiously, socially, and politically discriminated against and who belongs to religious and ethnic minority groups against whom the ruling elites are practicing systemic persecution. The book's historical studies are guided by my desire to bring about constructive transformation in Myanmar. My academic journey would not have been possible without the ever-abiding guidance of God. I would like to thank all of my teachers and mentors, from my primary education through to the present day. I am grateful to my alma mater, the Myanmar Institute of Theology, where my theological foundation was formed. I am also grateful to Princeton Theological Seminary, where I spent two years from 2008 to 2010 studying European Reformation History under the supervision of Kenneth G. Appold, who also encouraged me to apply for the doctoral program at United Lutheran Seminary.

I am deeply grateful to the faculty and staff of United Lutheran Seminary for my admission with a scholarship throughout my doctoral program. The generous support and warmhearted campus life I found there made my life and study in the United States a wonderful experience. I would like to express my sincere gratitude to my primary advisor, Dr. J. Jayakiran Sebastian, who has made himself accessible to me with a big heart whenever I have needed his help, providing insightful comments and suggestions at every stage of my research project and helping me learn the history of my own country. I would also like to thank Dr. J. Paul Rajashekar, Dr. Katie Day, and Dr. David Grafton for their support during my studies at United Lutheran Seminary. Their immense knowledge and bountiful experience have greatly impacted my academic research and opened my eyes to different perspectives. I would also like to offer special thanks to library director Evan E. Boyd, and acquisitions, cataloging, and systems specialist Ron Townsend, who helped me access resources from other universities and seminaries across the United States, even in the midst of the COVID-19 pandemic.

My heart-felt thanks also go to Dr. Timothy C. Geoffrin, president of Faith, Hope, and Love Global Ministries, not only for financial assistance but also for continuous prayers and support throughout my studies. I also extend my special thanks to the Myanmar Baptist Convention for partial financial assistance for three consecutive years. I am deeply grateful to Anna Biak Tha Mawi, owner of AIDII weaving house in Myanmar, who designed the cover of my book at no cost. Finally, I would like to thank my wife, Betty Cangkom Tang, who has been standing behind me, taking care of our loving son, Nathan Yaw, during my absence from home. Without her incredible encouragement and understanding, it would have been impossible for me to complete my studies and write this book.

Introduction

Religion is a set of beliefs and practices that help form our relationship to God and to our fellow human beings. It includes meditation, prayer, ritual, sermon, sacrifice, dance, music, liturgy, way of life, and morality. The essence of religion is a commitment to nonviolence and a peaceful coexistence in a pluralistic world. However, throughout history, efforts to protect religion, the nation, and the foundations of belief have often made violence a part of religion. As a result, religion becomes a source of both violence and nonviolence. In other words, in its institutional capacity almost every religion has engaged in or condoned some form of violence. Therefore, because religion sometimes becomes a source of violence there is a need to respect other religious traditions.

Myanmar was visible on the international stage after the National League for Democracy led by Aung San Suu Kyi had a landslide win over the military-backed ruling party, the Union Solidarity and Development Party, in the general elections held on November 8, 2015. Along with ethnic inclusiveness in the process of democratic reform, people expected that the new government would be able to revise the 2008 military-backed constitution, implement national reconciliation to bring an end to decades of ethnic conflict, bring economic development and a better educational system, and develop the living conditions of the whole people collectively. Unfortunately, the ultranationalist Buddhist movement known as Ma Ba Tha,[1] founded in June 2013 in the name of protecting race and religion and backed by the military generals, was mounting attacks against people of other faiths for fear of losing the Buddhist identity in a diverse society. Meanwhile, ethnonationalism among ethnic minority groups was also on the rise, as they began expressing their critical feelings of political repression, religious oppression, and ethnic discrimination in the public sphere.

The people's expectation of a better future turned into an ugly darkness, especially when an armed Muslim extremist group called Harakat al-Yaqin (later renamed Arakan Rohingya Salvation Army [ARSA]) carried out an attack on the Border Guard Police in Maungdaw Township, Rakhine State, on October 9, 2016, followed by the Myanmar military's overreaction in carrying out security operations. The fighting between the Myanmar military and ARSA resulted in the flight of tens of thousands of Bengali Muslims to Bangladesh and displaced many people inside the country. All blame was placed on Aung San Suu Kyi's shoulders for not criticizing the Myanmar military's overreaction in carrying out security operations. The government's attempt to revise the 2008 constitution, including to reduce the representation of the unelected military appointees in the parliament, was unsuccessful. The Nationwide Ceasefire Agreement, the first step for national reconciliation in the roundtable talk needed to bring an end to decades of ethnic conflict, was also inactive. Racist, jingoistic, nativist, and supremacist theologies from both the ultranationalist Buddhist group and the hardline ethnic minority groups were filling the air. People's expectations for the NLD government to transform the country are as high as a miracle, while the civilian government does not technically have much power under a hybrid constitution. In this context of political and religious conflicts, how does the church define its relationship to the state? To address this problem, I propose that we turn to the writings of Martin Luther that explicitly speak about the relationship between church and state.[2] I am aware that the two contexts are vastly different, but a constructive reflection on Luther's Theology of Two Kingdoms can help us understand the responsibility of the Christian disciple toward the secular state.

The first chapter introduces Myanmar as one of the world's largest diverse societies, which is multireligious, multiethnic, multilinguistic, and multicultural. Unfortunately, instead of celebrating the diversity of the country, the ultranationalist Buddhists have perpetrated numerous incidents of intimidation, harassment, and violence against ethnic and religious minority groups. Religious persecution and ethnic discrimination, including Islamophobia, are all too common in Myanmar. I will show Myanmar as a religiously and ethnically diverse society where people of living faiths should live in mutual recognition, acceptance, understanding, and belonging to each other.

The second chapter carefully examines Luther's Theology of Two Kingdoms within the historical context in which he sought to find the most appropriate way in a highly conflictual situation. I will look closely at English translations of certain primary writings of Luther on the role of Christians in society during the sixteenth-century European Reformation. An analysis of Luther's primary writings in sixteenth-century Germany and the present-day Lutheran interpretation of Luther's Theology of Two Kingdoms will guide this book's exploration of the problem of religion and politics and by extension, the problem of religion and politics in the Myanmar context. I will explore how Luther developed his two-kingdoms theology to throw light on religion and politics in his confrontation with the Roman Catholic Church and in the radical public movement of the sixteenth-century Reformation period.

Introduction 3

As such, Luther's interpretations of religious and secular authorities, and the role of the state in the reform process, will be carefully examined. I will posit the role of Luther as an intermediary between princes and peasants in his pursuit of a resolution for a highly conflictual situation, although his attempt was unsuccessful, and examine his ethics of resistance against a repressive state that violates God's mandate. I will also investigate secondary sources on how contemporary Lutheran scholars and others interpret Luther's Theology of Two Kingdoms, using a contemporary perspective without departing from Luther's original theology.

Chapter 3 examines Dietrich Bonhoeffer's theology of resistance against the repressive Nazi government in Germany from 1933 to 1945. I will closely look at English translations of certain primary writings of Bonhoeffer on the role of Christians in society. Bonhoeffer became a public figure as an engaged Christian to protect the ethnic and religious minority Jews and others in Germany. Utilizing Luther's Theology of Two Kingdoms as his theological ground, Bonhoeffer wanted the German church to return to a right understanding of the role of Christians in society. Although Bonhoeffer himself did not formulate a comprehensive understanding of the relationship between religion and politics, his views and works challenge a rigid separation between them, and thereby linked them for the well-being of people in society.

The fourth chapter examines social and religious engagement in Myanmar society. Taking the socially engaged Buddhist spirituality of a Vietnamese Buddhist monk, Thich Nhat Hanh, who first coined the term *engaged Buddhism*[3] in the 1960s, and the spirituality of Aung San Suu Kyi, who has been fighting for the liberation of the people of Myanmar from the tyranny of the military regime since 1988, as illustrations for my argument, I will carefully examine the sociopolitical movement for peace and democracy in the country by utilizing both theological and nontheological writings by national and international scholars and critics of Myanmar politics. As such, I will deal with socially engaged Buddhist and Christian communities from 1988 when the people's demonstration for democratization of the country broke out until the present.

One can see the sociopolitical engagement of the Buddhist monks who, after the 1990 elections for the SLORC, broke their promise to hand over power to the winning party, the NLD. I will also examine the Saffron Revolution, which broke out in 2007 because of the denial of basic freedoms as well as economic issues and the declining living standards of those living under the poverty line while the military generals and their cronies lavishly consumed the country's resources. Furthermore, I will look at the Spring Revolution in 2021 after the military coup on February 1, 2021. One will see national and international responses to the military takeover, asking the coup leaders to return power to the legitimate government. I will also explore the rise of engaged interfaith religious movements in Myanmar, in which religious leaders from Buddhism, Christianity, Islam, and Hinduism, including government officials, were actively engaging in many ways to combat religious and ethnic hate speeches. One will see Suu Kyi's tireless efforts to negotiate with the Myanmar military while inviting ethnic minority armed groups to come to the Twenty-First-Century Panglong Conference. Socially engaged religion emphasizes social justice and peace by engaging society nonviolently for the benefit of the community, rather than withdrawing from it.

In chapter 5, I will challenge the traditional Myanmar Baptist understanding of a rigid dichotomy between religion and politics, and the absolute submission of the church to the state, especially in the predominantly Buddhist context of Myanmar, and assess its shortcomings that call for a new understanding of the role of religion and politics in the public sphere. Accordingly, I will attempt to rethink possible modes of Christian engagement in society beyond the church. My argument understands religion and politics as institutions meant to contribute to the well-being of human beings in society. I will also explore the intersection of religion and politics in the public sphere for the betterment of humanity, and challenge supremacist theologies with a strong intention to embrace inclusiveness in our theological journey with God and people of other faiths.

To this end, I will examine both theological and nontheological resources from socially engaged Buddhist and Christian faith communities in the context of Myanmar, such as books, journals, and newspapers written by national and international scholars and critics of Myanmar politics. I will attempt to apply Luther's Theology of Two Kingdoms to the present context in Myanmar, which is religiously and culturally a diverse society. Comparative study of the two contexts will help the reader not just to identify similar theological concerns but also to promote social justice to our neighbors, with special attention to the most vulnerable in society. Juxtaposing and studying two different sets of writings will help find the lacunae in the attitude of Myanmar Christians on the matter of their responsibility as Christian citizens, and to pave new ways to bring transformation in society.

The conclusion of the book is largely confined to both religious and ethnic minorities and majority Burman Buddhists in Myanmar. I strongly believe that this book will open the views of Myanmar Christians and Buddhists to see their prophetic role in society, thereby constructively reflecting on Luther's Theology of Two Kingdoms, which maintains "institutional separation and functional interaction,"[4] or "two distinct but interconnected ways"[5] to address the challenges of the present-day Myanmar context. I hope that my work can offer a dynamic transformation of Myanmar society with the combined efforts of socially engaged Buddhist and Christian communities

Introduction   5

in the country. It will certainly give special attention to the Burmese scholars, pastors, and lay people who are committed to become socially engaged people of faith in the country in their pursuit of the democratic society that the nation is trying to build.

NOTES

1. Nyi Nyi Kyaw, "Islamophobia in Buddhist Myanmar: The 969 Movement and Anti-Muslim Violence," in *Islam and the State in Myanmar: Muslim-Buddhist Relations and the Politics of Belonging*, ed. Melissa Crouch (Oxford: Oxford University Press, 2016), 202. The Burmese acronym *Ma Ba Tha* stands for "Amyo, Batha, Thatana," that is to say, Bama-lumyo or Burman ethnicity, Bama-batha-saka or Burmese language, and Bama Thatana of Buddha-Bata or Buddhism.

2. Augustine, *The City of God against the Pagans*, trans. R. W. Dyson (Cambridge: Cambridge University Press, 1998), 609. As an Augustine monk Luther draws his two kingdoms theology from Augustine's two cities but with a different concern. Augustine's concern is the relationship between heavenly city and earthly city, while Luther's concern is the relationship between religion and politics or church and state. In other words, Augustine's concern is cosmological or eschatological, whereas Luther's concern is protological and historical. Augustine argues that the heavenly city shaped by the love of God, and the earthly city shaped by love of self will interact together until the final judgment. More specifically, the earthly city is shaped by the *libido dominandi* (the will to dominate) while the heavenly city is shaped by *caritas* (love of God and neighbor). The relationship between the two cities and their respective peace is not contrary or contradictory. Earthly peace is incomplete and imperfect. It is frail and fleeting. Moreover, it usually comes only at the tip of the sword or the point of the gun. In contrast, heavenly peace is complete and perfect. However, it is not a present reality. It is an eschatological hope. Therefore, in this life, Christians know no other peace than this earthly peace even as they hope and long for heavenly peace. Both Augustine and Luther have similar concern that Christians not only can, but must, participate in civic life.

3. Thich Nhat Hanh, *Vietnam: Lotus in a Sea of Fire* (New York: Hill and Wang, 1967), 42.

4. John R. Stumme, "A Lutheran Tradition on Church and State," in *Church and State: Lutheran Perspectives*, ed. John R. Stumme and Robert W. Tuttle (Minneapolis: Fortress Press, 2003), 51.

5. Evangelical Lutheran Church in America, *A Social Message on Government and Civic Engagement in the United States: Discipleship in a Democracy*, June 24, 2020, 4.

Chapter One

Persecution of Ethnic and Religious Minorities in Myanmar

Myanmar as an Ethnically and Religiously Pluralistic Society

For many Westerners, Myanmar has become a neglected country. They can quickly point out India, China, and Thailand on a map, but have no idea of the location of Myanmar. Myanmar, "shaped like a diamond with a tail,"[1] is in the middle of these countries. From Myanmar, China is to the north, India and Bangladesh to the west, and Thailand and Laos to the east. Myanmar, also well known as the "golden land or the land of pagodas,"[2] is one of the most diverse societies in the world in terms of religion, culture, and ethnicity, comprising 135 different ethnic groups. Major ethnic groups include the Kachin, Kayah, many Karens, Chin, Mon, Burman, Rakhine, and Shan. The majority of Burman, Mon, Rakhine, and Shan are Buddhists, while Kachin, Chin, and Karen are primarily Christians. According to 2014 statistics, Myanmar is comprised of "87.3 percent Buddhists, 6.2 percent Christians, 4.9 percent Muslims, 0.5 percent Hindus, 0.8 practitioners of indigenous religions, 0.2 percent other religions, and 0.1 percent no religion."[3] Examining the introduction of four major world religions into Myanmar will show how they have inevitably shaped the country into an ethnically and religiously pluralistic nation.

When tracing the early history of the arrival of Buddhism in Myanmar, the influence of India is indisputable. The introduction of Buddhism into Myanmar is related to the Buddhist missionary movement of Indian Emperor Asoka (c. 270–c. 230 BCE)[4] of the Mauryan dynasty as well as a great patron of Buddhism. During the reign of Emperor Asoka, a number of overseas missionaries were sent to other countries to propagate Buddhism, and two of the missionaries, Sona and Uttara, arrived in Suvannabhumi-Thaton on the southeastern coast of Myanmar and established Buddhism in that area.[5] Evidence of the early presence of Buddhism in Myanmar is also provided by archaeological excavations found at Beikthano near Taungdwingyi in central Myanmar. Tun Aung Chain, a Myanmar historian, writes:

> Beikthano, which is dated by radiocarbon tests to the 1st to 5th century A.D., yields various evidences on the presence of Buddhism. Among the most significant of these are two brick structures: one, a large cylindrical brick structure which functioned as a stupa; another a rectangular brick structure with eight cell-like rooms which functioned as a monastery. These brick structures help to establish a relationship between Beikthano and the archaeological site of Nagarjunakonda in southern India where a number of Buddhist sects flourished but in which the Theravada tradition predominated.[6]

The next development of Buddhism in Myanmar began with King Anawrahta who founded the kingdom of Pagan in 1044 CE. When Anawrahta came to the throne several forms of religion coexisted in Pagan. It is believed that both Mahayana and Theravada Buddhism were also practiced among the Burman at the time Anawrahta became king. There was also the prevalence of heretics known as Aris during the reign of Anawrahta. It is unknown whether they were disgraced Buddhists or indigenous priests. Charles Eliot, who studied Hinduism and Buddhism in Asia, described the character of Aris, stating, "They [Aris priests] wore black robes, let their hair grow, worshipped serpents, hung up in their temples the heads of animals that had been sacrificed, and once a year they assisted the king to immolate a victim to the *Nats* on a mountain top. They claimed power to expiate all sins, even parricide. They lived in convents but were not celibate."[7] Donald E. Smith, professor emeritus of political science at the University of Pennsylvania, whose work also focuses on religion and politics in Myanmar, describes the Aris as "a lawless group of monks who probably followed a corrupted form of Mahayana Buddhism."[8] Although Anawrahta tried to abolish the Aris, he could not uproot them all. It was Shin Arahan, a Mon Theravada Buddhist monk from Thaton, who urged Anawrahta to adopt Theravada Buddhism to be the state religion among the Burman in his kingdom, probably between 1054 and 1057. Maung Htin Aung, a Burman historian, stated the reasons why the Burman could easily baptize into the Buddhist faith, saying, "Buddhism became the official religion of the Burmese, not only because the principles of Buddhism fitted in with the existing pattern of Burmese society. The emphasis given to the individual in Buddhism, its insistence on the equality of all men and women, and its implied criticism of the caste system of the Hindus were doctrines which the average Burmese could appreciate and understand at once."[9]

Persecution of Ethnic and Religious Minorities in Myanmar 9

According to Aung's statement, there was and is no discrimination in the Burman Buddhist society based on gender and social orientations. However, another Burman historian, Thant Myint-U, suggests something quite different: "Until British rule, education for the vast majority would remain firmly male and monastic,"[10] indicating that there was and is no equality between men and women in terms of education, and Burmese women are missing from leadership positions in religious, political, and economic life. Furthermore, Aung's argument suggests the superiority of Buddhism to Hinduism because of the latter's caste system and discrimination based on social orientation. In other words, Aung's statement indicates that there was and is no social discrimination or caste system in the Burman Buddhist society. Contrary to his argument, social discrimination in the Burman Buddhist society was discussed by an American Baptist missionary, Henry Park Cochrane, in 1904. Cochrane asserted that there were five classes of outcasts in the Burman Buddhist society, namely: former pagoda-slaves and their descendants, grave diggers, lepers, beggars, and the deformed or maimed.[11] Cochrane argued that instead of lifting up the lives of the excluded and disadvantaged in society, the common Burman Buddhists regarded them as a class under a curse whose terrible sins of a former existence had brought this great calamity upon them,[12] adding, "Their touch was considered contaminating."[13] Furthermore, common Burmese proverbs such as, "The sun never rises when a hen crows, it only rises when the rooster crows," "If a woman is bent on mischief, she can destroy a country," "Things not to be trusted are a thief, the bough of a tree, a ruler, and a woman," testify to the inferiority of women to men in society.[14] In traditional Burman history, the Burman people feared their king and therefore followed the religion of their king. As Father Gaetano Mantegazza, a Roman Catholic missionary who came to Myanmar in 1772, stated, "The [Burman] people regarded the king as something to be feared like fire or the devil."[15] Therefore, there is no doubt that the people followed the religion of their king as the king played a key role in both religion and politics.

The story of Buddhism becoming the state religion in the Pagan dynasty implies that Shin Arahan, coming to Pagan from Thaton had a meeting with Anawrahta and knew that the prevalent creed was inadequate. Therefore, they looked upon Thaton and Ceylon (now Sri Lanka) as religious centers. Thus, Anawrahta broke up the communities of Aris and then sent an envoy to Manohari, king of Pegu, and asked for a copy of the Tripitaka and relics. He received a contemptuous reply, indicating that he was not to be trusted with such sacred objects. In indignation, Anawrahta collected an army, marched against the Mon—probably between 1054 and 1057 CE—and carried off to Pagan all the Mon monks, thirty thousand captives, and thirty-two white elephants laden with relics and Scripture.[16] The Mon craftsmen, artisans, artists, architects, goldsmiths, and wood carvers captured at Thaton taught

10   *Chapter One*

the Burman their skills and arts. It is believed that Mon monks and scholars taught the Burman the Pali language and the Buddhist Scripture, and the Burman soon became scholars themselves. In this way, Anawrahta and Shin Arahan propagated Theravada Buddhism throughout the kingdom, and Pagan rapidly became a great center of religion and culture. King Anawrahta's zeal in promoting Theravada Buddhism led him to attempt the suppression of Nat worship,[17] especially the thirty-six leading *Nats* which were worshipped all over his kingdom. He pulled down Nat shrines at Pagan, but he found that the indigenous cult was too firmly established to uproot completely. Therefore, he finally made a compromise by adding Thagyamin, the guardian god of Buddhism, to the list of spirits (making thirty-seven), and declared him the new head of the Pantheon. The images of the thirty-seven Nats were set up on the platform of the Shwezigon pagoda in Pagan to show their subservience to the Buddha. Anawrahta's reasoning was, "Let the people come to worship their old gods and then they will discover the truth of the new faith of Buddhism."[18]

The introduction of Hinduism into Myanmar is also related to India. During the first century of the Common Era the overland trade route between China and India passed through the borders of Myanmar, and merchant ships from India, Sri Lanka, and even farther west converged on its ports. Myanmar, therefore, became the gateway of Southeast Asia. The Indian merchants brought with them not only precious cargoes but also religion from their homeland, and within a few decades, Indian cultural traditions had remolded native society, native thought, and native arts and crafts.[19] In the Myanmar chronicles, the first Burman kingdom was at Tagaung in northern Myanmar and it was founded by the Hindu Sakiyan prince Abhiraja in the ninth century BCE.[20] There is no doubt that the Indian cultural traditions had influenced Myanmar to a certain extent. Indian names began to be applied to Myanmar localities. For instance, the two merchants, Tapussa and Bhallika, who were the first to salute the Buddha after his enlightenment, are said to have come from Ukkala.[21] Prome (now Pyi) was called Srikshetra, and the name Irrawaddy represents Iravati (the modern Ravi). The ancient town of Sravasti or Savatthi appears in the three forms: Tharawaddy, Tharawaw, and Thawutti.[22]

The ancient city of Pyu,[23] located in central Myanmar, was called Beikthano. It is said that the name Beikthano is a Myanmar version of the name of the Hindu god, Vishnu.[24] There are different styles of pagoda, and the ones at Srikshetra are similar to the ones built in India during the Gupta dynasty, which ruled from the fourth to the sixth centuries CE.[25] Therefore, it is reasonable to believe that there was the worship of Vishnu there in the time of Pyu. It is also said that the capital of Myanmar, Yangon, was once called Dagon, which was the name of a Hindu temple. In 1755, Aung Zeyya, who was called Alaungpaya (the future Buddha) by some of his followers, attacked the Mons, who retreated to the cities of Pegu and Syriam, and took the old pagoda town of Dagon and renamed it "Yangon," meaning "the end of enemy,"[26] with the expectation of ending the civil war. The name "Rangoon" is the English corruption of the Burmese name "Yangon."[27] All these facts prove that the coming of Hinduism into Myanmar is very ancient. It came to the land of Myanmar before the Pagan dynasty. However, when Anawrahta adopted Theravada Buddhism throughout his kingdom, it seems that Hinduism remained in the background for ages. It was revitalized by the Indian immigrants to Myanmar in the early fourteenth century.

Regarding the introduction of Islam into Myanmar, Bertil Lintner, a Swedish journalist who studies Myanmar politics, asserts that the first Muslims who came to Myanmar were actually Moorish, Arab, and Persian traders who arrived by sea in the ninth century.[28] This view is supported by Moshe Yegar, a historian of Islam in Southeast Asia, in his book *The Muslims of Burma: A Study of a Minority Group*, who wrote, "Muslim seamen first reached Burma in the ninth century."[29] Yegar continued, "The first Muslim trade colonies were established in Pegu by the ninth century and . . . Arab merchant vessels often visited there. Not all of them came by choice; some of them, because of shipwreck, were forced to seek refuge on shore, and remained to settle there."[30] As the years went by the number of Muslims increased relatively in Myanmar partly as a result of the growing descendants from mixed marriages with local women and partly because of the continued arrival of Muslim traders. However, it was after the British conquest of the Burman kingdom in 1885 that massive numbers of Indian Muslim immigrants were brought into Myanmar to work as "general laborers, clerks, teachers, engineers, workers for railroads, and . . . in river shipping, post offices, rice mills, mines, oil fields, and banks."[31] Yegar highlighted the crucial roles of the Indian immigrants in the new British colony when he wrote, "No new public, army, police, or civilian administrative office was established in Burma without Indians."[32] Ni Ni Myint, a Burman historian, also describes the roles of Indians in the British colony, stating, "India provided the British with the human and the material resources for an advance into other regions of Asia."[33] As Myanmar became an open door to any immigrants under the British colonial scheme, the Indians formed the biggest body of settlers and immigrants.

The history of Myanmar Christianity began in the middle of the sixteenth century with the arrival of Father Peter Bonfer in Myanmar in 1554 as the first official Roman Catholic missionary. After the Roman Catholic mission came the Protestant mission, which had great success, especially with the ministry of the American Baptist missionaries Adoniram Judson and his wife, Ann, who came to Myanmar in 1813 and were followed by fellow American

Baptist missionaries. Although the Christian mission first came among the Burman Buddhists in mainland areas, it was not as successful as expected for a number of reasons: first, when the Christian mission came into Myanmar, Buddhism was firmly established in the lives of Buddhists, and it was extremely difficult to uproot and replace it with the Christian faith. Judson lamented this extreme difficulty, saying, "To gain a convert from Buddhism is like pulling the tooth of a tiger."[34] Second, religion and nationalism are inseparable and blended together in Burman Buddhist thought. As Paul Ambrose Bigandet, a Roman Catholic missionary to Myanmar, said, "Religion cannot be forsaken without giving up nationality, and the fact of embracing the religion of another people is equivalent to becoming a member of the same social or political body."[35] Third, the Burman Buddhists saw Christianity as a totally foreign religion, and conversion to Christianity was considered as an insult to Buddhism in general and to the royal household in particular.

Therefore, the initial attempt of the missionaries to convert the Burman Buddhists in mainland areas was not as successful as expected, resulting in the shift of mission among three main ethnic minority groups—Karen, Kachin, and Chin—with great visible success as they responded to Christianity. A combination of indigenous religion and the Gospel, social change, and political context among ethnic minority groups played key roles in their conversion to Christianity collectively in Myanmar. Their acceptance of Christianity also protected them from Burmanization, or Burman assimilation. These ethnic minority groups could have been assimilated into the religion, culture, and language of the majority Burman if they refused to convert to Christianity from their indigenous religion. It is notable to consider that the native religion of the ethnic minority people is more open to Christianity than to Buddhism in the context of Myanmar, and it prepared the way for the Gospel so that many Christian missionaries were pleased to find what they saw as "pro-Christians."[36]

THE CONFLICT BETWEEN ETHNIC MINORITIES AND MAJORITY

Myanmar is known for the world's longest civil war, from the time of independence in 1948 until the present day, primarily caused by the failure of the successive governments to follow the spirit of the Panglong Agreement that General Aung San, the father of independence, signed with the leaders of ethnic minorities on February 12, 1947. The Panglong Agreement sought to build the Union of Myanmar based on three principles: political equality, self-determination, and voluntary association.[37] The successive governments of U Nu (1948–1962), Ne Win (1962–1988), Than Shwe (1992–2011), and

Thein Sein (2011–2016) failed to follow the Panglong Agreement, both in the constitution and in practical implementation, resulting in the emergence of ethnic minority armed groups, who have been fighting for liberation from the Burman majority's domination and for selfhood in their own homeland. In 1988, in a country with no external enemies, the Myanmar military spent some 40 percent of the national budget on fighting against the ethnic minority armed groups, neglecting education, health care, and socioeconomic growth.[38]

Before the British invasion, the ethnic minority groups were ruled by their own local chiefs: the Chins were ruled by *Khua-bawi* (the village headman), the Kachins by *Duwa* (chief), and the Shans by *Sawbwa* (prince). The British had occupied these colonies in different years and applied different administrative systems depending on the context. The "Burma Proper" or "Ministerial Burma,"[39] that is, the Burman kingdom, fell under the British rule after the third Anglo-Burmese war in 1885. Following their conquest of the ethnic minorities, the British drafted separate constitutions for each ethnic group, ratifying the "Chin Hills Regulation" in 1896,[40] the "Kachin Hill Tribes Regulation" in 1895,[41] the "1919 Act of Federated Shan States" in 1920,[42] and the "1935 Burma Act" in 1937,[43] using what scholars call "divide and rule"[44] tactics. Maung Htin Aung also described British "divide and rule" tactics, saying, "The British separated the hill regions of the Chins and the Kachins, and the plateau of the Shans entirely from the rest of Burma, with the excuse that the people in those regions were politically not advanced and must be kept under the direct control of the British governor of Burma."[45] Under the Burma Act of 1935, "Excluded Areas" that were not within "Ministerial Burma" included the Shan States, the northern Kachin country, the Chin Hills, and the territory of the Hills Karen.[46]

Local and international scholars and historians who are interested in the true history of modern Myanmar agree that the Union of Myanmar was founded by Aung San and leaders of ethnic minority groups, particularly Burman, Chin, Kachin, and Shan in February of 1947, at Panglong Conference, Shan State. Before the 1947 Panglong Conference, the ethnic minority groups had their own rulers, suggesting that the Burman had not ruled over them before independence from the British in 1948. Highlighting the independent rule of each state before the 1947 Panglong Conference, Chin scholar Lian H. Sakhong also says:

> The Union of Burma was founded at Panglong on February 12, 1947, by four former British colonies, namely Chinram, Kachin Hills, Federated Shan States and Burma proper. The British had occupied these four colonies separately as independent countries in different periods of time and had applied different administrative systems in accordance with the different constitutions that the colonial power had promulgated for them.[47]

14 *Chapter One*

With the expectation that independence from the British was on the horizon, it was General Aung San who reached out to the leaders of non-Burman ethnic groups in the hill areas to form the Union of Myanmar. In his speech, entitled "Defense of Burma, January 30, 1945,"[48] General Aung San spelled out the rights of the ethnic minorities in the future independent state of Myanmar, stating:

> Ethnic minorities must be given proper place in the state. They must have their political, economic and social rights definitely defined and accorded. They must have employment. They must have their own rights of representation. They must have equal opportunity in all aspects of the state. There must be no racial or religious discrimination. Any books, songs, signs, symbols, names, etc., which foster such ideas must be officially banned. And we must carry out special uplift work amongst them so that they can be brought to our level and finally to the world level together with us.[49]

According to Aung San, there should be no oppression or discrimination based on racial or religious identity. During January 17–23, 1946, the All-Burma Congress of AFPFL was held in the precincts of Shwedagon Pagoda, Yangon. The Congress was presided over by Aung San, and Than Tun acted as general secretary. The Congress was attended by thirteen hundred delegates from all over the country. Representatives of Shan, Chin, and Kachin were also present. Resolution No. 6 of the All-Burma Congress of AFPFL states, "The All-Burma Congress welcomes the awakening political consciousness of the national minorities in Burma and recognizes the following principles in order to foster a better understanding between the Burmese majority and national minorities which together form the Burmese nation: (a) Freedom of worship; (b) cultural autonomy; (c) equality of opportunities; (d) voluntary union, with the right of self-determination."[50]

In addition to this principle, the Congress heartily welcomed the Myanmar Muslims for their change of attitude, as they no longer considered themselves a foreign element in the country and were taking an active part in the struggle for national freedom.[51] During the preparation for independence from the British, the Delegation from Myanmar, led by Aung San, and the British prime minister, Clement Attlee, met on January 13, 1947, in London. Aung San's fellow delegates included Thakin Mya, U Ba Pe, Thakin Ba Sein, U Saw, U Tin Tut, U Kyaw Nyein, U Aung Than, Thakin Chit, U Ba Yin, and U Shwe Baw. In his opening speech, Aung San stated, "When we speak of Burma, we envisage a Burma united and free. There are no insurmountable obstacles in the way of achieving that unity. If all the racial groups in the country are offered full freedom, and if they but meet together and work together without outside interference, they will unite. We strongly hold the view that religion or race should not deprive any citizen in Burma of his right to freedom."[52]

On the question of the unification of the "Frontier Areas" and "Ministerial Burma," Aung San said that he thought it would be a comparatively simple matter, but the frontier peoples, if they desired it, would be granted autonomy.[53] Reaching out to the ethnic minorities before the Panglong Conference, Aung San gave a Radio Address on February 4, 1947, stating, "The matter of Hills Regions is a matter of Hills peoples. They will get equal rights if they want them. . . . If you will follow my leadership with trust and confidence, Burma will gain independence within one year. I do not break promises."[54] In another speech to the nation before his departure for the Panglong Conference, Aung San stated, "The affairs of the Frontier Areas are the concern of the peoples of those areas. If they declare that they want the same rights and privileges as ourselves, they will get them."[55] He restated this political scheme at the conference by saying that the Hill people will be allowed to administer their own areas in any way they please and the Burmese will not interfere in the internal administration.[56] Aung San also offered a place to immigrants from India and China who desired to make Myanmar their permanent home. To Indian immigrants in particular, he said, "We have no axe to grind, we nurture no feeling of racial bitterness and ill-will."[57] Aung San stated in a speech at a gathering of leaders from the "Frontier Areas" on February 11, 1947, at Panglong Conference in the Shan State:

> There is this thing called "racism" that I want to talk about. In the past we shouted slogans: Our race, our religion, our language! Those slogans are obsolete now. . . . We have in Burma many indigenous peoples: the Karens, the Kachins, the Shans, the Chins, the Burmese and others. . . . We can preserve our own customs and cultures, enjoy our own freedom of belief, but on the broader national life we must be together. We must be one. . . . The supreme commander of the armed forces may be a Karen, a Kachin or a Chin, but we must all rise and fight under his leadership.[58]

Aung San's nationalism was a secular nationalism, which did not depend on a particular religion or ethnicity. In other words, he did not conceive of nationalism in terms of religion and race. He absolutely favored national unity based on equal treatment regardless of race and religion. On June 16, 1947, at the Constituent Assembly, Aung San moved for a directive resolution adopting the seven basic principles of the new constitution. Article 4 of the constitution states, "The constitution shall guarantee justice, social, economic and political; liberty of thought, expression, belief, faith, worship, vocation, association and action; equal status, of opportunity and before the law; subject only to law, public order and morality."[59] Article 5 states, "The

16 *Chapter One*

constitution shall provide adequate protection for the rights of the minority peoples."[60] Aung San assured the Frontier Leaders of equal treatment at Panglong, saying, "If Burma receives one kyat [Myanmar currency], you will also get one kyat."[61] Maung Maung said, "The constitution was drafted. The Shans, the Chins, the Kachins, the Kayah, the Karens, all decided to join the Union, largely because of the trust they reposed in Aung San."[62] Aung San spoke on July 13, 1947, at a public meeting in Yangon, after which he and his six cabinet colleagues were assassinated by U Saw on July 19, 1947, at the Executive Council meeting.[63] He said:

> We must build and preserve unity between the peoples in our country, people of the frontier areas and other peoples, and in unity we must work together to build our national strength. Without unity and strength, independence will be meaningless; the nation will be weak and vulnerable. . . . There is a lot of nation-building to be done, and you must remember that you are building over the ashes of the war. Everywhere, we are behind, and to catch up with the world we must work far harder than other nations. . . . You must work hard, be united and disciplined. Otherwise, the fruits of freedom will not be yours to enjoy. . . . You must mend your ways and build a new Burma together. These words I leave with you today.[64]

Indeed, both the British and Aung San are responsible for the subjugation of ethnic minority groups into the majority Burman's domination since the British agreed to grant Myanmar independence only if the ethnic minority groups agreed to participate in a federal union.[65] Meanwhile, it was Aung San who reached out to the leaders of non-Burman ethnic groups in the hill areas and organized the multiethnic conference at Panglong, which was attended by Kachin, Chin, and Shan representatives, although Karen attended only as observers.[66] The conference came up with a political structure, which both the Burmans and non-Burman ethnic leaders accepted. The concept of a federal union was agreed upon, and ethnic states were to be created with autonomy over their own internal affairs. The constitution stipulated that the new Union of Myanmar would be ruled by a democratically elected parliament and prime minister. The ethnic states would have their own state councils, whose members would also serve in the union government's parliament, and the head of each state would automatically be a member of the union government's cabinet.[67] In short, the ethnic minorities joined the Union of Myanmar as equal partners with the majority Burman.

Unfortunately, people's great expectation for a bright future upon the achievement of national independence from the British in 1948 never came true. After the unexpected assassination of Aung San and his cabinet colleagues, the successive governments of Myanmar failed to follow the spirit of the Panglong Agreement both in the constitution and practical implementation. Regarding the assassination of Aung San by U Saw, Aung San Suu Kyi wrote:

> U Saw had not been able to accept the rise to national leadership of Aung San, whom he described as a mere boy. Shortly before Saw had joined the Burmese delegation to London, he had been shot at and wounded in the eye by men dressed in khaki. There were those who surmised that Saw had believed Aung San's PVO members to have been responsible for the shooting and therefore sought revenge. But the trial would reveal that the instructions had been for the whole Executive Council to be destroyed, and it seemed that Saw had sought the death of Aung San and his colleagues in the strange belief that once they had been removed, he would become the head of the Burmese government.[68]

If Aung San had not been assassinated and had led the country after independence from the British, the reality of Myanmar might not be the same as we see today. His vision of the country as a secular state, one that would embrace religious pluralism and ethnic diversity as strength, could have been realized. Unfortunately, when Chan Htun took office as the attorney general of the Myanmar government on January 4, 1948, he reversed the Panglong Agreement of the 1947 constitution, intentionally removing the provisions for separate constitutions for ethnic minority groups. Consequently, the 1947 constitution created a unitary state system in which the power lies in the hands of the central government held by the majority Burman until the present day.

After the general elections held on November 8, 2015, Myanmar's political transformation became very important when the National League for Democracy (NLD) led by Aung San Suu Kyi, the daughter of Aung San, had a landslide win over the ruling military-backed Union Solidarity and Development Party (USDP). During her political campaigns Suu Kyi promised her supporters that she and her government would focus on national reconciliation if her party won the 2015 general elections. To keep this promise, she persuaded ethnic minority leaders to attend the Twenty-First-Century Panglong Conference held from August 31 to September 3, 2016, which has once again drawn international attention to Myanmar's struggle for national reconciliation in a new chapter of the country. It has also reawakened the original spirit of the 1947 Panglong Agreement that the father of Suu Kyi, and the leaders of ethnic minorities made together to build a federation in the country. Suu Kyi, with the full acknowledgment of ethnic persecution and discrimination under the majority Burman's domination, continues her father's dream to find ways to end decades of ethnic conflict and to form a federation within Myanmar.

18   *Chapter One*

Indeed, the ethnic minority groups faced difficult decisions in the 2015 elections. Their own experiences under the repressive military regime, held by the majority Burman, in a unitary political system taught them to support their own ethnic political parties, which might succeed in their own states. However, this decision might not lead to the overthrow of the military regime. The best decision was to support the National League for Democracy, because the NLD had a greater chance of winning nationwide elections. Therefore, some ethnic minority people voted in support of the NLD, with a great expectation for change, while others supported their own ethnic political parties. I believe that the ethnic minorities who supported the NLD made a wise decision to dethrone the military leaders, who had ruined the country for decades for their own benefit.

In her opening remarks at the Twenty-First-Century Panglong Conference, Suu Kyi declared that the country's ongoing armed conflicts could be solved by "working together with mutual understanding and trust among Myanmar's political parties to seek solutions for lasting internal peace."[69] She added, "Peace cannot be achieved without the involvement of all groups in society. . . . No peace process can succeed without the support of the people. Peace is not something that leaders impose. It is not something that can be achieved only in a conference room. It requires the active involvement and support of all peoples."[70] Highlighting the crucial point of national reconciliation in Myanmar to end civil war, UN Secretary General Ban Ki-Moon also addressed delegates at the conference on August 31, 2016, stating, "The long civil war has cost numerous lives and robbed successive generations of their dignity, tranquility and normalcy. It is now clear that there can be no military solution to your differences."[71] In his opening remarks at the conference Myanmar military chief Senior General Min Aung Hlaing also stressed the need for "national unification"[72] and warned away from "ethnocentric dialogue,"[73] while ethnic minority delegates pushed for a greater autonomy. Underlining the role of the *Tatmadaw* (military) in peace processes, he said, "The *Tatmadaw* has contributed to the nation-building process through the ages and will continue to its utmost ability to achieve peace. . . . We should have a dialogue for peace without being too ethnocentric."[74] The question here is what his means of negotiation with ethnic armed groups will be? Will it be political dialogue? Or will the military use war and violence as an instrument for imposing tyranny?

During the conference, ethnic minority leaders openly criticized the majority Burmans in general, and more specifically the military generals who held the most power in the country under the 2008 constitution. At the conference, the head of the United Nationalities Federal Council and vice chair of the Kachin Independent Organization, Maj. General N' Ban La, said in his speech, "The reason why we, the non-Bamar ethnic people, are staging armed revolution is because of the loss of the Panglong Agreement's guarantees for democracy, national equality and self-determination of ethnic people. . . . The Federal Union that the armed ethnic organisations are demanding is not a request to secede from the Union but is a call for equality for the ethnic nationalities."[75] It was the first time in the history of modern Myanmar that the ethnic minority groups were able to air grievances that had rarely been heard in public after the military regime took power in 1962. For more than half a century they did not have the opportunity to express their critical feelings of political oppression and ethnic discrimination in public. Now, they could freely share their experiences of political inequality and ethnic discrimination under the successive military regimes over about half a century and ask for equal representation between the Burman majority and the non-Burman ethnic minority groups.

Under Union Solidarity and Development Party government, eight ethnic armed groups signed a Nationwide Ceasefire Agreement with the military on October 15, 2015, for political dialogue. On October 15, 2016, during the one-year anniversary celebration of the Nationwide Ceasefire Agreement, held at Myanmar International Convention Center (MICC), Nay Pyi Taw (the administrative capital of Myanmar), Suu Kyi encouraged the government, the military and ethnic armed groups to strive for a new method of peacebuilding, saying:

> All people around the country are watching our peacemaking process. They have high hopes for peace. They are watching what the government, the military and ethnic armed groups are doing, but I would like to say . . . don't underestimate our people. What I want to tell the government, the military and ethnic armed organizations is to compete [to see] who is more open-minded, who is more tolerant and who places more value on the future rather than the past.[76]

According to this statement, she was actually calling both the military and ethnic armed groups to opt for a third-way nonviolent negotiation for political dialogue.[77] Nevertheless, she was still reluctant to officially and publicly condemn the military's constant attacks on the ethnic armed groups, even as she calls the ethnic armed groups to sign the Nationwide Ceasefire Agreement. During her political campaign, she often confidently stated that no political party except her party, the NLD, condemned the military regime for ruining and spoiling the country for decades. In one of her rallies in Mandalay she accused the military of incompetence, saying, "The government has always said the Burmese still don't deserve democracy. They [the military] have ruled the country for nearly fifty years, and if they have failed to educate people about the norms of democracy during that period, they'd better not keep governing the country now."[78] People of ethnic minority groups might see

20 *Chapter One*

different politics in Suu Kyi before and after the 2015 election, since she did not condemn the military for its continued attacks on ethnic armed groups. However, I view Suu Kyi's politics at this point as "pragmatic pacifism,"[79] in the words of American scholar and peace activist, David Cortright. Instead of war, he prefers a third way nonviolent resistance, which is not surrender or appeasement, but the fight for justice through nonviolent action.[80] He, therefore, prefers more contemporary terms such as *peace-making* and *peacebuilding through political dialogue*.[81] While Suu Kyi has "power," her power is not "tough" but rather "soft," and she needs the people, notably the ethnic armed groups, to give a sign of their support for her leadership.

The commander in chief of the Myanmar military, Min Aung Hlaing, also called for more ethnic armed groups to sign the ceasefire agreement, and said, "If we accept democracy, we need to break down the obsession with armed struggle which is against democracy. To do so, we already have the NCA which has been ratified by many forces."[82] On November 2, 2016, Suu Kyi commented on ethnic conflict in Myanmar in the presence of the Burmese people during her visit to Japan, saying, "There are some ethnic armed groups who do not want to stop fighting. We are still trying to find the root causes of this fighting."[83] Suu Kyi's position on the Myanmar military is also ambiguous for ethnic minority groups. During her political campaigns, she condemned the military when she wanted to persuade people to support her party. Yet, she at other times referred to the military "my father's army," and all soldiers as "his sons,"[84] suggesting that they are part of her family. Surely, this is not a surprise, since she has to pacify both the military and the ethnic armed groups as an engaged Buddhist.

It was a misguided attempt by the military to use their authority to shore up privilege for themselves. As a member of an ethnic minority group, I perceive the attacks of the military as intimidation tactics, meant to pressure ethnic armed groups to sign the NCA. It did not produce mutual trust between them, but rather mistrust and enmity, which was a stumbling block in the peace process that the government was trying to achieve. The NLD government has been questioning the reservation of 25 percent of seats for the military officials in the parliament, which is not in accord with democratic principles. The government still cannot change the 2008 military constitution into a purely democratic constitution. The military remains autonomous and takes orders not from the government but only from its commander in chief. The changing of the constitution could result in the removal of the military officials from the parliament. As they still see their representation in the parliament as necessary and are unwilling to be removed, the military officials want to perform the role of the military in the country.

After years of reconciliation work by Suu Kyi and former US president Barack Obama, the United States finally lifted its economic sanctions on the former pariah state of Myanmar on October 7, 2016.[85] Suu Kyi might believe that the lifting of US economic sanctions on Myanmar will encourage the military officials to return to the barracks. Even before the lifting of economic sanctions, the Obama administration was interested in showing its generosity to the Myanmar military by providing non-lethal assistance and education.[86] The US economic sanctions on Myanmar had definitely missed the mark since it did not affect the military officials, but rather the ordinary citizens. The military generals and their cronies were lavishly and foolishly wasting the country's resources, while ordinary people were living far below the poverty line.

It is inspiring to see that civilians, young and old, are airing their grievances and calling not only the Myanmar military to stop its offensives but also some ethnic armed groups to stop abducting government officials and killing innocent civilians.[87] Some ethnic armed groups who had not signed the NCA yet, were waiting for a complete restoration of the original Panglong Agreement of 1947 in the Twenty-First-Century Panglong Agreement; that is, political equality, self-determination, and voluntary union. They are particularly concerned with chapter 10, article 201 of the 1948 constitution, which states, "Every state shall have the right to secede from the Union."[88] However, the Burman majority are suspicious of a complete restoration of the original Panglong Agreement and are particularly distrustful of the very sections of the agreement that are most important to the ethnic minority groups. They worry that a complete restoration of the original spirit of the Panglong Agreement could lead the ethnic minority groups to secede from the Union in the future, which would result in a national disintegration of the Union. Because of this disagreement, hostilities between the Myanmar military and the ethnic armed groups will likely continue.

PERSECUTION OF CHRISTIAN RELIGIOUS MINORITIES

Monarchical Period (1500–1885)

In traditional Burman Buddhist thought, there is an interdependence between the king and the sangha (a Buddhist order of monks or Buddhistic brotherhood).[89] The king is the protector of Buddhism, responsible for its preservation and purification, intervening in monastic affairs to settle disputes when needed. At the same time, the king must follow Buddhist ethical principles when ruling the country. Theoretically the monk serves as a mediator between the state and the people, to protect the people from arbitrary or oppressive kings and reconcile the people to the king's rule. Melford E. Spiro, an

22   *Chapter One*

American anthropologist, outlines the reciprocal relationship between the state and the sangha, writing:

> The relationship between state and *Sangha* during the monarchy was a reciprocal one. By supporting the monks, on the one hand, while on the other hand, purifying the order of dissident elements, the government minimized the potentiality of the *Sangha* for becoming an independent nucleus of political power. On the monastic side, by upholding the legitimacy of the government, while at the same time protecting the people from tyranny, the *Sangha* exercised a restraining influence on excessive abuse of power by the government.[90]

Into this context, the first Christian mission came to Myanmar in the middle of the sixteenth century. Roman Catholic missionaries were the first Christian missionaries in Myanmar. The rich natural resources of Myanmar, with her cereals, precious stones, and useful woods, attracted several Portuguese merchants and settlers from Malaya—the British controlled states now known as Peninsular Malaysia. Therefore, there is no doubt that the Catholic activity in Myanmar began with the advent of the Portuguese merchants and settlers. They were later joined by their own Catholic priests and chaplains. Although they came to Myanmar primarily for economic purposes, they also engaged in mission activities. Most of the earliest Roman Catholic missionaries practiced a "courtship" model in their mission strategy, seeking to convert the Burman king first with the expectation that people might follow. According to the history of Catholic Church in Myanmar, Nat Shin Naung, king of Taungoo, converted to Christianity through his intimate relationship with Philip de Britto, a Portuguese sailor, serving as a gunner under the king of Arakan (now Rakhine).[91] Instead of handing over Syriam (now Thanlyin), across the Yangon River to king of Arakan, de Britto established a small kingdom for himself there and ruled as an independent monarch for thirteen years until Annaukpet Lun-Min, King Maha Dhamma Raja of Ava (ancient royal city of the Burman kingdom at Kyaukse District now in Mandalay region) defeated and executed both de Britto and Naung in 1613. After the killing of Naung and de Britto, King Maha Dhamma Raja restricted foreigners to six villages between the Chindwin and Mu Rivers in Upper Myanmar. Any Europeans captured by the Myanmar kings were settled in that colony, which was called *Bayingyi Ywa*.

In contrast to King Maha Dhamma Raja's persecution of Christians in Myanmar, the letter of Father Calchi from Ava, to the Barnabite Society in Italy, dated March 11, 1723, conveys the Burman king's wishes for trade with Europe, friendship with all Christian princes, and the help of foreign technicians, saying:

As soon as I got to Ava, I presented myself to His Majesty, who was very pleased with our expedition, and after giving us permission to build churches and preach he gave us some money to build a church, and the next day I began the plan. The king desires to correspond with, to have amity and commerce with, all Christian princes, and especially with the Pope; he desires to have other missionaries and painters, weavers, glass makers, astronomers, mechanics, and geographers to instruct his subjects. He kept one of us in the Royal City and sent the other to present his sentiments of respectful homage to the Pope. He sends the pope a small present of rubies, sapphires and other stones in a box of red taffeta.[92]

During the early period of the Roman Catholic mission in Myanmar, religious persecution was not universal, but sporadic. There was often a good relationship between the Burman kings and the Christian missionaries. The Christian missionaries received permission from the Burman kings to preach freely and to build churches and schools. However, they sometimes suffered imprisonment and even death, caused both by civil wars and the three Anglo-Burmese wars. After the Roman Catholic mission, the Baptist mission came with Adoniram Judson and his wife, Ann. In order to win converts from Buddhism in mainland Myanmar, Judson and other American Baptist missionaries used various means, such as distributing literature, person-to-person evangelism, and building schools and hospitals. Alexander McLeish, who was a convener of the Survey Committee of the National Christian Council of India, Burma and Ceylon (now Sri Lanka), in his book *Christian Progress in Burma*, remarked upon Judson's contextual approach to mission in Myanmar and stated, "Judson wore a yellow gown in Rangoon to indicate that he was a religious teacher, as were the yellow-gowned Buddhist priests. In Ava, where he went next, he wore a white gown, not desiring to be mistaken for a Buddhist."[93] Although Judson worked very hard among the Buddhists in mainland Myanmar, he did not gain many converts from Buddhism. The first Burman convert to Christianity, a single man of thirty-five years named Maung Naw, was baptized on June 27, 1819, six years after the Judsons began their work in Yangon, well after he had changed his mission strategy.

One of the reasons for the failure of Judson's early mission was that living in his mission compound, which was far away from the main road and from any neighbors, Judson and his family were isolated from outside contact. In 1819, Judson began to change his mission strategy and built a small *zayat* in the Burman fashion near a public road where pedestrians and visitors could stop and hear the Gospel.[94] The zayat then became a stage where he could converse with visitors. He held his first worship service at the zayat on Sunday, April 4, 1819. His congregation consisted of about fifteen adults, whom he had invited from the neighborhood, as well as some uninvited

24   *Chapter One*

children. Judson's mission strategy was person-to-person evangelism in an informal setting in which the listeners could feel free to express their own views. In other words, the approach was neither a monologue nor a pulpit model, but rather a dialogue or a round-table model.

Unfortunately, Judson found that some visitors were afraid of public ostracism and the anger of the royal family. This included Judson's own teacher, Aung Min, who was threatened in public for teaching Judson the Burmese language. The last visitor to the zayat was Shwe Ngong, who was baptized on the night of July 18, 1820. Judson also baptized two other Burman converts, Maung Pye and Maung Tha Hla, on November 7, 1819, meeting with them at dusk in order to avoid public resentment. Through his own experiences, Judson saw the fear of persecution as the primary obstacle to gaining converts, rather than stubborn loyalty to Buddhism. Judson, therefore, with mixed feelings, concluded that all missionary attempts would be out of the question unless the king guaranteed protection from molestation to interested Burmans.[95] He concluded that it would be prudent to gain the king's favor for his mission work in Myanmar, since no local government would persecute the Christian missionaries if the king treated them with complacency or tolerance. The missionaries and new converts, therefore, decided to travel to the royal city to ask King Bagyidaw for religious toleration. Judson and James Colman of Boston, who arrived in Yangon in September 1818, accompanied by Maung Naw, the first Burman convert during Judson's mission, left Yangon on December 21, 1819, carrying with them a six-volume edition of the Bible in Burmese, intended as a gift for the king. They arrived at Ava in January 1820 and went to the palace, asking for religious toleration. But the king replied, "Why do you ask for such permission? Have not the Portuguese, the English, the Moslems [*sic*] and people of all other religions, full liberty to practice and worship according to their own customs? In regard to the objects of your petition, His Majesty gives no order. In regard to your sacred books, His Majesty has no use for them. Take them away."[96] The king wanted to inquire whether Colman had medical expertise. He therefore ordered Judson and Colman to proceed to the residence of his physician who happened to be the Portuguese priest, and asked the physician to see whether Colman could be helpful to the king's health. After learning that Colman had no magic art that would protect the king's health and make him live forever, they were dismissed. They returned to Yangon on February 18, 1820, after having been away for two months. A few days later, Judson called his three converts, Maung Naw, Maung Tha Hla, and Maung Byay, and told them he had failed to gain them religious freedom and that from now on Burman Christians could expect persecution.

Judson's second trip to Ava was as a translator for Jonathan Price, a medical missionary, in 1822. Upon the invitation of the king, they arrived in Ava on September 27, 1822. Although the center of interest was Price, King Bagyidaw unexpectedly asked Judson a number of questions on the spot: "And you in black, what are you? A medical man too?" When Judson responded to the king that he was a teacher of religion, the king asked Judson whether any persons had become Christians. Trying to evade the question, Judson replied, "Not here." The king persisted, asking "Are there any in Rangoon?" Judson replied, "There are a few." The king's next question was, "Are they foreigners?" Judson, thinking the consequence his answer might have for his church, carefully replied, "There are some foreigners and some Burmese."

The king also asked Judson cultural questions, as he and Price appeared before him dressed in European costume with the exception of their shoes, which they took off outside. The king wanted to know whether Christian Burmans still dressed like Buddhist Burmans. Judson assured the king that Christian Burmans were real Burmans and that they wore *longyis* (sheets of cloth) and *aingyis* (shirts).[97] The king's main concern was whether the new converts were still Burmans or if their conversion to Christianity had denationalized them. On returning to Yangon, Judson, therefore, took a very sensible attitude on the matter of religious conversion in his mission approach to make sure that being a Christian did not make a person love his own country less. Judson encouraged the new converts still to retain the costume of the country, and to respect national traditions which were common to the people.

During the monarchical period, the most liberal Burman king was King Mindon, who reigned from 1853 to 1878 in Mandalay, Upper Myanmar. In 1863 there was a political uprising in the palace, which caused Prince Thonze, one of King Mindon's sons, to flee to Yangon as a fugitive. In Yangon, he met with Anglican missionary John Ebenezer Marks and was very much impressed by his work at St. John's College Boys School. After reconciliation with his father, Prince Thonze returned to Mandalay and told his father about Marks and his mission school. Upon the invitation of the king, Marks visited the royal city in 1863. King Mindon not only warmly welcomed Marks but also provided funds for a new school just outside the palace walls in 1869, which was attended by the nine sons of King Mindon and those of his ministers, including Thibaw, the last Burman king. King Mindon was tolerant to people of other faiths. Myint-U remarked upon the open-mindedness of King Mindon to people of other faiths and said, "King Mindon also patronized the Islamic community in Mandalay, building a mosque and even a guest house at Mecca for the convenience of Burmese Muslim pilgrims."[98]

As a whole, during the monarchical period Christians were tolerated to some extent. However, this religious tolerance was meant only for Christian foreigners, not for the native Burman Christians, as stated in Judson's record, written on June 14, 1821: "When the emperor and others in government said

26   *Chapter One*

that all might believe and worship as they please, the toleration extended
merely to foreigner resident in the empire, and by no means to native
Burmans, who, being slaves of the emperor, would not be allowed, with
impunity, to renounce the religion of their master."[99] This strong role for
the state in relation to religion is crucial to understand the current situation
for Christians in Myanmar, and questions of church and state and religion
and politics.

Colonial Rule (1885–1948)

The British colonization of Myanmar began with the first Anglo-Burmese
war in 1824–1826, which resulted in the annexation of some parts of Lower
Myanmar under British control. The whole of Lower Myanmar fell under
British rule after the third Anglo-Burmese war in 1885. King Thibaw and
his family were exiled to India. During the colonial period, the Protestant
Churches (such as Baptist, Anglican, Methodist, and Presbyterian) became
firmly established in Myanmar. Donald E. Smith, professor emeritus of political science at the University of Pennsylvania who studies Myanmar politics,
in his book *Religion and Politics in Burma* writes that the British maintained
the principle of religious neutrality, interpreted as strict noninterference by
the government in religious matters.[100] Smith quotes Lieutenant General
Albert Fytche, who said, "The English government, while tolerating every
form of religion, will not appoint spiritual heads, or enforce the canons of
any religious sect by the secular arm, and schisms have crept in since the
establishment of our rule, which threatens to disorganize the ecclesiastical
structure."[101]

However, the principle of noninterference of course was interference
and preference for Christians in effect. The impact of British rule caused
Buddhism to seriously decline. In practice, the British government did not
promote Buddhism. Instead, they destroyed the Buddhist principle of interdependence between religion and politics. Joseph Silverstein, who studies
Myanmar politics, aptly recorded the impact of the British colonization in
Burma (Myanmar), saying, "The coming of the British destroyed the traditional pattern of authority. The British encouragement and protection of
minorities at the expense of the dominant Burmans, plus large-scale immigration of Indians as laborers and financiers gave rise to a new problem. The
removal of the local chieftains and the deterioration of Buddhist order were
two of the main causes for the breakdown of traditional society in Burma."[102]

Before the British conquest, Buddhist monasteries were the centers of
secular and religious education in Burman Buddhist society. However, when
the Christian missionary education was introduced, the mission schools over-
took the monasteries, particularly in the cities. The mission schools charged

admission fees, and children who could not afford to go to the new mission schools in the cities studied at monasteries. Western education styles were introduced in mission school curriculum, in which students, regardless of religion, were required to memorize the Ten Commandments. As a result, the Buddhist children knew more about the Ten Commandments of the Christian Scriptures than their own Five Precepts of Buddhism. Aung criticizes the Christian missionary education system, saying, "The centuries-old custom of the pupil showing respect to the teacher and the happy-pupil relationship disappeared from Burmese society. The missionaries' show of favoritism to a handful of Christians in their classes resulted in resentment against the teachers on the part of non-Christian pupils."[103] Aung's argument may be true to a certain extent. However, it is worth noting the work the missionaries did for the native people, especially in the areas of education, medicine, and other social services. The mission schools accepted all students regardless of religion or gender, which the Buddhist monastic education had failed to do.

Under the traditional Burman kings, the royal city was located in the heartland of the country away from contact with the outside world. It thus became both the political and religious centers of the country. The specific location of the capital, therefore, was determined both on the basis of religion and astrology. Under British rule, the capital was moved from Mandalay to Yangon, close to the sea, which was not only the center of the British administration, but also the hub of trade and finance. For Burman Buddhists, Mandalay remains the center of religious and spiritual life. Unlike the previous Burman capital, Yangon was populated predominantly by immigrants and its activities were secular. The unity of politics and religion—the interdependence between king and monk, in which the king protected Buddhism and monks prayed for the long reign of the king—was disrupted during the British colonial period. As a consequence, political monks emerged as a resistance movement against the British rule.

It is an undeniable fact that there was less consciousness among Christians of their minority position during the British colonial period, which lasted from 1885 to 1948. At that time, the Christian churches enjoyed some status and prestige because of the identification of Christianity with the West and modernization. Christians were particularly active in building schools and hospitals. However, there has been more Christian self-consciousness about their minority position in subsequent regimes when encouragement was given to a Buddhist resurgence as part of the effort to establish a Myanmar national identity.

28 *Chapter One*

Democratic Government (1948–1962)

After independence, when U Nu became prime minister in 1948, Myanmar became in many ways the acknowledged center of the Buddhist world. U Nu encouraged religion in his personal attitudes and in the politics of the country. Buddhism was deeply rooted in his expressions and actions. Many Buddhists even looked upon him as a "Bodhisattva" or "future Buddha."[104] U Nu held the Sixth Great Buddhist Council in Yangon, from May 1954 to May 1956, which was attended by 2,478 monks from Myanmar and 144 monks from Sri Lanka, Thailand, Laos, and Cambodia. The Mahayana Buddhists from China and Japan also sent their representatives. The significance of the council is the state promotion of Buddhism after its decline during sixty years of the British rule. Yet the abuse of religion for political ends had been clearly addressed in the 1947 constitution. Article 21, section 4, states, "The abuse of religion for political purpose is forbidden, and any act which is intended or is likely to promote feelings of hatred, enmity, or discord between racial or religious communities or sects is contrary to this constitution and may be made punishable by law."[105]

However, under U Nu this constitution became a dead constitution. He mixed religion and politics in state affairs for his own political gain. At the close of the Sixth Great Buddhist Council, U Nu proposed Buddhism to be the state religion. He argued that as prime minister, he was responsible for advancing the welfare of the people not only in this earthly existence, but also in endless future existence by pointing the way to Nirvana.[106] Several Asian leaders agreed to U Nu's proposal of Buddhism as the state religion at the council. Makoto Nagai of Japan declared to the government, "Your country has now escaped from the bondage of a foreign nation and has attained complete independence. Accordingly, you are now holding this Great Buddhist Council."[107] Similarly, Dudley Senanayake of Sri Lanka, also spoke of "the resurgence of Asia free from the yoke of foreign bondage, awake once more after centuries of servile slumber."[108] The Buddhists swore to give peace to the world by propagating the teaching of Buddhism, and they claimed Buddhism as the only religion capable of creating the peaceful world that Christianity had failed to create throughout its long history.[109]

After the council, the Buddhists expanded their mission work. Monks were sent out in the hill regions for the propagation of the Buddhist faith. New Buddhist monasteries and missionary schools were built in different parts of Myanmar among the ethnic minority groups. The Ministry of Religious Affairs, formed in 1950, played an important role in the state religion program. U Nu formed the State Religious Advisory Commission, consisting of eighteen Buddhist monks and seventeen Buddhist laymen. The decision was made to present the state religion proposal throughout the country by the commission before the end of 1960. Therefore, the commission went to every part of the country to consult with the leaders of both Buddhist and non-Buddhist religious associations. The commission had two principal objectives: first, to survey the opinions from individuals and organizations; second, to interview religious leaders personally.[110] The commission met with 300 Buddhists, 44 Christians of various denominations, 33 Muslims, 33 Hindus and 6 practitioners of indigenous religion.[111] A great demonstration against the state religion proposal took place in Myitkyina, Kachin State. About five thousand demonstrators from Christian and indigenous religious communities protested against the State Religion Commission at the train station. As a result, the train turned back to Yangon. A few days after this event, the commission had completed its tour throughout the country. After submitting the report to the government, U Nu reassured the religious minorities that the adoption of Buddhism as the state religion would not damage their citizenship rights or religious freedom. In October 1960, the Burmese Baptist Convention, representing two hundred fifty thousand Baptists in Myanmar, issued a statement saying that they feared that Christians would lose their fundamental rights if the Union of Myanmar officially adopted Buddhism as the religion of the state.[112] The Myanmar Council of Churches (Baptist, Anglican, and Methodist) also strongly opposed the state religion proposal, making a firm statement in May, 1960, stating, "If Buddhism becomes the state religion, the government will have to take adequate measures to safeguard the fundamental rights of the non-Buddhists."[113] U Nu declared in response, "I am not a man of violence, and therefore I cannot match the threat to kill anyone or let anyone's blood, but I am determined to bring in state religion, even if I have to die in the attempt."[114] The Roman Catholic Church kept silent about the state religion proposal, and as a result U Nu referred to the Catholics as a "model church in Burma."[115]

The Kachins and Chins, who are predominantly Christians, understood this state religion proposal as an attempt to assimilate them into the majority Burman religion of Buddhism. Not only in Kachin state, but also in Chin state, people demonstrated against the state religion proposal. In December 1960, the Chin Affairs Council, consisting of all members of Parliament representing the Chin people, adopted a resolution that opposed the government's proposal to make Buddhism the state religion.[116] The statement promoting Buddhism as the state religion was officially published in the press on August 1, 1961. The amended section 21.1 of the Myanmar Constitution reads, "Buddhism, being the religion professed by the great majority of the citizens of the Union, shall be the state religion. The recognition extended to Islam, Christianity, Hinduism, and Animism in a new sub-section; 21(5) provided that the Union government would render financial aid amounting to

30 *Chapter One*

a minimum of .5 percent of its annual current expenditure for matters connected with religion."[117]

However, promoting Buddhism as the state religion did not eradicate the existence of other religions; instead, it made them stronger. Those who opposed the state religion proposal based their argument on five points:[118]

1. It was against modern democratic principles.
2. It would create two classes of citizenship.
3. It was contrary to Aung San's convictions.
4. It was being forcibly imposed on the ethnic minorities.
5. It would disrupt national unity.

The National Religious Minorities Alliance was set up at the beginning of 1961 to oppose U Nu's state religion proposal. It included Christian, Muslim, indigenous, and even Buddhist representatives, mostly from the Shan and Kachin States.[119] They made a resolution to share powers equally between the minority states and the Burman majority areas, which would both guarantee self-government for each nationality and prevent the monopolization of all political and economic power by the center in Yangon.[120] U Nu agreed to meet with the leaders of the National Religious Minorities Alliance, and finally in mid-February 1962, a federal seminar was held in Yangon where the ethnic minority leaders put their resolution. However, on March 2, 1962, on the eve of U Nu's scheduled speech to respond to the Federal Movement, Burma's defense chief, General Ne Win, seized power for a different plan. His troops arrested U Nu at his residence at 2:00 a.m., along with other members of the government. Zahre Lian, minister for the affairs of the minority Chin people, was also arrested and taken to the army headquarters at 3:00 a.m.; he was sent back home six hours later. While at the army headquarters, Zahre Lian met with Ne Win, who told him, "Federalism is impossible. It will destroy the Union."[121] Brigadier General Aung Gyi, the main spokesman for the Revolutionary Council, explicitly stated, "We name economic, religious and political crises with the issue of federalism as the most important for the coup."[122]

U Nu's government mixed religion and politics for his political purposes, abolishing Aung San's secular state. U Nu attempted to develop a homogenous national identity by assimilating other religions and cultures into Buddhism. There is no doubt that the ultra-nationalist Buddhists agreed with the state religion program. The state religion issue created new tensions between Buddhists and non-Buddhist ethnic minorities. The sudden consequence was the emergence of the Kachin Independence Army (KIA), who are still fighting for religious freedom and self-identity in their own land today.

Persecution of Ethnic and Religious Minorities in Myanmar 31

It is clear that under his government, U Nu used religion as a steppingstone for his political gain.

Socialist Government (1962–1988)

On March 2, 1962, General Ne Win seized state power and militarized the country. He had full confidence that the rich natural resources in Myanmar and their technological ability would be enough to develop the country to be one of the richest countries in Southeast Asia. However, his plan backfired, and under his leadership Myanmar became one of the poorest countries in the world. In attempting to find the most Burmese form of socialism, Ne Win and his colleagues shut the country off from the outside world so that no outsider could disturb them while they lavishly and foolishly consumed the country's resources and impoverished the country for their own gain at the expense of the people. The socialist government believed that they were obligated, on the one hand, to eliminate religious attitudes and practices, which were obstacles to the building of a modern socialist society, and, on the other hand, to promote spiritual values, which would encourage progress. Ne Win abolished U Nu's State religion proposal, including the Buddha Sasana Council three weeks after the coup. The State Religion Promotion Act, which was in effect in October 1961, had provided for the closing of all government offices and schools on Buddhist Sabbath days and on Sundays. The socialist government believed that this system broke up the continuity of the work week and greatly affected the output of work since the Buddhist Sabbath days fall irregularly on any day of the week. Four days after the takeover, the military regime ordered the abolition of this system. The State Religion Promotion Act affirmed that the Burmese Broadcasting Service would broadcast Buddhist sermons on all Buddhist Sabbath days. The new government reduced the number of the Buddhist sermons by Buddhist monks to be broadcasted only on special occasions such as religious festivals.

Burmese socialism, which began on April 30, 1962, broke away from parliamentary democracy. In 1962 the government ordered the Buddhist monks to register, and when a great number of monks refused and tried to take their case to the people, the government responded with the creation of three basic laws: the exclusion of clergy from direct participation in politics as either voters or officeholders, the restriction of religious activities, and the banishment of clergymen of all religious organizations from political participation.[123] In order to meet his political ends, Ne Win and his government also nationalized Christian institutions like schools, hospitals, and training colleges from 1963 to 1966. They all came under state control. The church felt that the government dealt more harshly with them than with other religious institutions. One of the American Baptist missionaries to Myanmar,

32　　　　　　　　　　　　　　　*Chapter One*

Herman G. Tegenfeldt, recorded the nationalization of Christian schools and hospitals, stating:

> Of the approximately 850 private schools in Burma, 129 of the finest were taken over on April 1, 1965. The majority of these were Christian institutions, Protestant and Roman Catholic, some with long and outstanding histories. In each case, with no previous warning, a military officer appeared at the school and announced its nationalization, including all the assets of the institutions. Twenty-four Baptist schools were among those nationalized in 1965. In 1966 the remaining schools were similarly absorbed into the state school system, thus the bringing to an end of the contribution to Burma of Christian and other privately operated primary, middle and high schools. . . . In similar fashion the largest private hospitals in Burma were nationalized in July 1965. These included one Baptist, one Seventh-day Adventist, and one Roman Catholic. The assets of these institutions were taken over by the state, and their staff members were absorbed into government service. Smaller hospitals were not so affected at that time, but when missionaries were expelled from Burma in 1966, several of these hospitals were forced to close.[124]

Not only foreign missionaries, but nearly all foreigners were expelled from Myanmar in the 1960s. The socialist government restricted the entry of foreigners and the exit of Burmese, except those specially approved. Foreign missionaries who left were not permitted to return. Internal travel was also greatly restricted. Ne Win virtually cut the country off from the rest of the world, and Myanmar entered into a period of isolation from the outside world. Under Ne Win's military government, Myanmar became isolationist and filled with xenophobia. In the mid-1960s, Ne Win abolished even teaching English or using it as a medium of instruction in public schools as he linked the English language with the British colonial rule and thought that true nationalists should speak only in Burmese. University students who believed the government's propaganda mocked their fellow students who used English in their conversations. However, the government's propaganda did not last long as teaching English in public schools was reinstated after 1979 as a result of one of Ne Win's daughters, Sandar Win, failing her entrance exam into the British medical school in Europe because of her poor English.[125]

The military regime imposed restrictions on the activities of the church, requiring Christian publications such as magazines, tracts, pamphlets, and Sunday school materials to pass through censorship, and all of them to be written either in Burmese or English, when ethnic minority Christians—Kachin, Chin, and Karen—needed these manuscripts in their own languages. Tegenfeldt describes this difficult situation, writing, "As can well be imagined, having to translate manuscripts from these languages into Burmese or English entails much work, increased time for preparation, and added

Persecution of Ethnic and Religious Minorities in Myanmar 33

expense. Once the application to the government has been made, after a period of three weeks as a minimum and perhaps several months as a maximum one can expect word as to whether or not the government has approved the manuscript."[126] This statement shows Ne Win's attempt not only to oppress the Christian minority but also to eradicate the languages of ethnic minorities completely and replace them with the language of the Burman majority. Furthermore, Ne Win regarded ethnic minority groups with great suspicion, writing in 1979:

> Today you can see that even people of pure blood are being disloyal to the race and the country but being loyal to others. If people of pure blood act this way, we must carefully watch people of mixed blood. Some people are pure blood, pure Burmese heritage and descendants of genuine citizens. Karen, Kachin, and so forth, are of genuine pure blood. But we must consider whether these people are completely for our race, our Burmese people: our country, our Burma.[127]

Ne Win's wicked attempt to absorb the non-Burman peoples (ethnic minority groups) into one common Burman race in culture, belief, ways of living, and language was completely unacceptable to the non-Burman peoples. After the exodus of the Christian missionaries, the government thought that the church would fail in its mission. They expected that the Christian churches would weaken without missionaries. However, they saw the opposite result, as the Christian witness was as strong as ever and in fact it gained confidence as the churches tried to swim by themselves rather than sink.

Military Regime (1988–2015)

After the new military regime came to power in 1988, discrimination, forced labor, extortion, torture, murder, imprisonment, forced conversion, and rape have tragically increased in Myanmar, especially among ethnic minority Christians. The US Commission on International Religious Freedom, in its letter dated July 28, 2000, recommended Myanmar to be designated as a "country of particular concern"[128] under the "United States International Religious Freedom Act of 1998."[129] The Ministry of Foreign Affairs, Yangon, in denying this accusation, countered:

> The U.S. Commission's characterization of Myanmar as a land lacking in religious freedom is a misinterpretation of the highest degree and the Myanmar government completely refutes the allegation. Anyone who has lived and worked in Myanmar or visited the country even as a tourist will be able to attest to the harmony that exists among the diverse religious communities in the country. Even though nearly ninety percent of the population are devout Buddhists, Christians, Muslims, Hindus, and others are free to practice their faith without

34   *Chapter One*

hindrance. It is not uncommon to see pagodas, churches, mosques and temples coexisting peacefully side-by-side in cities and towns across the country. This striking situation so impressed the first United Nations Independent Expert on Human Rights to visit Myanmar that she was moved to place on record that in regard to religious tolerance, Myanmar may be regarded as a model society. Religious tolerance is a recognized hallmark of Myanmar society. The people and government of Myanmar attach great importance to promoting harmony among religions in the country and are proud of their achievement. A Government Ministry solely devoted to religious affairs exists. It works closely with leaders of different religions and strives to ensure that harmony is maintained. Material and financial assistance is provided to religious groups without discrimination to help promote their work. Religious tolerance is a reality in Myanmar. To allege otherwise, as the U.S. Commission on International Religious Freedom does, is to turn a blind eye to reality.[130]

This was not true, and this statement was written only as a show to the international communities. The Ministry of Religious Affairs prohibited Christians from using some Pali words such as *phonn taw gyee* (priest), *dukka* (suffering), *karuna* (compassion), and *anicca* (impermanence), to mention a few, in the publication of their own religious literature. The impact of these vocabulary restrictions is obvious. As a consequence, Christians now produce their own literature for limited circulation within the church and avoid getting into the clutches of the Board of Censorship. They cannot sell their books outside the churches and Christian organizations. This is not the case for Buddhist publications, as everyone has easy access to Buddhist literature in bookstores. As a result, Christian theology has very little presence in public life. Chin Christians in Myanmar used to build crosses on mountaintops of the cities as a symbol of their faith. The military regime forced them to tear down those crosses, and in some places replaced them with Buddhist pagodas and statues of Buddhist monks.[131]

Strict rules were set, and government permission was required for Christian meetings, campaigns, and conferences. In 2003, the State Peace and Development Council denied the Kachin Baptist Convention permission to meet for several months, delaying a convention that normally takes place every three years. When the authorities finally granted the permission, they ordered the convention to be moved, intentionally disrupting the activities of the church.[132] The government denied some Christian churches permission to build and renovate their own church buildings, even when they followed the official procedure, while the military generals themselves increasingly built pagodas and Buddhist monasteries as an act of merit for the remission of sin and to win the support of the Buddhist majority. Some ethnic Christians, therefore, built their churches under a hidden name such as "mission center," "cultural center," and so forth. For instance, Pastors B and C from Thantlang,

Persecution of Ethnic and Religious Minorities in Myanmar 35

Chin State, explained to the Chin Human Rights Organization how hard it was to obtain permission to build the church in their place. In their interview with the Chin Human Rights Organization on March 24, 2012, they state:

> If you want to construct a church building, permission must be obtained from the Ministry of Religious Affairs. You will never get it even if you ask. It is important that an understanding is established with the local authorities, so that the matter does not go any further, beyond the local government level. All of this can only be done through personal understanding and friendship; there is no change in the religious policy in terms of . . . church building.[133]

This is a clear example of the corruption of the local authorities, suggesting that permission could be obtained through kickbacks. Along with the resurgence of the Hill Region Buddhist Mission among ethnic minority Christians, a number of Chin children were enticed to study in Yangon with the promise of free education and other material advantages. Unfortunately, when they came to Yangon, their expectations were never met. In an interview with the Chin Human Rights Organization, former students A.Z. and A.F.A. explained how they fled to Malaysia after staying in the school for three months:

> A.F.A. explained, "*For the first three of four weeks, the teachers were very kind to us. They took us to the cinema, the zoo, the Shwedagon and Sule Pagodas, the national museum, and the ethnic nationalities village. We also got new shirts and trousers, and a new watch. But after that, I felt like I was in prison because they wouldn't let us go out. They forced us to do hard labour to build one new dormitory. We had to dig the construction site, carry bricks, and move heavy planks of wood. The Burmese students were mostly working in the kitchen or flower garden* [A.Z. also said that only the Chin and Naga were required to do the hard labor.] *It was so unfair. We were also forced to memorize and recite Pali [words].*"
>
> A.Z. related "* . . . If we couldn't memorize the Pali properly, or refused to bow down before the Buddha image, he would punish us. He ordered us to do 'stand-up-sit-down' exercises about 3,000 times. He said to us, 'If you are so stubborn and refuse to be Buddhists, you need to exercise like this so that you will be strong when you are in the military training.' Later on, we were so afraid of him that we just did whatever he asked us to do. . . . After two months he asked us, 'Do you regard yourself as a monk?' and we replied 'No, we are Christians.' Then he said, 'Those who want to be a monk, go to that side, and those who do not, move to the other side,' and we were divided into two groups. He said, 'If you don't want to be a monk, you must join the military.'*"[134]

Further, Christians in Myanmar are discriminated against in secular life. For instance, Christian children are not admitted to study at the military engineering and medical colleges, even if they meet the other requirements.

36   *Chapter One*

All adult citizens in Myanmar hold a National Registration Card, which carries information about their ethnic identity and religion. Whenever a person applies for school or job, they are required to submit their National Identity Card. The NIC plays a key role in the final decision process, for better or worse. Underlining the domination of the majority Burmans in Myanmar, Kanbawza Win, a political analyst of Myanmar governments, also criticizes Burmanization policy, saying, "Burma has been undergoing a process of ethnic cleansing for nearly half a century even before the country gained independence from Britain in 1948," adding, "Religious persecution is not new to Burma and currently, it is the Christians on whom the government has now trained its guns."[135]

In public schools, the military regime prescribed the curriculum and stressed Burman culture, history, and religion, excluding the history and culture of ethnic minorities from the curriculum. The regime banned the teaching of all non-Burman ethnic languages and literatures in public schools in the 1990s with the intent to assimilate all ethnic minorities into a homogenous Burman identity. As an act of resistance to the banning order of ethnic minority languages and literatures in public schools, the Christian churches began opening summer language schools where their children could study their own language and literature. With the acknowledgment of discrimination and persecution of ethnic minority Christians in Myanmar, Konrad Raiser, general secretary of the World Council of Churches, visited four Asian countries (Laos, Thailand, Myanmar, and Pakistan) from February 26 to March 9, 2003. His twelve-day visit to the countries assured Christian communities living in a minority situation that they had the support of the worldwide ecumenical family; it included meetings with churches and Christian institutions, leaders of the majority Buddhist and Muslim religions, representatives of civil society, and government officials. In addition to expressing solidarity, the visit helped to strengthen interfaith links and improve the relationship between religion and politics. Myanmar was the third stop on the journey. During his three-day visit to Myanmar (March 3–5), Raiser had an hour-long meeting with the top military generals. Focusing on the main issues of freedom of religion and persecution of ethnic and religious minorities in Myanmar, Raiser said to General Khin Nyunt, Secretary 1 of the military regime, "I would be failing in my task if I did not indicate to you concerns about intentional or involuntary discrimination in certain parts of the country against Christian minorities and ethnic groups. I am raising these concerns not out of any political interest, but concern with the well-being, peace and stability of the whole country."[136]

Stressing his awareness of the strongly Buddhist character of Myanmar and the people, Raiser affirmed the importance of "inter-religious dialogue"[137] in Myanmar. However, lip service has never changed the reality inside the country.

The National League for Democracy (2016–2020)

After the National League for Democracy (NLD), led by Aung San Suu Kyi, had a landslide win over the military-backed ruling party, the Union Solidarity and Development Party (USDP) in the general elections held on November 8, 2015, the situation has changed significantly in Myanmar. Some of the supporters of the NLD were still not confident about the smooth transition of power by the USDP to the NLD even after the result of the elections was out, as people had experienced the military regime's refusal to hand over power to the NLD in the 1990 elections. Amid this anxiety and uncertainty, members of the NLD and their supporters were delighted when the smooth transition took place on March 30, 2016. Out of 629 members of parliament at a national level in both Upper and Lower Houses, 45 are Christians. The NLD also elected Henry Van Thio, who is a Christian, as vice president. This is, indeed, a drastic change in the Myanmar political landscape, especially for Christians to be in the top leadership role. Indeed, under the NLD leadership there are subtle signs of change for freedom of religion for all citizens in the country. Unlike the military regime, the NLD government was trying to protect all religions and thereby celebrated the plurality of diverse religions and cultures. For instance, the government officially banned the leader of the ultra-nationalist Buddhist movement, Wirathu, from delivering public sermons for one year, effective March 10, 2017, due to his religious hate speech.[138] This ban was a first time in the history of modern Myanmar in terms of hate speech against non-Buddhist religions. Along with ethnic inclusiveness in the process of democratic reform, ethnic religious minorities also expected full religious freedom after the 2015 elections in Myanmar.

However, ethnic religious minorities are still patiently enduring religious persecution. The new Buddhist nationalist movement known as Ma Ba Tha, backed by the military generals, is mounting a campaign against people of other faiths for the protection of race and religion in Myanmar, similar to former US president Donald J. Trump, who does not take "diversity as strength but embraces the idea of exclusion to make America great again."[139] In spite of these challenges, the NLD government was working to fight against hate speech and establish justice and equal treatment of all citizens in the country regardless of religious, ethnic, and gender orientations. The reality is that some ultranationalist Buddhist monks and their supporters still take advantage of their majority position. For example, social and news media captured

38   *Chapter One*

the outcry of Christians when U Thuzana, a Buddhist monk, rallied his supporters to build a pagoda on land belonging to St. Mark Anglican Church at Kun Taw Gyi village in southeastern Karen State in April of 2016. This incident shows the lack of commitment the new government has to establishing peace through national reconciliation. Bishop Saw Stylo who is technically representing the church in his interview with *Morning Star News* said:

> Christian leaders don't want to inflame religious and ethnic conflicts in a country where a newly elected democratic government is striving for national reconciliation. The new democratic government that came into power is trying for national reconciliation and ending armed conflict. If we ignite religious dispute while the country is moving forward to a new chapter of the journey, it is likely that we will pass down a bad inheritance to our next generations. We don't want to pass down this kind of inheritance, so we don't respond. We have to forgive each other. We can only see God if we forgive. So, we always have to keep forgiveness with us.[140]

However, Stylo's forgiveness does not necessarily mean that the Buddhist pagoda should stand there forever. He attempted to meet with the monk at his monastery to request that he stop building the pagoda. Unfortunately, U Thuzana was not present. A senior monk told Bishop Stylo that U Thuzana longed to place pagodas where he believed they had existed some two thousand years ago, despite lacking any reasonable arguments or archeological evidence. The senior monk described this as U Thuzana's "dream." Stylo responded, "All the places he has dreamed of are in Christian church compounds. We pray that he doesn't dream anymore of building more pagodas on our Christian properties." Rather than submit fully to this treatment, Stylo called upon the minister of religious affairs to take responsibility to remove the pagoda and said, "If the new government doesn't take action against the illegal constructions, the menace will likely grow as Buddhist organizations are among the most powerful institutions in Myanmar."[141] U Thuzana's plan is more than a dream. He has many places to build pagodas. Specifically, why did he choose the land of the Christian church? His plan is the subjugation of the Christian lands illegitimately without any reasonable justification.

In fact, this is not the first pagoda that U Thuzana had built in the Christian lands. Prior to this, he also instructed the Buddhist community to build a Buddhist stupa in the Baptist church compound of Mi Zine village, Hpa-an township, Karen State. As a result, the Buddhist community began building the stupa on August 21, 2015, without prior notice to the Baptist church of their intention. Karen State government turned the issue over to the Ministry of Religious Affairs since they could not resolve it. Karen State minister for agriculture and livestock, Saw Christopher, told the *Myanmar Times*,

"The Union government should solve this issue immediately. It is big for us because of religious issues. And the Buddhist people should not act like that. They should give respect to people of other religions. Otherwise, the interfaith process cannot be a success."[142] According to historical record, the church has stood there since 1920.

After his meeting with members of the Christian community on September 7, 2015, Minister of Religious Affairs Soe Win promised the Baptist delegation that the government would stop construction of a stupa inside the church compound.[143] The minister of culture and religious affairs, Aung Ko, criticizing extreme Buddhist monks who made problems with other religions, spoke to reporters on the second day of the tenth national conference of Myanmar's sangha (monkhood/priesthood), which was convened by the State Sangha Maha Nayaka Committee, popularly known by the Burmese-language acronym, Ma Ha Na, in July of 2016, stating, "No monk is above the law. . . . I am just saying to any monk that, if you or anyone else violates the law, we will take action against you."[144] However, people obviously see the government's ambiguous relationship with the priesthood. They do not hesitate to take action against any monks who might interfere with their political leadership. Yet at other times, they are reluctant to take action against monks who attack people of non-Buddhist religions. Christians in those areas have taken on extra responsibilities to protect the pagodas from being destroyed as they might be blamed for the destruction. Although the government affirms that they will take action against any monks who violate the existing law and thereby invent religious conflict, they do not take any actions upon the building of pagodas on Christian land. Where is Myanmar's Religion Act that is intended to promote religious plurality?

On March 17, 2015, three men were sentenced to two-years imprisonment in Myanmar for posting an image of the Buddha wearing headphones on the Facebook page of the VGastro Bar and Restaurant in Yangon in their effort to promote an event.[145] They were the bar's thirty-two-year-old general manager, Philip Blackwood, from New Zealand, and two Burmese men, forty-year-old Tun Thein, the bar's owner, and its manager twenty-six-year-old, Htut Ko Ko Lwin. The men were arrested after public outcry from the hardline Buddhist group. They had immediately removed the image and issued an apology in their critical confession, saying "It was not intended to cause offense. Our ignorance is embarrassing for us, and we will attempt to correct it by learning more about Myanmar's religions, culture and history, characteristics that make this such a rich and unique society."[146] However, the court stated that the image of the Buddha with headphones insulted Buddhism and was a violation of "Myanmar's Religion Act,"[147] which prohibits insulting religion, with Judge Ye Lwin stating, "It is clear the act of the bar offended the majority religion in the country."[148]

40   *Chapter One*

After this incident, another religious issue took place in Mandalay on October 6, 2016. Klaas Haijtema, a thirty-year-old Dutch tourist who unplugged an amplifier that was broadcasting Buddhist chants, which he said disrupted his sleep, was sentenced to three months of hard labor in prison on the charge of insulting religion by a Mandalay court on October 6, 2016. Haijtema had been staying at a hotel in Mandalay on September 23 when a nearby Buddhist center began broadcasting the recitations of religious devotees. During a hearing in the court, Haijtema said, "I was really tired that night and woke up to the noise. I was very angry and assumed that children were playing music. I told them to lower the volume of the loudspeakers before I unplugged the amplifier, and they didn't understand me. That's why I unplugged it."[149]

It is typical in Myanmar to see that Buddhists often use loudspeakers at a high volume in broadcasting sermons from monasteries, and in performing rituals and soliciting donations in the streets. According to the Myanmar Police Force, Ward or Village Tract Administration Law allows the use of loudspeakers between 6:00 a.m. and 9:00 p.m. in order to avoid disturbing the neighborhood.[150] Thus, two lawyers who were not involved with the case said, "The Buddhist center or Dharma community hall that woke Haijtema appeared to have violated the law by using loudspeakers after 9 p.m. The law also bans their use before 6 a.m. and requires a permit." One lawyer, Zaw Win, said, "The one that broke the law is the dharma community hall, not the Dutch man." And a resident who lives near the Buddhist center, Ko Hla Myo Aung, said, "There were six others in his ward and all of them broadcast chants at a high volume late at night and early in the morning. If the Buddha were still alive, he would go deaf from the noise from the loudspeakers."[151]

I also experienced the same type of Buddhist broadcasting religious sermons and chants sometimes for twenty-four hours a day and seven days a week, with loudspeakers pointing directly at my house. It disrupted my regular sleeping hours after I had worked and studied the whole day. Although I also wanted to tell them at least to lower the volume I never did because I did not want to confront them as an ethnic minority and Christian person. As a result, I had to patiently endure the high volume of the loudspeakers. Many times, the final decision for law enforcement doesn't depend on existing law, but rather, on the person who makes it. If the government takes Haijtema's case as insulting religion, what about the destruction of Christian churches and monuments by the Myanmar army? Although I do not know Haijtema's original reason, I question the inconsistency in enforcing Myanmar's religious policy. His issue could be a cultural issue that people experience while they are in a different country from their own or it could be white supremacy over the Asian people. Whatever the case, I believe the case could have been settled with a fine, rather than imprisonment and hard labor. If he really

Persecution of Ethnic and Religious Minorities in Myanmar   41

deserves this kind of action, what about the Myanmar soldiers who intentionally destroyed the Christian churches and monuments? What about U Thuzana and his followers who intentionally built pagodas on Christian land without asking permission? Isn't this insulting Christianity? If unplugging an amplifier that broadcast the Buddhist chants deserves imprisonment with hard labor, what kind of action must be taken upon those who unplugged the lives of people from all potential sources of education, economy, health, religion, and security?

On March 16, 2018, Kyaw Moe, assistant director of the Ministry of Religious Affairs, issued an official letter that was sent to Christian Religious Organizations, Islamic Religious Organizations, and Hindu Religious Organizations as a response to two specific Christian religious events in Loikaw, Kayah State, and Yay Oo, Sagaing Division in Upper Myanmar.[152] St. Paul Anglican Church in Loikaw held a special occasion on January 31, 2018, for donating clerical robes for priests and on the backdrop of the pulpit had the words "Sangha Taw Mya-aa Wut-lon Hlu-Dann Pwe" (Ceremony of Donating Clerical Robes for Priests). Similarly, a Roman Catholic Church in Yay Oo, Sagaing Division in Upper Myanmar also used the phrase, "Phonn Taw Gyee Peter Myo Myint Ya Hann Khan Gon Pyu Pwe" (Ordination Ceremony of Peter Myo Myint) in its invitation letter. As these two Christian religious ceremonies went viral on social media, forty-seven Buddhist monks from the State Sangha Maha Nayaka Committee (a government appointed body of high-ranking monks that oversees all Buddhist monks) held a meeting on February 21, 2018, in which they made a unanimous decision not to allow non-Buddhist religions to use Pali words in their religious literatures. They argued that if non-Buddhist religions use Pali words, which Theravada Buddhists have already used in their doctrinal texts, it will create misunderstanding, enmity, and conflict among religions. After the meeting, the Ministry of Religious Affairs officially informed non-Buddhist religious organizations in Myanmar that they must stop using Pali words in their own religious literatures and ceremonies. In fact, there is no good reason for the Burman Buddhists to exclusively claim the Pali words as their own. They should also admit the fact that the Pali words did not originate in Myanmar, but rather came from India. One can see that under the NLD, while government officials, infrastructure, and education have changed to a certain extent, many things still remain the same.

ISLAMOPHOBIA AND THE INTER-COMMUNAL VIOLENCE BETWEEN BUDDHISTS AND MUSLIMS IN RAKHINE STATE

Islamophobia is not a new phenomenon but draws its roots from the British colonization of Myanmar. In 1938, anti-Muslim riots were sparked by the publication of a book *The Abode of a Nat* by a Burman Buddhist man named Maung Htin Baw, which included extracts from a pamphlet written in 1931 by a Muslim man named Shwe Hpi.[153] Maung Htin Baw included the passages most offensive to Buddhism from Shwe Hpi's book in an appendix of his book. He refuted Shwe Hpi's criticism of Buddhism, saying, "It is most earnestly asked that this sort of book should be stopped, and action taken with regard to these books which have already been distributed, that is to say the books which have been published to disparage our religion, our Paya (God), our community and our pagoda."[154] The final report of the riot inquiry committee also called Shwe Hpi's pamphlet a "piece of bigotry and bad taste,"[155] which contained defamatory remarks against Lord Buddha, his images, and pagodas.[156]

The All-Burma Council of Young Monks Association called a mass meeting on July 26, 1938, at the Shwedagon pagoda to protest against Shwe Hpi's offensive pamphlet. Over ten thousand people, including fifteen hundred monks, passed a resolution demanding that the author be punished, saying, "If the government fails to take necessary action in the matter as demanded, this meeting warns the government that steps will be taken to treat the Muslims who insult the Buddhist community and their religion as enemy number one, and to bring about the extermination of the Muslims and the extinction of their religion and language."[157] A protest against the government and Indians, both Muslims and Hindus, led by the leaders of the Young Monks Association broke out in Yangon first and then spread to other parts of the city and country. They indiscriminately attacked Muslims and looted their shops, which resulted in 181 deaths of people all over the country, of whom 139 were Muslims, 25 were Hindus, and 17 were Burmans.[158] Moshe Yegar, a historian of Islam in Southeast Asia, in his book *The Muslims of Burma: A Study of a Minority Group* writes that during the anti-Muslim riots there were some Hindus who cooperated with the Burmese Buddhists against the Muslims.[159] When the Burman nationalist movement rallied for the separation of Myanmar from British India in the 1920s and 1930s, the Indian Muslims in Myanmar opposed the separation of Myanmar from India, which heightened the Burman Buddhists' hostility toward the Muslims.[160]

Under the Union Solidarity and Development Party government, former president Thein Sein's administration enacted a very controversial

"Religious Conversion Law,"[161] which sparked criticisms from non-Buddhist groups. The ultra-nationalist Buddhist monks under the name of "Race and Religion Protection" proposed a law that sought to protect Buddhist identity by regulating religious conversion. The state-run newspaper published the proposed religious conversion law on May 27, 2014, and asked for public opinion. Despite strong opposition from ethnic minority groups and lawmakers, Myanmar's Lower House eventually approved the law on March 20, 2015. Under the law, any citizen who wishes to convert from his/her religion to another religion must be over eighteen years old. He/she must apply to a local registration board on religious conversion, which consists of four local representatives from government ministries that will interview the applicant and ascertain his or her beliefs and reasons for conversion. The board will determine whether the applicant is making the conversion of his or her own free will and conviction. The applicant has a period of ninety days to study the teachings of the religion, and then, if he or she still wishes to convert, and is not converting under pressure, he or she will be issued a certificate of religious certification.[162] Anyone found guilty of violating a list of prohibitions such as persuading, threatening, and proselytizing could face fines, imprisonment, or both.[163]

The Religious Conversion Law indicates that the ultranationalist Buddhist movement, Ma Ba Tha, led by Wirathu, aims to oppress, repress, and discriminate against religious minorities in the country. Calling the Muslims "the enemy,"[164] Wirathu spoke about the dangers of Muslims to a crowd of Buddhists in Taunggyi, Shan State, on June 20, 2013, saying, "You can be full of kindness and love, but you cannot sleep next to a mad dog."[165] Wirathu sees Muslims as the most dangerous threat to Buddhism and the nation. After the 2015 elections, Islamophobia became stronger as the ultranationalist Buddhists are afraid of the foundations of a pluralist society and believe that their nationalist monks could help them get rid of it. Therefore, they support the ultranationalist Buddhist movement against the Muslims. For instance, a Buddhist man named Kyi Lin assassinated Ko Ni, a Muslim human rights lawyer, outside Yangon International Airport on June 29, 2017. Ko Ni was returning to Myanmar from Indonesia with about twenty other government officials and civic leaders after completing a weeklong study tour on democratic transition and conflict resolution. He had been a legal advisor to State Counselor Aung San Suu Kyi and had been very active particularly in amending the 2008 constitution. As leader of Ma Ba Tha, Wirathu not only excused the killing of Ko Ni by Kyi Lin, but officially thanked Kyi Lin on social media.[166] Wirathu also thanked ex-military officers Zeya Phyo, who was accused of giving Kyi Lin one hundred million kyats, and Aung Win Zaw, who was also accused of being a collaborator of Kyi Lin. Aung Win Khaing, a former lieutenant colonel accused of masterminding the assassination, disappeared after the assassination, and his whereabouts remain top-secret. He allegedly asked his elder brother, Aung Win Zaw, to kill Ko Ni in 2016. According to the airport's CCTV footage, both Aung Win Zaw and Aung Win Khaing were at Yangon International Airport at the time of the assassination.[167] Needless to say, the Myanmar military generals also played an implicit role in allowing the ultranationalist Buddhists' hate speech against Muslims across the country. The assassination of Ko Ni was not religious but political, as he was a strong advocate to revising the 2008 constitution, which the military generals had written for their own protection. However, there is no doubt that Muslims in Myanmar also feel that they are intentionally targeted and threatened.

The intercommunal violence between Buddhists and Muslims in Rakhine State, which resulted in the deaths of 192 people (134 Muslims and 58 Buddhists) began in June and October of 2012 as a response to the gang rape and murder of a Buddhist woman by Muslim men.[168] On May 28, 2012, a Rakhine Buddhist woman, Thida Htwe, twenty-seven years old, of Thabyechaung village, Yanbye Township, was raped and ruthlessly stabbed to death by three Muslim men named Rawshi, Rawphi, and Kochi. Enraged by the brutal killing, about three hundred Rakhine Buddhists pulled the Muslims from a bus in Toungup, and ten Muslims were killed in the clash.[169] Following the 2012 riots and subsequent violence, the Myanmar government formed a Commission of Inquiry, which included both Buddhists and Muslims, to investigate the root causes of violence, verify loss of life and property, examine efforts to restore peace and promote law and order, develop strategies to reconcile differences, establish mutual understanding, and advise on promotion of social and economic development.[170] By the end of 2012, the Myanmar government gave permission to international organizations such as UN agencies, INGOs, and Muslim Aid to visit the affected areas and observe the situation themselves. In 2013, the Organization of Islamic Conference (OIC) made plans to establish a liaison office in Myanmar. However, thousands of Buddhist monks in Yangon and Mandalay protested on October 15, 2013, and President Thein Sein then did not grant permission for the OIC to open a representative office.[171]

The Advisory Commission on Rakhine State, chaired by Kofi Annan, was established on September 5, 2016, at the request of State Counselor Aung San Suu Kyi. The Commission is a national body, and the majority of its members are from Myanmar. It was authorized to examine the complex challenges facing Rakhine State and to propose responses to those challenges. The security situation in Rakhine State deteriorated sharply after October 9, 2016, when the Muslim armed group Harakat al-Yaqin (later renamed Arakan Rohingya Salvation Army) attacked three Border Guard Police Posts in Rakhine State, which resulted in the deaths of nine police officers.[172] Violence between the military and the Arakan Rohingya Salvation Army, particularly the over-reaction of the military, resulted in the destruction of private property and a significant number of Muslims fleeing across the border to Bangladesh. Some members of the Rakhine community were also forced to flee.

According to the Commission, there has been a Muslim community in Rakhine State since before the Burmese invasion in 1784–1785. The size of the Muslim community increased during the British colonial period (1885–1948) as the British brought Muslim workers from Bengal. The Commission remarked, "While many came on a seasonal basis, some settled down permanently, altering the ethnic and religious mix of the area."[173] The British ruled Myanmar as a province of India, which made Indian immigration easy. Eventually, Myanmar was freed from India in 1937 when it was made a separate colony. According to Alistair D. B. Cook, coordinator of the Humanitarian Assistance and Disaster Relief Program, and research fellow at the Center for Non-Traditional Security Studies, S. Rajaratnam School of International Studies, Nanyang Technological University, Singapore, the British had made a promise to the Muslims that they would establish a Muslim national area in northern Rakhine State. Based on this promise, some Muslims mobilized themselves politically.[174] Cook states that in the initial post-independence era, U Nu acknowledged the Muslims' claim to be a separate ethnic group within Myanmar.[175]

However, this recognition was denied by the military government when it took power in 1962 and that denial continues.[176] Muslims in Rakhine State insist that the government should recognize them as "Rohingya" in Myanmar. However, the government has consistently refused to include them in the list of 135 national races. Deputy Immigration and Population Minister Kyaw Kyaw Win in Pyithu Hluttaw said on February 20, 2013, "There is no so-called Rohingya ethnic race in Myanmar."[177] Burman historian Khin Maung Saw also rejected the term *Rohingya*, used by Muslims in Rakhine State to refer to themselves. He claims that Muslims in Rakhine State appropriated the name from the real natives of Rakhine, saying, "In the Chittagonian dialect of Bengali language, the land of Rakhine is called 'Rohan' and the Rakhine people or Arakanese are called 'Rohangya' (Rohan—Rakhine, Gya—man). Since the word is of Bengali origin, some of the Muslims used the name to identify themselves as natives of Rakhine and named themselves 'Rohingya' by hijacking the name of the real natives of Rakhine in Bengali language."[178] Saw's argument is also affirmed by a Western-educated Burman historian, Thant Myint-U, who says, "The British never used the term Rohingya. It was the word some Muslims, especially in the north of Arakan, used to refer to themselves in their own Bengali-related language. It simply meant 'of Rohang,' their name for Arakan. It implied that Arakan was their home."[179] Successive governments have contested that the

Rohingya are not an indigenous ethnic group but are Bengali Muslims who first entered Myanmar during British colonial rule and have been a threat to Myanmar since its independence.[180]

The final report of the Advisory Commission on Rakhine State declared, "Shortly after Myanmar's independence in 1948, a Muslim mujahidin rebellion erupted in Rakhine State, demanding equal rights and an autonomous Muslim area in the north of the state. While the rebellion was eventually defeated, they revived the armed struggle in the 1980s, but lost its military force in the 1990s."[181] From 1995, the authorities began issuing Temporary Residency Cards (known as white cards) to Muslims in Rakhine State who did not have identity documents, as well as to returning refugees from Bangladesh.[182] According to government figures, approximately four thousand Muslims have been recognized as citizens, out of a population of around one million Muslims in the state. Around ten thousand Muslims have also received National Verification Cards (NVC), considered a preparatory step toward applying for citizenship. The process was again introduced in 2014, where Temporary Resident Card (TRC) holders were allowed to apply for citizenship on the condition that they listed their ethnicity as "Bengali."[183] The process was suspended following protests from both communities, but was restarted and expanded to all of Rakhine State in January 2015. After announcing the cancellation of the TRCs in February 2015, the government started issuing its replacement, Identity Cards of National Verification (ICNV), in June 2015. To obtain this card, applicants were again required to register as "Bengali"[184] on the application form.

The Arakan Rohingya Salvation Army (ARSA) claims that they are like other ethnic armed groups in Myanmar who are fighting for their self-determination and should not be branded as a terrorist organization. There is a gap between local discourse and international rhetoric on the crisis in Rakhine State. The State Counselor, Aung San Suu Kyi, has been heavily criticized by the international communities for keeping silent and not speaking up for Muslim minorities. The United Nations has defined the security operation in Myanmar as "a textbook example of ethnic cleansing,"[185] while the commission chaired by Kofi Annan referred to the crisis as "intercommunal violence" or "inter-communal conflict."[186] Suu Kyi also said that the crisis was being distorted by a "huge iceberg of misinformation."[187] The international media captured only the Muslim refugees. They failed not only to condemn the ARSA's attack on the Border Police posts but also to look at the whole communities—Kamans, Chins, Hindus, and Mros—affected by the violence in Rakhine State. Suu Kyi's biographer Peter Popham criticized Suu Kyi's leadership, writing, "As Aung San Suu Kyi's biographer, I have to say that the only good thing she can do is resign."[188] After the Buddhist monks led demonstrations and advocated for the removal of the Muslims

Persecution of Ethnic and Religious Minorities in Myanmar 47

from Myanmar, international Buddhist leaders urged Burmans to show respect and compassion to Muslims, stating, "The Burmese are noble people, and Burmese Buddhists carry a long and profound history of upholding the *Dharma*. We wish to reaffirm to the world, and to support you in practicing, the most fundamental Buddhist principles of nonviolence, mutual respect, and compassion."[189]

The ARSA describes Northern Rakhine State as their land by right, calling it Rohinya State, which is completely intolerable for the people of Myanmar. John F. Cady, professor of history at Ohio University, who studied Southeast Asia, also stated that since the time of British colonial rule in Myanmar, Muslim interests have centered on the Arakan region, where around a third of the population was Mohammedan (Muslim).[190] The All-Myanmar Islamic Religious Organization (AMIRO) has condemned ARSA's attacks in Rakhine State and labeled them as terrorists who deviate from the true teachings of Islam. The AMIRO has pledged to collaborate with the government, interfaith groups, and the public to prevent such violence.[191] The international communities should know that the state counselor and president are not commander in chief of the Myanmar military, which means that they do not have much power over the military. The military retains control over the three most important ministries, namely Defense, Home, and Border Affairs. In other words, the military controls all security matters, while the elected government is responsible for health, education, agriculture, infrastructure, and foreign policy. Myanmar's military is thus not on the side of the civilian government. If the parliament could amend the undemocratic 2008 constitution to make it a democratic one, the president would be commander in chief of the military, and the military would return to the barracks. For now, the country is still wrapped up in its core fight: democracy versus military dictatorship. The military generals will take advantage of international communities' criticisms of Suu Kyi to bring down Myanmar's democracy. If the international community keeps criticizing Suu Kyi, it effectively means that they are supporting the old military regime and want to turn the country's power back to them. Suu Kyi, as a nonviolent peacemaker, has been trying to pacify all sides. In reality, the government is not building a new house, but rebuilding and repairing a ruined building left behind by the old regime. In such a context, international communities should find different ways to support Suu Kyi and her leadership as they work to solve the crisis so that everyone can live peacefully in the country.

Unquestionably, people of good faith have an urgent duty to defend the rights of those suffering violence. The victims are not only the Muslim refugees in Bangladesh but also other ethnic and religious groups within Rakhine State. The Bengali Muslims have continued fleeing to Bangladesh even after the Myanmar military operation is over. Why? In addition to escaping

48   *Chapter One*

the military's racist attacks, they struggle very hard for their livelihood in Myanmar. According to 2012 statistics, 44 percent of the population of Rakhine State live below the poverty line, almost 20 percent higher than in most parts of Myanmar.[192] Western countries should not negatively pressure the Myanmar government to solve the issue overnight. They should be aware that the issue is more complex than they can imagine. The government alone might not be able to solve the crisis in Rakhine State without the participation of the faithful citizens from all religious and ethnic backgrounds. There are fears and anxieties from both Buddhist and Muslim communities in Rakhine State. The rhetoric of the ultranationalist Buddhists portrays Muslims as a demographic threat to Myanmar in general, and Buddhism in particular, as they are allegedly waging a "love jihad" or "Romeo jihad" against the Buddhists.[193] Yegar also says that monogamy is the custom among Burmese Muslims, but not among Indian Muslims.[194] The fear is that if the Muslims actually practice polygamy, they will come to outnumber the Rakhine Buddhists in the area. As a result, the Rakhine Buddhists fear becoming a minority in the future.

Lily Kadoe and Fatimah Husein, after extensive research on Buddhist-Muslim conflict in Rakhine State say that some Muslim political leaders in Myanmar also criticize Muslim communities in Northern Rakhine State for their outdated ideas and lack of modern education, especially in learning only their own language, Urdu, and suggest that Muslims in Rakhine State also need to learn Rakhine and Burmese languages, which is a requirement for Myanmar citizenship.[195] In addition, an anonymous Muslim political leader, highlights the causes of conflict in Rakhine State, saying:

> Rohingya religious leaders are conventional. Many of them embrace an extreme theology as they receive their education from conservative schools in India, Pakistan and Bangladesh. Girls are not encouraged to study for higher education as their parents ask them to get married at the average age of fourteen. The religious leaders oppose family planning which is against Islam so that their birthrate is higher than Rakhine people and Rohingya population is one-third of total population in Rakhine State. The Rohingya and the Rakhine population became half by half in Sittwe, the capital city of Rakhine State before the communal violence broke out in 2012. The rapid growth of Rohingya population is one of the causes of conflict in that area. Rohingya religious leaders can neither lead the social and economic affairs of their own communities nor integrate other communities.[196]

Aye Lwin, a prominent Muslim leader at the Islamic Center of Myanmar also criticizes both the ultranationalist Buddhists for their racism against the Muslims, and the Bengali Muslim religious leaders and elders in Rakhine State for encouraging their own people to stay aloof and separate from others, including not only non-Muslims but also people of Muslim origins.[197] The Burmese Muslims also speak Burmese, while the Indian Muslims speak mostly Urdu. There are tensions between the Burmese Muslims and Indian Muslims. Yegar states, "The Indian Muslims objected to the introduction of the Burmese language because of their desire to safeguard their ties with India and a semi-holy association with Urdu, as well as because of the fear of most teachers who were Indian Muslims lest they lose their job."[198] Accordingly, Muslims in Rakhine State need, first, intra-religious dialogue with other Muslims within the country; second, inter-religious dialogue with people of other faiths.

As a Christian public theologian, I believe that the Bible teaches us to offer hospitality to sojourners, refuge to the needy, and security to immigrants as much as we can. However, the rights of citizenship also depend upon adaptation into a new culture and context. Meanwhile, the ultranationalist Buddhists and the military have perpetrated racist violence in their attempt to expel all Bengali Muslims from Rakhine State. The escalation of intercommunal violence between the two groups is also due to the overreaction and incompetence of the military. However, I believe that the government should actively combat all forms of hate speech and discrimination, regardless of ethnic and religious identity, to build mutual respect, understanding, and recognition among different ethnic and religious groups. Religious leaders of Buddhist, Muslim, Hindu, Christian, and others should also actively combat hate speech and racial/religious discrimination. When acts of violence are committed by members of one particular ethnic/religious group, their leaders should promptly and publicly denounce such actions. In this way, faithful citizens of the country can also help the government in building a nation where everyone can live without fear.

NOTES

1. Maung Htin Aung, *A History of Burma* (New York: Columbia University Press, 1967), 1.

2. Aung San Suu Kyi, *Freedom from Fear and Other Writings* (New York: Penguin Books, 1995), 66.

3. Thein Ko Lwin, "Religious Data from 2014 Census Released," *New Light of Myanmar*, July 22, 2016.

4. A. L. Basham, "Asoka," in *The Encyclopedia of Religion*, vol. 1, ed. Mircea Eliade (New York: Macmillan Publishing Company, 1987), 466. Emperor Asoka was known as the Constantine of Buddhism.

5. John S. Strong, *The Legend of King Asoka: A Study and Translation of the Aso-kavadana* (Princeton, NJ Princeton University Press, 1983), 25.

50 Chapter One

6. Tun Aung Chain, "The Christian-Buddhist Encounter in Myanmar" (paper presented at the Inauguration Ceremony of Judson Research Center at Myanmar Institute of Theology, Yangon, Myanmar, July 13, 2003).

7. Charles Eliot, *Hinduism and Buddhism: An Historical Sketch*, vol. 3 (London: Routledge & Kegan Paul Ltd, 1954), 54.

8. Donald Eugene Smith, *Religion and Politics in Burma* (Princeton, NJ: Princeton University Press, 1965), 12–13.

9. Maung Htin Aung, *The Stricken Peacock: Anglo-Burmese Relations, 1752–1948* (The Hague: Martinus Nijhoff, 1965), 6.

10. Thant Myint-U, *The Making of Modern Burma* (Cambridge: Cambridge University Press, 2001), 113.

11. Henry Park Cochrane, *Among the Burmans: A Record of Fifteen Years of Work and Its Fruitage* (New York: Fleming H. Revell Company, 1904), 147.

12. Cochrane, 148.

13. Cochrane, 148.

14. Anna May Say Pa, "A Place at the Round Table: Equipping Burmese Women for Leadership," *MIT Journal of Theology* 5 (January 2004): 18. Anna May Say Pa argues that the proverb, "If a woman is bent on mischief, she can destroy a country," gained popularity at the annexation of Myanmar by the British in 1885, which some blamed on King Thibaw's aggressive wife, power-hungry Queen Supayalat, who ordered the execution of Mi Hkin-gyi, Thibaw's concubine, and Yanaung, who introduced the king to Mi Hkin-gyi and encouraged him to take on more wives. Supayalat also ordered the execution of Yanaung's members and imprisoned Mi Hkin-gyi's uncles and grandfathers.

15. Vivian Ba, "The Early Catholic Missionaries in Burma," *The Guardian* (1962): 92.

16. Smith, *Religion and Politics in Burma*, 13.

17. Thant Myint-U, *The Making of Modern Burma*, 49. *Nat* is a generic word for any spirit or deity, and they are seen as potentially malevolent and in need of constant propitiation, usually through the ritual offering of food and water.

18. Smith, *Religion and Politics in Burma*, 14.

19. *The New Encyclopaedia Britannica*, 15th ed. (1993), s.v. "History of Myanmar."

20. Eliot, *Hinduism and Buddhism: An Historical Sketch*, 50. A Burmese historian, Thant Myint-U said that Thibaw, the last Burman king, would trace his descent ultimately to Abhiraja and the Sakiyan clan. Also see Thant Myint-U, *The River of Lost Footsteps: A Personal History of Burma* (New York: Farrar, Straus and Giroux, 2006), 44.

21. Eliot, *Hinduism and Buddhism*, vol. 3, 50. In Yangon, there are two Ukkala towns: North Ukkala and South Ukkala, which is identified with Orissa and Myanmar tradition locates it in Myanmar as well.

22. Eliot, 50.

23. Suu Kyi, *Freedom from Fear and Other Writings*, 46. The Pyus were a Tibeto-Burman people of Mongolian stock whose culture was very similar to that of India. It is not known exactly when they came into Myanmar. However, it is fairly accepted that they founded the city of Pagan around 850 CE In the ninth century, the

Persecution of Ethnic and Religious Minorities in Myanmar 51

kingdom of Pyus was destroyed by raiders from Nanchao in Southern China. Since then, the Pyus faded away in history. It is thought that they moved elsewhere or perhaps were absorbed by the Burman.

24. Suu Kyi, 45.

25. Suu Kyi, 46.

26. Myint-U, *The River of Lost Footsteps*, 93. Aung Zeyya also changed the name of his hometown from Moksobo, which means "the hunter chief" to Shwebo, meaning "the golden chief."

27. Suu Kyi, *Freedom from Fear and Other Writings*, 41.

28. Bertil Lintner, *Outrage: Burma's Struggle for Democracy* (London: White Lotus, 1990), 19.

29. Moshe Yegar, *The Muslims of Burma: A Study of a Minority Group* (Wiesbaden: Otto Harrassowitz, 1972), 2.

30. Yegar, *The Muslims of Burma*, 2.

31. Yegar, 30.

32. Yegar, 30.

33. Ni Ni Myint, *Burma's Struggle against British Imperialism, 1885–1895* (Rangoon: The Universities Press, 1983), 12.

34. Cochrane, *Among the Burmans*, 211.

35. Paul Ambrose Bigandet, *Outline of the History of the Catholic Burmese Mission from the Year 1720 to 1857* (Rangoon: Hanthawaddy Press, 1967), 4.

36. Michael Fredholm, *Burma: Ethnicity and Insurgency* (London: Praeger, 1993), 26. A better term for the conversion of the ethnic minority groups might be *proto-Christians* instead of *pro-Christians*, because the former would mean the ethnic minority people easily converted into Christians, while the latter would mean they are in favor of Christians.

37. Lian H. Sakhong, *In Defense of Identity: The Ethnic Nationalities' Struggle for Democracy, Human Rights, and Federalism in Burma* (Bangkok: Orchid Press, 2010), 15. Panglong is the name of a city in Southern Shan State where the founding fathers of modern Myanmar held a Conference to build a federal State.

38. Martin Smith, *Burma: Insurgency and the Politics of Ethnicity* (London: Zed Books, 1991), 24.

39. Sakhong, *In Defense of Identity*, 120. After its official separation from the British India in 1937, the "Burma Proper" was well known as "Ministerial Burma."

40. Sakhong, 14.

41. Sakhong, 14.

42. Sakhong, 14.

43. Sakhong, 14.

44. John F. Cady, *A History of Modern Burma* (Ithaca, NY: Cornell University Press, 1960), 228.

45. Aung, *A History of Burma*, 285.

46. Hugh Tinker, *Burma: The Struggle for Independence, 1944–1948*, vol. 1, 1 January 1944 to 31 August 1946 (London: Her Majesty's Stationery Office, 1983), xviii. The term *Excluded Areas* was later changed to *Frontier Areas*.

47. Sakhong, *In Defense of Identity*, 14.

48. Josef Silverstein, *The Political Legacy of Aung San* (Ithaca, NY: Southeast Asia Program, Cornell University, 1993), 23.

49. Silverstein, 27.

50. Tinker, *Burma: The Struggle for Independence*, 621.

51. Tinker, 1:621.

52. Maung Maung, *Aung San of Burma* (The Hague: Martinus Nyhoff, Southeast Asia Studies, Yale University, 1962), 106.

53. Maung, 110.

54. Silverstein, *The Political Legacy of Aung San*, 55–56.

55. Silverstein, 10.

56. Silverstein, 10.

57. Silverstein, 141.

58. Maung, *Aung San of Burma*, 123–24. Panglong Conference was held from February 7, 1947, to February 12, 1947.

59. Maung, *Aung San of Burma*, 125.

60. Maung, *Aung San of Burma*, 125.

61. Smith, *Burma: Insurgency and the Politics of Ethnicity*, 78.

62. Maung, *Aung San of Burma*, 119.

63. Tinker, *Burma: The Struggle for Independence*, 1:769–907. The Governor of Burma, Reginald Dorman-Smith's letter to Clement Attlee, Rangoon, May 6, 1946, stated that U Saw has had two of his political party (Myochit Party) leaders murdered recently, and in his opinion by Aung San's followers. U Saw who was dubbed an ambitious power-hungry man thought that he had sufficient power and ability to crush Aung San, whom he considered his rival. His main political platform was to vigorously attack Aung San.

64. Maung, *Aung San of Burma*, 141–42.

65. Jay Milbrandt, "Tracking Genocide: Persecution of the Karen in Burma," *Texas International Law Journal* 48, no. 1 (September 2012): 68.

66. Christina Fink, *Living Silence in Burma: Surviving under Military Rule* (London: Zed Books, 2009), 17.

67. Fink, 17.

68. Aung San Suu Kyi, *Aung San of Burma: A Biographical Portrait by His Daughter* (Edinburgh: Kiscadale, 1991), 50–51.

69. *New Light of Myanmar*, "Only If Our Country Is at Peace Will We Be Able to Stand on an Equal Footing with Other Countries in Our Region and across the World," September 1, 2016.

70. Ibid.

71. Lun Min Mang and Ei Ei Toe Lwin, "Speech Highlights from Panglong Conference Opening Ceremony," *Myanmar Times*, September 1, 2016.

72. Ibid.

73. Ibid.

74. Ibid.

75. Ibid.

76. *Myanmar Times*, "Ceasefire Anniversary Prompts Calls for More Signatories," October 17, 2016.

Persecution of Ethnic and Religious Minorities in Myanmar

77. Walter Wink, *Jesus and Nonviolence: A Third Way* (Minneapolis: Fortress Press, 2003), 27. Walter Wink states that in the face of persecution and oppression some Christians have taken the position of flight, while others have chosen the position of fight with armed revolt against the perpetrators. His argument takes a different position that challenges the ideas of both flight and fight and takes the position of a third way that refuses the absolute subjugation to the perpetrators and exposes the injustice of the system through nonviolent movement.

78. Marie Lall, *Understanding Reform in Myanmar: People and Society in the Wake of Military Rule* (London: Hurst & Company, 2016), 88.

79. David Cortright, *Peace: A History of Movements and Ideas* (Cambridge: Cambridge University Press, 2008), 211.

80. Cortright, 213.

81. Cortright, 336–37.

82. *Myanmar Times*, "Ceasefire Anniversary Prompts Calls for More Signatories," October 17, 2016.

83. *Democratic Voice of Burma (DVB) in Burmese*, November 2, 2016.

84. Lall, *Understanding Reform in Myanmar*, 83.

85. Matthew Pennington, "Obama Orders U.S. Economic Sanctions on Myanmar Lifted," *Washington Post*, October 7, 2016.

86. Bertil Lintner, "There Is a New Cold War in Asia," *Irrawaddy*, September 12, 2016.

87. Nan Lwin Hnin Pwint, "Myanmar Military, AA Swap Blame for Civilian Deaths in Chin State," *Irrawaddy*, January 14, 2020. A teacher from Se Phalaung village and two civilians from Kyet U Wa village in Paletwa, Chin State were abducted by a group of men on January 14, 2020, and were found on January 17 with their hands tied and dead from knife wounds in a forest about three kilometers from Paletwa. Both the Myanmar military and the Arakan Army (AA) denied responsibility for the deaths. The Khumi Affairs Coordination Council (KACC), a local civil society organization, said that the AA was responsible for the death of three civilians.

88. Constituent Assembly of Burma, *The Constitution of the Union of Burma* (Rangoon: Government Printing and Stationery, 1948), 48.

89. P. V. Aoley, "Sangha," *Encyclopedia of Hinduism*, vol. 9, ed. K.L. Seshagiri Rao and Kapil Kapoor (New Delhi: India Heritage Research Foundation in Association with Rupa & Co., 2011), 182–83. The word *sangha* is derived from classical Sanskrit and Pali.

90. Melford E. Spiro, *Buddhism and Society: A Great Tradition and Its Burmese Vicissitudes* (Berkeley: University of California Press, 1982), 382.

91. Myanmar Catholic Dioceses, "A Brief History of Catholic Church in Myanmar," https://www. catholicchurchmyanmar.wordpress.com (accessed January 12, 2023). Also see Aung, *A History of Burma*, 140.

92. Ba, "The Early Catholic Missionaries in Burma," *The Guardian* (1962): 3.

93. Alexander McLeish, *Christian Progress in Burma* (London: World Dominion Press, 1929), 21.

54   *Chapter One*

94. A zayat is a small building or a public rest house built at the roadside. It has a roof and floor, but no walls. It serves as a shelter for travelers and a meeting place for villagers to discuss the needs of the village.

95. Helen G. Trager, *Burma through Alien Eyes: Missionary Views of the Burmese in the Nineteen Century* (London: Asia Publishing House, 1966), 76.

96. Courtney Anderson, *To the Golden Shore: The Life of Adoniram Judson* (Grand Rapids, MI: Zondervan, 1976), 251.

97. Maung Shwe Wa, *Burma Baptist Chronicle* (Rangoon: Burma Baptist Convention, 1963), 41–42.

98. Myint-U, *The River of Lost Footsteps*, 136.

99. Francis Wayland, *A Memoir of the Life and Labors of the Rev. Adoniram Judson,* vol. I (Boston: Phillips, Sampson, and Company, 1853), 300.

100. Smith, *Religion and Politics in Burma*, 40.

101. Smith, 44–45.

102. Joseph Silverstein, *Burma: Military Rule and the Politics of Stagnation* (New York: Cornell University Press, 1977), 13.

103. Aung, *A History of Burma*, 269.

104. Smith, *Religion and Politics in Burma*, 138.

105. Constituent Assembly of Burma, *The Constitution of the Union of Burma, 1948*, 4.

106. Smith, *Religion and Politics in Burma*, 308.

107. Smith, 123.

108. Smith, 123.

109. Smith, 123–24.

110. Smith, 243–44.

111. Smith, 244.

112. Frank N. Trager, "The Failure of U Nu and the Return of the Armed Forces in Burma," *The Review Politics* 25, no. 3 (July 1963): 314.

113. Kanbawza Win, "Colonialism, Nationalism and Christianity in Burma: A Burmese Perspective," *Asia Journal of Theology* 2, no. 2 (October 1988): 277.

114. Smith, *Religion and Politics in Burma*, 246.

115. Smith, 248.

116. Smith, 250.

117. Smith, 253.

118. Smith, 266–67.

119. Smith, *Burma: Insurgency and the Politics of Ethnicity*, 195.

120. Smith, 195–96.

121. Smith, 196. Also see *Brandon Sun Newspaper*, March 2, 1962.

122. Smith, 196.

123. Silverstein, *Burma: Military Rule and the Politics of Stagnation*, 98.

124. Herman G. Tegenfeldt, *Through Deep Waters* (Valley Forge, PA: Foreign Mission Society, 1968), 11–12.

125. Lintner, *Outrage*, 62.

126. Tegenfeldt, *Through Deep Waters*, 18.

127. Smith, *Burma: Insurgency and the Politics of Ethnicity*, 37.

128. Ministry of Foreign Affairs, "Religious Tolerance Recognized Hallmark of Myanmar Society," *New Light of Myanmar*, August 4, 2000.

129. U.S. Commission on International Religious Freedom, *Annual Report 2021* (Washington, DC: USCIRF, 2021). The report still recommends Myanmar to be a "country of particular concern."

130. Ministry of Foreign Affairs, "Religious Tolerance Recognized Hallmark of Myanmar Society," *New Light of Myanmar*, August 4, 2000.

131. Benedict Rogers, *Burma: A Nation at the Crossroads* (London: Rider Books, 2012), 108–9.

132. Rogers, 95.

133. Rachel Fleming, "Persecution and Coerced Conversion of Ethnic Chin Christians in Burma," 13 (paper presented at the Second International Conference on Human Rights and Peace, and Conflict in Southeast Asia in Jakarta, Indonesia, October 17–18, 2012).

134. Fleming, 23–24.

135. Kanbawza Win, "Are Christians Persecuted in Burma?" *Asia Journal of Theology* 14, no. 1 (April 2000): 170.

136. World Council of Churches, "Myanmar: Raiser Points Out Discrimination against Christian Minorities, Affirms Role of Interfaith Dialogue," WCC News, March 7, 2003, https://www.oikoumene.org/news/myanmar-raiser-points-out -discrimination-against-christian-minorities-affirms-role-of-interfaith-dialogue.

137. World Council of Churches.

138. Htun Htun, "Government Bans U Wirathu from Preaching Sermons," *Irrawaddy*, March 11, 2017.

139. *Irrawaddy*, "Ma Ba Tha's U Wirathu: Trump Similar to Me," November 18, 2016. In his political campaign against his opponent Hilary Clinton, Trump reiterated his racist rhetoric to "Make America Great Again" by embracing the idea of exclusion in his support of white supremacy, racism, and anti-Muslim and anti-immigrant rhetoric. The well-known leader of Ma Ba Tha, Wirathu, drew parallels between his views on Islam and those of Trump, saying, "Trump is similar to me."

140. *Morning Star News*, "Christians in Burma Patiently Endure Building of Pagodas on Church Lands," May 3, 2016.

141. "Christians in Burma Patiently Endure."

142. Ye Mon, "Minister Promises Christians Removal of Dream-Inspired Stupa," *Myanmar Times*, September 8, 2015.

143. Mon.

144. *Irrawaddy*, "Religious Affairs Minister Says No Monk Is Above the Law," July 14, 2016. The State Sangha Maha Nayaka Committee, known by the Burmese acronym Ma Ha Na, is a government appointed body of high-ranking monks that oversees all Buddhist monks in Myanmar.

145. Wai Moe and Austin Ramzy, "Myanmar Sentences 3 to Prison for Depicting Buddha Wearing Headphones," *New York Times*, March 17, 2015.

146. Moe and Ramzy.

147. Ministry of Information, "Constitution of the Republic of the Union of Myanmar, 2008," 152. Myanmar's Religion Act states that any act which is intended or is

56 *Chapter One*

likely to promote feelings of hatred, enmity or discord between racial or religious communities or sects is contrary to this Constitution. A law may be promulgated to punish such activity.

148. Moe and Ramzy, "Myanmar Sentences 3 to Prison."

149. Saw Nang, "Myanmar Gives Tourist Who Pulled Plug on Buddhist Chants 3 Months in Prison," *New York Times*, October 6, 2016.

150. Htet Naing Zaw, "Police: Loudspeakers Require Permission," *Irrawaddy*, October 4, 2016. According to Ward or Village Tract Administration Law, an application to use a loudspeaker must be submitted to local authority three days in advance with detailed information about the purpose, date, and time of use. Failure to do so will result in a punishment with a fine of up to five thousand kyats or up to seven days in prison.

151. Saw Nang, "Myanmar Gives Tourist Who Pulled Plug on Buddhist Chants 3 Months in Prison," *New York Times*, October 6, 2016.

152. This official letter was written on March 12, 2018, signed by Kyaw Moe, an assistant director of the Ministry of Religious Affairs, and issued to Christian religious organizations, Islamic religious organizations, and Hindu religious organizations on March 16, 2018.

153. The word *nat* in Burmese is used to refer to any spirit or deity.

154. *Paya* in Burmese means "God." In 1931, there was a religious controversy between a Moulvi named Hassan Shah and Maung Pan Nyo. As a response to the controversy, Maung Pan Nyo wrote a pamphlet entitled "Moulvi Yogi Sadan," in which he countered the attacks by the Moulvi on Buddhism. The book contained passages extremely offensive to Islam. As a result, a Zerbadi, Alias Maung Sin, also wrote a book entitled *Moulvi-Yogi Sadan Vinnissaya Kyan*, in which he challenged Maung Pan Nyo's book as being false and an insult to Mohammed in particular and to Muslims in general. In the same year, Shwe Hpi also wrote a pamphlet entitled "Moulvi-Yogi Aw-wada Sadan" as a refutation of Maung Pan Nyo's original offensive book. The first edition of Shwe Hpi's book did not gain public attention as it remained exclusively in the hands of Muslims. In 1938, a Muslim butcher named Abdul Rashid gave Maung Htin Baw a copy of Shwe Hpi's book. Then, Maung Htin Baw included offensive passages on Buddhism from Shwe Hpi's pamphlet as an appendix in his book. See Riot Inquiry Committee, *Final Report* (Rangoon: Govt. Printing and Stationery, 1939), 1–5.

155. *Final Report*, 11.

156. *Final Report*, appendix, x.

157. *Final Report*, appendix, x.

158. *Final Report*, 281.

159. Yegar, *The Muslims of Burma*, 48.

160. Yegar, 60–65.

161. Ministry of Religious Affairs, "Invitation to Submit Suggestions from the Public in Relation to the Draft Law on Religious Conversion," *New Light of Myanmar*, May 27, 2014.

162. *New Light of Myanmar*.

163. *New Light of Myanmar*.

164. Thomas Fuller, "Extremism Rises among Myanmar Buddhists," *New York Times*, June 20, 2013.

165. Fuller. Wirathu refers to the Muslims as mad dogs and troublemakers in his sermon.

166. *The Straits Times*, "A Monk Gagged, but Can Hate Be Silenced? The Nation," March 14, 2017.

167. San Yamin Aung, "Highlights of the U Ko Ni Murder Case," *Irrawaddy*, January 29, 2019.

168. Kofi A. Annan, *Towards a Peaceful, Fair, and Prosperous Future for the People of Rakhine: Final Report of the Advisory Commission on Rakhine State*, Advisory Commission on Rakhine State, August 2017, 19, https://www.kofiannanfoundation .org/app/uploads/2017/08/FinalReport_Eng.pdf.

169. Myanmar News Agency, "10 Muslims Killed in Bus Attack," *New Light of Myanmar*, June 5, 2012.

170. Alistair D. B. Cook, "The Global and Regional Dynamics of Humanitarian Aid in Rakhine State," in *Islam and the State in Myanmar: Muslim-Buddhist Relations and the Politics of Belonging*, ed. Melissa Crouch (Oxford: Oxford University Press, 2016), 265.

171. Cook, 268.

172. Hyuk Kim, "A Complex Crisis: The Twisted Roots of Myanmar's Rohingya Conflict," *Global Asia* 12, no. 3 (September 2017): 266.

173. Annan, *Towards a Peaceful, Fair, and Prosperous Future*, 18.

174. Cook, "The Global and Regional Dynamics," 262.

175. Cook, 262.

176. Cook, 262.

177. *New Light of Myanmar*, "No Rohingya Race in Myanmar, Says Deputy Minister," February 21, 2013.

178. Khin Maung Saw, "Islamization of Burma through Chittagonian Bengalis as Rohingya Refugees," Burma Library, https://www.burmalibrary.org/docs21 /Khin-Maung-Saw-NM-2011-09-Islamanisation_of_Burma_through_Chittagonian _Bengalis-en.pdf.

179. Thant Myint -U, *The Hidden History of Burma: Race, Capitalism, and the Crisis of Democracy in the 21st Century* (New York: W.W. Norton, 2020), 26–27. Myint-U denies a common perception that the Rohingya were stripped of their citizenship by the 1982 citizenship law.

180. Cook, "The Global and Regional Dynamics," 263.

181. Annan, *Towards a Peaceful, Fair, and Prosperous Future*, 19.

182. Annan, 30.

183. Annan, 26.

184. Annan, 27.

185. "Rohingya Crisis: UN Sees Ethnic Cleansing in Myanmar," BBC News, September 11, 2017, https://www.bbc.com/news/world-asia-41224108.

186. Annan, *Towards a Peaceful, Fair, and Prosperous Fair*, 19.

187. "Rohingya Crisis: Suu Kyi Says Fake News Helping Terrorists," BBC News, September 6, 2017, https://www.bbc.com/news/world-asia-41170570.

188. Peter Popham, "As Aung San Suu Kyi's Biographer, I Have to Say that the Only Good Thing She Can Do Now Is Resign," *Independent*, December 7, 2017.

189. *Irrawaddy*, "World Buddhist Leaders Pen Letter to Burma," December 11, 2012.

190. Cady, *A History of Modern Burma*, 295.

191. *Xinhua*, "Myanmar Islamic Organization Condemns Extremist Terror Attacks in Northern State," September 11, 2017.

192. Naw Lily Kadoe and Fatimah Husein, "Ulama, State, and Politics in Myanmar," *Al-Jamiah Journal of Islamic Studies* 53, no. 1 (2015): 140.

193. Nyi Nyi Kyaw, "Islamophobia in Buddhist Myanmar: The 969 Movement and Anti-Muslim Violence," in *Islam and the State in Myanmar: Muslim-Buddhist Relations and the Politics of Belonging*, ed. Melissa Crouch (Oxford: Oxford University Press, 2016), 202.

194. Yegar, *The Muslims of Burma*, 107.

195. Kadoe and Husein, "Ulama, State, and Politics in Myanmar," 151–52.

196. Kadoe and Husein, 151.

197. Kadoe and Husein, 152.

198. Yegar, *The Muslims of Burma*, 107.

Chapter Two

Martin Luther's Theology of Two Kingdoms as a Tool for Transformation in Myanmar Society

The Intersection of Religion and Politics in Luther's Reform Movement

In order to understand Luther's political thought, one must look at the intersection of religion and politics in Luther's context in the sixteenth century. In the Middle Ages, the crisis of religion and politics was the power struggle between pope and king. For instance, Pope Boniface VIII clashed with the French and English monarchy over ecclesiastical property and taxation. He issued the papal bull *Unam Sanctam* in November 1302, one of the most forceful statements of papal supremacy in the Middle Ages, which historian Brian Tierney calls "probably the most famous of all the documents on church and state that has come down to us from the Middle Ages."[1] The bull stated, "There is one holy, Catholic and apostolic church. Outside this church there is no salvation or remission of sins."[2] The bull contains general theological propositions about the nature of the church and the position of the pope within it. Pope Boniface VIII was concerned about the primacy of the papacy above all worldly rulers. This tradition still continued in the sixteenth century. Luther was fully aware that the pope controlled every aspect of life in society. Therefore, Luther's political thought can be viewed from two historical phases: before and after he broke away from Rome.

In his earlier treatises, including *To the Christian Nobility of the German Nation Concerning the Reform of the Christian Estate*, *The Babylonian Captivity of the Church*, *On the Freedom of a Christian*, and *Two Kinds of Righteousness*, Luther attacked the power of the Roman papacy over secular

60 *Chapter Two*

authorities, the sacramental system of the church, the doctrine of transubstantiation, the doctrine of the Mass as a sacrifice, the Roman Catholic Church's doctrine of justification, and Christian liberty. In other words, Luther's concern during this period was not only theological criticisms of the pope but also the liberation of secular authorities from the tyranny of the Roman papacy.

Luther also witnessed the corruption of the papacy by practices such as simony (the practice of buying and selling ecclesiastical positions), and concubinage as an escape from celibacy. For instance, Albrecht of Brandenburg (1490–1545) is one of the undisputable examples of simony in Luther's own time. In 1513, Albrecht, the second son of the elector of Brandenburg, saw a golden chance to become archbishop of Magdeburg and Mainz. There were two obstacles keeping him from attaining the position: first, he was not a priest; second, he was only twenty-three years old, much younger than the required minimum age of thirty. Nevertheless, he managed to find a way past these two obstacles. While his older brother was the electorate of Brandenburg, Albrecht could quickly get himself ordained as archbishop of Magdeburg in 1513 by bribing curial officials. Roughly a year later, Albrecht obtained an even higher position, becoming archbishop of Mainz, the most important ecclesiastical position in Germany. The latter position required yet another exemption because canon law did not allow bishops to occupy more than one seat. Fortunately for Albrecht, money had the power to solve these obstacles. Since he did not have enough funds to buy the desired exemptions from the curia, he took out a loan from the extremely wealthy Fugger banking family of Augsburg. He secured the monies to pay off Rome and become archbishop of both Magdeburg and Mainz.[3]

When the time came to pay off his debt to the Fugger family, a terrific opportunity came to Albrecht. Pope Leo X (1475–1521) was busy raising funds for the construction of a magnificent new papal church in Rome, St. Peter's Basilica, and announced a general indulgence, available to qualified customers.[4] Albrecht and Pope Leo X made a great deal, albeit a secret one, in which Albrecht offered to help the pope in raising funds. Albrecht also took half of the income to pay off the Fugger family. Albrecht formed a commission of indulgence preachers to travel throughout his dioceses and market the papal offer. The most famous and skillful of these indulgence preachers was a Dominican friar named John Tetzel (1465–1519). According to Tetzel's preaching, indulgences could be purchased not only for the living, but also on behalf of those who had already departed but were suffering in purgatory. Traveling from town to town and calling upon the living to purchase indulgence slips, Tetzel preached, "You should know that all who confess and in penance put alms into the coffer according to the counsel of the confessor, will obtain complete remission of all their sins. . . . Why are you then standing there? Run for the salvation of your souls!"[5] Manipulating concerns for those loved ones who had already departed as well, Tetzel's highly emotional sermons painted graphic pictures of purgatorial suffering capped by personal appeals to his listeners, stating:

> Don't you hear the voices of your wailing dead parents and others who say, "Have mercy upon me, have mercy upon me, because we are in severe punishment and pain. From this you could redeem us with a small alms and yet you do not want to do so." We have created you, fed you, cared for you, and left you our temporal goods. Why then are you so cruel and harsh that you do not want to save us, though it only takes so little? You let us lie in flames so that we only slowly come to the promised glory.[6]

Elector Frederick the Wise, who ruled Luther's Saxony, banned Tetzel from entering his territory. Luther observed Tetzel's manipulated preaching and responded to him in 1517 by writing his theological premises *Disputation on the Power and Efficacy of Indulgences* commonly known as the *Ninety-Five Theses*. He attacks the commercialization and abuses of indulgences in his disputation because people thought of indulgences as "tickets to heaven."[7] Actually, the practice of indulgences was an ancient practice. In the Middle Ages, the official theology of indulgences was accompanied by repentance. Importantly, Luther did not attack the official theology of indulgences. What he did attack was clerical abuse of indulgences, including the authority of the pope over the dead, saying, "The pope neither desires nor is able to remit any penalties except those imposed by his own authority or that of the canons."[8] The pope had authority to forgive only those sins prescribed in the canon laws. Accordingly, Luther saw that the church needed to be purified from its abuse of indulgences.

Another clerical abuse was concubinage, which means living with a concubine, which was different from legal or church-affirmed marriage. Celibacy is not an ancient practice of the church, but is a later practice required of clergy after the twelfth century, although some church leaders encouraged it much earlier as part of ascetic discipline. Despite this requirement, some clergymen carried on sexual relationships with women whom they did not marry, that is, concubines, while others married openly. Those clergies who married openly were not left without negative criticism and were pejoratively named "Nicolaitists."[9] On the subject of concubinage by clergy, Kenneth Appold, professor of Reformation Church History at Princeton Theological Seminary, states, "Throughout the centuries leading up to the Reformation, even bishops and popes kept concubines, and most rural villagers would have been surprised to find a priest without a common-law wife."[10] All this evidence proved the corruption of the papacy, which Luther strongly attacked without hesitation before he broke away from Rome.

62   *Chapter Two*

However, after Luther broke away from Rome his political thought was shaped by the unnecessary interference of princes over religious matters in the Wittenberg Reforms of 1522 and the peasants' revolt of 1525. The Edict of Worms, promulgated by Emperor Charles V in 1521, branded Luther as a heretic, ordering both his arrest and the destruction of his writings. Returning to Wittenberg, Frederick the Wise, the elector of Saxony, ordered that Luther be kidnapped and brought to Wartburg Castle for his own protection, where he remained for nearly a year. While Luther was at Wartburg, church leadership in Wittenberg fell to the hands of three men: Philip Melanchthon, professor of Greek and Luther's dearest friend; Karlstadt, professor of theology and archdeacon at the Castle Church; and Gabriel Zwilling, a monk of Luther's own order. Karlstadt and Zwilling too easily influenced Melanchthon, who was neither a strong organizer nor a personal leader. Karlstadt urged three important reforms at the Castle Church: first, Mass was to be abolished; second, Communion in both kinds was to be given to the laity; third, Marriage was urged for the clergy, priests and monks alike.[11] He distributed Communion in both kinds and urged the removal of images and altars. Some people welcomed these innovations exuberantly, while others were horrified by the rapid reform movement. As a result of the chaos, which needed immediate attention, the Town Council met with faculty representatives from the University of Wittenberg and drafted *The Worthy Ordinance for the Princely City of Wittenberg*, which laid out four main points: first, Mass was to be conducted in German, which included Communion in both kinds; second, begging was forbidden within the city limits; third, a common fund was to be established for the maintenance of the poor, which would eliminate the need for begging; fourth, all images were to be removed.[12]

Upon returning to Wittenberg on March 6, 1522, Luther held Karlstadt responsible for initiating a rapid reform program that Luther deemed too aggressive. Although Luther himself approved the abolition of images, the serving of Communion in both kinds, and the marriage of clergy, he believed that these reforms should not come by force, but by individual freedom of choice. He believed that reforms should be conducted through preaching the Word of God. Meanwhile, Luther condemned the interference of territorial rulers upon religious matters. This is affirmed by J. Paul William Rajashekar, an Asian Luther scholar and professor of systematic theology at United Lutheran Seminary, Philadelphia. He writes:

> Once Luther broke away from Rome, the issue was no longer the liberation of secular power from ecclesiastical control. The ruling class had begun to consolidate its power, and in the absence of a countervailing ecclesiastical authority comparable to that of the papacy in the evangelical churches, Luther was faced with the issue of exaggerated prerogatives of the princes. He was now forced

Martin Luther's Theology of Two Kingdoms as a Tool for Transformation 63

to articulate his political thought as well as his theological thought in order to state the relationship between the church and the state and to underscore the limitations of the latter.[13]

Although Luther's primary vocation was religious reform, it would be misleading to conclude that Luther stayed aloof from the sociopolitical issues of his time. Again, Rajashekar supports this, writing, "The extraordinary intermixture of religion and politics in Luther's time compelled him to think politics and even to think politically in religious matters."[14] As such, Luther's reform movement was a response to the demands of both the religion and the politics of his own time.

MARTIN LUTHER'S THEOLOGY OF TWO KINGDOMS AND RESISTANCE

There is no concept of the "state" at the time of Luther. The "state" refers to "temporal authority/government," "civil government," and "the kingdom of the world" in Luther's writings.[15] Regarding the relationship between religion and politics, Luther gave his lectures on the Book of Romans from November 3, 1515, through September 7, 1516, in which he spoke of "spiritual government" and "temporal government," or "inward man" and "outward man," to refer to "religion and politics" and "church and state" in his own theological context. He strongly believed that God institutes both spiritual government and temporal government, where the former directs people as Christians, and the latter directs them as citizens. Luther emphasizes the interdependence of the two, saying, "In this life the inward man cannot be without the outward, that is, the believer serves Christ in his kingdoms of grace and of power."[16] Paul Althaus, a twentieth-century German theologian, argues in his book *The Ethics of Martin Luther* that Luther draws his theology of two kingdoms from Augustine's doctrine of "earthly city and heavenly city," and Luther lays out his understanding of religion and politics as a dualistic approach between the kingdom of God and the kingdom of the world.[17] I view Althaus's interpretation to be a deviation from Luther's own theology, since Luther does not favor a twofold governmental structure, one divinely instituted and the other not; Luther suggests something quite different, stating, "For there is no government that is not divinely instituted."[18]

In August 1520, Luther wrote his treatise *To the Christian Nobility of the German Nation Concerning the Reform of the Christian Estate.* In it he accused the Roman Catholic Church of ecclesiastical abuse for building three walls around themselves for protection: first, they had declared that temporal power had no jurisdiction over them but that on the contrary, the spiritual

64 *Chapter Two*

power was above the tempora power; second, when the attempt was made to reprove them with the scriptures, they raised the objection that only the pope could interpret the Scriptures; third, they claimed that no one could summon a council but the pope.[19] Moreover, Luther accuses the Roman Church of inventing two unnecessary estates, "Pope, bishop, priests, and monks are called the spiritual estate, while princess, lords, artisans, and farmers are called the temporal estate."[20] Luther saw this invention as a piece of deceit and hypocrisy that frightened Christians. On the contrary, Luther believed that all Christians are truly of the spiritual estate, and there is no difference among them except that of office.[21]

Luther's argument is based on the doctrine of the priesthood of all believers—that all Christians are equal before God in terms of justification by grace through faith alone, stating,

> There is no true, basic difference between laymen and priests, princes and bishops, between religious and secular, except for the sake of office and work, but not for the sake of status. . . . We are all one body of Christ the Head, and all members one of another. Christ does not have two different bodies, one temporal and the other spiritual. There is but one Head and one body.[22]

For Luther, the difference between spiritual authority and temporal authority lies only in terms of work and office, meaning that they do not do the same work. Accordingly, spiritual authorities are charged with the administration of the Word of God and the sacraments, while temporal authorities bear the sword and law in their hands to punish the wicked and protect the good.[23] Luther believes that as all the members of the body serve one another (I Cor. 12:14–26), and the hand shall help the eye when it suffers pain, the temporal authority and spiritual authority are to help one another. Since the temporal authority is ordained of God to punish the wicked and protect the upright, it should be left to perform its office in the whole body of Christendom without restriction and without respect to office, whether it affects pope, bishops, priests, monks, nuns, or anyone else.[24] If the pope failed to fulfill his office properly, what should the temporal authorities do? In such a case, Luther believes that temporal authorities could also summon a Christian council to discuss religious matters, as they are also "fellow-Christians, fellow-priests, fellow-members of the spiritual estate,"[25] adding, "Would it not be unnatural if a fire broke out in a city and everybody were to stand by and let it burn on and on and consume everything that could burn because nobody had the authority of the mayor, or because, perhaps, the fire broke out in the mayor's house?"[26] Luther is convinced that there is no authority in the church except to promote the good; and therefore, if the pope uses his authority to prevent

Martin Luther's Theology of Two Kingdoms as a Tool for Transformation   65

religious reform, his "power is not to be obeyed, but rather resisted with life, property, and with all our might and main."[27]

In his treatise *The Babylonian Captivity of the Church*, written in 1520, Luther rejects the Roman Catholic sacramental practice of withholding of the cup from the laity, the doctrine of transubstantiation, and the doctrine of the Mass as a sacrifice.[28] Luther's criticism of the withholding of the cup from the laity is based on individual freedom. He says, "It is certainly an impious act to withhold the cup from the laymen when they desire it."[29] For Luther, the clerical refusal to offer the wine to the laity is unbiblical and a violation of the commandment of Christ. Luther does not condemn the use of just the bread, but he prefers both the bread and wine in Communion because Christ Himself gave both the bread and wine to his disciples (Mt. 26:26–28; Mk. 14:22–24; Lk. 22:17–20). Luther worried that if the church could withhold the wine from the laity, it could also withhold the entire sacrament. He says, "The sacrament does not belong to the priests but to all men. The priests are not lords, but servants in duty bound to administer both kinds to those who desire them, as often as they desire them."[30] Luther does not force anybody to take the sacrament or not to take it. He opts for each individual to make the choice.

In his treatise *The Freedom of a Christian*, written in November 1520, Luther explains his understanding of the relationship between good works and justification by grace through faith. In order to substantiate this relationship, Luther gives his example of the relationship between "inner man" and "outer man,"[31] in which the former stands for our relationship with God, in the belief that Christ died for us on the cross, and the latter stands for good works in our relationship to others as our spontaneous love in obedience to God. Grounding his argument on the doctrine of justification by grace alone through faith, Luther declares the liberation of all Christians from the bondage of the pope, who tries to control them from the cradle to the grave.

Luther's resistance against the tyranny and ecclesiastical abuses of the Roman papacy reached its height on December 10, 1520, when he attended a bonfire outside the city gates of Wittenberg and threw a copy of the papal bull *Exsurge Domine* (Arise, O Lord) into the flames rather than submit to its demands.[32] *Exsurge Domine*, issued on June 15, 1520, condemned Luther's 95 Theses, and its release was followed by the burning of his writings. Luther justified the burning of the papal bull by arguing, "If they are allowed to burn my articles, in which there is more gospel and more of the true substance of Holy Scripture . . . than in all the pope's books, then I am justified much more in burning their unchristian law books in which there is nothing good."[33] Therefore, Pope Leo X issued the bull *Decet Romanum Pontificem* (It pleases the Roman Pontiff) on January 3, 1521, excommunicating Luther, who had refused to recant from his reform movement.

66 *Chapter Two*

Turning his attention to temporal authority after he broke away from Rome, in his treatise *Temporal Authority: To What Extent It Should Be Obeyed*, written in 1523, Luther presented two kingdoms: the kingdom of God and the kingdom of the world, dividing his treatise into three parts, "First, he upholds the divine origin of temporal authority; second, he defines the limits within which the temporal power may act, pointing out that it has no power over faith or conscience, although it does have power over men's bodies and property; third, he discusses the manner in which a prince should exercise his power."[34]

Luther believed that God ordains both spiritual and temporal authorities to exercise its own authority within its own God-given field. Luther gives a good tree as an example, saying that it needs no instruction on how to bear good fruit and not thorns. Luther contends that true believers do not need the instruction of temporal authority for themselves, saying:

> Those who belong to the kingdom of God do not need temporal law or sword. If all the world were composed of real Christians, that is, true believers, there would be no need for or benefits from prince, king, lord, sword, or law. Christians have in their heart the Holy Spirit, who both teaches and makes them to do injustice to no one, to love everyone, and to suffer injustice and even death willingly and cheerfully at the hands of anyone. Where there is nothing but the unadulterated doing of right and bearing of wrong, there is no need for any suit, litigation, court, judge, penalty, law, or sword. For this reason, it is impossible that the temporal sword and law should find any work to do among Christians, since they do of their own accord much more than all laws and teachings can demand.[35]

Luther's argument is based on the doctrine of justification by grace through faith that is a free act, to which no one can be forced, and the power and guidance of the Holy Spirit who teaches true believers to produce good fruits. Yet, he still believes that true Christians need secular authority for the good of others since the temporal sword and law should be used for the punishment of the wicked and the protection of the upright, adding:

> If anyone attempted to rule the world by the gospel and abolish all temporal law and sword on the plea that all are baptized and Christian, and that, according to the gospel, there shall be among them no law or sword—or need for either— pray tell me, friend, what would he be doing? He would be losing the ropes and chains of the savage wild beasts and letting them bite and mangle everyone, meanwhile insisting that they were harmless, tame, and gentle creatures. But I would have the proof in my wounds.[36]

Martin Luther's Theology of Two Kingdoms as a Tool for Transformation   67

Although true Christians do not need the government for themselves, they still need to support the government for the sake of their neighbors who need the government for their protection and safety. Underlining the political calling of true Christians in society, Luther said:

> You are under obligation to serve and assist the sword by whatever means you can, with body, goods, honor, and soul. For it is something which you do not need, but which is very beneficial and essential for the whole world and for your neighbor. Therefore, if you see that there is a lack of hangmen, constables, judges, lords, or princes, and you find that you are qualified, you should offer your services and seek the position, that the essential governmental authority may not be despised and become enfeebled or perish. The world cannot and dare not dispense with it.[37]

Luther affirms that although Christ did not bear or prescribe the sword, it is sufficient that he does not forbid or abolish it, but actually confirms it. Yet Luther defines the limits within which secular authority and religious authority may act. Luther sees that spiritual authorities and temporal authorities act in the wrong way, saying, "Worldly princes rule in a spiritual way, and spiritual princes rule in a worldly way. They rule the souls with iron and the bodies with letters."[38] Hence, according to Luther, the purpose of temporal authorities is to bring peace and stability in society. More importantly, Luther speaks about the need for a mutual service between spiritual authority (religion) and temporal authority (politics), saying:

> Both must be permitted to remain: the one to produce righteousness, and the other to bring about external peace and prevent evil deeds. Neither one is sufficient in the world without the other. No one can become righteous in the sight of God by means of the temporal government, without Christ's spiritual government. Christ's government does not extend over all men; rather, Christians are always a minority in the midst of non-Christians. . . . A Christian submits most willingly to the rule of the sword, pays his taxes, honors those in authority, serves, helps, and does all he can to assist the governing authority, that it may continue to function and be held in honor and fear.[39]

Since political authority is ordained by God, those who govern can be called "gods,"[40] in line with the language of the Psalms; that is, they sit in God's place.[41] Therefore, disobedience and resistance against the government represent disobedience and resistance against the true supreme God.[42] However, Luther's instruction to obey the government does not necessarily mean that the government deserves absolute obedience, and the citizens must remain silent with blind obedience in the face of human evils. Luther understood that he could not entangle himself in governing and prescribing laws for

68   *Chapter Two*

the government. However, he suggested the fourfold duty of a prince. He wrote, "First, toward God there must be true confidence and earnest prayer; second, toward his subjects there must be love and Christian service; third, with respect to his counselors and officials he must maintain an untrammeled reason and unfettered judgment; fourth, with respect to evil doers he must manifest a restrained severity and firmness."[43]

With this suggestion, Luther expects the government to rule the country with justice for the well-being of humanity. Nevertheless, Luther doubts that the government will ever rule the country with justice, and it is difficult to find the upright rulers. He writes, "You must know that since the beginning of the world a wise prince is a mighty rare bird, and an upright prince even rarer. They are generally the biggest fools or the worst scoundrels on earth; therefore, one must constantly expect the worst from them and look for little good, especially in divine matters which concerns the salvation of souls."[44]

Therefore, in the case of the wicked rulers who failed to rule the country properly with justice, Luther believes that God will bring them down by tearing out their roots and destroying their names and memories.[45] Who is technically responsible to rebuke the wicked rulers according to Luther's thought? Luther assures us that God has appointed a particular group of people to take this responsibility to rebuke the wicked rulers boldly—namely, priests and preachers.[46] Luther continues affirming the responsibility of preachers to rebuke the wicked rulers, stating, "It would be far more seditious if a preacher did not rebuke the sins of the rulers; for then he makes people angry and sullen, strengthens the wickedness of the tyrants, becomes a partaker in it, and bears responsibility for it. Thus, God might be angered and might allow rebellion to come as a penalty."[47]

Luther's works witness to his care about the betterment of society in his time and beyond. Nevertheless, Reinhold Niebuhr, an American theologian and writer on ethical and social issues, has mistakenly portrayed Luther as divorcing private morality from public morality and religion from politics in the public sphere, considering Luther's works "quietistic tendencies,"[48] and unsympathetic to the political and social movements of his time. Luther was not a politician, but rather a religious reformer whose primary vocation was religious reformation. However, he did not keep silent in response to the social and political calling of the church if the situation demanded. In the Diet of Worms in 1521, when presented with a pile of his writings Emperor Charles V charged Luther with teaching "rebellion, division, war, murder, robbery, arson, and the collapse of Christendom" and asked him to recant from his reform movement.[49] However, Luther responded to him boldly, saying:

> Unless I am convinced by the testimony of the Scriptures or by clear reason (for I do not trust either in the pope or councils alone, since it is well known that

Martin Luther's Theology of Two Kingdoms as a Tool for Transformation 69

they have often erred and contradicted themselves) I am bound by the Scriptures I have quoted and my conscience is captive to the Word of God. I cannot and I will not retract anything since it is neither safe nor right to go against conscience. I cannot do otherwise, here I stand, may God help me.[50]

As a whole, Luther maintains a mutual service between religion and politics, though with different responsibilities in human society. In his reform movement, both religious and secular authorities play important roles. Luther does not claim a dichotomized separation of religion and politics in his theology. In his view, there are two ways in which God rules: through the law in the worldly kingdom and through the Gospel in the spiritual kingdom. They are distinct ways of ruling, but a distinction is not a rigid dichotomy. Both the worldly and the spiritual kingdoms are God's. The church belongs in both realms as an institution in the world and as a proclamation of the Gospel of God's mercy and grace.

As such, is there the basis for a theology of resistance to the government in Luther? Or does Luther believe that the church must give absolute obedience to the repressive government? Although Luther believes in mutual service between religion and politics for the well-being of human beings in society, we can also find some elements of a theology of resistance in him. He does not believe that the repressive government deserves absolute obedience. In other words, Luther defends not only the duty of obedience but also of resistance when the government does not respect personal belief. For instance, in 1521, at the Diet of Worms, Luther himself refused to comply with the order of the highest secular authority, the emperor, to recant the books he had written and published. In other words, resistance by means of the Word is not only permitted but required when individual faith is not respected. Accordingly, Luther does not admit the interference of temporal authorities in religious matters to prescribe laws intended for the soul, and such laws would give the citizens the rights to disobey and resist them.

MARTIN LUTHER'S POSITION AS A NECESSARY EVIL BETWEEN PRINCES AND PEASANTS

In order to understand Luther's position in the conflict between the peasants and their rulers in sixteenth-century Germany, one has to look at the background history of the Peasants' War of 1524–1525. In several parts of Germany, the antagonism between the peasantry and the feudal nobility grew in the last decades of the fifteenth century. The cause of this antagonism was the attempt to bring the peasantry into an even stronger feudal dependency. These changes occurred during the development of the capitalist mode of

70 *Chapter Two*

production on a large scale, which had direct impact upon the agricultural sector.[51] The contributing factors of the peasants' war were based on economic, political, and religious oppression. The protests originated in Southern Germany in 1524 and spread quickly to other parts of the country. Different groups of peasants were protesting against the rulers and each group of the peasants acted completely independently of others and as a result, the grievances and demands were not uniform. At the beginning of March 1525, peasants in Upper Germany formulated the "Twelve Articles of the Peasants in Swabia,"[52] which were circulated widely in the middle of March. They are:

> The community should have the power and authority to choose and appoint its own pastor with the right to depose him; the peasants are willing to pay a just tithe. A church provost, appointed by the community, should collect this. From this tithe a sufficient sum should be given to the elected pastor; the rest should be given to the poor. Provision should be made for those people forced to leave the community, due to poverty and lack of jobs. No improper tithes will be paid; men should be free and not considered property of another; they should be allowed to fish and hunt, which right did not belong to the privileged alone; they should have access to woods and be allowed to cut timber; excessive imposition of services should cease; they should be free from oppression in the form of unspecified services; there should be a readjustment of rents; the constant making of new laws being a burden, all cases should be judged according to their merits; enclosing and expropriation of the commons being an evil, they should be reopened; the *Todfall* (heriot) should be abolished; if these articles were not in agreement with God's Word, let them be changed when proven so.[53]

Luther was acquainted with the Twelve Articles and responded to them with the *Admonition to Peace: A Reply to the Twelve Articles of the Peasants in Swabia* in 1525. In the "Articles," the peasants express their belief that their demands are rooted in divine law. They appeal to Luther by name for practical advice. Luther explains his reason for writing his treatise, stating, "Since I have a reputation for being one of those who deal with the Scriptures here on earth, and especially as one whom they mention and call upon by name in the second document, I have all the more courage and confidence in openly publishing my instruction. I do this in a friendly and Christian spirit, as a duty of brotherly love."[54] With the knowledge of the "Twelve Articles" of the peasants who have taken up arms, Luther addresses his treatise first to the princes, lords, bishops, priests, and monks, for their blindness and vanity. He points out the corruption of temporal rulers, which has become the root cause of the peasants' war, saying, "As temporal rulers you do nothing but cheat and rob the people so that you may lead a life of luxury and extravagance. The poor common people cannot bear it any longer."[55] In his criticism of the temporal rulers for their unfair rule, Luther sees the peasants

Martin Luther's Theology of Two Kingdoms as a Tool for Transformation 71

as God's instruments, and he is sure that if the peasants failed to tear down the temporal rulers because of their corruption, God would raise up others to do so. Luther further sees that it is not the peasants who are resisting the temporal rulers, but God himself, saying, "God will raise up others. It is his will to defeat you, and you will be defeated. It is not the peasants, dear lords, who are resisting you; it is God himself."[56] Luther knows the destitute situation of the peasants and urges the temporal rulers to seek their welfare. He, therefore, advises the princes to choose certain counts and lords from among the nobility and certain councilmen from the cities and ask them to arbitrate and settle the dispute amicably.[57]

Then, Luther turned his attention to the peasants and argued against them for their violence. Having read the "Twelve Articles," which the peasants had already submitted to their rulers, Luther acknowledges that some of the articles, but not all, are fair enough. For instance, in the first article the peasants ask the rights to hear the gospel and choose their own pastor, suggesting that the rulers are opposing the rights of the peasants to appoint their own local pastor with their own financial support. However, Luther denies the peasants' violence, which he believes will bring unnecessary suffering to the innocent. He realizes the oppression of the peasants by their temporal rulers. Yet Luther believes that violence against God's instituted authority is not the best means of solving the conflict. In other words, it is not a good Christian spirituality for true Christian subjects to take arms against God's instituted rulers, because true Christian spirituality for Luther is, "Suffering! Suffering! Cross! Cross!"[58] The main arguments of Luther's first treatise for peasants' revolution are patience and obedience to God's instituted authority until their demands are heard and met partially if not fully. Instead, Luther saw with his own eyes the results of the peasants' violent revolution against their landlords and rulers in three main centers in Germany, Swabia, Franconia, and Thuringia, where peasants looted monasteries and churches, plundered castles, and left fields lying unattended.

Luther, therefore, writes his treatise *Against the Robbing and Murdering Hordes of Peasants*, in 1525, as an indictment of the peasants' violence. In his treatise, Luther accuses the peasants on three charges: first, that they have deliberately violated their oath to obey their rulers and are therefore subject to temporal punishment; second, that they have violently plundered the properties of others and are therefore subject to death in body and soul; and third, that they have committed terrible crimes under the cover of the gospel, and thereby shamefully blasphemed against God.[59] The worst peasants' revolt had taken place in Thuringia, where Thomas Muntzer had preached violence against the authorities as the only means to create a new order. In his sermon before Duke John on July 13, 1524, Muntzer had warned the princes that if they did not protect the common people, the sword would be taken away

72   *Chapter Two*

from them and given to the elect.[60] Muntzer's theological critique of Luther's instruction to the people to obey secular authority arose primarily out of Muntzer's belief that the eschatological transformation of the world was approaching.[61] Muntzer's text, from the second chapter of Daniel, suggested to him that the final earthly age had already begun. He called for the use of the sword against the princes. Identifying his group with the Israelites when entering the Promised Land, Muntzer said, "They [the Israelites] did not conquer the land by the sword but rather through the power of God. But the sword is the means, as eating and drinking is for us a means of living. In this way the sword is necessary to wipe out the godless."[62] Muntzer viewed the temporal world as the center of God's redeeming activity and the peasants' revolt as the battleground on which God had chosen to fulfill his purposes.

The peasants' revolt had been exploding in various parts of Germany. In the context of this uncontrollable situation, Luther made the difficult decision to declare that it was time for temporal rulers to respond to the peasants' revolt with the use of violence. Walter Altmann, a Latin American liberation theologian, called Luther's view the "lesser evil to massacre the rebelling peasants."[63] Condemning the peasants' revolt, Luther said:

> For rebellion is not just simple murder; it is like a great fire, which attacks and devastates a whole land. Thus, rebellion brings with it a land filled with murder and bloodshed; it makes widows and orphans, and turns everything upside down, like the worst disaster. Therefore, let everyone who can, smite; slay, and stab, secretly or openly, remembering that nothing can be more poisonous, hurtful, or devilish than a rebel. It is just as when one must kill a mad dog; if you do not strike him, he will strike you, and a whole land with you.[64]

Luther urges the princes to employ their power to establish law and order by smiting and slaying the rebelling peasants with all the resources at their disposal and his last sentence demonstrates, "If anyone thinks this too harsh, let him remember that rebellion is intolerable and that the destruction of the world is to be expected every hour."[65] The peasants' revolt was unsuccessful as they achieved the opposite of what they had hoped. Because of his claim that temporal authorities had the right to kill the rebelling peasants, Luther was accused of justifying the ruthless killing of peasants by the temporal authorities. Hence, Luther felt that it was necessary to clarify his position between the two conflicting sides. Therefore, he writes his treatise *An Open Letter on the Harsh Book against the Peasants* in late June or early July, 1525, in which he says:

> There are two kingdoms, one the kingdom of God, the other the kingdom of the world. . . . God's kingdom is a kingdom of grace and mercy, not of wrath and punishment. In it there is only forgiveness, consideration for one another, love,

Martin Luther's Theology of Two Kingdoms as a Tool for Transformation 73

service, the doing of good, peace, joy, etc. But the kingdom of the world is a kingdom of wrath and severity. In it there is only punishment, repression, judgment, and condemnation to restrain the wicked and protect the good.[66]

Furthermore, Luther reiterates his earlier position, condemning the peasants' rebellion and calling it a danger that needs immediate attention in order to restore law and order. He presents a compelling example, saying:

> Suppose I had a wife and children, a house, servants, and property, and a thief or murderer fell upon me, killed me in my own house, ravished my wife and children, took all that I had, and went unpunished so that he could do the same thing again, when he wished. Tell me, who would be more in need of mercy in such a case, I or the thief and murderer? What a fine mercy to me it would be, to have mercy on the thief and murderer, and let him kill, abuse, and rob me![67]

Indeed, true mercy is not to free the wicked unpunished, but to punish them on the one hand, and to protect the upright, on the other. By upholding society in law and order, the government serves God and human beings. One can see that Luther's view did not favor one side arbitrarily in his first treatise. In fact, Luther was trying to pacify both sides, the princes and peasants, for a peaceful solution. He urged both parties, princes and peasants, to reach an agreement. However, they were unwilling to listen to Luther's counsel. Luther, therefore, reassured both the peasants and the princes that they had reaped what they had sowed, saying, "The peasants were unwilling to listen, and now they have their reward; the lords, too, will not hear, and they shall have their reward also."[68]

Furthermore, there was no real unity even among the peasants themselves. Some groups wanted a peasant dictatorship, some a classless society, some a return of the old feudalism where everything was regulated by a contract between lord and peasant, and others wanted the abolition of all rulers except the pope and the emperor.[69] One can imagine that if the Peasants' War had been successful, a new conflict may have arisen among the peasants themselves because of their different opinions. At the same time, one can see that Luther's response to the violence between the peasants and the rulers is the *necessary evil* to bring about law and order in society. There was no neutral ground for Luther in this particular uncontrollable situation. Meanwhile, nonviolence is not an absolute principle in Luther's writings. Luther defended the use of violent resistance to the wicked government in some situations.

74   *Chapter Two*

MARTIN LUTHER'S CRITIQUE OF ANABAPTISM

After the Peasants' War, Luther may have thought that there was no more threat in his reform movement. However, he now faced a new threat: the Anabaptist movement, emerging from a variety of sources. One such source was the rising tension between the city of Zurich and its rural dependencies over tithes. People in the countryside paid their tithe to Zurich city churches. Now, they wanted to keep their tithes in their own small community, in which they could elect their own priest. The Anabaptists perceived the tithe they paid to the Zurich city churches as an instrument of control by the Zurich government over the country parishes. Therefore, in December 1522, the village of Witikon, outside Zurich, elected its own pastor, Wilhelm Reublin, without obtaining permission from the Great Minster Church, which was one of the four major churches in Zurich. In fact, Reublin had been expelled from Basel, a central city for the Reformation movement in Switzerland, Germany, and France, for his reform movement in 1522 before his appointment in Witikon. In March 1523, the Zurich city council decided to allow Reublin to be a parish pastor in Witikon as long as the parish paid its tithe to the Great Minster Church. In June 1523, other villages influenced by Reublin also challenged the tithing system to the Zurich city churches. Nevertheless, the Zurich city council refused the demand of its rural dependencies to keep their tithes. The council responded that the old tithe payments were to remain in place.[70]

In such a situation, Ulrich Zwingli,[71] as a leader of reformation in Switzerland, felt obligated to address the tithing system of the Zurich city council. He, therefore, preached his famous sermon "Divine and Human Righteousness" on St. John the Baptist Day, in June 1523, in which he supported the Zurich city council's decision about the existing practice of tithes. He argued, "I say that everyone is obliged to pay it [the tithe] as long as a magistrate orders it generally. The magistrate is entitled to punish the defaulter who refused to pay it."[72] Not only the villagers, but also some of Zwingli's supporters in Zurich, including Conrad Grebel, a Swiss reformer who is called the "father of Anabaptism,"[73] were disappointed with Zwingli's position. The conflict over tithes became stronger between Zwingli and Grebel's circles. Grebel, disappointed with Zwingli's position, began to organize his own splinter group that included Felix Mantz, cofounder of Zurich Anabaptism, and others. They met in small circles in private homes to study Scripture. One particular issue caught their attention: baptism. Highlighting the voluntary conviction of baptism, Mantz argued that infant baptism was "unbiblical."[74] In 1524, Grebel and Mantz began developing their conception of baptism: it should be an "outward sign" of an "inward reality," together with a public commitment to live in the community of believers.[75]

Martin Luther's Theology of Two Kingdoms as a Tool for Transformation 75

The controversy escalated when Mantz challenged Zwingli to defend infant baptism. At the same time, Reublin also advised parents in Witikon to delay the baptism of their children until they could make the decision by themselves to receive baptism. As a result, on January 17, 1525, the Zurich's city council held a disputation between the groups with Zwingli on one side, and Grebel, Mantz, and Reublin on the other. Grebel, Mantz, and Reublin argued that an infant cannot understand the gospel or exercise faith. Zwingli defended infant baptism from the concept of covenant, in which for him the old covenant is circumcision and the new covenant baptism. There is unity between circumcision and baptism in Zwingli's baptismal theology. Since the old covenant of circumcision was given to infants, thus the new covenant of baptism should also be given to the infants. Zwingli cited Colossians 2:10–12 as conclusive proof that baptism has replaced circumcision.[76]

The council supported Zwingli's view and issued two mandates on January 18 and 21. The first mandate decreed that all children shall be baptized as soon as they are born; those parents who delay baptizing their children shall have eight days to comply or be banished.[77] The second decree called upon those who were not citizens of Zurich to leave within eight days. Grebel and Mantz were banned from public speaking and even meeting in Zurich.[78] What happened next was the birth of the Anabaptist church in the home of Felix Mantz's mother on the evening of January 21, 1525, when Grebel baptized George Blaurock,[79] as the latter asked the former to give him baptism. The chronicle of the Hutterian Brethren states, "After the prayer, George Blaurock stood up and asked Conrad Grebel in the name of God to baptize him with true Christian baptism on his faith and recognition of the truth. With this request he knelt down, and Conrad baptized him, since at that time there was no appointed servant of the Word. Then the others turned to George in their turn, asking him to baptize them, which he did."[80]

Thus, a new church was born. The Anabaptist movement penetrated to some parts of Germany—especially Franconia and Thuringia—in 1526, then in Saxony in 1527. Luther saw the Anabaptists win some converts among the common people. On February 24, 1527, the Swiss and Southern German Anabaptists gathered in the border of Schleitheim (Southern Germany), with Michael Sattler, a notable leader of the Swiss and Southern German Anabaptist movements. They issued the statement of Anabaptist belief, known as the *Schleitheim Articles*. The *Articles* state:

> Baptism contingent upon repentance and amendment of life; the ban or excommunication of brethren who do not keep the commandments; the Lord's Supper as a memorial meal expressing Christian community; a radical separation of believers from the evil world, for "truly all creatures are in but two classes, good and bad . . . and none can have part with the other"; the "shepherd," as the model

76   *Chapter Two*

of the godly life, to be elected by the community; absolute rejection of bearing arms and holding civic offices because Christians' citizenship is in heaven and their weapons are spiritual; and the prohibition of oaths.[81]

Balthasar Hubmaier, a German Anabaptist, viewed baptism as an "inward transformation of outward expression,"[82] which means an internal trans-formation that shows itself outwardly, to be witnessed by the church. He believed that coming to faith in Christ, an inward transformation, was the prerequisite of true baptism. In other words, Hubmaier believed that bap-tism should be a voluntary commitment motivated by free choice and real conviction without being compelled by others. Hubmaier's opposition to infant baptism became stronger after he and sixty others were baptized by Wilhelm Reublin, one of the leading figures of the Anabaptist movement, on Easter Saturday, April 15, 1525. By that time, Hubmaier was encouraging his parishioners to postpone the baptism of their children until they could make their own voluntary request for baptism.[83] In his treatise *On the Christian Baptism of Believers*, dated June 11, 1525, Hubmaier discusses the orders of baptism: word, hearing, change of life or recognition of sin, baptism, and works.[84] Hubmaier's belief, which is based on hearing the Word preached, implies a certain degree of physical maturity and as a consequence, infants are excluded. According to these orders, preaching the Word precedes water baptism. The Anabaptists required people to give a sermon before they could be baptized. Hence, according to Hubmaier, baptism applies only to adult believers who are capable of hearing and believing the Gospel.

Luther countered the Anabaptist belief in his sermons, letters, and tracts. One of Luther's theological letters is addressed exclusively to a refutation of the Anabaptist's views. In his 1528 letter, *Concerning Rebaptism*, Luther spe-cifically mentions Hubmaier, whose booklet on "rebaptism," included Luther as if he agreed with Hubmaier on his view. Hubmaier writes, "Luther wrote a sermon six years ago on the mass, wherein he points out in the seventeenth article how symbols like baptism and the Supper mean nothing without prior faith. They are like a sheath without a knife, a case without a jewel, a hoop before an inn without wine."[85] Luther was angry because Hubmaier had referred to him as if he shared his view on baptism. It is in *A Treatise on the New Testament*, that Luther writes, "In every promise of God there are two things which one must consider: the word and the sign."[86] Luther considers the words and the promise of God as important. Without them the sacraments are dead and nothing at all, like a body without a soul, a cask without wine, a purse without money, a type without a fulfilment, a letter without the spirit, a sheath without a knife, and the like.[87] Hubmaier misinterprets Luther's pas-sage that does not support his view.

Luther refutes the Anabaptist's teaching of adult baptism on the one hand and defends infant baptism on the other. He insists that the Anabaptists make baptism dependent on human work and the inner certainty of one's own conviction. Luther's defense of infant baptism is based on Scripture and the apostolic tradition, saying:

> First, child baptism derives from the apostles and has been practiced since the days of the apostles; second, if child baptism were wrong, God would not certainly have permitted it to continue so long, nor let it become so universal and thoroughly established in all Christendom, but it would have sometime gone down in disgrace . . . while all kinds of heresies have disappeared which are much more recent and later than child baptism; third, children have been given great and holy gifts in baptism, which will enlighten and strengthen them to understand the teaching of Scripture; fourth, if child baptism were not right, it would follow that for more than a thousand years there was no baptism or any Christendom; fifth, the apostles baptized the entire households (Acts 16:15) and there is no other baptism than child baptism under the pope, among the Turks, or in all the world; sixth, if circumcision is the old covenant between God and the children of Abraham, baptism is a new covenant between God and his people.[88]

The Anabaptists base their faith on Mark 16:16, "He who believes and is baptized will be saved," and claim the need for personal profession of faith before baptism. Luther interprets this to mean that no one should be baptized before he/she believes. He argues that the Anabaptists are guilty of a great presupposition, saying, "For if they follow this principle, they cannot venture to baptize before they are certain that the one to be baptized believes. How and when can they ever know that for certain? Have they now become gods so that they can discern the hearts of men and know whether or not they believe?"[89] Luther understands baptism as the work of God, not invented by human beings but commanded by God and witnessed by the gospel.[90]

In response to the Anabaptist's view, Luther's understanding is based on Matthew 19:14, "The kingdom of heaven belongs to children," identifying children as pure and holy—this they could not be without spirit and faith.[91] Luther also sees baptism as a covenant between God and the child's human family, saying, "We read in Acts and the Epistles of Paul how whole households were baptized, and children are surely a good part of the household."[92] Luther sees the Anabaptist understanding of baptism as the reintroduction of the Donatist heresy, which based baptism on the holiness of the baptized and salvation on human works, when Christ based baptism on his Word and commandment.[93] To say that faith is prerequisite for baptism, then, leads either to uncertainty of salvation, together with the longing for it, or to a great presumption. Luther focuses on God choosing the sinner and the commandment of Christ in baptism, while the Anabaptists emphasize one's own

78   *Chapter Two*

personal internal transformation. Indeed, infant baptism is not only a rule of the church but has been a law of the state since the days of Roman law under the emperors Theodosius and Justinian, which, according to Luther, suggests that the refusal of infant baptism is heretical and rebellious to both church and state, and can be considered a capital offense.[94]

The Anabaptist's weakness lies in the fact that they criticize infant baptism for its role as a pledge of faith to be. This implies that they are not confident in infants to become good Christians after baptism. According to their belief, baptism must be administered only after faith is made perfect, which means that one should not sin after baptism. In fact, baptism is a personal commitment between God and the person baptized. It is also communal, as it commemorates the entrance of the baptized, whether infant or adult, into the Christian community. With regard to the subject of private property, Luther, in his lecture on Genesis chapter thirteen, compares the Anabaptists to monks who believe beggary as an act of true worship toward God, saying, "The Anabaptists, too, think that those who have any possessions of their own are not Christians."[95] Luther criticizes the Anabaptists for forsaking money, goods, marriage, houses, and wife and child as well.[96] He urges his readers not to withdraw themselves from human society like the Anabaptists, stating:

> Do not choose separation or the cloister or any other innovation voluntarily. But if the government seizes you and drives you from your possessions, then you must endure it, provided this happens without any faults of yours. Years ago, under the papacy, servants deserted the service of their masters, and wives ran from the household of their husbands and from submission to them, went on pilgrimages, and became monks and nuns. Those were real Donatists. The Anabaptists are reviving this practice.[97]

Luther knows that the Anabaptists do not want to take normal human responsibilities, even in the family, claiming, "They [the Anabaptists] forsake wife and child, house and home; they surrender everything; they act as though they were senseless and mad."[98] In a *Table Talk* entitled "Not Solitude but Social Intercourse Advised"[99] between January 8 and March 23, 1532, Luther charges the Anabaptists with teaching that those who know Christ must separate themselves from human society, stating, "If you wish to know Christ, try to be alone, don't associate with men, become a separatist."[100] In a letter to Johann Hess dated January 27, 1528, Luther reports to Hess that the Anabaptists are the devil's captives, who leave their wives, children, and worldly goods in order to wander about in their teaching ministry.[101] Luther declares further that the Anabaptists agree with Muntzer that Christians should kill the wicked. They are, he claims, completely seditious. Again, in his letter to Justus Menius and Friedrich Myconius in February 1530, Luther states that the Anabaptists are not only blasphemers and disobedient but also seditious.[102] What does the word *seditious* mean in Luther's context? In his expository writing on the eighty-two Psalms, Luther defines that seditious heretics were those who teach that: first, no rulers are to be tolerated; second, no Christian may occupy a position of political authority; third, no one should have private property; fourth, the Christian ought to leave his home and family; fifth, all property should be held in common.[103] Luther contends that the temporal rulers should punish these teachers who attack the rulers and their government.

Luther also critiques Anabaptism for its position on the role of Christians in society. The Anabaptists were viewed as politically and religiously exclusive for refusing to accept normal obligations of citizenship—oaths, taxes, military service—who were seen to be forming a state within the state.[104] Seeing taking oaths as a major part of the glue that held society together in late medieval society, citizens swore oaths to the common good and defense of the town, to the societies to which they belonged, and to the truth.[105] Luther, therefore, sees taking oaths imposed by the government as in agreement with the command of God, who has commanded us to obey the government.[106] Therefore, Luther saw the Anabaptists as a threat to both church and state, and society in general for withdrawing themselves from others into their own contact zone. Carter Lindberg, professor emeritus of Church History at Boston University School of Theology, also characterizes the Anabaptist as "a steepleless Christianity,"[107] a Christianity with corporate loyalties and internal disciplines transcending any earthly state and never to be subsumed under one, a people characterized by the pursuit of holiness, separated from the world. As such, the entire sociopolitical order was jeopardized by their insistence on no Christian participation in the affairs of human beings for the welfare of all humanity. Luther, therefore, saw the Anabaptist as a disruptive force to the sociopolitical and religious tenets of his day, who held themselves above human society.

NOTES

1. Brian Tierney, *The Crisis of Church & State, 1050–1300: With Selected Documents* (Englewood Cliffs, NJ: Prentice-Hall, 1964), 182.

2. Tierney, 188.

3. Kenneth G. Appold, *The Reformation: A Brief History* (Malden, MA: Wiley-Blackwell, 2011), 45.

4. Appold, 46.

5. Carter Lindberg, *The European Reformations Sourcebook* (Oxford: Blackwell Publishing, 2000), 31.

80 *Chapter Two*

6. Lindberg, 31.

7. Carter Lindberg, *The European Reformations* (Oxford: Blackwell Publishing, 2010), 72.

8. Martin Luther, "Ninety-Five Theses or Disputation on the Power and Efficacy of Indulgences," in *Luther's Works*, vol. 31, trans. C. M. Jacobs, ed. Harold J. Grimm (Philadelphia: Muhlenberg Press, 1957), 26.

9. James L. Price Jr., "Nicolaitans," in *The HarperCollins Bible Dictionary*, ed. Mark Allen Powell (New York: HarperCollins Publishers, 2011), 700. The term *Nicolaitism*, is derived from a Christian sect in Ephesus and Pergamum whose members are denounced in Revelation 2:6, 15 for eating food sacrificed to idols and for sexual license. In the Middle Ages the term was sometimes used to refer to married priests by the upholders of clerical celibacy.

10. Appold, *The Reformation*, 23–24.

11. Robert N. Crossley, *Luther and the Peasants' War: Luther's Actions and Reactions* (New York: Exposition Press, 1974), 3.

12. Crossley, 6–7.

13. J. Paul William Rajashekar, "Faith Active in Love and Truth Realized in Love: A Comparative Study of the Ethics of Martin Luther and Mahatma Gandhi" (PhD thesis, The Graduate College of the University of Iowa, July 1981), 156–57.

14. Rajashekar, 152.

15. Karl H. Hertz, *Two Kingdoms and One World* (Minneapolis: Augsburg Publishing House, 1976), 310–12.

16. Martin Luther, *Commentary on the Epistles to the Romans*, trans. J. Theodore Mueller (Grand Rapids, MI: Zondervan Publishing House, 1954), 164.

17. Paul Althaus, *The Ethics of Martin Luther*, trans. Robert C. Schultz (Philadelphia: Fortress Press, 1972), 51.

18. Luther, *Commentary on the Epistles to the Romans*, 165.

19. Martin Luther, "To the Christian Nobility of the German Nation Concerning the Reform of the Christian Estate," in *Luther's Works*, vol. 44, trans. Charles M. Jacobs, ed. James Atkinson (Philadelphia: Fortress Press, 1966), 126.

20. Luther, 127.

21. Luther, 127.

22. Luther, 129–30.

23. Luther, 130.

24. Luther, 130.

25. Luther, 137.

26. Luther, 137.

27. Luther, 138.

28. Martin Luther, "The Babylonian Captivity of the Church," in *Luther's Works*, vol. 36, trans. A. T. W. Steinhauser, ed. Abdel Ross Wentz (Philadelphia: Muhlenberg Press, 1959), 11–57.

29. Luther, 21.

30. Luther, 27.

31. Martin Luther, "The Freedom of a Christian," in *Luther's Works*, vol. 31, trans. W. A. Lambert, ed. Harold J. Grimm (Philadelphia: Muhlenberg Press, 1957), 358.

32. Martin Luther, "Why the Books of the Pope and His Disciples Were Burned by Doctor Martin Luther," in *Luther's Works*, vol. 31, trans. Lewis W. Spitz, ed. Harold J. Grimm (Philadelphia: Muhlenberg, 1957), 381.

33. Luther, 394.

34. Martin Luther, "Temporal Authority: To What Extent It Should Be Obeyed," in *Luther's Works*, vol. 45, trans. J. J. Schindel, ed. Walther I. Brandt (Philadelphia: Muhlenberg Press, 1962), 79.

35. Luther, 89.

36. Luther, 91.

37. Luther, 95.

38. Luther, 116.

39. Luther, 92–94.

40. Martin Luther, "Selected Psalms II," in *Luther's Works*, vol. 13, trans. C. M. Jacobs, ed. Jaroslav Pelikan (Saint Louis: Concordia Publishing House, 1956), 44.

41. Rajashekar, "Faith Active in Love and Truth Realized in Love," 160.

42. Luther, "Selected Psalms II," 44.

43. Luther, "Temporal Authority," 126.

44. Luther, 113.

45. Luther, "Selected Psalms II," 46.

46. Luther, 49.

47. Luther, 50–51.

48. Reinhold Niebuhr, *The Nature and Destiny of Man* (New York: Charles Scribner's Sons, 1943), 187.

49. Roland H. Bainton, *Here I Stand: A Life of Martin Luther* (London: Hodder and Stoughton, 1951), 189.

50. Martin Luther, "Luther at the Diet of Worms, 1521," in *Luther's Works*, vol. 32, trans. Roger A. Hornsby, ed. George W. Forell (Philadelphia: Muhlenberg Press, 1958), 112–13.

51. Janos Bak, "The Peasant War in Germany by Friedrich Engels—125 Years After," in *The German Peasant War of 1525*, ed. Janos Bak (London: Frank Cass, 1976), 112.

52. The Twelve Articles were the Manifesto of the Upper Swabian peasants written by Sebastian Lotzer, a lay Reformer, and Christoph Schappeler, a pastor, which summarized lists of peasant grievances.

53. Crossley, *Luther and the Peasants' War*, 41–42.

54. Martin Luther, "Admonition to Peace: A Reply to the Twelve Articles of the Peasants in Swabia," in *Luther's Works*, vol. 46, trans. Charles M. Jacobs, ed. Robert C. Schultz (Philadelphia: Fortress Press, 1967), 17.

55. Luther, 19.

56. Luther, 20.

57. Luther, 42.

58. Luther, 29.

82   *Chapter Two*

59. Martin Luther, "Against the Robbing and Murdering Hordes of Peasants," in *Luther's Works*, vol. 46, trans. Charles M. Jacobs, ed. Robert C. Schultz (Philadelphia: Fortress Press, 1967), 50.

60. Thomas Muntzer, "Sermon before the Princes," in *Spiritual and Anabaptist Writers*, vol. 25, ed. George Huntston Williams and Angel M. Mergal (Louisville, KY: Westminster John Knox Press, 1957), 68.

61. Muntzer, 62.

62. Muntzer, 68.

63. Walter Altmann, *Luther and Liberation: A Latin American Perspective* (Minneapolis: Fortress Press, 2015), 287.

64. Luther, "Against the Robbing and Murdering Hordes of Peasants," 50.

65. Luther, 55.

66. Martin Luther, "An Open Letter on the Harsh Book of Peasants," in *Luther's Works*, vol. 46, trans. Charles M. Jacobs, ed. Robert C. Schultz (Philadelphia: Fortress Press, 1967), 69–70.

67. Luther, 71.

68. Luther, 84.

69. Crossley, *Luther and the Peasants' War*, 49.

70. C. Arnold Snyder, "Swiss Anabaptism: The Beginnings, 1523–1525," in *A Companion to Anabaptism and Spiritualism, 1521–1700*, ed. John D. Roth and James M. Stayer (Leiden: Boston, Brill, 2007), 52.

71. *The Oxford Dictionary of the Christian Church*, 3rd edition (2005), s.v. "Zwingli, Ulrich." Zwingli was a Swiss Reformer, who was ordained priest in 1506. On December 11, 1518, he was elected People's Preacher at the Old Minster in Zurich, where he remained for the rest of his life. He began the Reformation in Switzerland in 1519 by attacking the doctrines on purgatory, invocation of saints, and monasticism. In 1522, he advocated the liberation of Swiss Christians from the control of the Papacy and bishops.

72. Huldrych Zwingli, "Divine and Human Righteousness," in *Selected Writings of Huldrych Zwingli*, vol. 2, trans. H. Wayne Pipkin (Allison Park, PA: Pickwick Publications, 1984), 31.

73. Walter Klaassen, "Grebel, Conrad," in *The Oxford Encyclopedia of the Reformation*, vol. 2, ed. Hans J. Hillerbrand (New York: Oxford University Press, 1996), 191–93.

74. Snyder, "Swiss Anabaptism," 63.

75. Appold, *The Reformation: A Brief History*, 120.

76. Ulrich Zwingli, *Zwingli and Bullinger*, vol. 24, trans. G. W. Bromiley (Philadelphia: Westminster Press, 1953), 124. Colossians 2:10–12, "And you have come to fullness in him, who is the head of every ruler and authority. In him also you were circumcised with a spiritual circumcision, by putting off the body of the flesh in the circumcision of Christ; when you were buried with him in baptism, you were also raised with him through faith in the power of God, who raised him from the dead."

77. Snyder, "Swiss Anabaptism," 64.

78. Snyder, 64.

Martin Luther's Theology of Two Kingdoms as a Tool for Transformation 83

79. H. Wayne Pipkin, "Blaurock, George," in *The Oxford Encyclopedia of the Reformation*, vol. 1, ed. Hans J. Hillerbrand (New York: Oxford University Press, 1996), 177. George Blaurock was a Swiss Anabaptist founder whose significance lies in his leadership of Swiss-Austrian Anabaptists. He participated in baptismal debates in January 1525. He was the first to be baptized by Conrad Grebel as an adult believer during a gathering at the home of Felix Mantz on January 21, 1525. He in returned baptized those present who requested it.

80. Hutterian Brethren, *The Chronicle of the Hutterian Brethren*, vol. 1 (Rifton, NY: Plough Publishing House, 1987), 45. The name "Hutterian Brethren" is derived from Jacob Hutter, Anabaptist leader in Austria. There were three Anabaptist branches: the Swiss Brethren, the Dutch Anabaptists (called Mennonites), and the Hutterites (the followers of Jacob Hutter). The Hutterian Brethren were Austrian in origin. Their movement began in Moravia.

81. Lindberg, *The European Reformations*, 205.

82. Balthasar Hubmaier, *Balthasar Hubmaier: Theologian of Anabaptism*, trans. H. Wayne Pipkin & John H. Yoder (Scottdale, PA: Herald Press, 1989), 85.

83. Rollin Stely Armour, *Anabaptist Baptism: A Representative Study* (Scottdale, PA: Herald Press, 1966), 22.

84. Hubmaier, *Balthasar Hubmaier*, 106.

85. Hubmaier, 256.

86. Martin Luther, "A Treatise on the New Testament, that is, the Holy Mass, 1520," in *Luther's Works*, vol. 35, trans. Jeremiah J. Schindel, ed. E. Theodore Bachmann (Philadelphia: Muhlenberg, 1960), 91.

87. Luther, 91.

88. Martin Luther, "Concerning Rebaptism," in *Luther's Works*, vol. 40, trans. Conrad Bergendoff, ed. Conrad Bergendoff (Philadelphia: Fortress Press, 1958), 254–57.

89. Luther, 239.

90. Luther, 239.

91. Luther, 242.

92. Luther, 245.

93. Luther, 250.

94. Lindberg, *The European Reformations*, 202.

95. Martin Luther, "Lectures on Genesis," in *Luther's Works*, vol. 2, trans. George V. Schick, ed. Jaroslav Pelikan (Saint Louis: Concordia Publishing House, 1960), 326. Luther gave his lectures on the book of Genesis to his students at University of Wittenberg. His students took down lecture notes.

96. Martin Luther, "Sermons on the Gospel of St. John," in *Luther's Works*, vol. 23, trans. Martin H. Bertram, ed. Jaroslav Pelikan (Saint Louis: Concordia Publishing House, 1959), 66.

97. Luther, 205.

98. Luther, 356.

99. Martin Luther, "Table Talk," in *Luther's Works*, vol. 54, trans. Theodore G. Tappert, ed. Theodore G. Tappert (Philadelphia: Fortress Press, 1967), 140.

100. Luther, 140.

84   *Chapter Two*

101. Martin Luther, *D. Martin Luthers Werke: Kritische Gesamtausgabe*, 4. Band (Weimar: Germann Bohlaus Nachfolger, 1933), 371–72.

102. Martin Luther, *D. Martin Luthers Werke: Kritische Gesamtausgabe*, 5. Band (Weimar: Germann Bohlaus Nachfolger, 1934), 244. Menius was a leading polemicist against the Anabaptists in Eisenach (Wittenberg circle). In 1519 he studied under the supervision of Melanchthon in Wittenberg where he also became acquainted with Luther personally.

103. Luther, "Selected Psalms II," 61.

104. Hutterian Brethren, *The Chronicle of the Hutterian Brethren*, vol. 1, 52–62. Also see Lindberg, *The European Reformations*, 192.

105. Lindberg, *The European Reformations*, 192.

106. Martin Luther, "Lectures on Genesis," in *Luther's Works*, vol. 4, trans. George V. Schick, ed. Jaroslav Pelikan (St. Louis: Concordia Publishing House, 1964), 78.

107. Lindberg, *The European Reformations*, 190.

Chapter Three

Dietrich Bonhoeffer's Theology of Political Resistance in Light of Luther's Theology of Two Kingdoms

Historical Context of Dietrich Bonhoeffer

In order to understand Dietrich Bonhoeffer's political engagement, one needs to look at the political, social, and religious contexts of Germany in Bonhoeffer's day. Bonhoeffer lived in the time when xenophobic nationalism was on the rise in Germany. World War I, which ended with the Treaty of Versailles on June 28, 1919, when Bonhoeffer was thirteen years old, had an enormous effect on Germany and its relations with other nations, in Europe and beyond. The Treaty of Versailles had required Germany to accept sole responsibility for reparations of other nations. Article 124 of the Treaty states, "Germany hereby undertakes to pay, in accordance with the estimate to be presented by the French Government and approved by the Reparation Commission, reparation for damage suffered by French nationals in the Cameroons or the frontier zone by reasons of the acts of the German civil and military authorities and of German private individuals during the period from January 1, 1900, to August 1, 1914."[1]

Accordingly, Germany had to pay for damage caused to allied civilians and their property. As a consequence, the German people were suffering under the harsh measures imposed on them by the Allies, leading to drastic economic decline in the country. Furthermore, Article 160 of the Treaty of Versailles states, "The total number of the German Army must not exceed one hundred thousand men, including officers and establishments of depots. The Army shall be devoted exclusively to the maintenance of order within the territory

86   *Chapter Three*

and to the control of the frontiers."[2] Germany was required to reduce the strength of its armed forces, which allowed only a small professional army of one hundred thousand men, restricted to preserving order within the country, and was forbidden from maintaining military aircraft or submarines.

Considering the Treaty of Versailles one-sided and unfair, some of the German people embraced xenophobic nationalism, looking for scapegoats to blame for their troubles. They were also searching for a strong leader who would fuel these deeply passionate feelings. In such a situation, Adolf Hitler quickly rose to fill in that blank, taking the chance to fuel the false sense of national identity by blaming the Jews for Germany's defeat in WW I. As a leader of the National Socialist German Workers' Party, *Nationalsozialistische Deutsche Arbeiterpartei* (NSDAP),[3] Hitler said in a 1923 speech that the Treaty of Versailles was not only unfair but criminal, which enslaved Germany, saying, "We were the first to declare that this peace treaty was a crime."[4] When the Nazi regime took power in 1933, Adolf Hitler viewed the rest of Europe as enemies of Germany, and saw the Jews as the driving force behind the German defeat in 1918, and saw the Russian communist movement, which might spread throughout Europe, as a danger for Germany.[5] In his speech to the German nation on February 1, 1933, in Berlin, Hitler emphasized the danger of Communism in Germany, stating:

> Communism with its method of madness is making a powerful and insidious attack upon our dismayed and shattered nation. It seeks to poison and disrupt in order to hurl us into an epoch of chaos. This negative, destroying spirit spared nothing of all that is highest and most valuable. Beginning with the family, it has undermined the very foundations of morality and faith and scoffs at culture and business, nation and Fatherland, justice and honor.[6]

In such an emotional context, some Germans believed that Hitler could help them get rid of the Communists as well. As a result, many of the German people supported Hitler and his agenda to transform Germany into a world power. Then, after the death of German president Paul von Hindenburg on August 2, 1934, Hitler attempted to unify the whole German nation into one solid monolithic system directed by one will, his own, and governed by one small group of people—the Nazi dictatorship. The Nazis perverted justice and exploited the government structure for their own purposes in the name of resurrecting their "humiliated" nation. On February 28, 1933, Hitler announced his laws, which abolished all personal rights of the citizens previously protected by the constitution, in the name of the protection of people, and declared all those who opposed the Nazi regime traitors to the country, saying, "Restriction of personal freedom, of the right of free speech, including the freedom of the press, of the right of association and of public assembly, intervention in the privacy of post, telegraph and telephone, authorization of house searches and the confiscation and restriction of property, beyond the hitherto legal limits, will henceforward be admissible."[7]

According to the declaration, the police could arrest persons without a warrant and without stating any reasons; they could hold persons indefinitely, search their homes, and confiscate their property.[8] Hitler legalized a series of discriminatory policies against the Jews, which excluded people of Jewish origin from holding government office. He founded the "Sturmabteilung," (the SA militia, meaning Storm Troopers),[9] which was a paramilitary organization of the Nazi Party, that fought against the Jews. The Nazi regime also took charge of the nation's schools. On July 21, 1931, the *Nationalsozialistischer Deutscher Studentenbund* (National Socialist German Student League), which was an organization of university students who got more power under the Nazis, elected as their chair a Nazi student who decided to support Hitler's Nazi regime and the segregation of Jews. The National Socialist German Student League became groups of brown-shirted shock troops on university and graduate school campuses.[10] Students who supported the Nazi government were strongly active at all institutions of learning, always ready to attack their opponents. The Nazi regime prescribed the curriculum, especially in the teaching of biology and history. Teachers known to be suspicious of the Nazi regime were removed from their positions. From the age of ten boys were pressured into joining the *Hitlerjugend* (Hitler Youth), the only youth organization allowed by the Nazis, which spent much of its time imparting basic military skills to its members. For girls there was a parallel organization, *Bund Deutscher Madel* (Band of German Maidens).[11] Young men between eighteen and twenty-five were obliged to spend six months in the *Arbeitsdienst* receiving further military training, followed by two years' compulsory military service.[12] From 1931 to 1932, Bonhoeffer was a lecturer at Friedrich Wilhelm University. He was not happy with what was happening in his university since many faculty members and students at the University of Berlin supported Hitler and his agendas.

Hitler went much further than denouncing the Treaty of Versailles, spreading his long-held antisemitic beliefs. He gave fiery speeches calling Jews evil and harmful, like a cancer for the health of the Germany. Considering Jews to be the embodiment of evil, Hitler called for a national boycott of Jewish businesses on April 1, 1933. This involved boycotting, looting and destroying Jewish businesses, verbally ridiculing Jews, and physically attacking Jewish physicians and lawyers in particular.[13] The SA militiamen held up signs in front of Jewish stores that read, "Germans! Defend yourself, don't buy from Jews."[14] Marriage between Jews and Germans was prohibited. Jewish children were expelled from school and university, and they were all obliged by law to wear a badge showing a yellow star in public as a mark of

88   *Chapter Three*

degradation.[15] Again, on November 9–10, 1938, now known as *Kristallnacht* (Crystal Night), Hitler's SA militiamen and civilians brutalized Jews, broke the windows of Jewish houses and stores, and burned the synagogues, all in the presence of the police, who watched the violence passively without any interventions. On January 30, 1939, Hitler addressed his supporters in the Reichstag, about "the Jewish question." He said:

> It is a shameful spectacle to see how the whole democratic world is oozing sympathy for the poor tormented Jewish people, but remains hard-hearted and obdurate when it comes to helping them, which is surely, in view of its attitude, an obvious duty. . . . Today I will once more be a prophet: If the international Jewish financiers inside and outside Europe should succeed in plunging the nations once more into a world war, then the result will not be the Bolshevization of the earth, and thus the victory of Jewry, but the annihilation of the Jewish race in Europe.[16]

The Nazis perverted the Christian virtues of compassion, kindness, love, charity, and humility, on the one hand, and on the other hand exalted the use of violence for their own ends. In October 1939, Hitler gave a formal order to kill the mentally ill and the disabled. Hitler introduced the notion of the German people as a superior and unique race in his political rhetoric. According to Nazism, the true German people who would be part of rebuilding Germany were Aryan, which excluded the Jews. As a result, Jews were excluded in nation building. Hitler delivered a speech on November 10, 1933, in Siemensstadt, saying, "I am interested only in the German people. To the people alone I belong and for the people I spend my energies."[17]

Regarding religious matters, many Catholic bishops were deeply concerned about the future of the church in Germany under the Nazi regime, and they wanted to advocate a conciliatory policy to Hitler. Hitler used this as an opening to co-opt the church for his political ends. He neutralized the Roman Catholic Church by offering to negotiate with the Vatican directly, intending to gain international prestige for his regime and to cut the Catholic clergy out of German politics. On July 20, 1933, Hitler made a concordat with the Vatican, signed by Cardinal State Secretary Eugenio Pacelli (later Pope Pius XII from 1939 to 1958) and Vice Chancellor Franz von Papen. Since the Catholic Church in Germany was less closely linked with the government than the Protestant Churches, the Vatican signed the concordat in exchange for their obedience to the Nazi regime and the rights to maintain and run the Catholic schools and the freedom of Catholics to worship in Germany. For Hitler, however, the concordat was little more than a symbol, meant to show the rest of the world that his government was respectable and trustworthy in the eyes of the highest authority within Catholicism.[18] The

Nazi regime promised the Catholics the right to run Catholic schools, the right to send uncensored communication back to Rome, and the right to publish pastoral letters. In return, the church ordered bishops to take an oath of loyalty to the state and prohibited the clergy from taking part in political activities.[19] However, Hitler broke the concordat. He interfered in the rights of bishops to communicate with Rome and publish pastoral letters, and he shut down some of the Catholic schools. Several bishops denounced the discriminatory policies of the Nazis, particularly in March 1937, after Pope Pius XI criticized the Nazis. As a result, the campaign against priests was intensified, and by 1939 hundreds of clergymen were taken to concentration camps.

Relations with the Protestant churches were not better either. At an assembly of the "Brown Synod"[20] in September 1933, the church adopted Hitler's agenda of the "Aryan Paragraph,"[21] denying Jewish ministers from pastoral ministry. Hitler excluded Christians of Jewish descent from churches and forbade Christian mission activities among them. Many Christians within Germany had adopted Hitler's jingoistic nationalism as part of their creed. In this context, Bonhoeffer attempted to persuade delegates from churches not to vote for pro-Hitler candidates. Despite Bonhoeffer's efforts, an evangelical group who wanted to synthesize Hitler's National Socialism and Christianity secured large majorities with Nazi assistance. Those who were declared "non-Aryan" pastors—that is, Jewish pastors, were dismissed and the new national synod, meeting at Wittenberg, elected Ludwig Muller, a former military chaplain and current Nazi sympathizer, to be the first national bishop. He promptly appointed like-minded clergy to the various churches, giving the Nazis complete control of the church. At the assembly of the "Brown Synod," which was the pro-Nazi national synod, the German Christians made a provision that clergy were to be of "Aryan descent" and would be required to declare support for the National Socialist State and the German Protestant Church.

Shortly after the assembly of the "Brown Synod," Bonhoeffer, together with Martin Niemoller, who was ordained in 1924 and became a pastor of Berlin parish of Dahlem in 1931, formed the Pastors' Emergency League. The Confessing Church was established at Barmen in 1934 by the Pastor's Emergency League, which became the opposition church that stood against policies of the German Christians. The "Aryan Paragraph" imposed the belief that the German churches should be purely German and excluded Christians of Jewish descent from them. In other words, Hitler had racialized religion, which was totally unacceptable for Bonhoeffer and the Confessing Church. At a meeting of the Barmen Synod in 1934, the Confessing Church affirmed the famous Barmen Confession of Faith. Authored in large part by Karl Barth, it said, "We repudiate the false teaching that there are areas of our life in which we belong not to Jesus Christ but to other lords."[22] The Barmen

90   *Chapter Three*

Confession was focused on restoring the integrity of the church and standing against the Nazi regime. In other words, the Confession opposed the Nazi regime's intention to go beyond its own office and exercise control over the church's vocation as well.[23] However, it did not speak out for those outside the church who were suffering. Karl Barth would later regret that he had overlooked the increasing social and religious conflicts of his time since the Confession's emphasis on Christ alone was inadequate to help the persecuted Jews and others.

DIETRICH BONHOEFFER'S RECEPTION OF LUTHER'S TWO KINGDOMS THEOLOGY

As a Lutheran, Bonhoeffer was strongly influenced by Luther's theology during his theological studies at the University of Tubingen. However, prominent Bonhoeffer scholar Clifford Green distances Bonhoeffer from Luther's theology of two kingdoms. In his editorial introduction to the scholarly edition of Bonhoeffer's *Ethics*, Green argues that Bonhoeffer breaks away from Luther's two-kingdoms theology. Green writes, "Bonhoeffer is proposing an alternative to the two kingdoms doctrine. He introduces the doctrine of mandates right after his polemics against the two-kingdoms doctrine."[24] He continues, "Bonhoeffer's doctrine of mandates—marriage, work, church, state—grew from grappling with several ideas in traditional Lutheran theology as they were found wanting in his historical experience. One was the doctrine of orders of creation, another the doctrine of the three estates, and a third the doctrine of two-kingdoms."[25]

I do not agree with Green in his argument that Bonhoeffer's use of the four mandates is a totally distinct idea, which replaces Luther's two-kingdoms theology. In fact, Bonhoeffer is renewing and reclaiming Luther's original two-kingdoms theology with a new term and dynamic explanation. Bonhoeffer defines the word *mandate* as:

> The concrete divine commission grounded in the revelation of Christ and the testimony of Scripture; it is the authorization and legitimization to declare a particular divine commandment, the conferring of divine authority on an earthly institution. A mandate is to be understood simultaneously as the laying claim to, commandeering of, and formation of a certain earthly domain by the divine command. The bearer of the mandate acts as a vicarious representative, as a stand-in for the one who issued the commission.[26]

In Bonhoeffer's view, God has entrusted government officials under his mandates. Therefore, government officials must serve God with every action.

Bonhoeffer's Theology of Political Resistance in Light of Luther's Theology 91

After providing this definition, Bonhoeffer considers three traditional terms—order, estate, office—but prefers the term *mandate* to renew and reclaim the old concepts with better language.[27] He then says, "Lacking a better word we thus stay, for the time being, with the concept of mandate. Nevertheless, our goal, through clarifying the issue itself, is to contribute to renewing and reclaiming the old concepts of order, estate, and office."[28] With this statement, Bonhoeffer commits to reclaiming Luther's original two-kingdoms theology without departing from it.

In his 1932–1933 essay "Thy Kingdom Come," Bonhoeffer presents each of Luther's "two-kingdoms" as balancing and supporting each other in mutual service and respect. He states, "The church limits the state, just as the state limits the church. And both must remain aware of this mutual limitation and support this tense juxtaposition, which should never be a coalescence. Only thus do both *together*, and never one alone, point to the kingdom of God, which is here attested in such a splendid twofold form."[29]

It is clear from this statement that Bonhoeffer is integrating his "mandates" idea with Luther's two kingdoms idea. According to Luther's view, God rules the world in two ways—through the law in the worldly kingdom and through the Gospel in the spiritual kingdom. Both worldly and spiritual kingdoms are God's. The church belongs in both kingdoms as an institution in the world and as a proclamation of the Gospel of God's mercy and grace. Bonhoeffer affirms this view by saying, "The mandate of the church embraces all people as they live within all other mandates. . . . The church mandate reaches into all the other mandates. The Christian is at the same time worker, spouse, and citizen."[30] This statement is clear evidence that Bonhoeffer does not break away from Luther's two-kingdoms theology, but rather draws from it, and criticizes his contemporaries for what he considers their misunderstanding of Luther's intent.

Combining two-kingdoms theology and the four mandates to form his basic theological ground, Bonhoeffer wrote his essay "The Church and the Jewish Question" in April 1933 as a response to the "Aryan Paragraph," which barred Jewish people from various organizations such as political parties, from holding government office, and from Christian churches and theological study. Coming from the state, the "Aryan Paragraph" excluded the Jewish people forcibly from the church. Removing Christians of Jewish descent from the pastorate contradicts the Lutheran understanding of the priesthood of all believers, thereby making Christians of Jewish descent inferior to the German Christians. In the face of such exclusion, Bonhoeffer calls upon the church to speak up for the oppressed Jews, saying, "The church must open new doors to the ministry for Christians of Jewish descent and thereby protest, through its proclamation, against such measures that attack the substance of the ministry. If the church does not do so, it is guilty of responsibility for the entire "Aryan

92   *Chapter Three*

Paragraph."[31] Bonhoeffer considers keeping silent in the face of oppression as equivalent to supporting violence or renouncing responsibilities.

In "The Church and the Jewish Question," Bonhoeffer raises two questions for the church. First, how does the church judge this action by the state, and what is the church called upon to do about it? Second, what are the consequences for the church's position toward the baptized Jews in its congregations? Bonhoeffer states that both these questions can only be answered on the basis of a right concept of the church and its response to state action in particular.[32] Bonhoeffer's theoretical response to the first question is, "There is no doubt that the church of the Reformation is not encouraged to get involved directly in specific political actions of the state."[33] In other words, it is not the task of the church to prescribe laws and policies for the state. To do so would mean turning the gospel into law, thereby undermining the gospel. The state preserves the world through law and order, and the church preaches the gospel of grace. It is the function of the state to maintain order by "creating law and order by force."[34] It is to the state, not the church, that God has given the judging sword of power.[35] However, while discouraging the church from direct political action on particular state policies, Bonhoeffer goes on, saying:

> But that does not mean that the church stands aside, indifferent to what political action is taken. Instead, it can and must, precisely because it does not moralize about individual cases, keep asking the government whether its actions can be justified as *legitimate state* actions, that is, actions that create law and order, not lack of rights and disorder. It will be called upon to put this question as strongly as possible wherever the state seems endangered precisely in its *character as the state*, that is, in its function of creating law and order by force. The church will have to put this question with the utmost clarity today in the matter of the Jewish question.[36]

Accordingly, the church should speak out against the state on the question of its character as God's entrusted institution to maintain law and order for the well-being of human beings in society, since the church knows that the role of the first use of the law is to restrain sin and promote the good, that is, to punish the wicked and protect the upright. As such, Bonhoeffer continues to say that either too little law and order or too much law and order compels the church to speak.[37]

In his 1932 lecture "The Nature of the Church," Bonhoeffer affirms the distinction between church and state as fulfilling their respective mandates by standing side by side. He states:

> God's word has power also over the state. Through this the state is set as a critical warning for the church, that God has not given the judging sword of power

to the church. Its sword is the word and the prayer. Thereby it serves the state. When it is threatened by the state, it fights against the state. It will not try to govern the state. The goal is the proclamation of the lordship of Christ over the whole world in faith and in the word. The church and the state are side by side. The church may not become the state; the state is recognized as an autonomous worldly power. . . . [It is] a call to completely responsible, true action, each according to its own office. Obedience to the state exists only when the state does not threaten the word. The battle about the boundary must then be fought out! The decision will be difficult in the development of our future state. The office of the state is neither Christian nor godless; the office must be carried out in a responsible and objective way (the state's proper purposes). The existence of the church depends on whether its criticism can come from listening to the gospel alone. Criticism of the state is demanded where it threatens the word.[38]

Bonhoeffer describes both the limitation and the support church and state should provide to each other in a mutual service without a dichotomized separation or unnecessary interference. He presents the church and the state as two different entities, each with its own office under God's governance. Using the two kingdoms as the center of his argument, Bonhoeffer continues elaborating on the relationship between church and state, saying, "Miracle and order are the two forms in which God's kingdom on earth presents itself and in which it is scattered. The miracle as the breaking through of all order, and the order as the preservation in preparation for the miracle. . . . The form in which the kingdom of God is attested as miracle we call—the *church*; the form in which the kingdom of God is attested as order we call—the *state*."[39]

According to Bonhoeffer's argument, the church witnesses to the miracle of God—that is, the resurrection of Christ breaking death to life and the power of God in the new creation. The state maintains and preserves the earth with its laws. In this way, both the church and the state are not dichotomized, but rather, are necessarily linked to each other. The state is responsible for maintenance of law and order in society with the use of law and sword, while the church is ordained by God to preach the gospel of grace.

This does not mean, however, that God's word does not have power over the state. Rather, the church and the state should not interfere in other's tasks unnecessarily. The state's power comes into question if it fails to fulfill God's mandate. The church is the place where the gospel is preached and heard. Bonhoeffer articulates the church's resistance to the state in his theology of mandates. He does not distance himself from Luther's two-kingdoms theology. In his 1933 lecture "Christology," Bonhoeffer states, "This is why Luther can say that the state is the kingdom of God on the left hand. As long as Christ was on earth, he alone was the kingdom of God. Since he was crucified, it is as if his form is broken into the right hand and the left hand of God. He can now be recognized only in twofold form, as church and state."[40] Bonhoeffer

94   *Chapter Three*

has inherited Luther's theology of two kingdoms in a mutual form as opposite to a rigid dichotomized form. Bonhoeffer, therefore, believes that if the state unnecessarily threatens the church, the battle about the boundary must then be fought out.[41] He affirms that if the state interferes with the church in religious matters, two-kingdoms theology should be utilized to make the distinction between them. Bonhoeffer describes the unity of church and state, in the language of Luther's two-kingdoms thinking, saying:

> There is unity of faith only under the true word of Jesus Christ. The sword, however, belongs to the worldly government, which in its own way, in the proper exercise of its office, serves the same Lord Jesus Christ. There are two kingdoms, *Zwei Reiche*, which, as long as the earth remains, must never be mixed together, yet never torn apart: the kingdom of the proclaimed word of God and the kingdom of the sword, the kingdom of the church and the kingdom of the world, the kingdom of the spiritual office and the kingdom of worldly authority. The sword can never bring about the unity of the church and of faith; preaching can never rule the peoples. But the lord of both kingdoms is God revealed in Jesus Christ. God rules the world by the office of the word and the office of the sword. The bearers of both of these offices are accountable to God. There is only one church, the church of faith ruled by the word of Jesus Christ alone. This is the true Catholic church that has never disappeared and is still concealed in the church of Rome. It is the body of Christ—Corpus Christi. It is the true unity of the West.[42]

Bonhoeffer maintains neither a rigid dichotomy between church and state nor the mixing up of the two. He affirms that God rules the world in two ways—through the sword in the worldly kingdom and through the preached word in the spiritual kingdom. Both worldly and spiritual kingdoms are united under God's rule. Bonhoeffer sees that this authentic unity has been corrupted through the process of secularization, resulting in the pseudo-Lutheran misunderstanding of the two kingdoms. He says:

> Protestants found in a misunderstood Lutheran doctrine of the two kingdoms a liberation and sanctification of the world and the natural order. Government, reason, economy, and culture each claimed the right to autonomy, but in this autonomy understood themselves to be not at all at odds with Christianity. Rather, they saw the service of God that is truly demanded by Reformation Christianity in their very autonomy. The original Reformation message, that human holiness is found neither in the sacred nor in the profane as such, but only through the gracious sin-forgiving word of God, was thoroughly forgotten. The Reformation was celebrated as the liberation of the human beings, of conscience, reason, and culture, as the justification of the worldly as such.[43]

This pseudo-Lutheran misunderstanding of the two kingdoms is characterized by the complete autonomy of the worldly kingdom, and a rigid dichotomy between church and state in which one is fully divine, holy, supernatural, and Christian, while the other is profane, natural, and unchristian.[44] Bonhoeffer identifies this view as one first articulated during the High Middle Ages and then repeated in the post-Reformation period as pseudo-Reformation thought. As such, the German-Lutheran secularization misunderstands the distinction between the two kingdoms, and thereby the church becomes reduced to purely spiritual devotion in submission to state power. Bonhoeffer, therefore, is in fact returning to the understanding that Luther espoused in the sixteenth century. In Bonhoeffer's context, the complete separation of church and state, was a ploy used by the Nazis and some of the German churches, resulting in the absolute submission of the church to the state. Bonhoeffer is trying to bring the church back in line with Luther's views.

DIETRICH BONHOEFFER'S POLITICAL RESISTANCE

Dietrich Bonhoeffer learned theology of solidarity with the oppressed in an expected place: the Abyssinian Baptist Church, New York, in 1930 during his study at Union Theological Seminary as a postdoctoral student for one year before returning to Germany to protect the oppressed and fight against the dehumanizing forces of the Nazi regime. Reggie L. Williams, assistant professor of Christian Ethics at McCormick Theological Seminary, presents in his book *Bonhoeffer's Black Jesus: Harlem Resistance Theology and an Ethic of Resistance* Bonhoeffer's significant experience of the Harlem Resistance, which became a catalyst for him to become an engaged Christian in Germany during the Nazi period. One of Bonhoeffer's classmates, Albert Fisher, worked in the Abyssinian Baptist Church in Harlem. Fisher introduced Bonhoeffer to the Black church where he witnessed human suffering in general, and Black suffering in specific, as the beginning of theology of suffering. Williams states that most liberal whites ignore the constant dangers of daily life in America for Black people who live under the constant threat of white supremacy,[45] adding, "The white Christ was the theological muscle of the power structure of the color line and its global manifestations: colonization, imperialism, nationalism, and white terrorism in America."[46] In the Abyssinian Baptist Church, Bonhoeffer saw the Black church engagement in four dialectics: priestly and prophetic functions, otherworldly and this-worldly tensions, universalism and particularism, and accommodation and resistance.[47] The African American churches in Harlem played a significant role in the development of ideas, initiatives, and ethics around poverty and social welfare to reach out to less privileged Black people. About thirteen

96   *Chapter Three*

years later, on November 5, 1942, Bonhoeffer writes that his year in New York has been highly significant for him up to the present day.[48]

Furthermore, Bonhoeffer's own lived experiences during his childhood also play a significant role in his journey toward socially engaged Christianity. World War I directly impacted Bonhoeffer, driving him to search for the meaning of life because of the death of his brother, Walter Bonhoeffer, on April 28, 1918, after being fatally wounded in battle on April 23. His mother, Paula Bonhoeffer, could not bear the loss of her son and laid in bed for weeks. The Bonhoeffer family did not celebrate holidays for years. Three years after the death of his brother, at Bonhoeffer's confirmation, his mother gave Bonhoeffer the Bible that Walter had received at his confirmation in 1914. Bonhoeffer used it throughout his life for his personal meditations and in worship.[49] Speaking in New York City on November 9, 1930, Bonhoeffer recalled the tragedy of WWI, saying, "Death stood at the door of almost every house and called for entrance. . . . Germany was made a house of mourning."[50] As a result, human suffering is the starting point of theology for Bonhoeffer. Therefore, when we turn to Bonhoeffer's use of Luther's two-kingdoms theology in twentieth-century Germany, we see a more compelling picture of a socially engaged Christian movement as Bonhoeffer reaches beyond Luther in order to protect the most vulnerable members of his society, breaking racial, religious, and cultural boundaries and embracing the politics of inclusiveness in his theology of empathic solidarity with the oppressed.

German resistance to the Nazi regime emerged as a direct response to its fundamental injustice and destructive forces. Corruption, dictatorial oppression, racial discrimination, persecution of religious leaders and political opponents, and the persecution of "non-Aryans" were the principal causes of the resistance movement. Bonhoeffer's resistance movement took different forms, such as publicly denouncing and condemning the dehumanizing forces of the Nazi regime, asking others to resist the Nazis at all costs, helping persecuted Jews to escape from Germany, a refusal to contribute even a small amount of money to Nazi fund drives, founding the Confessing Church and seminary, refusing to serve in the military service, and participating in conspiracy activities.

The installation of Adolf Hitler as Chancellor on January 30, 1933, was a turning point for Bonhoeffer, beginning his efforts to boldly and responsibly resist against Hitler's dehumanizing forces. On February 1, 1933, Bonhoeffer gave a radio address entitled "The Fuhrer and the Individual in the Younger Generation," in which he outlines his understanding of political authority. He argues that political authority runs "from above to below."[51] He then highlights proper relations between the individual leader and the office. He says, "Leader and office that turn themselves into gods mock God and the solitary individual before him who is becoming the individual and must collapse. Only the leader who is in the service of the penultimate and the ultimate authority merits loyalty."[52] God, as the ultimate authority, gives the penultimate authority not to the person, but rather, to the political office in the state, and a good political leader recognizes that authority does not rest in his own person but in his office. Bonhoeffer states, "The leader points to the office; leader and office, however, point to the ultimate authority itself."[53] With this understanding, Bonhoeffer believes that every action of the office of the state must serve God. However, Bonhoeffer sees Hitler's Nazism as the reversal of right political leadership, where authority is seen as deriving not from "above," from God, but from "below," the people who transfer it to the Fuhrer. He says, "This leader, arising from the collective power of the people, now appears in the light as the one awaited by the people, the longed-for fulfillment of the meaning and power of the life of the *Volk* [people]. Thus, the originally prosaic idea of political authority is transformed into the political-messianic idea of leader that we see today. All the religious thinking of its supporters flows into it as well."[54]

Bonhoeffer strongly criticizes Hitler for "[making] himself an idol"[55] and becoming a misleader by granting himself the ultimate authority, which should be reserved for God, thereby destroying the office of the ultimate authority. The Nazi regime sought to take the mechanism of church government under its control and create a united national church under a national bishop appointed by the party. Hitler wanted his people to participate in his agenda. Therefore, the late 1930s were turbulent years for Bonhoeffer. The Gestapo closed down the Finkenwalde seminary, which he had founded and directed, in late 1937. As a result, Bonhoeffer and his seminarians were forced to form a secret network in order to continue their work. Since the end of 1937, the pastors whom Bonhoeffer trained had been pressured to minister under the authority of the provincial church consistories. Those who denied were not recognized as legal pastors, resulting in the loss of their parsonage and salaries. Many of them compromised in order to achieve legal status as pastors. The director of the evangelical consistory, Friedrich Werner, issued an order on April 20, 1938, which required all German pastors to pledge a loyalty oath not only to the National Socialist Party but also to Hitler personally by saying, "I swear that I will be faithful and obedient to Adolf Hitler, the Fuhrer of the German Reich and people, that I will conscientiously observe the laws and carry out the duties of my office, so help me God."[56] Some of the German Lutheran churches who sided with the Nazi totalitarian regime saw Hitler as a new spiritual leader who would restore Germany's cultural greatness by excluding Christians of Jewish descent and others from Germany. Paul Althaus, a German Lutheran theologian of the twentieth century, in

98   *Chapter Three*

support of the Nazi regime also said, "Our Protestant churches have seen the German year of 1933 as a gift and miracle of God."[57]

Utilizing Luther's two-kingdoms theology, Bonhoeffer believes that God ordains the state to exercise its own authority within its own God-given field. According to him, God entrusts the state, on the one hand, to punish the wicked, and, on the other hand, to commend and protect the good and the righteous. In other words, God gives the state the task of establishing justice and righteousness on earth. Bonhoeffer sees persons in government as "God's liturgists, servants, vicarious representatives."[58] In other words, Bonhoeffer's position is that every action of the state must serve God and represent God's actions, which means that the violation of the divine commandment will result in punishment from God. Underlining the actions of the state in society, Bonhoeffer says, "The task of government consists in serving the dominion of Christ on earth by worldly exercise of the power of the sword and of the law. Government serves Christ inasmuch as it establishes and preserves an external righteousness by wielding the sword given to it, and to it alone, in God's stead."[59] Bonhoeffer believes that the dominion of Christ includes both church and state, that is, both serve the same Christ, stating, "Government and church are bound, and bound together, by the same Lord. . . . Government and church have the same sphere of action, human beings."[60] Meanwhile, government and church are distinguished from each other in their tasks. The church should not interfere with the work of the state. In his 1932 essay "What is the Church?" Bonhoeffer says, "The church proves its worth through nothing other than properly spreading the message of the gospel, through properly proclaiming grace and commandment."[61] Although Bonhoeffer believes that the church should not try to govern the state, the church has a situational political responsibility if the state fails to fulfill its divine mandate. Bonhoeffer's key question for the government is, if the state does not manage God's given task properly, what should the church do? Believing that God has entrusted the church under his mandates[62]—work, marriage, government, and church—Bonhoeffer states three important possibilities in his essay "The Church and the Jewish Question" in 1933, in which the church can respond to the state in the face of killing, and oppression, "First, the church can ask the state whether its actions are legitimate and in accordance with its character as state, that is, the church can throw the state back on its responsibilities; second, the church can aid the victims of state action regardless of religion; third, there is a possibility not just to bandage the victims under the wheel, but also to put a spoke in the wheel itself."[63]

In short, Bonhoeffer believes that God has mandated both church and state, but if the state is causing or ignoring the suffering of the people, the church must hold the state accountable. If the state will not respond to its higher calling, then the church is not only to aid the victims but to put "a spoke in the wheel" of the state. Seeing Hitler's agenda as a severe danger to the health of the nations, Bonhoeffer petitions the armed forces for anti-Hitler agendas and protection of the persecuted Jews and others in November 1941, stating, "In view of the acute dangers, the Protestant church requests that the military effect the following, namely: first, all antichurch measures be halted for the duration of the war; second, imprisonments, expulsions, bans on speaking, etc. resulting from ecclesial and/or church-political grounds be rescinded; third, help and protection at home be extended to the church for its responsible mission during the war."[64] Bonhoeffer was to be disappointed, since his petition was not met, and indeed, some of the German churches were hailing the rise of Hitler. He, therefore, strongly resisted Hitler's agendas at all costs in order to protect the persecuted Jews and others in Germany to save not just Christian civilization as a whole, but all Western civilization, including Jewish cultures. He argued that driving the Jews out from the West must result in driving out Christ with them, for Jesus Christ was a Jew.[65] In a context where fellow-human beings, the Jews in specific, were discriminated against, Bonhoeffer quotes Luther, saying, "God would rather hear the curses of the godless than the hallelujahs of the pious."[66] Bonhoeffer believes that the German national church has cut itself off from the true church of Jesus Christ. Therefore, he does not hesitate to draw the connection between the Confessing Church and salvation. The question of church membership is the question of salvation: whoever knowingly cuts himself off from the Confessing Church in Germany cuts himself off from salvation.[67] Bonhoeffer critiques not just the government but the church itself, since it is enmeshed with the Nazi government. Using the Confessing Church as an example of the church in resistance, Bonhoeffer considers that only the church in resistance, distinct from the state, is the true church.

Furthermore, Bonhoeffer finds a correlation between discipleship and justification by costly grace. Drawing from Luther's understanding of the doctrine of justification by costly grace, Bonhoeffer says in his classic book *Discipleship*, "The grace was costly, because it did not excuse one from works. Instead, it endlessly sharpened the call to discipleship."[68] He continues saying that Luther's teachings are quoted everywhere but twisted from their truth into self-delusion.[69] Bonhoeffer is, therefore, disappointed with some of the German churches when they overstressed grace into what he calls "cheap grace," stating, "Like ravens we have gathered around the carcass of cheap grace. From it we have imbibed the poison which has killed the following of Jesus among us. The doctrine of pure grace experienced an unprecedented deification."[70] Bonhoeffer argues that the German Lutherans have distorted the truth of justification by faith into an emphasis on "cheap grace," which means grace sold on the market, grace without discipleship, grace without the Cross, grace without the incarnate Christ, forgiveness without repentance,

100 *Chapter Three*

baptism without church discipline, Communion without confession, and absolution without contrition. Bonhoeffer instead calls for "costly grace," stating:

> It is costly, because it calls to discipleship; it is grace, because it calls us to follow Jesus Christ. It is costly, because it costs people their lives; it is grace, because it thereby makes them live. It is costly, because it condemns sins; it is grace, because it justifies the sinner. Above all, grace is costly, because it was costly to God, because it costs God the life of God's Son—"you were bought with a price"—and because nothing can be cheap to us which is costly to God. Above all, it is grace because the life of God's Son was not too costly for God to give in order to make us live. God did, indeed, give him up for us. Costly grace is the incarnation of God.[71]

Bonhoeffer notes with deep frustration how the German churches have been reduced to purely spiritual devotion in submission to state power and are thus led to overlook their public responsibility to promote the value of human life. He, therefore, warns the churches that the consciences of Christians can be dulled by churchly assurances that their routine, periodic sacred performance of listening to a sermon or participating in a harmless, nonthreatening liturgy is sufficient responsibility.[72] Rather than the privatization of religion, he called for the public engagement of the Christian faith in the secular world and urged the church not to flee from, but to enter a worldly life. We can also clearly see Bonhoeffer's altruism in his letter to Reinhold Niebuhr, which was written at the end of June 1939, when he was determined to leave the United States of America and return to Germany in order to share the pain and suffering of his people, stating, "I have made a mistake in coming to America. I must live through this difficult period of our national history with the Christian people of Germany. I will have no right to participate in the reconstruction of Christian life in Germany after the war if I do not share the trials of this time with my people. My brothers in the Confessional Synod wanted me to go."[73] Bonhoeffer made the right decision to return to Germany, instead of enjoying a comfortable life in America, to speak up for the persecuted Jews and others. He blamed the German churches for not speaking out against the Nazi regime and declared that German Christians were partially guilty for the deaths of countless Jewish people. Bonhoeffer urged the church to acknowledge its failure to speak, saying:

> The church was mute when it should have cried out, because the blood of the innocent cried out to heaven. The church did not find the right word in the right way at the right time. It did not resist to the death the falling away from faith and is guilty of the godlessness of the masses. The church confesses that it has misused the name of Christ by being ashamed of it before the world and by not resisting strongly enough the misuse of that name for evil ends. The church has

Bonhoeffer's Theology of Political Resistance in Light of Luther's Theology 101

looked on while injustice and violence have been done, under the cover of the name of Christ. It has even allowed the most holy name to be openly derided without contradiction and has thus encouraged that derision.[74]

Bonhoeffer reveals the failure of the church to fulfill its calling as the true church of Jesus Christ by resisting the atrocities committed by the Nazis. To Bonhoeffer, the refusal to participate in contemporary issues in society comes not from religious piety but from a lack of moral courage. Criticizing the church for keeping silent in the face of oppression, Bonhoeffer defines the role of the church in society, stating:

> The church is the church only when it exists for others. To make a start, it should give away all its property to those in need. The clergy must live solely on the free-will offerings of their congregations, or possibly engage in some secular calling. The church must share in the secular problems of ordinary human life, not dominating, but helping and serving. It must tell men of every calling what it means to live in Christ, to exist for others.[75]

Bonhoeffer underlines the public engagement of the church in society without withdrawing narrowly into a comfort zone. His lecture at the University of Berlin on November 19, 1932, "Thy Kingdom Come" indicates his burning desire to stress the public engagement of the Christian faith in a secular society. He states, "Christianity was neither an archaic replica of the heavenly world nor a cluster of sacred shrines and hallowed sanctuaries, magic escape routes from earthly turmoil. Rather, the Christian is to live faith as much in the marketplace and factory as at church altars. Faith is thus to be embedded in the way each Christian becomes strong in his or her service of earth and its people."[76] Bonhoeffer called upon the church to shape the world in the image of Jesus Christ by implementing Christ's compassion for the oppressed, the marginalized, the exploited, the downtrodden, and the defenseless. When Christians stand up against oppression, Bonhoeffer is quite aware that they can potentially face severe consequences, as he believes that "when Christ calls a man, He bids him come and die."[77] Bonhoeffer believes that in following Christ, Christians must be prepared not to withdraw themselves but to go into a challenging human society in order to respond to Christ's calling, stating, "A Christianity that withdraws from the world falls prey to unnaturalness, irrationality, triumphalism, and arbitrariness. . . . There is no real Christian existence outside the reality of the world and no real worldliness outside the reality of Jesus Christ. For the Christian, there is nowhere to retreat from the world, neither externally nor into the inner life."[78]

Regarding ethical principles Bonhoeffer believes that yesterday cannot ever be decisive for his moral action today. Rather, a direct relationship to God's

102   *Chapter Three*

will must be ever sought afresh. He says, "I do not do something again today because it seemed to me to be good yesterday, but because the will of God points out this way to me today. This is the great moral renewal through Jesus, the renunciation of principles, of rulings, in the words of the Bible, of the law, and this follows as a consequence of the Christian idea of God."[79] Bonhoeffer strongly believes that there can be ethics only in the concrete situation, and at the moment of the divine call, of the claim which one has to answer and for which one has to make himself responsible. He says, "There cannot be good and evil as general ideas, but only as qualities of will making a decision."[80] In his thought, Jesus is not concerned with an abstract idea of ethics. Jesus is concerned with God's love for human beings, and thereby entering into human life and bearing humans' guilt. He, therefore, maintains that human beings are not called to realize ethical ideals, but are called into a life that is lived in God's love, which must be a life lived in reality.[81]

When he defines his ethics of responsible action, Bonhoeffer uses the German word *Stellvertretung*, which literally means "to represent in place of another," to act, advocate, intercede on behalf of another that could be translated as "vicarious representative action."[82] As a theological concept it is, therefore, deeply rooted in Christology and refers to the free initiative and responsibility that Christ takes for the sake of humanity in His incarnation, crucifixion, and resurrection.[83] As a whole, the word *Stellvertretung* involves acting responsibly on behalf of others and on behalf of one's community. Taking Jesus Christ's vicarious representative action for human beings as the structural principle of the Christian ministry, Bonhoeffer called upon Christians to be actively with-one-another and for-one-another. As a consequence, it is no longer possible to separate ecclesiology from Christology, because both are connected through the principle of vicarious representative action.[84] Addressing the necessity of vicarious representative action of the church in public engagement, Bonhoeffer strongly insists that the true church of Jesus Christ exists only where the vicarious representative witness of faith takes on a concrete form.[85]

In *Sanctorum Communio*, Bonhoeffer sees Christ's action in terms of *Stellvertung*, saying, "Though innocent, Jesus takes the sin of others upon himself, and by dying as a criminal he is accursed, for he bears the sins of the world and is punished for them."[86] However, vicarious representative love triumphs on the criminal's cross, as obedience to God triumphs over sin and thereby sin is actually punished.[87] Christ, as vicarious representative, justifies the sinners. Michael DeJonge, whose scholarship has focused on Bonhoeffer, argues that *Sanctorum Communio* presents *Stellvertung* in more communal terms, addressing the church, while *History and Good* in *Ethics* presents it in relatively individualistic terms, addressing the world beyond the church.[88] In action, the idea of *Stellvertung* embraces both individuals and communities.

Speaking against absolute obedience to the repressive laws of the totalitarian state power, Bonhoeffer strongly encourages responsible Christians to do the daring deed freely amid the risky consequences of their own lives, for the sake of the oppressed, the weak, and ultimately for Jesus Christ. Citing the biblical text Luke 17:33, he articulates that those who want to lose their lives will save them, adding, "This is the only way in which surrendering myself to what God wills for my neighbor really leads to the community of the *Sanctorum Communion* established by God; to realize this each person serves as an instrument of God."[89] Bonhoeffer deepened his understanding of the church as being the-one-for-others as Christ is. Christ is more than a role model. The church is Christ. Bonhoeffer also correlates Christian freedom with service, that is, freedom from something is complete only through freedom for something. Freedom solely in order to be free leads to anarchy. Biblically, freedom means being free for service to God, and to one's neighbor, freedom for obedience to the commandments of God.[90] He also spoke of immersing himself in the life, words, actions, suffering, and death of Jesus, and continued saying, "It is certain that our joy is hidden in suffering, and our life in death."[91] Indeed, Bonhoeffer saw joy in his own suffering in solidarity with the oppressed, and advocated for theology from below, from the perspective of the outcasts, the suspects, the maltreated, the powerless, the oppressed, the reviled, the despised, the discriminated, and the marginalized.[92]

Although Bonhoeffer did not formulate the relationship between church and state systematically, his work proves his political resistance against the repressive regime and challenges the absolute submission of the church to the state. However, three Mennonite scholars—Mark Thiessen Nation, Anthony G. Siegrist, and Daniel P. Umbel—question Bonhoeffer's active resistance against Hitler, giving him the simplistic label "pacifist." They brand Bonhoeffer as a consistent pacifist throughout his life's journey and distance him from active resistance in conspiracy activities against the Third Reich, and argue that the central issue of Bonhoeffer's trial was his refusal to enter military service, as well as encouraging others in the same refusal.[93] In order to understand this argument, we have to look at the whole picture of Bonhoeffer's active engagement in public beyond the church by looking at his own writings and those of his colleagues. Indeed, conspiracy was very clandestine and complicated. It involved gathering information, exchanging information, engaging with ecumenical movements to establish peace between Germany and the Allies, and eventually moving to overthrow Hitler's Nazi regime before Hitler launched his offensive against others.

Eberhard Bethge, Bonhoeffer's close friend and biographer who extensively collected Bonhoeffer's monographs, also notes the twists and turns of active resistance and pacifism in Bonhoeffer. He recalls Bonhoeffer saying sometime in September 1941, that "if it fell to him to carry out the deed

104   *Chapter Three*

[the assassination], he was prepared to do so, but that he must first resign, formally and officially, from his church. The church could not shield him, and he had no wish to claim its protection. It was a theoretical statement, of course, since Bonhoeffer knew nothing about guns or explosives."[94] Is it true that Bonhoeffer really knew nothing about guns or explosives? Bethge's last sentence contrasts with Bonhoeffer's own words, since his own writing shows something quite different. While a theological student at Tubingen, Bonhoeffer did two weeks of military training where he learned how to use various weapons. He wrote to his parents on November 16, 1923, saying, "Today I am a soldier. Yesterday as soon as we arrived, we were invested with a uniform and were given our equipment. Today we were given grenades and weapons."[95] Just two weeks later on December 1, Bonhoeffer wrote to his parents again, saying, "Today I am a civilian. . . . I told the lieutenant on Wednesday that I wanted to leave after two weeks. . . . It was, after all, very reasonable to perform one's duty for two weeks. We began with group training, and then progressed fairly quickly to proper field duty and to shooting exercises."[96] Clearly, Bonhoeffer's own letters prove Bethge's misreading of Bonhoeffer's life on this point.

On February 8, 1929, Bonhoeffer gave a lecture titled "Basic Questions of a Christian Ethics" to a German-speaking congregation in Barcelona, Spain. In his lecture, Bonhoeffer speaks against the literal application of the commandments of the Sermon on the Mount in his specific context because such an application would violate the spirit of Christ and freedom from the law.[97] Bonhoeffer believes that to apply the Sermon on the Mount literally in times of war would mean surrendering one's own neighbors into the hands of enemies. He reflected the crisis and hope in the face of war and provided a rationale to protect one's family and people, saying, "I no longer have the choice between good and evil; regardless of which decision I make, that decision will soil me with the world and its laws. I will take up arms with the terrible knowledge of doing something horrible, and yet knowing I can do no other. I will defend my brother, my mother, my people, and yet I know that I can do so only by spilling blood; but love for my people will sanctify murder, will sanctify war."[98] He added that he must love his enemies yet will kill them because of love and gratitude toward his own people. There is no doubt that Bonhoeffer was not a pacifist at this historical time. However, at other times Bonhoeffer shifted his stand from active resistance to passive resistance. His attitude of passive resistance could be seen in his letters and lectures. In 1930 during his study at Union Theological Seminary, Bonhoeffer came to know a deeper understanding of the commandments of the Sermon on the Mount through his friendship with Jean Lasserre, a French Reformed pastor and pacifist. Bethge says that Lasserre confronted Bonhoeffer with an acceptance of Jesus's peace commandment that he had never encountered before.[99] On November 1, 1934, Bonhoeffer secured a personal invitation from Mahatma Gandhi, with Bishop George Kennedy Allen Bell of Chichester, England, as intermediary, to come to India to stay with him and study with him if Gandhi was not in prison or traveling, or otherwise to stay in his Sarbamati Ashram in Ahmedabad, in northwest India.[100] However, the two could not meet personally because the growing crisis in Germany demanded Bonhoeffer's attention. Reinhold Niebuhr told Bonhoeffer that Gandhi's nonviolent method would not be applicable in the context of the Nazi regime in Germany. He warned Bonhoeffer that Gandhi's success depended upon British political liberalism, and passive resistance against the Nazi regime would end in utter failure.[101] In his 1932 lecture on "Christ and Peace," Bonhoeffer said, "The commandment—You shall not kill, the word that says—Love your enemies,—is given to us simply to be obeyed. For Christians, any military service, except in the ambulance corps, and any preparation for war, is forbidden."[102] Again in 1936, Bonhoeffer wrote about Christian pacifism, stating, "I had still passionately attacked the position of Christian pacifism during a debate in which Gerhard also was present. Now I suddenly came to recognize it as self-evident. And this process continued, step by step. I no longer saw or thought anything else anymore."[103] It seems that Bonhoeffer was a pacifist at this particular point.

We see the twists and turns of Bonhoeffer's stance and thoughts. In his 1932 lecture "The Theological Foundation of the Work of the World Alliance," Bonhoeffer said:

> Our contemporary war does not fall under the concept of battle because it means the certain self-destruction of both warring sides. For that reason today it is utterly impossible to characterize it as an order of preservation toward revelation, simply because it is absolutely destructive. The power of destruction reaches the inner life as well as the external life of human beings. Today's war destroys soul and body. Because there is no way for us to understand war as God's order of preservation and therefore as God's commandment, and because war needs to be idealized and idolatrized in order to live, today's war, the next war, must be *condemned* by the church. . . . We must face the next war with all the power of resistance, rejection, condemnation. . . . We should not balk here at using the word "pacifism." Just as certainly as we submit the ultimate *pacem facere* (to create peace) to God, we too must *pacem facere* to overcome war.[104]

There are no winners, but only losers, in war with regard to humanity since it results in the loss of human lives from both warring sides. Therefore, Bonhoeffer reflects war from the perspective of the preservation of God's creation and understands it as a total destruction of humanity. Bonhoeffer was, therefore, calling upon the church to opt for peace with all the power of resistance to war. His understanding of the word "pacifism" is not associated

106   *Chapter Three*

with total withdrawal from sociopolitical engagement, but rather, a call to participation to condemn war for the welfare of all humanity. In other words, Bonhoeffer is calling upon the church to engage actively in the sociopolitical affairs of human beings to value human lives.

Although Lasserre influenced Bonhoeffer to a certain extent, they had disagreed on the path to social engagement. Their disagreement inspired Bonhoeffer to write his book *The Cost of Discipleship*, published in 1937, in which Bonhoeffer himself saw the dangers of his stance.[105] On March 25, 1939, Bonhoeffer wrote a letter to Bishop Bell during his visit to England, bringing him two concerns: first, the relationship of the Confessional Church to the overseas churches; second, a more personal concern. Regarding the latter, Bonhoeffer states:

> The second point is of entirely personal character, and I am not certain if I may bother you with it. Please, do take it quite apart from the first point. I am think- ing of leaving Germany sometime. The main reason is the compulsory military service to which the men of my age (1906) will be called up this year. It seems to me conscientiously impossible to join in a war under the present circumstances. On the other hand, the Confessional Church as such has not taken any definite attitude in this respect and probably cannot take it as things are. So, I should cause a tremendous damage to my brethren if I would make a stand on this point which would be regarded by the regime as typical of the hostility of our church towards the state. Perhaps the worst thing of all is the military oath which I should have to swear. So, I am rather puzzled in this situation, and perhaps even more because I feel, it is really only on Christian grounds that I find it difficult to do military service under the present conditions, and yet there are only very few friends who would approve of my attitude. In spite of much reading and thinking concerning this matter I have not yet made up my mind what I would do under different circumstances. But actually as things are I should have to do violence to my Christian conviction if I would take up arms here and now.[106]

It is true that Hitler put a new law for compulsory military service for men effective on May 1, 1935. Many Christians in Germany, including those in the Confessing Church, joined the military service despite Bonhoeffer's objec- tion. In this situation, Bonhoeffer was convinced by Jesus's commandment to love our neighbor. Therefore, he did not want to volunteer in the military service in which he would kill the Nazi regime's enemies in the name of Hitler. Therefore, in August 1939, at the beginning of the war, Bonhoeffer applied for a military chaplaincy but was turned down on the basic reason that it was reserved only for a pastor who had already served as a soldier in the military. Hans von Dohnanyi, Bonhoeffer's brother-in-law, a lawyer who had taken a position in the Military Intelligence Agency on August 25, 1939, persuaded Bonhoeffer to join the *Abwer* (the Military Intelligence Agency).

Bonhoeffer's Theology of Political Resistance in Light of Luther's Theology 107

Then, the Military Intelligence office discussed employing Bonhoeffer as an agent in September 1940. On October 30, 1940, Bonhoeffer joined the *Abwer* in the Munich office as a confidential agent after which the Military Intelligence Agency granted him a "UK" classification *unabkommlich*, or "indispensable," thereby making him unavailable for conscription into the army.[107] Bonhoeffer gained international relations through his involvement in ecumenical activities throughout the European and American ecumenical world. Therefore, in order to cut Bonhoeffer's contact with people outside of Germany, Bishop Theodor Heckel, the leader of the Ecclesiastical Foreign Office of Hitler's Nazi regime, demanded a written declaration from Bonhoeffer that he would withdraw from all ecumenical activities. But he did not get Bonhoeffer's signature.[108] Bonhoeffer refused to sign it because he considered it as a revocation of his ordination vow and his commitment to ecumenical activities in which he engaged for years.

We can also see Bonhoeffer's involvement in conspiracy activities in Bishop Bell's writings. Bell and Bonhoeffer had known each other intimately since 1933 when Bonhoeffer served as pastor of German-speaking congregations in England. Bell writes that Bonhoeffer works for the Confessing Church by day and engages in political activity by night.[109] On May 31, 1942, Bonhoeffer met with Bishop Bell at Sigtuna, Sweden. During their meeting, Bonhoeffer told Bishop Bell the names of chief conspirators such as Colonel-General Beck, Colonel-General von Hammerstein, Karl Goerdeler, Wilhelm Leuschner, and Jakob Kaiser. Bell says that when the plot to assassinate Hitler took place on July 20, 1944, the men named to him just over two years before by Bonhoeffer were among the chief conspirators who, in Hitler's words, were "exterminated mercilessly."[110] Bishop Bell says that during their meeting in 1942 Bonhoeffer was obviously distressed in his mind as to the lengths to which he had been driven by force of circumstances in the plot for the elimination of Hitler.[111] Bonhoeffer told Bishop Bell that it was his Christian conscience which was driving him to eliminate Hitler, saying, "There must be punishment by God. We should not be worthy of such a solution. We do not want to escape repentance. Our action must be understood as an act of repentance."[112]

Again in 1945, Bishop Bell writes about his meeting with Bonhoeffer in Sweden in 1942, and gives an account of the foundations of the plot to kill Hitler that had been laid in 1940. He says:

> Bonhoeffer started his political activities with his friends (especially von Dohnanyi) at the outbreak of war. We know of the despair which seized all those who were engaged in subversive activities in July and August 1940. We know of a meeting held at that time where it was proposed that further action should be postponed, so as to avoid giving Hitler the character of a martyr if he should be

108   *Chapter Three*

killed. Bonhoeffer's rejoinder was decisive: If we claim to be Christians, there is no room for expediency. Hitler is the anti-Christ. Therefore, we must go on with our work and eliminate him whether he be successful or not.[113]

There is no doubt that Bonhoeffer did oppose Hitler. His involvement in conspiracy activities to take down Hitler is not by chance, but rather, it was the result of his theological reflection and decision as a socially engaged Christian who was seeking social justice through emphatic solidarity with the oppressed Jews and others. Studying Bonhoeffer's life and thoughts shows his struggle with the twists and turns of passive and active resistance in life. However, it is important to remember that we should never understate a hidden reality inside Bonhoeffer, that is, nonviolence is not an absolute principle for either Bonhoeffer or Luther. Bonhoeffer involved himself in conspiracies against Hitler and the Third Reich in 1940 not as a representative of the church, but rather, as an individual. Why did Bonhoeffer join the *Abwer*? The answer is to stop Hitler by whatever means. Bonhoeffer was convinced that Hitler had to be stopped or eliminated in whatever ways because he was not just bad, but terrible. A country that elected and hailed Hitler was in turmoil. In such a horrible situation, Bonhoeffer as a pastor could not remain silent. He therefore attempted to stop Hitler by different means in order to restore peace, and eventually ended up in joining the *Abwer*, the Military Intelligence Agency, as a last resort.

NOTES

1. United States Senate, *Treaty of Peace with Germany* (Washington: Government Printing Office, 1919), 63–64.

2. United States Senate, 71.

3. David Bankier, "Nazi Party," *Encyclopedia of the Holocaust*, vol. 3, ed. Israel Gutman (New York: Macmillan Publishing Company, 1990), 1039–40. *Nationalsozialistische Deutsche Arbeiterpartei* (NSDAP) was the official name of the Nazi Party.

4. Adolf Hitler, *My New Order*, ed. Raoul de Roussy de Sales (New York: Reynal & Hitchcock, 1941), 25.

5. Ferdinand Schlingensiepen, *Dietrich Bonhoeffer: Martyr, Thinker, Man of Resistance* (New York: T & T Clark, 2010), 115.

6. Hitler, *My New Order*, 143.

7. Eberhard Bethge, *Dietrich Bonhoeffer: A Biography* (Minneapolis: Fortress Press, 2000), 263.

8. Peter Hoffmann, *German Resistance to Hitler* (Cambridge, MA: Harvard University Press, 1988), 20.

9. Bankier, "Nazi Party," *Encyclopedia of the Holocaust*, vol. 3, 1039.

Bonhoeffer's Theology of Political Resistance in Light of Luther's Theology 109

10. The name *brown-shirted unit* is derived from the brown color of the Nazi's uniform.

11. William Carr, *A History of Germany, 1815–1945* (New York: St. Martin's Press, 1969), 372–73.

12. Carr, 373.

13. Hoffmann, *German Resistance to Hitler*, 37.

14. Schlingensiepen, *Dietrich Bonhoeffer*, 121.

15. The star was intended to easily identify the Jews for deportation and humiliate them for discrimination.

16. Hitler, *My New Order*, 582–85.

17. Hitler, 226.

18. Hoffmann, *German Resistance to Hitler*, 32.

19. Carr, *A History of Germany*, 376.

20. The Prussian General Synod was called the "Brown Synod" because German attendees wore brown Nazi uniforms in the assembly in support of the Nazis.

21. Israel Gutman, "Arierparagraph," in *Encyclopedia of the Holocaust*, ed. Israel Gutman (New York: Macmillan Publishing Company, 1990), 83. The Nazi regime issued the "Aryan Paragraph" in April 1933, regulation barring "non-Aryans" (that is, Jews) from membership in German political parties, economic establishments, student and sport groups. The idea of an "Aryan" race is a Nazi invention. The church also adopted it and dismissed the Jews from pastoral ministry. Also see Schlingensiepen, *Dietrich Bonhoeffer*, 121–24.

22. Geffrey B. Kelly et al., "As Hitler Manipulated the German Churches and Oppressed the Jews, Most Christians Remained Silent. Not Dietrich Bonhoeffer," *Christian History* 10, no. 4 (1991): 11.

23. James Y. Holloway, *Barth, Barmen and the Confessing Church Today: Katallagete* (Lewiston, NY: The Edwin Mellen Press, 1995), 5–8.

24. Dietrich Bonhoeffer, "Ethics," in *Dietrich Bonhoeffer Works*, vol. 6, trans. Reinhard Krauss, Charles C. West, and Douglas W. Stott, ed. Clifford J. Green (Minneapolis: Fortress Press, 2005), 21.

25. Bonhoeffer, 18.

26. Bonhoeffer, 389.

27. Bonhoeffer, 389–90. Luther did not use the same terms consistently but varied between *order*, *estate*, and *hierarchy*. He uses the three orders in his 1542–1543 "table talk" to articulate his biblical interpretation: the household, the government, the church. His understanding of the three orders is seen in his interpretation of Genesis 2:16–17 in 1535, saying, "We have the establishment of the church before there was any government of the home and of the state. . . . The church is established without walls and without any pomp, in a very spacious and very delightful place. After the church has been established, the household government is also set up. . . . Thus the temple is earlier than the house, and it is also better this way. There was no government of the state before sin, for there was no need of it. Civil government is a remedy required by our corrupted nature." Also see Martin Luther, "Lectures on Genesis," *Luther's Works*, vol. 1, trans. George V. Schick, ed. Jaroslav Pelikan (Saint Louis: Concordia Publishing House, 1958), 103–4.

110 Chapter Three

28. Bonhoeffer, 390.

29. Dietrich Bonhoeffer, "Berlin, 1932–1933," in *Dietrich Bonhoeffer Works*, vol. 12, trans. Isabel Best and David Higgins, ed. Larry L. Rasmussen (Minneapolis: Fortress Press, 2009), 294.

30. Bonhoeffer, "Ethics," 73.

31. Bonhoeffer, "Berlin, 1932–1933," 431.

32. Bonhoeffer, 362.

33. Bonhoeffer, 362.

34. Bonhoeffer, 364.

35. Dietrich Bonhoeffer, "Ecumenical, Academic, and Pastoral Works, 1931–1932," in *Dietrich Bonhoeffer Works*, vol. 11, trans. Anne Schmidt-Lange, Isabel Best, Nicolas Humphrey, and Marion Pauck, ed. Victoria J. Barnett, Mark S. Brocker, and Michael B. Lukens (Minneapolis: Fortress Press, 2012), 332.

36. Bonhoeffer, "Berlin, 1932–1933," 363–64.

37. Bonhoeffer, 364.

38. Bonhoeffer, "Ecumenical, Academic, and Pastoral Works, 1931–1932," 332.

39. Bonhoeffer, "Berlin, 1932–1933," 292–93.

40. Bonhoeffer, 326–27.

41. Bonhoeffer, "Ecumenical, Academic, and Pastoral Works, 1931–1932," 332.

42. Bonhoeffer, "Ethics," 112.

43. Bonhoeffer, 113–14.

44. Bonhoeffer, 56.

45. Reggie L. William, *Bonhoeffer's Black Jesus: Harlem Resistance Theology and an Ethic of Resistance* (Waco, TX: Baylor University Press, 2014), 21.

46. William, 41.

47. William, 89.

48. Dietrich Bonhoeffer, "Conspiracy and Imprisonment, 1940–1945," in *Dietrich Bonhoeffer Works*, vol. 16, trans. Lisa E. Dahill, ed. Mark S. Brocker (Minneapolis: Fortress Press, 2006), 367–68.

49. Bethge, *Dietrich Bonhoeffer*, 28.

50. Dietrich Bonhoeffer, "Barcelona, Berlin, New York, 1928–1931," in *Dietrich Bonhoeffer Works*, vol. 10, trans. Douglas W. Stott, ed. Clifford J. Green (Minneapolis: Fortress Press, 2008), 582.

51. Bonhoeffer, "Berlin, 1932–1933," 278.

52. Bonhoeffer, 282.

53. Bonhoeffer, 281–82.

54. Bonhoeffer, 278.

55. Bonhoeffer, 280.

56. Bethge, *Dietrich Bonhoeffer*, 600.

57. Robert P. Ericksen, *Theologians under Hitler*, DVD, A Film by Steven D. Martin, 2006.

58. Bonhoeffer, "Conspiracy and Imprisonment, 1940–1945," 513.

59. Bonhoeffer, 514.

60. Bonhoeffer, 526.

61. Bonhoeffer, "Berlin, 1932–1933," 264.

Bonhoeffer's Theology of Political Resistance in Light of Luther's Theology   111

62. Bonhoeffer, "Ethics," 68.

63. Bonhoeffer, "Berlin, 1932–1933," 365.

64. Bonhoeffer, "Conspiracy and Imprisonment, 1940–1945," 245.

65. Bonhoeffer, "Ethics," 105.

66. Bonhoeffer, 124. Regarding the question of theodicy of God—why do the righteous suffer and the wicked prosper—Luther believed that blasphemies have been sometimes forced out by the devil against the will of the people. Even if one would commit blasphemy because of the overwhelming violence of his temptation, he would not therefore perish. For our God is not a God of impatience and cruelty, even toward the ungodly. Luther is saying this for the comfort of those who are perpetually troubled by thoughts of blasphemies and are in great anxiety about such blasphemies, because they are violently exhorted from men by the devil against their will. See Martin Luther, "Lectures on Romans," in *Luther's Works*, vol. 25, trans. Jacob A. O. Preus, ed. Hilton C. Oswald (Saint Louis: Concordia Publishing House, 1972), 390.

67. Dietrich Bonhoeffer, *A Testament to Freedom: The Essential Writings of Dietrich Bonhoeffer*, ed. Geffrey B. Kelly and F. Burton Nelson (New York: Harpers Collins Publishers, 1995), 166. Bonhoeffer contextualized the axiom *extra ecclesiam nulla salus* originated from Cyprian of Carthage. Bishop Cyprian fled his diocese and guided his church through correspondence during the persecution of Decius in 250 CE. When he came back to his diocese at the end of the persecution, thereby the church enjoying a relative peace, his authority in the church was challenged by the so-called "Confessors" (those who did not offer sacrifice to the gods as a symbol of their loyalty to the Christian faith). As a result, Cyprian called a council of bishops at Carthage in 251 CE in which important decisions were made on the readmission of the lapsed: first, those who had purchased certificates but actually performed no sacrifice to the Roman gods were immediately to be readmitted to the church; second, those who had sacrificed could only be readmitted on their deathbed if they repented or withstood another persecution; third, those who had sacrificed and were unrepentant could never be readmitted. Cyprian believed that all those actions were to be taken by the bishops, not by the confessors. Reaffirming his authority for the unity of the church, Cyprian said, "Outside the church, no salvation." See Mark Ellingsen, *Reclaiming Our Roots: An Inclusive Introduction to Church History*, vol. 1 (Harrisburg, PA: Trinity Press International, 1999), 80.

68. Dietrich Bonhoeffer, "Discipleship," in *Dietrich Bonhoeffer Works*, vol. 4, trans. Barbara Green and Reinhard Krauss, ed. Geffrey B. Kelly and John D. Godsey (Minneapolis: Fortress Press, 2001), 49.

69. Bonhoeffer, 53.

70. Bonhoeffer, 53.

71. Bonhoeffer, 45.

72. Bonhoeffer, *A Testament to Freedom*, 356.

73. Dietrich Bonhoeffer, "Theological Education Underground, 1937–1940," in *Dietrich Bonhoeffer Works*, vol. 15, trans. Victoria J. Barnett, Claudia D. Bergmann, Peter Frick, and Scott A. Moore, ed. Victoria J. Barnett (Minneapolis: Fortress Press, 2012), 210. Bonhoeffer was adamant to remain in America although his American

112   *Chapter Three*

friend, Paul Lehmann, and his former teacher, Reinhold Niebuhr, arranged for the tour with unspoken intention to rescue him from the evils of the Nazi Germany.

74. Bonhoeffer, "Ethics," 138.

75. Dietrich Bonhoeffer, *Letters and Papers from Prison*, trans. Eberhard Bethge (New York: The Macmillan Publishing, 1971), 382–83. Bonhoeffer's *Letters and Papers from Prison* was smuggled out by guards who wanted to help Bonhoeffer during his imprisonment.

76. Bonhoeffer, *A Testament to Freedom*, 88.

77. Dietrich Bonhoeffer, *The Cost of Discipleship*, trans. R. H. Fuller (New York: The Macmillan Company, 1949), 73.

78. Bonhoeffer, "Ethics," 61.

79. Bonhoeffer, *A Testament to Freedom*, 345.

80. Bonhoeffer, 350–51.

81. Bonhoeffer, "Ethics," 232.

82. Dietrich Bonhoeffer, "Sanctorum Communio: A Theological Study of the Sociology of the Church," in *Dietrich Bonhoeffer Works*, vol. 1, trans. Reinhard Krauss and Nancy Lukens, ed. Clifford J. Green (Minneapolis: Fortress Press, 1998), 120.

83. Bonhoeffer, 120.

84. Bonhoeffer, 302–3.

85. Bonhoeffer, 304.

86. Bonhoeffer, 155–56.

87. Bonhoeffer, 155–56.

88. Michael P. DeJonge, *Bonhoeffer's Reception of Luther* (Oxford: Oxford University Press, 2017), 246.

89. Bonhoeffer, "Sanctorum Communio," 176.

90. Bonhoeffer, "Conspiracy and Imprisonment, 1940–1945," 532.

91. Bonhoeffer, *Letters and Papers from Prison*, 391.

92. Bonhoeffer, 17.

93. Mark Thiessen Nation, Anthony G. Siegrist, Daniel P. Umbel, *Bonhoeffer the Assassin? Challenging the Myth, Recovering His Call to Peacemaking* (Grand Rapids, MI: Baker Academic, 2013), 226.

94. Bethge, *Dietrich Bonhoeffer*, 751–52.

95. Dietrich Bonhoeffer, "The Young Bonhoeffer, 1918–1927," in *Dietrich Bonhoeffer Works*, vol. 9, trans. Mary C. Nebelsick, ed. Paul Duane Matheny, Clifford J. Green, Marshall D. Johnson (Minneapolis: Fortress Press, 2003), 70.

96. Bonhoeffer, 74.

97. Bonhoeffer, "Barcelona, Berlin, New York, 1928–1931," 367.

98. Bonhoeffer, 372.

99. Bethge, *Dietrich Bonhoeffer*, 153.

100. Dietrich Bonhoeffer, "London, 1933–1935," in *Dietrich Bonhoeffer Works*, vol. 13, trans. Isabel Best, ed. Keith Clements (Minneapolis: Fortress Press, 2007), 229–230. Bishop George Bell wrote to Gandhi on October 22, 1934, and introduced Bonhoeffer to him, thereby asking Gandhi's great kindness to let Bonhoeffer visit him and study with him.

101. Larry L. Rasmussen, *Dietrich Bonhoeffer: Reality and Resistance* (Louisville, KY: Westminster John Knox Press, 2005), 213.

102. Bonhoeffer, "Berlin, 1932–1933," 260.

103. Bonhoeffer, "Discipleship," 292.

104. Bonhoeffer, "Ecumenical, Academic, and Pastoral Works, 1931–1932," 366–67. Bonhoeffer is referring to Luther's distinction between the two parts of the human beings, the inner (the relation to God) and the outer (the relation to the world).

105. Bonhoeffer, *Letters and Papers from Prison*, 369.

106. Dietrich Bonhoeffer, *Gesammelte Schriften*, Band. 1, trans. Eberhard Bethge (Munchen: Kaiser Verlag, 1958), 281–82.

107. Schlingensiepen, *Dietrich Bonhoeffer, 1906–1945*, 245.

108. Bonhoeffer, "London, 1933–1935," 254.

109. Bonhoeffer, *Gesammelte Schriften*, 394. Regarding Bonhoeffer's involvement in conspiracy activities against the Third Reich, Bell said there could be no two options in Bonhoeffer, who was an uncompromising anti-Nazi.

110. Bonhoeffer, 412. Bonhoeffer had been already arrested by the Gestapo on April 5, 1943, and was in prison when the attempt was made. Bonhoeffer and Dohnanyi were both arrested on April 5, 1943, on the charge of currency violations, related to Operation 7 of August and September 1942. It was called "Operation 7" because originally only seven people were concerned, but later fourteen Jews fled Germany to Switzerland on the pretext that they were the Abwer agents. Dohnanyi arranged for the foreign currency needed to support the "Operation 7" group. The Reich Central Security Office had found the irregularities of currency transactions for the Jews of "Operation 7," Bonhoeffer's exemption from military duty, and the international relations.

111. Bonhoeffer, 395.

112. Bonhoeffer, 395.

113. Bonhoeffer, 397–98. Also see Bethge, *Dietrich Bonhoeffer*, 722–23. Bethge said that Bonhoeffer's expression of Hitler being an anti-Christ does not occur anywhere else. He, this time, confirms that Bonhoeffer's arrest on April 5, 1943, is associated with his actual complicity in the plot against Hitler with active resistance.

Chapter Four

Social and Religious Engagement in Myanmar Society

Engaged Buddhism in Myanmar Society

Sallie B. King, professor emeritus of philosophy and religion at James Madison University in Harrisonburg, Virginia, defines engaged Buddhism by saying, "Engaged Buddhism is a contemporary form of Buddhism that engages actively yet non-violently with the social, economic, political, social, and ecological problems of society. At its best, this engagement is not separate from Buddhist spirituality, but is very much an expression of it. Chauvinistic Buddhism cannot be considered to be engaged Buddhism; it is indeed the antithesis of it."[1] According to this definition, socially engaged Buddhists emphasize social justice and peace by nonviolently engaging with society rather than withdrawing from it. Engaged Buddhism is strongly rooted in traditional Buddhist notions of good governance based on the ten duties. They are, first, *dana* (charity, generosity, and liberality): the ruler should not have craving and attachment to wealth and property but should give it away for the welfare of the people; second, *sila* (a high moral character): he should never destroy life, cheat, steal and exploit others, commit adultery, utter falsehood, or take intoxicating drinks; third, *pariccaga* (sacrificing everything for the good of the people): he must be prepared to give up all personal comfort, name and fame, and even his life, in the interest of the people; fourth, *ajjava* (honesty and integrity): he must be free from fear or favor in the discharge of his duties, must be sincere in his intentions, and must not deceive the public; fifth, *maddava* (kindness and gentleness): he must possess a genial temperament; sixth, *tapa* (austerity in habits): he must lead a simple life and should not indulge in a life of luxury, he must have self-control; seventh, *akkodha* (freedom from hatred, ill-will, enmity): he should bear no grudge against anybody; eighth, *avihimsa* (nonviolence), which means not only that he should harm no one, but also that he should try to promote peace by avoiding and

116   *Chapter Four*

preventing war, and everything which involves violence and destruction of life; ninth, *khanti* (patience, forbearance, tolerance, understanding): he must be able to bear hardships, difficulties and insults without losing his temper; tenth, *avirodha* (non-opposition, non-obstruction): he should not oppose the will of the people and should not obstruct any measures that are conductive to the welfare of the people. In other words, he should rule in harmony with his people.[2]

If a country is governed by people endowed with such qualities, happiness and peace will be realized in the country. Thich Nhat Hanh, a Vietnamese Buddhist monk who was the most important figure of the Vietnamese "Struggle Movement" to bring an end to the war in Vietnam coined the term *Nhan Gian Phat Giao*, or "engaged Buddhism"[3] in the 1960s to describe his efforts to apply the Buddhist teaching of meditation to discern what actions need to be taken to meet the sociopolitical demands of his particular time and place. The Vietnamese peasants who constituted up to 90 percent of the country's population felt during the war that their religious leaders were keeping silent in the face of the suffering of the nation. They, therefore, turned to them to find ways that could bring an end to war. The sufferings of the people during the war in Vietnam, therefore, compelled Nhat Hanh to push back against the stereotype of monks as uneducated, superstitious indigents who shave their heads, forgo meat, and recite prayers for salvation from birth.[4]

During his visit to the United States and Europe in the 1960s, Nhat Hanh met with several people, including Al Hassler, executive secretary of the Fellowship of Reconciliation in the United States, John Heidbrink of the Fellowship of Reconciliation staff, Thomas Merton, the Trappist monk, Secretary of Defense Robert McNamara, and Martin Luther King Jr., and asked them help to achieve peace in Vietnam. Some of them supported US efforts to defeat the National Liberation Front of the North in order to restore peace, while others backed the Front in order to get the Americans out of Vietnam. Nhat Hanh saw that both groups did not truly understand the complicated situation in Vietnam. He wrote:

> Some of them feel that they ought to back the United States effort in order to defeat the Front and so secure peace in Vietnam. Others think that they ought to back the Front in order to get the Americans out of Vietnam to secure peace. . . . They do not truly understand the situation. In reality the war in Vietnam cannot be ended by people who support either side. By doing so what they really do is to help the war continue and help destroy the Vietnamese people. The most effective way is not to support either of the two sides, but rather to support those Vietnamese people who seek a third way of achieving peace.[5]

Social and Religious Engagement in Myanmar Society 117

Nhat Hanh, further, saw that Vietnam had become a victim of a power struggle between the United States and China at the expense of the Vietnamese people. He was convinced that the war in Vietnam could not be ended by people who supported either side. Instead, they were finding reasons for the war to continue, and the war would destroy the Vietnamese people. Nhat Hanh himself was one of those people siding neither with the National Liberation Front of the Communist North nor with the Capitalist South, but with the people and with life. Taking the role of mediator between the oppressed and the oppressors, Nhat Hanh did not perceive the oppressors as the real enemies per se. Instead, the real enemies were the corrupted ideologies in the hearts and minds of humans. Nhat Hanh, therefore, called upon the oppressors to change their hearts and minds. He said, "The real enemies are not man. They are intolerance, fanaticism, dictatorship, cupidity, hatred, and discrimination which lie within the heart of man. . . . Please kill the real enemies of man which are present everywhere, in our hearts and minds."[6] In solidarity with the victims of war, he said, "If you touch suffering deeply in yourself and in the other person, understanding will arise. When understanding arises, love and acceptance will also arise, and they will bring the suffering to an end."[7] Indeed, everyone involved in the conflict was a victim of corrupted ideology.

In his book *The Miracle of Mindfulness*, which was written during the war years for his students as an explanation of the connection between meditation and social action, Thich states:

> Take the situation of a country suffering war or any other situation of injustice. Try to see that every person involved in the conflict is a victim. See that no person, including all those in warring parties or in what appear to be opposing sides, desires the suffering to continue. See that it is not only one or a few persons who are to blame for the situation. See that the situation is possible because of the clinging to ideologies and to an unjust world economic system which is upheld by every person through ignorance or through lack of resolve to change it. See that two sides in a conflict are not really opposing, but two aspects of the same reality. See that the most essential thing is life and that killing or oppressing one another will not solve anything.[8]

According to Nhat Hanh's understanding, the people involved in the conflict were all victims of war. In engaged Buddhist spirituality, meditation is integral because the inner peace of a liberated heart is achieved through meditation. The liberated heart is filled with compassion and motivation to relieve the sufferings for themselves and others who are imprisoned by false views, hatred, ignorance, and anger.[9] Highlighting the utmost importance of applying the Buddhist teaching of compassion in social action, Nhat Hanh

118 *Chapter Four*

says, "If we teach Buddhist philosophy, but do not practice generosity to ease the suffering of others, we have not yet attained the essence of Buddhism. We should practice generosity with compassion and not disdain, without discriminating against people who, because of their poverty, have caused anger and hatred."[10] He continues saying that the life of a socially engaged Buddhist is like the lotus flower that blooms in the mud and yet remains pure and unstained.[11] Highlighting the relations between faith and action for social service, Nhat Hanh says:

> Our faith must evolve every day and bring us joy, peace, freedom, and love. Faith implies practice, living our daily life in mindfulness. Some people think that prayer or meditation involves only our minds or our hearts. But we also have to pray with our bodies, with our actions in the world. And our actions must be modelled after those of the living Buddha or the living Christ. If we live as they did, we will have deep understanding and pure actions, and we will do our share to help create a more peaceful world for our children and all of the children of God.[12]

As such, a socially engaged Buddhist does not withdraw from convoluted human society, but rather, lives in harmony with others and is eager to help them. Nhat Hanh explains two dimensions of relationship in engaged Buddhist spirituality: horizontal theology and vertical theology. The former describes our relationships to one another and the latter our relationship to God,[13] which is similar to Luther's explanation of the relation between "inner man" and "outer man" in Christian spirituality. According to Nhat Hanh, there is a deep relationship between the horizontal theology and vertical theology. They are interrelated, and if we do not succeed in getting in touch with the horizontal dimension, we will not be able to get in touch with the vertical dimension. Nhat Hanh says, "If you cannot love man, animals, and plants, I doubt that you can love God. The capacity for loving God depends on your capacity for loving humankind and other species."[14]

In Myanmar, U Ottama can be considered one of the first engaged Buddhist monks for his active yet nonviolent anti-colonial movement against British imperialism. In light of the Burmese enslavement to the British, he made a statement, saying, "The people should not ask for Nirvana yet. Nirvana is a release from cosmic slavery (the wheel of rebirth), but those who do not even enjoy earthly freedom cannot attain it. *Pongyis* (monks) pray for Nirvana but slaves can never obtain it, therefore, they must pray for release from slavery in this life."[15] It is notable to remember that engaged Buddhists played an important role in the national history of Myanmar not only in resistance against the British rule and in demand for national independence from the

Social and Religious Engagement in Myanmar Society   119

British colonialism, but also in resistance against the military dictatorship and in pushing for the democratization of the country.

After the military seized power in 1988, two opposing modern trends of Buddhism emerged in Myanmar: militant religious fundamentalism and socially engaged Buddhism.[16] The military turned to Buddhism as a source of legitimacy and popular support and disseminated extreme Burman Buddhist nationalism. Socially engaged Buddhists emphasized nonviolent resistance against the military and demanded a political dialogue between the military and the NLD. In engaged Buddhism, "inner" and "outer" practices are deeply interdependent as a path of social action in the world.[17] They should flow in one specific direction. Aung San Suu Kyi is one of the most inspiring examples of socially engaged Buddhism, emphasizing *vipassana* (meditation), *metta* (loving-kindness), and the ten benevolent moral duties of a *dhammaraja* (political monarch), as she adhered to a pious Buddhist morality in her political reform movement through nonviolent resistance against the military.[18] As such, religious meditation also plays a key role in her commitment to nonviolent civil resistance against the military. Reflecting on her house arrest for six years (1989–1995), she remarked, "Like many of my Buddhist colleagues, I decided to put my time under detention to good use by practicing meditation. . . . In my political work, I have been helped and strengthened by the teachings of members of the sangha."[19]

Suu Kyi defines engaged Buddhism as "active compassion or active *metta.* It's not just sitting there passively saying—I feel sorry for them. It means doing something about the situation by bringing whatever relief you can to those who need it the most, by caring for them, by doing what you can to help others."[20] As such, a socially engaged person protects others at the cost of one's own safety. Suu Kyi, as an engaged Buddhist, breaks through the idea of violence throughout the modern history of Myanmar and opts to pursue nonviolent means in her politics for Myanmar's democracy movement for two practical reasons: first, nonviolence will hurt fewer people; second, it will give a great deal of advantage to present and future generations to show that change can be brought without the use of arms.[21] She says, "I do not believe in an armed struggle because it will perpetuate the tradition that he who is best at wielding arms, wields power. Even if the democracy movement were to succeed through force of arms, it would leave in the minds of the people the idea that whoever has greater armed might wins in the end. That will not help democracy."[22]

Suu Kyi is not just focusing on the motivation, the means, and the goal, but also on the consequences of the means for present and future generations. She understands that nonviolent politics is not an easy task, but one that requires courage and strength. Indeed, Suu Kyi has been through a great deal of suffering at the hands of the military dictatorship in her political movement. She

120   *Chapter Four*

was put under house arrest for about fifteen years between July 20, 1989, and November 13, 2010. Soldiers of the Myanmar army and hired thugs threatened Suu Kyi's life multiple times during her political campaigns. On April 5, 1989, when Suu Kyi and her supporters were on tour for her political campaign in Danubyu Township, Irrawaddy Division, an army captain ordered them not to walk in procession at an army blockade. Defying the orders of a captain, Suu Kyi walked alone in the middle of the road, facing a row of armed soldiers who threatened to fire at her and was only stopped when a major intervened at the last minute. When the cofounder and director of the Burma Project USA, Alan Clements, asked her to recount her powerful determination to face armed soldiers at gunpoint Suu Kyi said:

> I was quite cool-headed. I thought, "What does one do?" Does one turn back or keep on going? My thought was one doesn't turn back in a situation like this. . . . It's a decision which you have to make there and then. Do I stand or do I run? Whatever you may have thought before, when it comes to the crunch, when you're actually faced with that kind of danger, you have to make up your mind on the spot . . . and you never know what decision you will make.[23]

Indeed, without a gun in her hands, Suu Kyi tried extremely hard to use her mind in a sense of compassion and intelligence to work out the solution on the spot. The symbolic image people have in their minds and Suu Kyi's descriptions of the event have attracted worldwide support for her political journey. Again, in November 1996, a mob of about two hundred people attacked a motorcade carrying Suu Kyi and NLD vice-chairman Tin Oo with iron bars and rocks near Kokkine junction, Yangon. Suu Kyi was unhurt, but Tin Oo suffered minor injuries as the attackers smashed the windows of the motorcade. It is believed that the attack was directed by the military government in an attempt to stop the NLD and its supporters from gathering.[24] The third attack took place at Depayin, a town in Sagaing Division in central Myanmar, on May 30, 2003. When Suu Kyi and the NLD members approached Depayin Township, a large number of Union Solidarity and Development Association (USDA) members and hired thugs carried out a deadly attack on Suu Kyi and her convoy with knives, iron bars, and bamboo sticks in a ruthless way. An eyewitness recounts the Depayin massacre, saying:

> The attackers beat women and pulled off their *longyi* (skirts) and their blouses. When victims, covered in blood, fell to the ground, the attackers grabbed their hair and pounded their heads on the pavement until their bodies stopped moving. The whole time, the attackers were screaming the words, "Die, die, die. . . . " There was so much blood. I still cannot get rid of the sight of people, covered in blood, being beaten mercilessly to death.[25]

The NLD vice chairman, Tin Oo, was dragged from the car, severely beaten, and then arrested. Suu Kyi was not severely injured but was subsequently put in jail. The incident cost the lives of about eighty people in all, but the exact death toll is not known.[26] Suu Kyi believes that people cannot have one fixed policy for all time, but must work according to a changing situation.[27] Without condemning those who fight the "just fight,"[28] Suu Kyi embraces nonviolent politics as the best way to bring about change in the current political context of Myanmar. As an active engaged Buddhist, Suu Kyi teaches the NLD party members to opt for nonviolent politics. It is not her politics to take revenge on the military dictators who persecuted her in different ways, such as putting her under house arrest for about fifteen years, cutting off her landline phone, preventing her from saying goodbye to her beloved husband at his last breath in March of 1999, and multiple attempts on her life.

Suu Kyi has shown a level of compassion that many people would consider unimaginable. Of her experience of captivity and violence, she has said, "I've always felt that if I had really started hating my captors, hating the SLORC and the army, I would have defeated myself."[29] Regarding the military, Suu Kyi says, "I would like to think of the army as a force of protection rather than a force of destruction."[30] As a result, Suu Kyi has been trying to convince the Myanmar army to be a dignified army who protect the people instead of taking advantage of their role to manipulate the people for their own gain. Furthermore, she has engaged with multiple armed groups to encourage them to move away from the idea of armed struggle and opt for nonviolent politics to effect change in Myanmar.

SOCIALLY ENGAGED RELIGIOUS MOVEMENT FOR PEACE AND DEMOCRACY IN THE 1988 UPRISING

When nationwide demonstrations for democratization of the country broke out in Myanmar in 1988, I was a high school student in Yangon. With the great expectation of better educational opportunities in the capital, I left my rural village in Chin State in 1987 which is over one thousand miles away from Yangon. My mother, who had lost her beloved husband in 1982, sent small amounts of money for my education on a monthly basis, with the expectation that one day I would become a medical doctor or an engineer. However, I could not fulfill her dream for various reasons. My steady education was interrupted by a shortage of money, especially when the military regime unexpectedly announced the demonetization of 25-, 35-, and 75-kyat banknotes on September 5, 1987. This affected my life greatly as I lost thousands of kyats, forcing me to rely on the cheapest street food I could find for my own survival.

122   *Chapter Four*

The early protest movement that began in 1988 was sparked by a fight between students from the Rangoon Institute of Technology (RIT) and local young men at Sanda Win teashop at Insein, close to the RIT campus. In Myanmar, a local tea shop is often one of the most popular places to meet, talk, watch television, and listen to music over a cup of tea or coffee for multiple hours at a time. Traditional Burmese tea was served at no cost. Most Burmese people at that time were unable to afford home luxuries like a tape player, so they often went to tea shops not only for food but also for entertainment and relaxation. On March 12, 1988, a group of RIT students entered the tea shop, bringing with them cassette tapes of a classical singer, Sai Htee Saing, and asked the tea shop's owner to play it on his tape deck. A group of intoxicated local young men seated at a nearby table objected to Sai Htee Saing's songs. The students disregarded the intoxicated men. Unfortunately, one of the drunks stood up and threw his chair toward the students, hitting one in the head. This escalated the argument, which finally ended up as a brawl. Although the man who initially threw the chair was arrested, he was released the following day, mainly because he was the son of a government official. With the knowledge of the immediate release of the culprit, many students felt that it was not fair enough. They, therefore, organized a protest at the local police station, resulting in a clash with riot police, who fired gunshots at the unarmed students. A number of students were hit; one of them, named Phone Maw, was hit seriously and died in his hostel a few hours later. Outraged by the death of Phone Maw, his fellow students demanded that the government officially announce the truth about the incident in Myanmar Radio and Television. However, a spokesman for the government blamed the students for inciting unrest.[31]

Soldiers and police raided the RIT campus on March 15, beating students with batons and arresting them en masse.[32] In the days that followed, demonstrations broke out not only at RIT but also at Rangoon Arts and Sciences University. On March 16, when students from Rangoon Arts and Sciences University marched toward the RIT campus about six miles away, demanding the end of one-party rule, they were trapped at *Ta Darr Phyu*, meaning "white bridge," on Pyi Road between soldiers in front of them and riot police behind. Some students managed to escape, but others were arrested and beaten unconscious by soldiers. Female students were dragged off by the soldiers and gang-raped.[33] Finally, the incident resulted in the tragic death of forty-one students as a result of being packed in an overcrowded prison van for two hours on the ten-mile journey to prison.[34] The incident came to be known as the Red Bridge Incident because it resulted in the "white bridge" being spattered with blood.[35]

This atrocity was a repeat of history in 1962 when university students in Yangon protested against the military regime, which resulted in the killing of

Social and Religious Engagement in Myanmar Society 123

hundreds of students. When students at the University of Yangon protested against the military regime, the student union building was blown up by the military and many students were killed; unofficial figures estimate that as many as 400 people lost their lives in this horrific event.[36] In their protests against the military regime in 1988, students held Aung San's portrait and repeatedly shouted their slogan, "Aung San did not train the military to kill its own people."[37] They were joined by civilians, social activists, monks, workers, school teachers, Christian nuns, and civil servants who all took to the streets and protested against the military dictatorship and demanded multiparty democracy instead of the one-party rule that had led the country into decline. Calling for a multiparty democracy instead of one-party system, Suu Kyi, during her campaign, addressed tens of thousands of people at the Myanmar's iconic Shwedagon Pagoda in Yangon on August 26, 1988, saying, "I believe that all the people who have assembled here have without exception come with the unshakable desire to strive for and win a multiparty democratic system. . . . In order to arrive at this objective, all the people should march united in a disciplined manner towards the goal of democracy."[38] Since the beginning of her engagement in politics, Suu Kyi has not proclaimed that she alone can bring change in Myanmar, but rather has been calling upon all people in Myanmar to contribute whatever they can, small or large, to bring a genuine democracy to the country.

In the face of the people's demonstrations against the military dictatorship, Ne Win aggressively threatened peaceful demonstrators in his televised address on state media, saying, "When the army shoots, it shoots to hit; it does not fire in the air to scare. Therefore, I warn those causing disturbances that they will not be spared if in the future the army is brought in to control disturbances."[39] Despite this threat, the people's demonstration, which Suu Kyi called "the second struggle for national independence,"[40] broke out across the entire city of Yangon on August 8, 1988, which came to be known as 8888 Uprising, or Four Eights Uprising, demanding an end to decades of military tyranny. Suu Kyi also recalls the Four Eights Uprising day, saying:

> Participating in these peaceful demonstrations were people of all ages, from all different strata of society; students, farmers, laborers, civil servants, including numbers of the armed forces, Buddhist monks, Christians, Muslims, intellectuals, professionals, businessmen, small traders, housewives and artists. Their united demand was for change: they wanted no more of the authoritarian rule, initiated by a military coup in 1962, that had impoverished Burma intellectually, politically, morally, and economically.[41]

The public protest continued for months, and the military regime systematically and harshly cracked down and hunted the protestors in the streets.

124   *Chapter Four*

Students, civilians, civil servants, and monks sacrificed their noble lives for the sake of their country's freedom, justice, and democracy. Bertil Lintner, a Swedish journalist, reported that some of the wounded were cremated while still alive.[42] Aung Zaw, political activist and the founder of the *Irrawaddy News*, said about the atrocities perpetrated against peaceful demonstrators by the military on September 18, 1988:

> The September 18 massacre was systematic and cold-blooded murder, as troops came with machine guns and automatic rifles, storming a protest center where demonstrators were staging hunger strikes and sit-in protests. Even a group of demonstrators who held a peaceful protest in front of the U.S. embassy, where they felt they would be protected, were slaughtered in a mass killing that was caught on camera. Some gunshot victims who were still alive were believed to have been secretly cremated, while the luckier ones were taken to hospital emergency wards with missing limbs and chest wounds. It seemed the regime did not care who saw this brutality.[43]

Unfortunately, the peaceful protests resulted in the killing of approximately three thousand innocent civilians. The peaceful demonstrators expected the US embassy to help protect them, but to no avail. In an address to the United Nations' General Assembly on September 28, 1988, Sir Geoffrey Howe, the British foreign secretary, condemned the massacre, stating, "In Burma we have been appalled at the killing of unarmed demonstrators, women and children, which has taken place. . . . The Burmese authority must recognize that the only way to a lasting solution to the country's internal crisis lies in meeting the desire of the Burmese people for greater freedom and multi-party democracy."[44]

Nevertheless, the military still refused to discuss and meet the desires of the people. Taking no responsibility or accountability in the country's chaotic situation, General Ne Win resigned from his presidency in the face of people's demonstration and handed over power to his trusted military generals on July 23, 1988. Sein Lwin, dubbed as "butcher of Rangoon"[45] for his role in the bloody suppression of demonstrators, took his position as president on July 27, 1988, but resigned less than a month later on August 12. Maung Maung, a lawyer and non-military man who had studied in the West, succeeded Sein Lwin on August 19, 1988. At the end of September he gave a televised address, saying, "The fire of anger can be extinguished with the cool waters of love and compassion."[46] Maung Maung called upon people to stop attacking and threatening the military officials, saying, "The time has now arrived to restore law and order all over the country."[47] He resigned from his office the next month on September 18, 1988, and was succeeded by General Saw Maung, the army chief of staff and minister of defense and

Social and Religious Engagement in Myanmar Society 125

a loyal subordinate of General Ne Win. General Saw Maung promised the people of Myanmar that his administration would hold multiparty elections and hand over power to the winning party, but only after restoring law and order, and peace and tranquility.[48] The military regime had established itself as the State Law and Order Restoration Council (SLORC) by September 26, 1988. However, student leaders understood Saw Maung's strategy as deflecting the movement for democracy in the name of law and order, saying, "By depicting Burma's crisis as essentially a question of law and order, the Burmese army hoped to legitimize their hold on power, drive the opposition underground and marginalize the fledgling democracy movement as a political force."[49] Needless to say, the power-hungry military regime repeatedly cheated the people with different excuses for fear of losing their power over Myanmar politics.

Socially engaged Buddhist movements led by monks, students, and civilians emerged as social and political forces in 1988 with massive demonstrations across the country, calling for democratization of Myanmar and a response to the suffering of the people after the unexpected demonetization of its currency the year before. During the 1988 uprising, Buddhist monks condemned the ruthless massacre of students and civilians by the authorities and appealed to the regime to rule the country in accordance with Buddhist principles. They offered shelter in their monasteries to protesters who were trying to evade the authorities. Protest songs used in the massive demonstrations reflected the longing for the basic human right to a tranquil, dignified existence free from want and fear, stating, "I am not among the rice eating robots. . . . Everyone should be entitled to human rights. We are not savage beasts of the jungle, we are all men with reason, it's high time to stop the rule of armed intimidation: if every moment of dissent were settled by the gun, Burma would only be emptied of people."[50]

Unfortunately, the outside world was unaware of the true reality of the inhuman massacres committed by the military regime in 1988 at the right time because security forces targeted anyone, they saw holding a camera. Furthermore, there was no mobile phone or internet access in 1988, only government-controlled landlines and only one landline phone in some small towns. People would need to go to the nearest city from their villages in order to talk to family members in other parts of the country over the phone. In such a context, the only source of news was the state-run television and radio stations, which always broadcast government propaganda. Since I was away from the city, I did not know what had happened to the people throughout my country. The only access I had to news updates was through radio broadcast from foreign-based stations, particularly the British Broadcasting Corporation (BBC). Even the BBC service was sometimes not very clear because the authorities would jam the radio frequency to disrupt its signal.

126   Chapter Four

Most of the time people did not listen to it in pubic, but rather clandestinely in their homes because of the fear of being arrested and imprisoned by the authorities, who were trying to withhold the reality of Myanmar from the public as much as possible.

THE UPRISING OF MONKS IN MANDALAY
AFTER THE 1990 ELECTIONS

In 1990, the SLORC under General Saw Maung played a political game with the National League for Democracy, using multiparty elections to gain legitimacy. The election date was set with the advice of astrologers, using 9, the favorite number of Ne Win: 2+7 = 9, and the fourth week of the fifth month in the year '90.[51] Because Suu Kyi was under house arrest and many other important NLD leaders had been imprisoned, the SLORC underestimated the organizational strength of and popular support for the NLD and felt confident in winning the election. On January 9, 1990, General Saw Maung reassured the public in a televised address, saying, "An election has to be held to bring forth a government. That is our responsibility. But the actual work of forming a legal government after the election is not the duty of the *Tatmadaw* (the military). We are saying it very clearly and candidly right now."[52] With this expectation, a notably free and fair election was held on May 27, 1990. The people of Myanmar, for the first time in modern Myanmar history, went to the polls to vote for their leader. The military regime was not granted the easy win they were expecting. The National League for Democracy achieved an extraordinary landslide victory, winning 392 of the 485 contested seats.[53] The military's ill-treatment of Suu Kyi and other political prisoners motivated the supporters of the NLD to vote generously for the NLD. The magnitude of the NLD's win in the election was very high. It was a nationwide political earthquake. As a result, the regime came up with a crafty agenda to retain political power.

The SLORC broke their promise to hand over power to the winning party. Instead of handing over power peacefully to the NLD, the SLORC nullified the result of the elections and declared that power could not be transferred until a new constitution was written.[54] In late July 1990, the SLORC issued "Order No. 1/90," in the name of the so-called "three main tasks," national unity, national security, and national sovereignty, claiming the rights of the *Tatmadaw* to intervene in Myanmar's politics.[55] According to Order No. 1/90, the SLORC would not accept the establishment of a civilian government based on an interim constitution, and therefore, the SLORC would maintain power until it could hold a National Convention, which would create guidelines for a new constitution. The SLORC declared that the army had to

Social and Religious Engagement in Myanmar Society

approve the guidelines prior to the actual drafting of the constitution by the National Convention, and only after that would the constitution be put to the people for a referendum.[56] Out of 702 delegates in the National Convention, only 99 were elected "MPs," and of these, only 81 belonged to the NLD. The rest were hand-picked by the SLORC.[57] Not only the NLD but also its supporters were disappointed and angry at the decision of the SLORC as they felt that they had been systematically cheated. When asked about the transfer of power to the NLD, General Saw Maung said in a radio broadcast on October 18, 1990, "I cannot say when. I cannot see into the future. I have to handle the situation as it comes. I cannot tell whether I will drown tomorrow."[58] General Saw Maung was replaced by General Than Shwe in March 1992 as chairman of the SLORC.

The uprising of monks emerged in 1990 as they commemorated the second anniversary of the 1988 uprising on August 8, 1990, by marching through the streets of Mandalay. The student unions came with black flags as a sign of mourning. The situation turned from peaceful commemoration to ugly violence after the military ordered the students to lower their flags. A student leader talked back to them and was severely beaten by soldiers in front of the crowd. When a monk who would not keep silent came forward to mediate between students and soldiers in search of a peaceful resolution of the problem, the soldiers started beating the monks and an angry mob began throwing rocks at the soldiers.[59] Some students also hoisted a peacock flag, a symbol of the NLD and pro-democracy movement.[60] The soldiers opened fire into the crowd, killing two monks and injuring many others. Several monks were wounded and detained, while some went missing and are presumed dead.[61]

The military regime flatly denied the shooting and the state-run radio reversed the truth by claiming that the students and the monks had attacked the security forces and that one monk had been slightly injured in the commotion.[62] On August 27, over seven thousand monks who gathered in Mandalay made a decision not only to refuse donations from soldiers and their families but also to perform religious rites as an act of resistance against the repressive military government. For instance, senior monks and abbots refused to attend a Buddhist religious ceremony to which they were invited by the Mandalay Division commander of that time, Major General Tun Kyi. As retaliation for the boycott, the authorities raided over 130 Buddhist monasteries in Mandalay, arresting and imprisoning several monks.[63] The boycott soon spread across the country and two thousand monks in Yangon sent an open letter to chairman of the State Law and Order Restoration Council, General Saw Maung, on September 27, 1990, to inform him that "the *Sanghas* within Rangoon City Development Area [would] boycott the military government and support the decision taken by the *Sanghas* of Mandalay to undertake a *patta nikkujjana kama* [excommunication] on the military government."[64] According to this

128 *Chapter Four*

practice, the monks turned their begging bowls upside down as a symbol of resistance to the repressive military regime on their strike.

Taking a piecemeal approach with the intention of causing a gradual collapse of the NLD, the SLORC arrested and imprisoned several important members of the party in September on trumped-up charges of inciting unrest. However, the regime had once again miscalculated the organizational strength of the NLD, as most of its members remained faithful to the democratization of the country. Suu Kyi was still put under house arrest, though the SLORC called it "restricted residence."[65] Toward the end of October 1990, armed troops raided 350 Buddhist monasteries in retaliation, 133 of them in Mandalay alone, seizing those monks suspected of being anti-regime and grabbing student dissidents taking refuge in the monasteries.[66] It was extremely risky to protest against the military dictatorship at that time, because the regime could do whatever they wanted, including threaten, beat, or arrest, which could result in death. It required great courage to take this extremely risky action. Despite these dangerous challenges, socially engaged Buddhist monks and students collectively risked their lives to alleviate the suffering of the people.

THE SAFFRON REVOLUTION IN 2007

The 2007 Buddhist monks' demonstrations in Myanmar have been called the Saffron Revolution, probably named by the media for the saffron-colored robes worn by Theravada Buddhist monks, although many monks object to the word *revolution* since it carries a denotation of violence.[67] The Saffron Revolution broke out in major cities of Myanmar based on both short- and long-term issues: in the short term, an economic crisis after the government suddenly raised fuel prices on August 15, which affected people's daily survival; the long-term cause was the increasing denial of basic freedoms and the declining living standards of the poor. The military regime had unexpectedly increased diesel prices from 1,500 to 3,000 kyats per imperial gallon and petrol prices from 1,500 to 2,500 kyats in an attempt to meet the country's economic deficits and continue their excessive luxurious lives. The SPDC moved the administration capital of Myanmar from Yangon to Nay Pyi Taw, meaning the "abode of the king" or "royal capital," on November 6, 2005, at 6:37 a.m., according to the advice of astrologers. Hundreds of government servants left Yangon in army trucks carrying important documents and furniture, shouting, "We are leaving! We are leaving,"[68] which could mean they were upset at having to relocate. In addition to lavishly spending the country's resources in building a new capital, the SPDC increased the salaries of civil servants and military officials in 2006 in order to win their support. These actions

Social and Religious Engagement in Myanmar Society   129

may have been the cause of the government's budget deficits. As a result, the SPDC levied more taxes and suddenly, instead of a gradual process, reduced subsidies on gasoline products, raising the price of diesel oil by 100 percent and compressed natural gas by almost 500 percent.[69]

Lee Kuan Yew of Singapore remarked that the generals had mismanaged the country's economy, and protest from the people was inevitable because of their excessive luxurious lives while the ordinary people lived in extreme poverty. He stated:

> In Myanmar, these are rather dumb generals when it comes to the economy. How can they so mismanage the economy and reach this stage when the country has so many natural resources? They are putting up expensive buildings for themselves and a golf course. Flaunting these excesses must push a hungry and impoverished people to revolt. But what will happen? I don't know because the army has got to be part of the solution. If the army is dissolved, the country has got nothing to govern itself because they have dismantled all administrative instruments.[70]

Indeed, the military generals and their cronies are internal colonizers who consume most of the country's resources, while the ordinary people live in extreme poverty. As a result of the unexpected increase of fuel prices, transportation costs also increased exponentially, and some urban poor literally could not afford to take public buses to work. Poor workers living on the outskirts of Yangon were forced to walk long distances to work since they could not afford the increased price of public transportation. Observing the country's devastating economic situation, the 88-Generation Students Group[71] began protest marches in Yangon a few days after the price hike, calling on the military regime to revoke the increase in fuel prices. The members of Union Solidarity and Development Association (USDA) and their Swan Arr Shin[72] militias attacked the protesters, resulting in the immediate arrest of most of the leaders of the 88-Generation Students Group, including some members of the NLD. They were charged with agitating to undermine the stability and security of the State and attempting to disrupt the ongoing National Convention.[73] Despite arrests by the military regime, sporadic protests continued in some major cities of the country.

The Buddhist monks were also aware of the suffering of the people, as they went out every morning to receive offerings of food from the laity for their livelihood. Aung Zaw, a political activist and the founder of the *Irrawaddy News*, noted the Buddhist monks were firsthand witnesses to the suffering of the Burmese people, stating:

> Monks who receive donations from laymen and who visit households every morning to receive *hsoon* [cooked rice and curry] witness at firsthand the

130   *Chapter Four*

suffering and poverty of ordinary Burmese people. They continue to witness the deteriorating situation in the predominantly Buddhist country, ruled by a military government.[74]

Offering food to monks is one of the principal forms of merit-making in Theravada Buddhism. Playing the significant role of mediator between the rulers and the ruled, hundreds of monks in Pakoku, a city in Upper Myanmar well known for its monastic education centers, took to the streets on September 5, denouncing the price hike. Thousands of residents came out in the streets to show their support. However, the USDA and Swan Arr Shin militias attacked, calling in soldiers who overreacted by firing their guns into the air and beating the monks, some of whom they had tied to poles.[75] In retaliation, monks held some local officials hostage for several hours at a monastery and burned their cars.[76] This escalated the national confrontation between the sangha and the military regime. The military regime accused the monks of inciting violence and warned them that the people of Myanmar would never tolerate inciting the 1988 unrest-like uprising.[77] On the contrary, however, in the eyes of the people, the military had committed one of the gravest sins possible by physically assaulting their monks. News of the incident quickly spread across the country and on September 9, 2007, the All Burma Monks' Alliance (ABMA) issued a statement calling on the SPDC to officially apologize to the monks, reduce the prices of fuel and other basic commodities, release all political prisoners, and begin a dialogue with the democratic movement for national reconciliation, giving the government until September 17 to comply.[78] On September 14, the ABMA issued the second statement, warning that all monks would initiate a religious boycott, refusing to receive alms from the SPDC officials and their supporters through a religious excommunication known as *patta nikkujjana kamma* (the overturning of the alms bowls).[79] However, the regime did not respond to the demands of the monks.

As a result, monks in Yangon, Mandalay, Sittwe, and other major cities gathered at temples and city centers and marched through the streets for hours every day, chanting the *Metta Sutta* and some monks carried alms bowls turned upside down as a symbol of protest against the military regime and of their commitment not only to refuse alms but also to refuse to perform religious rituals for government officials, army officers, or their families. On September 22, thousands of monks walked along the streets in a wet and rainy Yangon, chanting the *Metta Sutta*, which reads, "sabbe satta bhavantu skitatta . . . sukino va khemino hontu," meaning, may all beings enjoy happiness and comfort . . . may they feel safe and secure.[80] A group of five hundred monks marching down the streets of Yangon was allowed to pass through the security barriers surrounding Suu Kyi who was still under house arrest. As the monks approached her residence, Suu Kyi was also allowed to open her

Social and Religious Engagement in Myanmar Society 131

old steel gate and pay obeisance to the monks behind a row of police guards. The monks offered prayers for Suu Kyi, who was in tears.[81] On September 24, thousands of Buddhist monks were joined by the NLD members and 88-Generation Students as well as tens of thousands of civilian supporters, marching from Shwedagon pagoda to downtown Yangon, shouting political slogans and holding signs that read, "Free Aung San Suu Kyi!" and "Free all political prisoners."[82]

Day after day, the riot police, soldiers, and Swan Arr Shin worked together to beat, arrest, and detain protesters. The security forces raided monasteries day and night and arrested the monks. The government-controlled newspaper *New Light of Myanmar* claimed on November 7 that a total number of 2,927 persons had been detained throughout the country during the protests and the subsequent crackdown, and that only 91 persons remained in detention.[83] Obviously, some of detainees suffered brutal treatment. Some monks were forcefully disrobed and severely beaten by prison guards and their interrogators. The "Saffron Revolution" of 2007 was second to the 1988 people's uprising in terms of participation of monks and pro-democracy politicians and civilians. However, the "Saffron Revolution" of 2007 was different from 1988's massive demonstrations. This time, monks led demonstrations, not allowing lay people to join them, for they believed that if they kept their movement purely a religious one, the authorities would not react with violence. However, many young people kept begging the monks to let them join. Therefore, later on lay people were allowed to join the monks in peaceful marches, where they would form a human chain on both sides of the marching monks. Reflecting on the "Saffron Revolution" of 2007, Jeff Kingston, professor of history and director of Asian studies at Temple University, Japan, says:

> Religion is not abstract or something distant from everyday lives but rather woven together inextricably into them, and thus it organically evolves and adapts to the needs and circumstances of adherents. Involvement in political and economic matters may seem the antithesis of religiosity, but again this view overlooks local perceptions about Buddhism as an encompassing way of life that must be nurtured, respected, and protected.[84]

Indeed, religion does not teach its adherents to remain aloof from daily struggles. To do so would mean withdrawing from human society and into their comfort zone, which has been contrary to the true teachings of religion since its origin. Not only monks but also ordinary people risked their lives for political change during the "Saffron Revolution" of 2007 because they viewed the government as an obstruction to a better life. The immorality of the military generals and their families was the barrier between them and

132   *Chapter Four*

the people. The monks' refusal to accept the alms offered by the top military generals and anyone related to them by turning their alms bowls upside down was a strong symbol of defiance to the military regime. This public rebuke prevented the military personnel and their families from earning merit, which is considered crucial in Buddhism.

Unlike in 1988 and 1990, by 2007 the outside world could see the reality of the merciless violence perpetrated on monks and civilians by the security forces, thanks to the internet and mobile phone networks. In 1988, students led demonstrations and monks later joined them. The international communities did not see the true reality of the 1988 demonstrations in time because of the lack of technology. There were no social media, internet access, or even cell phones to capture the reality. A cell phone cost from $1,000 to $1,500 in 2007, so few people could afford it and internet access. Knowing that they could use cell phone and internet to a great advantage, protesters sent images and news to social media outside the country. Therefore, international social media quickly captured the outbreak of the 2007 Saffron Revolution, and the world saw the true reality inside the country as technology played key role in spreading images of the demonstrations.

ENGAGED RELIGIOUS MOVEMENT
IN MYANMAR SOCIETY

Socially engaged religious movements became more prevalent in Myanmar after the country had gone through political transition from the military regime to a semi-civilian government in 2011. As the country became more open to the outside world after this transition, the ultra-nationalist Buddhists began to fear the movement toward democracy, feeling that they would lose traditional Buddhist values in a democratic society. In such a context, they were looking for someone who could fill the void left by the military regime and help them protect their traditional values by whatever means. For this purpose, the Association for the Protection of Race and Religion, well-known by its Burmese acronym Ma Ba Tha was established in 2013. Ashin Wirathu, backed by the military generals, was a heavyweight champion of hate speech not only against people of non-Buddhist faiths but also against the NLD government. However, one good thing is that not all Buddhists share the same view of Ma Ba Tha and many even see that Wirathu's hate speech spread a horrible image of Buddhism. Left-wing Buddhist monks held a conference in Hmawbi, about thirty miles away from Yangon, for two days in June of 2013. Calling for peace and communal harmony in Myanmar, the conference denounced the passing of a very controversial law that restricted Buddhist-Muslim marriages. A senior monk and a spokesman for the convention, U Dhammapiya said, "To accept or not to accept the so-called restrictions on interfaith marriage will be decided in accordance with human rights (standards). Anybody can marry at their own will," adding, "I will not accept someone forcing others to convert to their religion. If it violates human rights, we cannot agree to it."[85]

At the outbreak of inter-communal violence between Buddhists and Muslims in Rakhine State, an Interfaith Academic Conference on Security, Peace, and Coexistence was held for two days in October 2013, at the Sitagu International Buddhist Academy, Yangon, in joint partnership with the US-based Institute for Global Engagement (IGE). It was attended by 226 participants, including religious leaders of Buddhism, Christianity, Islam, Hinduism, and Judaism, as well as government officials and academics. With the common goal of a greater commitment to peace in the country, Archbishop Charles Bo said, "We must send a strong signal to those who want to plant the seeds of discord in the country and build together a future that Myanmar is founded on justice, peace, and fraternal cooperation."[86] The participation of different religious leaders is a sign to people that they should combat hate speech and build a peaceful society in the country.

Ashin Nyanissara, founder and head of the Sitagu Buddhist Academies, and Al Haj U Aye Lwin, one of the founding members of Religions for Peace Myanmar (RfP-M), paid a visit to Thandwe, Rakhine State on October 7, 2013, to meet with the local people there. Nyanissara warned the local Buddhists, including town officials, of the bad consequences that await those who believe rumors, and cautioned that dangerous people with hidden agendas were out to incite violence for their own gain. He urged the assembled Buddhists to live peacefully with the Muslims who live on the same soil but have a different faith.[87] This visit underlines the paramount importance of mutual respect, a peaceful coexistence between the Buddhist and Muslim communities in Rakhine State, and a guard against those who would use religion as a political tool.

Not only religious leaders of different faiths, but also civic educators endeavored to reduce religious conflict in the country by creating and introducing an inclusive curriculum for students. A local NGO, the Center for Diversity and National Harmony (CDNH), which promotes racial and religious diversity, designed and published a civic education curriculum in December 2015 as a resource for the government. The curriculum is very inclusive, introducing the basic beliefs of four major religions—Buddhism, Christianity, Islam, and Hinduism—in Myanmar for kindergarten to tenth grade. However, the ultranationalist Buddhists have opposed it, labeling it an attempt at the Islamization of the country.[88] The CDNH prepared the curriculum under the guidance of civic trainers and relevant interfaith leaders with the aim of promoting religious knowledge for children so that they could

134 *Chapter Four*

start learning mutual respect and understanding in childhood. Wirathu posted about this on his Facebook page, saying, "Only one popular faith is urged to be included instead of outlining all four religions."[89] He was arguing that only one faith—that is, Buddhism—should be included in the curriculum.

Despite the efforts of interfaith movements to reduce religious and ethnic conflict in Myanmar, former President Thein Sein's USDP administration paid little attention to the interfaith tensions fueled by Ma Ba Tha. It was after the NLD took power in 2016 that interfaith movements increased in the country through prayer meetings and seminars intending to combat the harmful rhetoric of religious and ethnic extremists. For instance, on May 13, 2016, Suu Kyi met with State Sangha Maha Nayaka Committee Chairman Bhamo Sayadaw Bhaddanta Kumarabhivamsa. Suu Kyi said that her NLD government would commit itself to fulfilling the rational wishes and ambitions of people of all different races and faiths, suggesting that the NLD government would apply a policy of no discrimination based on ethnic and religious identities, and that this policy based on the four virtues—pure love, pure compassion, pure delight, and pure disregard—would promote Buddhism.[90] The meeting apparently led to good relations between the NLD government and Ma Ha Na, because the latter announced that Ma Ba Tha, the ultranationalist group was not a lawful monks' association since it was not formed in accordance with the country's monastic rules.[91] Eventually Ma Ha Na banned Ma Ba Tha on May 23, 2017, and ordered it to end its activities, including taking down its signboards throughout the country within forty-five days, because of its anti-Muslim rhetoric, which was fueling religious and racial conflict.[92] Consequently, monks from Ma Ba Tha held a meeting on May 27 in Yangon in which the group quickly rebranded itself as a philanthropic foundation called the Buddha Dhamma Parahita Foundation. The nativist politics of the ultranationalist Buddhists also includes strongly opposing amendments to the 2008 constitution. Due to his hate speech against people of non-Buddhist faiths, especially against the Muslims in the country, the government officially banned Wirathu from delivering public sermons effective March 10, 2017.[93] To promote religious harmony in Myanmar, Kyaw Soe Aung, secretary of the Democracy and Human Rights Party, said, "To live in harmony, it is not enough to educate people. Leaders of the country, like the President and State Counsellor, should participate in promoting interfaith campaigns by visiting churches and mosques. Also state-owned broadcast media should often air some of the customs and activities of different religions. Now when we turn on the television every morning, we always see programs related to Buddhist teaching."[94]

In pursuit of building a peaceful society in Myanmar, a local NGO, Ar Yone Oo, meaning "The Dawn," in collaboration with the Swedish Embassy and the Swedish Peace and Arbitration Society, organized the Pre-celebration of the International Day of Peace in Yangon on September 18, 2016. It was attended by peace activists, members of parliament, and religious leaders of Buddhism, Christianity, Islam, and Hinduism. Religious leaders called on people to cease the misunderstanding and hatred between different ethnic and religious communities. Ashin Issariya, a Buddhist monk, told the participants that previously there had been misunderstandings and hate speech spread among different communities because there had not been open discussions held in the country.[95] Criticizing the hate speech some ultranationalist Buddhist monks participated in, he said, "We all need to cooperate in building peace. We all have a duty to stop hate speech, which can cause unrest."[96] Underscoring the vital importance of peace in one's life and in society, Myanmar's First Catholic Cardinal Charles Bo said, "If there is no peace in your heart; if there is no peace in your family, if there is no peace in your place of work; there will not be peace in the world or in Myanmar,"[97] suggesting that peace begins from one's own heart and mind. Highlighting the paramount importance of peace, Al Haj U Aye Lwin also remarked, "I think we have suffered enough. We deserve peace. If we want to achieve peace, we need to clear all the doubts in all the communities and build mutual understanding and trust."[98]

About six months later, an interfaith forum aimed at fostering a peaceful coexistence of the different faiths in Myanmar was held on March 18, 2017, at the Mandalay city hall in central Myanmar. It was attended by religious leaders, government officials, and social service groups. The meeting denounced the use of violence and hate speech in the name of religion and issued a statement, declaring, "Anyone carrying out any actions that involve using weapons and violence as a solution is smearing the good relations between faiths. The preaching of hateful words is totally rejected as it creates more harm than good, and that any uprising problems and difficulties should be approached using the virtue of *metta* (unconditional love for all beings) and resolved and negotiated in the most peaceful way."[99] Indeed, religion should be a source of peace rather than a source of violence. The NLD government organized the gathering of religious leaders at Aung San Stadium in Yangon on October 10, 2017, after the outbreak of intercommunal violence between Buddhists and Muslims in Rakhine State. It was attended by religious leaders of Buddhism, Islam, Hinduism, and Christianity, along with thousands of supporters and government officials. Bhaddanta Iddhibala, Chairman of the Yangon Region Sangha Maha Nayaka Committee said, "If each of us only sees the mistakes of others, there will be no peace among us. We need to have inner peace in each of us first and avoid the actions which could affect the peace, while praying for the peace." And Muslim leader Alahaj Mofti Mohamad stated, "We, the Muslims, strongly hope for the immediate end of the current conflicts and the haters. We strongly desire to live in harmony as our ancestors

136 *Chapter Four*

lived in past centuries. We want back the situation where we shared the happiness together with humility, without haters and doubts of each other, without discrimination."[100] The NLD Secretary Hanthar Myint said, "Making wishes will not solve problems in Myanmar but it advocates for public participation in the government's affairs. The only advantage of the praying ceremony is that it shows the satisfaction of the public with the government to the international community."[101] Despite criticism that the interfaith gathering would not contribute to peace in Myanmar, it has attracted the participation of peacemakers and shows the NLD-led government's willingness to strengthen national unity with the participation of the interfaith community.

On April 2, 2019, the Interfaith Friendship and Unity Group (Myanmar) signed a Memorandum of Understanding to cooperate with Myanmar in Yangon, in the presence of the union minister for religious affairs and culture, Thura Aung Ko, who also welcomed the signing of the MOU.[102] Despite many challenges, these groups work to reduce ethnic and religious conflicts and to help the NLD government build democracy transition, and bring the country back to the international stage. Religions for Peace Myanmar convened the Second Advisory Forum on National Reconciliation and Peace in Myanmar, as the increased level of armed conflict on Rakhine State endangered the prospect of peace and further stalled the return of refugees.[103] Two hundred representatives from religious organizations, government and military offices, parliament, ethnic organizations, foreign governments, UN agencies, international and national NGOs, and civil society groups met in Nay Pyi Taw for two days in May 2019. Bishop Gunnar Stalsett, honorary president of Religions for Peace International, noted in his address:

> Religions for Peace Advisory Forum is one of many roads towards a future where the people of Myanmar will enjoy the full measures of democracy, truth and reconciliation in the beautiful land of promise and hope. . . . The abhorrent terrorist attacks and the mass murders against Christians in Sri Lanka two weeks ago, and the similar massacres on Muslim worshippers at a mosque in New Zealand and Jewish believers at prayer in a synagogue in Pittsburgh are among the many signs of religions being massively perverted. One of the most dangerous features of the 21st century is how religious extremists join murderous hands with likeminded nationalistic, ethnic and racist individuals and movements, destroying innocent lives worldwide. This is not religion—this is apostasy. This is not faith—this is perversion. This is not loving—this is hatred. This is not truth—this is deceit. This is not tolerance—this is discrimination. This is not respect—this is scorn. Against destructive expression of faith gone amok, we hold a different conviction, a genuine profession of faith: religion is pro-love, pro-life, pro-justice, pro-truth. Religion is freedom. Religion is peace.[104]

Social and Religious Engagement in Myanmar Society   137

The Forum is an important organization that believes in human dignity and seeks solutions to national challenges. In the face of international condemnation for human rights violations against ethnic minorities in the country, Myanmar's military commander in chief, Senior General Min Aung Hlaing, visited Muslim mosques and hospitals, Christian churches, and Hindu temples, along with Buddhist monasteries in August and September 2019. His visits to non-Buddhist organizations were accompanied by donating massive amounts of money. He was attempting to improve relations with non-Buddhist organizations to repair the damage that the military's offensives on Muslims in Rakhine State and on other ethnic minority groups had done to his image. An army spokesman, Brigadier General Zaw Min Tun, commented on the visits and donations made by General Min Aung Hlaing, saying, "Our country is now in need of political, social, and religious unity, so we have done what is needed in a time like this."[105] However, this is just an outward show to the world, which does not really come from inner reflection and change, but rather, from a desire to gain popular support in the face of national and international criticism. Indeed, under the NLD leadership there are subtle signs of increased freedom of religion for all citizens in the country. Unlike the military regime, the NLD government was trying to protect all religions and thereby celebrate the plurality of diverse religions and cultures. It is true that there was no interfaith dialogue in past decades except interfaith deadlock. This interfaith dialogue could play a key role in bridging the gap instead of building the dividing wall. But table talk alone won't work. This interfaith dialogue needs to penetrate all levels, from grassroots to top leadership positions.

THE POLITICS OF POST 2015 ELECTIONS

People's hopes that the NLD would defeat the military backed USDP came true in the 2015 general elections, as the NLD won by a wide margin, not only in Burman-dominated regions but also in five ethnic minority states except Rakhine and Shan States. Voters cast their votes for the NLD, with great hope for a better life brought about by economic development, educational reform, amendment of the 2008 constitution, national reconciliation to bring an end to decades-old ethnic conflict, liberation from the military rule, and improvements to the existing health care system. Despite the massive victory of the NLD, there were still "obstacles"[106] preventing Suu Kyi from becoming the president. Nevertheless, she was smart enough to create a new position for herself. Soon after a transfer of power, the NLD created a position called state counselor for Suu Kyi, placing her "above the president."[107]

138 *Chapter Four*

Suu Kyi, with her smiling face and clear confidence in her ability to win the general election, told reporters at her lakeside residence in Yangon on November 5, 2015, ahead of the election, "I'll run the government and we will have a president who will work in accordance with the policies of the NLD."[108] A bill proposing the creation of the new position of state counselor, which would be equivalent to prime minister, was circulated among parliamentarians on March 30, 2016, after which it was first passed at the Amyotha Hluttaw (Upper House) on April 1 and then at the Pyithu Hluttaw (Lower House) on April 5, 2016. The bill was then sent to President Htin Kyaw, who signed it into the law at the Pyidaungsu Hluttaw (Union Parliament) after its approval by the majority votes despite strong opposition from the military representatives. Brigadier General Maung Maung disagreed with the creation of the state counselor bill and called it "democratic bullying by the majority."[109]

The manifesto of the NLD envisions a better future for the country. President Htin Kyaw, in his first address at the Pyidaungsu Hluttaw (Union Parliament) on March 30, 2016, pledged to prioritize four main policies under the NLD government: national reconciliation, internal peace, pursuing a constitutional movement toward a federal union, and improving the living standards of the majority of the people.[110] After taking office, Suu Kyi also called for a national peace conference to bring an everlasting peace to the country. Speaking at the second meeting of the Union Ceasefire Joint Monitoring Conference on April 27, 2016, she stressed the need to hold the national peace conference by inviting both the signatory and non-signatory groups into the nationwide ceasefire agreement as a priority. Expressing her willingness to continue the peace process of her predecessor, she said:

> I see no reason not to succeed in the peace process if we all really desire peace and if we have genuine goodwill. In this regard, what counts is the approach to the give-and-take policy. If we come to the roundtable discussion with our minds bent on taking rather than giving, we won't succeed. That's why I'd like you to think of what you can give as the first priority, showing the correct attitude toward the country. As long as you're only thinking of what you'd like to take, it will not be an easy task to seek peace and unity in a Union that was composed of a plethora of indigenous races.[111]

Suu Kyi's strategy to bring an end to decades of ethnic conflict is a call to all people to contribute something, big or small, to nation building. However, some ethnic minority people argue that they have given more than enough to the majority Burman since independence from the British in 1948, suggesting that the only thing they have is to take or get from the majority Burman, as opposed to the give-and-take policy. In other words, Suu Kyi is proposing a two-way traffic, while some ethnic minority groups are demanding a one-way traffic. After taking office, the NLD continued the work of its predecessor, and endorsed the Nationwide Ceasefire Agreement, although they did not sign the NCA in 2015 based on three fundamental reasons: first, the nature of partial coverage or lack of inclusiveness to cover the entire nation; second, the NCA could create misunderstanding among signatory organizations and non-signatory organizations; third, the government would likely exert pressure on non-signatory armed organizations.[112] It is true that some ethnic armed groups were not invited or welcomed by the government to sign the NCA in 2015. Only eight ethnic armed organizations signed the NCA on October 15, 2015. Unlike its predecessor, the NLD government encouraged and invited all ethnic armed organizations to participate in the roundtable talk at the Twenty-First-Century Panglong Conference, for political dialogue intending to bring an end to decades of civil war and secure a sustainable and lasting peace. Suu Kyi had been trying to negotiate with the Myanmar armed forces, while inviting ethnic minority groups to come to the conference. However, the Myanmar army's renewed attacks on the ethnic armed groups in the midst of the government peace process seriously weakened any attempts at national reconciliation. As a result, the NLD government's efforts for national reconciliation as its top priority stalled. Among the many factors that weaken peace building are not only the fighting between the Myanmar armed forces and the ethnic minority armed groups, but also intercommunal violence between Buddhists and Muslims in Rakhine State. When the NLD government was slowly settling into political authority, the attacks of the ARSA on security forces and the overreaction of the Myanmar military in Rakhine State changed the image of the country.

Changing the 2008 constitution was not only a major talking point during the NLD's election campaign but was a pledge after taking office as well. Drafting of the 2008 constitution was begun in the wake of the tragic Cyclone Nargis and was highly criticized for being the outcome of a limited consultation with the regime's hand-picked personnel, so the referendum was marred by controversy. It did not represent a true reflection of public opinion, since citizens were not given a free and fair choice in accordance with the law. Ironically, on May 29, 2008, the SPDC announced from Nay Pyi Taw that 92.48 percent, out of the 98.12 percent of voters all over the country, supported the 2008 constitution in accordance with law.[113] The reservation of 25 percent of parliamentary seats for unelected military appointees, which is not in line with democratic principles, was a transparent attempt to systematically secure the military's position in politics. According to the 2008 constitution, neither the state counselor nor the president is commander in chief of the Myanmar military, which means that they do not have much power over the military. The military retains control over three important ministries, namely,

140   *Chapter Four*

defense affairs, home affairs, and border affairs. In other words, the military controls all security matters, while the elected government is responsible for health, education, agriculture, infrastructure, and foreign policy. More importantly, the constitution gives the Myanmar military the full authority to declare a national state of emergency in chaotic situations such as ethnic conflicts and public protests, and take the power from the civil government, suggesting that the Myanmar military can operate independently of the civil government. The military is autonomous, and it is very difficult for Suu Kyi and President Win Myint to tell the military what and how to do their job. As such, the military wants to see the NLD government fail and the country fall into a chaotic disaster as a way to stage a coup in the name of law and order.

In 2014 during Armed Forces Day, the military commander in chief Min Aung Hlaing addressed in his speech the need for a gradual reduction of the armed forces in politics until the country becomes mature in democracy.[114] Supporting efforts to change the 2008 constitution in the face of increasing pressure for greater political reform, former president Thein Sein during his presidency also said on January 2, 2014, in his monthly radio address, "A healthy constitution must be amended from time to time to address the national, economic, and social needs of society."[115] However, it is still extremely hard, though not impossible, to amend the 2008 constitution, which Burman historian Thant Myint-U called "a hybrid system, with the army and elected institutions sharing authority,"[116] since a more than 75 percent majority is required to amend the constitution, while military appointees occupy 25 percent of seats in both Houses. Myint-U continues to argue that the 2008 constitution will not solve the Myanmar democracy problem under a "new system with old people."[117] He unveils the hidden reality inside government sectors, saying, "There would be a genuinely new setup but, for the first five years, perhaps ten, ex-military men would dominate institutions, to break them in. They wanted to make sure reform didn't lead to revolt, to protect their families and safeguard their wealth. Not all generals were corrupt, but many had family members who had profited from their positions."[118]

It is obvious that before the NLD officially took power in March 2016, the military officials who changed their uniform from military to civilian like wolves in sheep's clothing, already occupied positions of power in every sector of government. Since then, power-sharing between the civilian government and the military has been taking place. In the ongoing deteriorating relationship between the civilian government and the military at least one military representative in the parliament was required to support the amendment of the 2008 constitution.

The movement to amend the 2008 constitution centers on questions related to the fundamental power balance between the unelected military appointees and the elected civilian leaders, between the center and the periphery, and a

Social and Religious Engagement in Myanmar Society   141

drastic change to allow Suu Kyi to assume the position of president. Under the national government in Nay Pyi Taw, there are fourteen state and regional assemblies. The administration system of Myanmar is more or less still centralized. Although the fourteen states and regions elect their own assemblies, all chief ministers are directly appointed by the president from the center. Ethnic minority people are demanding more decentralization to the regional states and divisions in order to manage their own internal affairs as part of the government's political reforms, desiring to limit the power of the top bureaucracy from the Burman dominated center over the ethnic minority periphery. On the second anniversary of the NLD's election win, Suu Kyi reiterated the NLD's motto, "Together with the people,"[119] and reaffirmed their commitment to a democratic federal state, as well as addressing the development of socioeconomic life and transparency alongside national reconciliation and internal peace and calling for the amendment of the 2008 constitution to provide the foundation for a democratic federal union.

Despite strong resistance from the unelected military appointees in the parliament, the NLD and ethnic parties submitted their proposed amendments to the 2008 constitution to the Union Parliament on February 25, 2020. The NLD proposed a reduction in the military's share of seats from the current 25 percent to 15 percent after the 2020 general elections, and then to 10 percent after 2025, and 5 percent after 2030.[120] The political reforms also propose to remove the commander in chief's right to take power during a state of emergency,[121] and repeal Article 59(f) that prevents anyone with a foreign spouse and children from becoming president. Furthermore, the NLD proposes that the president shall take charge instead of the commander in chief during an emergency. Unlike ethnic parliamentarians, who support the amendment, the USDP and military parliamentarians strongly oppose the proposed amendment based on the country's instability facing the ongoing ethnic conflicts. The USDP is trying to prevent international intervention in Myanmar's internal affairs. The USDP lawmaker Tin Aye said, "It is too early to reduce the percentage of military parliamentarians during a time of instability."[122] The military's lawmaker, Major Htet Lin, added, "It was important to have the military in leadership roles to establish a disciplined, multiparty democracy as the country's transition was facing threats to national sovereignty, the rule of law and stability. There would be undesirable consequences of reducing the number of military lawmakers before the armed conflicts are ended and peace is established."[123]

The Myanmar military justifies its role in politics based on two fundamental reasons: "first," their involvement in the struggle for independence, "second," the ongoing struggles with ethnic minority armed groups. Obviously, the military's top brass is not prepared or willing to hand over power completely to the civilian government. The assassination of Ko Ni, who had

142 *Chapter Four*

been a legal advisor to Suu Kyi and had been very active in the movement to amend the 2008 constitution, is a strong signal that the Myanmar's armed forces are still attempting to prevent the NLD dominated government from amending the 2008 constitution. One can undoubtedly see that a genuine political transition to democracy is also dependent upon the Myanmar military top brass. The NLD and ethnic minority parliamentarians alone could not do it without the cooperation of the military. Calling everyone to play a role in political reforms toward democracy as opposed to a one-lady show, Suu Kyi once said, "I can't do it alone. If you want democracy, it is no use depending on either me or the NLD alone. What democracy means is government of the people, by the people, and for the people. If you want democracy, you'll have to work for it. You've got to join in. The more people are involved the quicker we'll reach our goal."[124]

Indeed, a political transition toward democracy cannot be achieved without the participation of all faithful citizens. Because of her politics and effort to find ways to bring together all opposing sides, Suu Kyi is accused of being aligned with the interests of the military. However, it is also important to be aware that Suu Kyi, as an engaged Buddhist, has been engaging with two sides—the democratic forces and the military. Many facets of life in Myanmar have changed since the NLD took office in 2016. Yet, many things still remain the same under a new system with both new and old people. There is no doubt that both challenges and opportunities still await the NLD government. As Myanmar was preparing for the forthcoming election expected later in 2020, ultranationalist Buddhists backed by the USDP was on the rise. Former president Thein Sein, from relative obscurity, appeared in public to campaign for his party. Speaking to thousands of supporters at the USDP headquarters in January 2020 with a dire warning, he said, "Because of neocolonialism under the disguise of democracy and human rights, our country is on the brink of being consumed by foreigners. The country would soon be swallowed whole."[125] The Myanmar military's commander in chief, Min Aung Hlaing, was given an award by the Young Men's Buddhist Association for his work defending "race, language, and religion."[126] This is a strong signal that the USDP is attempting to take power back from the civilian government after the 2020 general elections.

With a strong intention of forming a stronger bloc, many ethnic minority parties are merging across the country in preparation for the 2020 general elections, hoping to beat the NLD and the USDP in the ethnic minority states. The Kayah Unity Democracy Party and the All Nationals' Democracy Party Kayah State merged to create the Kayah State Democratic Party, and registered with the Union Election Commission on August 4, 2017.[127] Three Karen State-based parties—the Karen Democratic Party, the Karen State Democracy and Development Party, and the United Karen

Social and Religious Engagement in Myanmar Society 143

National Democratic Party—dissolved and merged together to form the Karen National Democratic Party (KNDP), which was approved by the Union Election Commission on February 22, 2018.[128] The two Mon parties—the All Mon Democracy Party and the Mon National Party—also registered at the Union Election Commission after merging to form the Mon Unity Party.[129] The Kachin State People's Party (KSPP) was formed by a merger of the Kachin Democratic Party, the Kachin State Democracy Party (KSDP), and the Unity and Democracy Party of Kachin State. The Union Election Commission approved the new political party registration in June 2019.[130] The Chin Progressive Party (CPP), Chin National Democratic Party (CNDP), and Chin League for Democracy (CLD) have also merged and registered at the Union Election Commission as the Chin National League for Democracy (CNLD) on July 11, 2019. All these ethnic minority political parties challenged the NLD and USDP in the general elections in 2020 in ethnic minority states. Another political force who challenged the NLD and USDP in the 2020 general elections was the People's Party led by Ko Ko Gyi, who had spent seventeen years in prison under the military regime for his work as one of the senior leaders of the pro-democracy "88 Generation Students Group." The Union Election Commission approved the People's Party as a new political party for official registration on August 23, 2018.[131]

The ethnic minority political parties might believe that the NLD had lost popular support in ethnic minority states, where people felt that their expectations for increased decentralization had been neglected. Furthermore, the ethnic minority people were extremely exhausted by the rolling civil war, which resulted in the death of innocent civilians and increase of internally displaced people in refugee camps. Nevertheless, because of Suu Kyi's cult of personality and the people's deep-seated hatred for the military dictatorship, the NLD still gained overwhelming support, winning 83 percent of the seats in the Union Parliament.[132] It is also important to give credit to current office holders under the NLD government, many of whom are former political prisoners who have sacrificed their freedom and their lives for the democratization of the country. The NLD was taking a more democratic platform, focusing on the creation of a democratic federal union, while the USDP adopted a more traditional and nationalist stand by using the religion of the majority Buddhists as a political steppingstone. The USDP was still exercising political muscle to bolster its power over politics beyond the 2020 elections. There is no doubt that Myanmar's young democracy has yet a long way to go. Constitutional amendments, peace-building and national reconciliation will be still the main concerns.

SPRING REVOLUTION IN 2021

To speed up democratic reform in Myanmar, voters went to polling stations on November 8, 2020, and cast their votes amid a surge of COVID-19 cases. The National League for Democracy (NLD) won 399 of the 642 seats in the bicameral Parliament far more than the 322 needed to form a government that already exists. Unable to accept the NLD's victory, USDP chairman Than Htay questioned the legitimacy of the results and said that his party would mount a legal challenge to the NLD's victory, claiming the vote was marred by electoral fraud, despite international polling observers like the Carter Center (formed by former US president Jimmy Carter) finding "no major irregularities in the polls."[133] Making matters worse, the USDP in cooperation with the military called for a new election.[134] The NLD invited the USDP to go ahead with legal procedures, "if they have enough evidence."[135] However, the USDP did not begin legal procedures. A few days after its victory, the NLD called forty-eight ethnic political parties to join the NLD in building a democratic federal union and to work effectively for ethnic affairs to bring an end to civil war.[136]

Parliament was scheduled to approve the election results and form a new government on February 1, 2021. Unfortunately, the Myanmar military's commander in chief, Min Aung Hlaing, seized power in the early morning of February 1, 2021, using the USDP's unsubstantiated claims of electoral fraud. The military detained the NLD's leader Aung San Suu Kyi and President Win Myint, as well as several regional and state ministers. Myanmar soldiers entered President Win Myint's bedroom at around 5:00 a.m. and took him to the president's office, where two military generals asked him to resign on the grounds of ill health. When the president responded that he would not resign because he was in good health, one of the generals asked him to reconsider his decision, otherwise he would face harm. The president told them he would rather die than resign, telling them to act lawfully, not stage a coup.[137] The military-owned Myawaddy TV station announced that the military was taking control of the country, declaring that a state of emergency would remain in place for one year, and that a second general election would be held after it had ended.[138] The next day the military formed the so-called "State Administration Council" (SAC), made up of military officers and handpicked civilians. Mass protests followed, voicing the people's anger at the military coup, which would come to be called the Spring Revolution. A new pro-democracy movement called the Civil Disobedience Movement (CDM), led by medical and health care workers, emerged after the coup, beginning as a social media campaign, particularly on Facebook, attracting bankers, lawyers, teachers, engineers, and other civil staff workers nationwide.[139] They

Social and Religious Engagement in Myanmar Society   145

demanded the military return the power to the elected government and refused to work under the military coup. A surgeon in Nay Pyi Taw, Zwe Min Aung, told the Voice of America, "At the time, we really disagreed with the military coup, and we created a small group in Mandalay hospital and other hospitals too. We distributed the statement on February 2 from Facebook and the nationwide CDM began. There is no leader."[140]

The military and police forces did not hesitate to open fire on peaceful protesters. As of June 10, 2022, the military regime has destroyed around 12,719 houses and religious buildings, ruthlessly slaughtered over 1,900 people, and arrested or detained more than 14,000 people including democratically elected leaders, NLD party members, election commissioners, medics, writers, journalists, artists, and civilians since February 1, 2021.[141] Thousands of protesters have been arrested on false accusations of spreading unrest, and agitating directly or indirectly against the military regime. Many have been fleeing to refugee camps inside the country, while a few fortunate ones have managed to flee to other countries for their own safety. In spite of the military crackdown, people continue to take to the streets across the country in protest against the military regime. After the February coup, the State Administration Council (SAC) hired Ari Ben-Menashe and his Montreal-based firm Dickens and Madson, to help polish its image. According to documents filed with the US Department of Justice, the contract Dickens and Madson signed with Myanmar's military leadership is worth US$2 million and is designed to explain the real situation in the country and to communicate with the United States and other countries who had misunderstood them. However, in mid-July, Ben-Menashe announced that he had ceased working with the generals because sanctions from the United States prevented him from being paid.[142]

On February 5, the Committee Representing Pyidaungsu Hluttaw (CRPH) was made up of the elected NLD lawmakers and members of Parliament ousted in the military coup from the 2020 November election. On April 16, the CRPH formed the National Unity Government (NUG), a shadow government with President Win Myint and State Counselor Aung San Suu Kyi taking their original positions, and ethnic leaders and activists appointed as ministers.[143] The NUG formed the "People's Defense Force" (PDF) on May 5, 2021, as an armed group to fight against the military regime. The military regime has branded the NUG a terrorist organization, but the majority of the population of Myanmar supports it as their legitimate government. Ethnic armed groups also support an anti-military coup, as they can no longer keep silent and watch the unarmed civilians being brutally killed by the junta forces. They attack the military in border areas, provide shelter to those fleeing their homes for fear of arrest and possible torture, and offer military training to young people who have gone underground to join the armed struggle

146 *Chapter Four*

to fight against the junta and return the country to civilian rule. This is the first time in the history of modern Myanmar that the majority Burman young people support ethnic armed groups in their fight against the junta.

In the face of the military coup, the people of Myanmar are crying out for the intervention of the Association of Southeast Asian Nations (ASEAN) and the United Nations Security Council to save lives and restore democracy in Myanmar. However, things have not happened as expected, as these organizations have taken no action except to issue statements that condemn the military coup and claim to stand with the pro-democracy movement in Myanmar. At a meeting held on April 24, 2021, in Jakarta, Indonesia, ASEAN leaders reached a five-point plan in the presence of Myanmar junta's commander in chief, Min Aung Hlaing, on how to resolve the political crisis the country is facing. They agreed upon the following goals: the immediate cessation of violence in Myanmar, constructive dialogue among all parties concerned to seek a peaceful solution in the interests of the people, mediation to be facilitated by an envoy of ASEAN's chair, with the assistance of the secretary-general, humanitarian assistance provided by ASEAN's AHA Center, and a visit by the special envoy and delegation to Myanmar to meet all parties concerned.[144]

However, the military regime did not participate in reaching the ASEAN's consensus, instead escalating its brutal crackdown on civilians across the country. Instead of acting in the best interests of the people, the military regime focuses on its own interests to perpetuate its own status quo. Therefore, health care workers, engineers, teachers, and other civil staff workers continue their refusal to work under the military regime through the Civil Disobedience Movement, preventing the junta from running the country properly. Since the February coup, the country has been facing the collapse of the economy and the education system, high unemployment resulting in poverty, and disruption of health care services. Consequently, the military regime could not provide health care to civilians as the third wave of COVID-19 spread across the country. Myanmar's public hospitals had a shortage of medical workers, as they had joined the Civil Disobedience Movement in protest against the military coup. In the face of a surge of COVID-19 cases, Myanmar's health care system collapsed, leaving tens of thousands of people desperately struggling to obtain oxygen supplies for sick family members. The military blocked oxygen sales to private sellers. People struggled to obtain oxygen because the military hoarded it for their own family members and the military hospitals. Even worse, the military looted shops, private homes, and offices to steal oxygen concentrators and hospital beds.[145] Despite the military junta's ban on oxygen sales to the public, people line up day and night outside oxygen factories to buy or refill cylinders for their families. Many people believe that the military regime uses COVID-19 as a weapon to kill its opponents. For instance, as a result of being barred from treatment for COVID, NLD Central

Social and Religious Engagement in Myanmar Society 147

Committee member and longtime personal lawyer to Suu Kyi, Nyan Win; forty-five-year-old lecturer at University of Medicine, Mandalay, Maung Maung Nyein Tun; and elected NLD lawmaker Nyunt Shwe, chair of the NLD's Bago Township office, all died in prison of COVID-19.[146]

The coup would not have happened if the military-backed Union Solidarity and Development Party (USDP) had won the election. The military's initial intention was to rule the country through its proxy party, the USDP. If the USDP had managed to win the election, the military would be in control of the government: 25 percent of parliamentary seats are held by military representatives directly appointed by the commander in chief, Min Aung Hlaing, and 25 percent or more would have been held by the USDP's representatives. However, the USDP managed to win just 6.4 percent of seats, while the NLD secured more than 83 percent of seats in the Union Parliament.[147] The Myanmar military feared that the civilian government would slowly reduce its power over Parliament and abolish the 2008 constitution, which could finally bring an end to its role in Myanmar's politics. The military regime explicitly injected its political intentions into the 2008 constitution, as Article 6 (f) states, "Enabling the Defense Services to be able to participate in the national political leadership of the state as one of the Union's consistent objectives."[148] When the USDP was defeated by the NLD with a landslide victory, the military used plan B: starting the coup to take power back from the civilian government.

Six months after the coup, General Min Aung Hlaing announced the State Administration Council as the country's "Caretaker Government"[149] on August 1, 2021, appointing himself as its prime minister. He extended the country's state of emergency until August 2023. A "Caretaker Government" with Min Aung Hlaing as its prime minister is a sign that the military is determined to stay in power for many years. Free and fair elections in 2023 and a transfer power to the winning political party was a false promise to national and international communities, intended to lend the military regime more credibility. Even if an election is held in 2023, everything the junta is doing indicates that it will be acting without the NLD, as the military are using any means possible to ensure the party's collapse. The military regime will try to find a way for its proxy party, the USDP, to dishonestly win the election. To transfer power to the winning political party after the 2023 election is also the old promise of the military regime. General Saw Maung promised the same thing after the 1988 coup, saying that the military would return to their barracks and transfer power back to elected civilians after the 1990 election.[150] But in reality, the military regime broke their promise. Instead of handing over power to the winning political party, the NLD, who had achieved a landslide victory, winning 392 of the 485 contested seats, the junta came up with a crafty plan to retain power. They nullified the results of the election

148 *Chapter Four*

and declared that power could not be transferred until a new constitution was written, resulting in the 1990 Uprising. The UN special envoy to Myanmar, Christine S. Burgener, has said that the coup leaders appear determined to solidify their grip on power by annulling the 2020 election, won overwhelmingly by the NLD, extending their stay in power from a one-year emergency to August 2023, and declaring Min Aung Hlaing as the prime minister of the newly formed "Caretaker Government."[151] Recent evidence has demonstrated that the military is extremely hostile toward pro-democracy movements and does not hesitate to mercilessly kill political activists, including peaceful protesters, and then lie to national and international communities to help them continue to rule.

On August 4, 2021, foreign ministers from the Association of Southeast Asian Nations appointed Brunei's second minister for foreign affairs, Erywan Yusof, as a special envoy to Myanmar, tasked with creating dialogue between the military rulers and their opponents, in order to end the political crisis the country is facing.[152] In a videoconference with Myanmar's military-appointed minister of foreign affairs, Wunna Maung Lwin, on August 31, 2021, Yusof called for a four-month ceasefire until the end of 2021, by all sides to enable the smooth delivery of humanitarian assistance to the country.[153] However, Myanmar's military regime has denied the call for a ceasefire.[154] The ASEAN's action is very slow, as it took almost four months to appoint a special envoy to Myanmar. In opposition to Yusof's call for a ceasefire, the acting president of Myanmar's shadow National Unity Government, Duwa Lashi La, declared defensive war on Myanmar's military regime on September 7, 2021, calling on citizens to revolt against the rule of military terrorists led by coup leader Min Aung Hlaing, in every corner of the country, and defending the war as a necessary step. He calls the NUG's declaration of war on the military regime a just revolution, declaring, "This revolution is a just revolution, a necessary revolution for building a peaceful country and a federal Union."[155] After the declaration of a just revolution against the military regime, the fighting between the military regime and its opponents escalated across the country in both rural and urban areas. In some places the junta forces randomly opened fire and bombarded residential areas in towns and villages with their heavy weapons, burning houses and Christian churches to ashes. They randomly arrested and shot innocent civilians with zero justification. During the fighting between the junta forces and local civilian resistance fighters in Thantlang, Chin State, the junta forces launched heavy artillery shells at a residential area of the town, resulting in the burning of nearly twenty houses. As he could not look at the burning houses with folded arms, thirty-year-old, Chin Christian pastor Cung Biak Hum, organized a group of young men and tried to extinguish the blaze to save his town. Unfortunately, he was shot dead by soldiers, who also cut off Hum's ring finger and stole his

Social and Religious Engagement in Myanmar Society 149

wedding ring, along with his watch and mobile phone.[156] The United Nations Special Rapporteur Tom Andrews called the murder of Hum and bombing of houses in Thantlang, Chin State, "the living hell being delivered by junta forces against the people of Myanmar."[157] In some cases, pictures of victims posted on social media showed lifeless bodies with internal organs exposed, or with deadly bruises and cuts, and bullet wounds to the head.[158] The killing of unarmed and innocent civilians was not only totally unacceptable but also against the slogans of the Myanmar soldiers, which claim that they exist to protect the people. In other words, the junta forces do not abide by the slogans they recite every day, pledging to protect the people.

The people of Myanmar have learned from their own experiences that neither diplomacy nor political dialogue work against the military regime. The UN's special envoy for Myanmar, Christine S. Burgener, has also said that her efforts to facilitate an "all-inclusive dialogue in the interest of the people were not welcomed by the military," confessing that her months-long attempts, in the wake of the takeover, to persuade the coup leaders in Nay Pyi Taw to engage in dialogue to settle the ongoing political and social turmoil caused by the coup, had failed.[159] Furthermore, sanctions are not effective in convincing the Myanmar military to retreat from politics. The military regime uses extreme measures to make sure that democracy does not take hold in Myanmar. In other words, the military regime is willing to return to the dark old days of its rule. Without a doubt, the military regime has destroyed the political development achieved during five years under the NLD and has hauled the country toward the status of a failed state. Therefore, the goal of the ongoing Spring Revolution is to uproot the military dictatorship through revolution. Compared to the 1988 Uprising, the 1990 Uprising, and the Saffron Revolution in 2007, the Spring Revolution in 2021 is unique in three ways: first, young people, regardless of gender and ethnic group, from both minority and majority Burman ethnic groups, have joined the People's Defense Force and ethnic minority armed groups to overthrow the military regime; second, tens of thousands of civil workers such as medics, engineers, teachers, bankers, lawyers, and other staff workers have joined the Civil Disobedience Movement, refusing to work under the military rule; third, there is resistance within the military and police force. Some mindful soldiers and police, who see the coup as completely contradictory and unacceptable to the best interests of the majority of the population, resist the mindless orders of their supreme leaders to mercilessly kill unarmed civilians, leaving the military and police force and joining the PDF to fight against their former military employers. As a result, the military's bureaucracy cannot perform its job well. The NUG's declaration of war has accelerated the ongoing armed struggle against the junta to a higher level, with fighting expected to intensify across the country. The fighting will be in both rural and urban areas, as

150   *Chapter Four*

members of the PDF who have received weapons and training from ethnic minority groups are scattered across the country.

As an engaged religionist, I also support political dialogue and engagement through nonviolent movement. However, it will be ineffective against the Myanmar military until they recognize and respect the voices and best interests of the majority of the people. Everything the military has done is completely contradictory to the aspirations of the majority of the population of Myanmar. They are the destroyers of Myanmar's promising young democracy. Therefore, the Spring Revolution in 2021 is the last resort for the oppressed to uproot the military's ruthless rule. Christine Burgener, in the face of her failure to convince the leaders of the Myanmar military to engage in peaceful negotiation with the opposition groups through nonviolent means, also states, "I regret this clear lack of will for a peaceful solution which could have prevented other stakeholders from feeling they have no choice but to seek violent means."[160] The Spring Revolution in 2021 is an ongoing fight between a pro-democracy movement and a military regime, and history will determine who will celebrate victory in the end.

NOTES

1. Sallie B. King, *Socially Engaged Buddhism: Dimension of Asian Spirituality* (Honolulu: University of Hawai'i Press, 2009), 1–3.

2. Walpola Rahula, *What the Buddha Taught* (Bedford, UK: Gordon Fraser, 1959), 85. The term *king* (raja) could be replaced today by the term *government*.

3. Thich Nhat Hanh, *Vietnam: Lotus in a Sea of Fire* (New York: Hill and Wang, 1967), 42.

4. Nhat Hanh, 1.

5. Nhat Hanh, 92.

6. Nhat Hanh, 107.

7. Thich Nhat Hanh, *Going Home: Jesus and Buddha as Brothers* (New York: Berkeley, 1999), 37.

8. Thich Nhat Hanh, *The Miracle of Mindfulness: A Manual on Meditation*, trans. Mobi Ho (Boston: Beacon Press, 1987), 95.

9. Nhat Hanh, 58.

10. Thich Nhat Hanh, *The Sutra on the Eight Realizations of the Great Beings*, trans. Diem Thanh Truong and Carole Melkonian (Berkeley, CA: Parallax Press, 1987), 15–16. Nhat Hanh states that poverty brings anger and hatred, and therefore, poor people are more inclined to create evil in society.

11. Nhat Hanh, 16.

12. Thich Nhat Hanh, *Living Buddha, Living Christ* (New York: Riverhead Books, 1995), 136.

Social and Religious Engagement in Myanmar Society

13. Nhat Hanh, *Going Home*, 2–3. According to Luther's understanding, the "inner man" stands for our relationship with God in the belief that Christ died for us on the cross, and the "outer man" stands for good works in our relationship to others as our spontaneous love in obedience to God. See Martin Luther, "The Freedom of a Christian," in *Luther's Works*, vol. 31, trans. W. A. Lambert, ed. Harold J. Grimm (Philadelphia: Muhlenberg Press,1957), 358.

14. Nhat Hanh, 3.

15. Donald Eugene Smith, *Religion and Politics in Burma* (Princeton, NJ: Princeton University Press, 1965), 96.

16. Niklas Foxeus, "Contemporary Burmese Buddhism," in *The Oxford Handbook of Contemporary Buddhism*, ed. Michael Jerryson (New York: Oxford University Press, 2016), 226.

17. Christopher Queen, "From Altruism to Activism," in *Action Dharma: New Studies in Engaged Buddhism*, ed. Christopher Queen (Hoboken, NJ: Taylor and Francis, 2013), 1–2.

18. Foxeus, "Contemporary Burmese Buddhism," 227.

19. Juliane Schober, "Buddhist Visions of Moral Authority and Modernity in Burma," in *Burma at the Turn of the 21st Century*, ed. Monique Skidmore (Honolulu: University of Hawaii Press, 2005), 123.

20. Aung San Suu Kyi, *The Voice of Hope: Conversations with Alan Clements* (New York: Seven Stories Press, 2008), 43.

21. Suu Kyi, 155–56.

22. Suu Kyi, 31.

23. Suu Kyi, 53.

24. Wai Moe, "Aung San Suu Kyi's Security," *Irrawaddy*, December 23, 2004.

25. Aung Zaw, *The Face of Resistance: Aung San Suu Kyi and Burma's Fight for Freedom* (Chiang Mai, Thailand: Mekong Press, 2013), 23–24. Also see Peter Popham, "They were Screaming: Die, Die, Die! The Dramatic Inside Story of Aung San Suu Kyi's Darkest Hour," *Independent*, October 16, 2011. The incident came to be known as the "Depayin Massacre," which comes from the name of the place the incident took place.

26. Zaw, 24. Senior General Than Shwe later admitted having ordered the attack. In his letter to Asian governments, he justified the attack by claiming that Aung San Suu Kyi and her party were conspiring to create an anarchic situation with a view to attaining political power. Also see Popham, "They Were Screaming: Die, Die, Die!"

27. Suu Kyi, *The Voice of Hope: Conversations with Alan Clements*, 113.

28. Suu Kyi, 155.

29. Suu Kyi, 41. Suu Kyi's mother always taught her not to hate those who killed her father.

30. Suu Kyi, 48.

31. Christina Fink, *Living Silence in Burma: Surviving under Military Rule* (London: Zed Books, 2009), 47.

32. Michael W. Charney, *A History of Modern Burma* (Cambridge: Cambridge University Press, 2009), 149.

33. Charney, 149. It is said that the bodies were cremated the following day.

152 *Chapter Four*

34. Charney, 149.

35. Fink, *Living Silence in Burma*, 47.

36. David I. Steinberg, *Burma: The State of Myanmar* (Washington, DC: Georgetown University Press, 2001), 209.

37. Zaw, *The Face of Resistance*, 11.

38. Aung San Suu Kyi, *Freedom from Fear and Other Writings* (New York: Penguin Books, 1995), 193.

39. Charney, *A History of Modern Burma*, 152.

40. Suu Kyi, *Freedom from Fear*, 193. Martin Smith called massive the 1988 uprising "the eruption of a sleeping volcano." See Martin Smith, *Burma: Insurgency and the Politics of Ethnicity* (London: Zeds Books, 1991), xvii.

41. Aung San Suu Kyi, *Letters from Burma: With a New Introduction by Fergal Keane* (London: Penguin Books, 2010), 119.

42. Bertil Lintner, *Burma in Revolt: Opium and Insurgency Since 1948* (Chiang Mai, Thailand: Silkworm Books, 1999), 352.

43. Zaw, *The Face of Resistance*, 15.

44. Bertil Lintner, *Outrage: Burma's Struggle for Democracy* (London: White Lotus, 1990), 145.

45. Smith, *Burma: Insurgency*, 4.

46. Smith, 5.

47. Smith, 14.

48. Smith, 15.

49. Smith, 17.

50. Suu Kyi, *Freedom from Fear*, 174.

51. Justin Wintle, *Perfect Hostage: A Life of Aung San Suu Kyi, Burma's Prisoner of Conscience* (New York: Skyhorse Publishing, 2007), 334.

52. Wintle, 337.

53. Suu Kyi, *Freedom from Fear*, xxiv.

54. Thant Myint-U, *The Hidden History of Burma: Race, Capitalism, and the Crisis of Democracy in the 21st Century* (New York: W.W. Norton & Company, 2020), 43.

55. Smith, *Burma: Insurgency*, 415.

56. Wintle, *Perfect Hostage*, 342.

57. Wintle, 362.

58. Wintle, 341.

59. Fink, *Living Silence in Burma*, 67.

60. Human Rights Watch, *The Resistance of the Monks: Buddhism and Activism in Burma* (New York: Human Rights Watch September 22, 2009). In the Burmese tradition the peacock is always considered a lucky bird and also associated with militant nationalism of the past and a symbol of the NLD and pro-democracy movement. See Maung Htin Aung, *The Stricken Peacock: Anglo-Burmese Relations 1751–1948* (The Hague: Martinus Nijhoff, 1965), xii.

61. Aung, xii.

62. Aung, xii.

63. Aung Zaw, "The Power Behind the Robe," *Irrawaddy*, September 12, 2017.

64. Human Rights Watch, *The Resistance of the Monks.*

Social and Religious Engagement in Myanmar Society 153

65. Suu Kyi, *Freedom from Fear*, xxv. Also see Wintle, *Perfect Hostage*, 346.

66. Wintle, *Perfect Hostage*, 343–44.

67. Mikael Gravers, "Monks, Morality and Military: The Struggle for Moral Power in Burma—and Buddhism's Uneasy Relation with Lay Power," *Contemporary Buddhism* 13, no. 1 (May 2012): 15.

68. William J. Topich and Keith A. Leitich, *The History of Myanmar* (Santa Barbara, CA: Greenwood, 2013), 122. Topich and Leitich offered a number of possible factors for moving the capital to Nay Pyi Taw. First, Yangon was a security threat both internally and externally to forces for the regime. Internally, the regime feared the "88" unrest-like protests, which could bring down the regime. Externally, there was a growing fear of an international force attacking the regime. For this purpose, the regime had constructed underground tunnels to secure the leadership in case of invasion. Second, Yangon was an aging city with infrastructural problems that needed a lot of renovations but were not worth the investment. Third, the generals may have been following a pattern developed in precolonial times in which the kings had relocated the capital at particular historical moments.

69. Stephen McCarthy, "Overturning the Alms Bowl: The Price of Survival and the Consequences for Political Legitimacy in Burma," *Australian Journal of International Affairs* 62, no. 3 (September 2008): 307.

70. Tom Plate and Jeffrey Cole, "Tom Plate and Jeffrey Cole Interview Lee Kuan Yew," *Asia Media*, UCLA Asia Institute, October 9, 2007. In July 2006 Senior General Than Shwe had a lavish wedding for his daughter, Thandar Shwe, who decked out in layers of pearls and sparkling diamonds. This lavish wedding outraged the ordinary people who live under extreme poverty. Lee Kuan Yew remarked that the daughter was like a Christmas tree.

71. This group was formed with former political prisoners who had led the pro-democracy demonstrations in 1988. It still exists today.

72. Human Rights Watch, *Crackdown: Repression of the 2007 Popular Protests in Burma* (New York: Human Rights Watch, December 6, 2007), 109. The Union Solidarity and Development Association (USDA) was established in 1993 as a government formed and controlled organization with millions of members, many of whom are coerced or induced into joining to support the *Tatmadaw* for rallies in support of the military regime and to attack pro-democracy group, the NLD. *Swan Arr Shin* in Burmese means "Masters of Force" and is the government-backed private militia. The SPDC strategically recruited Swan Arr Shin members from poor areas, giving them rudimentary military training in marching, shouting slogans, organizing participants and basic hand-combat techniques. Most of them were daily laborers who were used to doing hard manual labor, such as working as porters in the markets or at the ports. They were paid 3,000 kyats and two meals a day by the SPDC.

73. Myanmar News Agency, "So-called '88' Generation Student Group Agitating to Undermine Stability and Security of the State," *New Light of Myanmar*, August 25, 2007.

74. Aung Zaw, "Burmese Monks in Revolt," *Irrawaddy*, September 11, 2007.

75. Christina Fink, "The Moment of the Monks: Burma, 2007," in *Civil Resistance and Power Politics: The Experience of Non-violent Action from Gandhi to the*

154   *Chapter Four*

Present, ed. Adam Roberts and Timothy Garton Ash (Oxford: Oxford University Press, 2009), 355.

76. Juliane Schober, *Modern Buddhist Conjunctures in Myanmar: Cultural Narratives, Colonial Legacies, and Civil Society* (Honolulu: University of Hawai'i Press, 2011), 124.

77. Myanmar News Agency, "So-called '88' Generation Students and NLD Released Announcement the Protest was a Non-Violent One," *New Light of Myanmar*, September 7, 2007.

78. Fink, "The Moment of the Monks," 355.

79. Human Rights Watch, *Crackdown*, 31. In Buddhism, the giving and receiving of alms is a fundamental expression of religious piety and is considered as one of the most meritorious acts. As such, the practice of *patta nikkujjana kamma* could be considered as a religious punishment to the person concerned.

80. Myint-U, *The Hidden History of Burma*, 77.

81. Human Rights Watch, *Crackdown*, 39. This was the first time for Suu Kyi to be seen in public since her house arrest in 2003. Her picture paying obeisance to the monks beamed around the world.

82. Human Rights Watch, 42.

83. Myanmar News Agency, "Clarification on Myanmar's Situation to UNSG's Special Envoy Mr. Ibrahim Agboola Gambari," *New Light of Myanmar*, November 7, 2007. The government claimed that out of 2,284 detainees in Yangon, 2,235 were released and there remained only 49 persons in detention. In other cities, out of 643 persons who had been called for questioning 601 were released and only 42 remained in detention for further questioning.

84. Jeff Kingston, *The Politics of Religion, Nationalism, and Identity in Asia* (London: Rowman & Littlefield, 2019), 115.

85. May Kha, "Monks Conference Calls for Harmony, Criticizes Interfaith Marriage Draft Law," *Irrawaddy*, June 17, 2013.

86. Francis Khoo Thwe, "Archbishop of Yangon to Religious Leaders: Build Together a Myanmar of Peace and Justice," *Asia News*, October 3, 2013.

87. Regional Interfaith Network, "Seeking Peace for Myanmar along Interfaith Lines," *Regional Interfaith Dialogue, Connecting and Cooperating for Peace and Harmony in the Asia-Pacific Region*, August 11, 2014.

88. Tin Htet Paing, "Nationalists Oppose NGO's Curriculum for Including Religious Education," *Irrawaddy*, March 7, 2017.

89. Paing.

90. Myanmar News Agency, "Daw Suu Kyi Speaks on Unity: Virtuous Leaders Serve Public Interests with Genuine Affection: Chairman Bhamo Sayadaw," *New Light of Myanmar*, May 14, 2016.

91. Kyaw Phyo Tha and San Yamin Aung, "State-Backed Monks' Council Decries Ma Ba Tha as Unlawful," *Irrawaddy*, July 13, 2016.

92. Htun Htun and Pe Thet Htet Khin, "State Buddhist Authority Stands Its Ground," *Irrawaddy*, July 18, 2017. It goes on to say that people, either as individuals or as a group, must end its activities under the name Ma Ba Tha.

Social and Religious Engagement in Myanmar Society 155

93. Htun Htun, "Government Bans U Wirathu from Preaching Sermons," *Irrawaddy,* March 11, 2017.

94. Ei Ei Toe Lwin, "NLD Considers Religious Harmony Law," *Myanmar Times,* May 20, 2016.

95. San Yamin Aung, "Interfaith Leaders Call on Individuals to Build Peace," *Irrawaddy,* September 19, 2016. The International Day of Peace fell on September 21, and that year's theme was "Sustainable Development Goals: Building Blocks for Peace."

96. Aung.

97. Aung.

98. Aung.

99. Si Thu Lwin, "Interfaith Forum Denounces Violence," trans. Kyaw Soe Htet, *Myanmar Times,* March 24, 2017.

100. Zarni Mann, "Thousands Gather for Interfaith Rallies," *Irrawaddy,* October 11, 2017.

101. Naw Betty Han, "Interfaith Celebrations Aim to Unite Myanmar, NLD Says," *Myanmar Times,* October 18, 2017.

102. Zaw Min, "Interfaith Friendship and Unity Group (Myanmar) and Religions for Peace—Myanmar Sign MOU," *New Light of Myanmar,* April 3, 2019.

103. "Religions for Peace Second Advisory Forum in Myanmar Focuses on Religion in Nation-Building," Religions for Peace, May 7–8, 2019, https://www.rfp .org/religions-for-peace-convenes-second-advisory-forum-in-myanmar-focuses-on -religion-in-nation-building/.

104. "Religions for Peace Second Advisory Forum."

105. Roseanne Gerin, "Myanmar Top General Raises Questions with Visits to Mosques, Other Places of Worship," *Radio Free Asia,* September 23, 2019.

106. Constitution of the Republic of the Union of Myanmar, 2008 (Yangon: Ministry of Information, 2008), 19–20. Article 59(f) of the 2008 constitution barred Aung San Suu Kyi from becoming president for being married to a foreign man and having two sons of foreign citizenship. The article states that "the President and Vice-Presidents shall he himself, one of the parents, the spouse, one of the legitimate children or their spouses not owe allegiance to a foreign power, not be subject of a foreign power or citizen of a foreign country. They shall not be persons entitled to enjoy the rights and privileges of a subject of a foreign government or citizen of a foreign country."

107. Simon Roughneen, "Suu Kyi Says I Will Be Above the President," *Nikkei Asia,* November 5, 2015.

108. Roughneen.

109. Republic of the Union of Myanmar, "President Signs State Counselor Bill into Law," April 6, 2016. UJMC was formed on November 18, 2015. The Myanmar Peace Center was renamed to National Reconciliation and Peace Center (NRPC) after the NLD took office.

110. Zar Zar Soe, "President U Htin Kyaw's Inaugural Address," *Myanmar Times,* March 31, 2016.

156 *Chapter Four*

111. Thein Ko Lwin, "Inching toward Peace: State Counsellor Calls for Peace Conference within Two Months," *New Light of Myanmar*, April 28, 2016.

112. Nay Thar, "Why Aung San Suu Kyi Did Not Sign the NCA," *Mizzima News*, December 8, 2015.

113. State Peace and Development Council, "Myanmar Ratifies and Promulgates Constitution," *New Light of Myanmar*, May 30, 2008. Former President Thein Sein repeatedly lied to the people about the 2008 constitution by claiming that it was written by the approval of the people. Also see Janelle Saffin, "Seeking Constitutional Settlement in Myanmar," in *Constitutionalism and Legal Change in Myanmar*, ed. Andrew Harding (Oxford: Hart Publishing, 2017), 20.

114. "Myanmar's Military: Back to the Barracks?" International Crisis Group, April 22, 2014, https://www.crisisgroup.org/asia/south-east-asia/myanmar/myanmar -s-military-back-barracks.

115. Lawi Weng, "Thein Sein Says a Healthy Constitution Must Be Amended," *Irrawaddy*, January 2, 2014.

116. Myint-U, *The Hidden History of Burma*, 70.

117. Myint-U, 118.

118. Myint-U, 118.

119. Myanmar News Agency, "State Counsellor Daw Aung San Suu Kyi's Speech on the 2nd Anniversary of NLD Government," *New Light of Myanmar*, April 2, 2018.

120. San Yamin Aung, "Myanmar's Military and USDP Reject NLD Attempts to Limit the Armed Forces' Political Power," *Irrawaddy*, February 27, 2020.

121. Article 40 (c) allows the military to take power, stating, "If there arises a state of emergency that could cause disintegration of the Union, disintegration of national solidarity and loss of sovereign power or attempts therefore by wrongful forcible means such as insurgency or violence, the Commander in Chief of the Defense Services has the right to take over and exercise State sovereign power in accord with the provisions of the constitution." Ministry of Information, Constitution of the Republic of the Union of Myanmar, 11.

122. Aung, "Myanmar's Military and USDP Reject NLD Attempts."

123. Aung, The USDP is the military-backed party.

124. Suu Kyi, *The Voice of Hope*, 169.

125. Andrew Nachemson, "Myanmar's Aggressive Nationalism in the Air Ahead of 2020 Elections," *Diplomat*, February 21, 2020. Former President Thein Sein is currently the chairman of the USDP.

126. Nachemson.

127. "New Kayah State Party Officially Registered," *Kantarawaddy Times*, Burma News International, August 14, 2017. https://www.bnionline.net/en/news/karenni -state/item/3372-new-kayah-state-party-officially-registered.html.

128. "New United Karen Party's Registration Accepted by Union Election Commission," *Karen News*, March 2, 2018, https://karennews.org/2018/03/new-united -karen-partys-registration-accepted-by-union-election-commission/.

129. *Mizzima News*, "Mon Unity Party Allowed to Be Registered as Official Political Party," July 15, 2019.

130. Swe Lei Mon, "New Kachin Party to Meet Public for First Time," *Myanmar Times*, July 26, 2019.

131. "Myanmar's Election Commission Approves 88 Generation Group's Bid to Form Political Party," Radio Free Asia, August 24, 2018, https://www.rfa.org/english /news/myanmar/myanmars-election-commission-approves-88-generation-groups-bid -08242018161039.html.

132. Kyaw Zwa Moe, "What Another NLD Victory Means for Myanmar and the World," *Irrawaddy,* November 23, 2020. The overwhelming support of the people for the NLD is even higher in the 2020 general elections than the 1990 elections when the NLD gained 82 percent of seats.

133. *Irrawaddy*, "In Myanmar, the NLD's Main Rival Finds It Hard to Accept Electoral Defeat," November 12, 2020.

134. San Yamin Aung, "Myanmar Opposition Party Demands Election Rerun with Military Involvement," *Irrawaddy*, November 11, 2020.

135. "In Myanmar, the NLD's Main Rival."

136. Nyein Nyein, "NLD Reaches Out to Myanmar's Ethnic Parties Seeking Federal Union and End to Civil War," *Irrawaddy*, November 13, 2020.

137. *Irrawaddy*, "Myanmar President Reveals Details of His Arrest," October 14, 2021.

138. Russel Goldman, "Myanmar's Coup and Violence, Explained," *New York Times*, May 29, 2021. Also see "European Leaders Condemn Coup as Myanmar's Military Seizes Power, Detains Aung San Suu Kyi," CBS News, February 1, 2021, https://www.cbsnews.com/news/myanmar-coup-military-detains-aung-san-suu-kyi -latest-updates/.

139. Tommy Walker, "How Myanmar's Civil Disobedience Movement Is Pushing Back against the Coup," *Voice of America*, February 27, 2021.

140. Walker.

141. *Irrawaddy*, "Myanmar Regime Committed Almost 2,800 War Crimes in Last Six Months: NUG," June 13, 2022.

142. Bertil Lintner, "All Lies: Myanmar's Junta Clumsy Propaganda Has a Disturbing Familiar Ring," *Irrawaddy*, August 16, 2021.

143. *Irrawaddy*, "Myanmar Coup Highlights in 90 Days," May 1, 2021.

144. *Bangkok Post*, "ASEAN Leaders Agree 5-Point Plan for Myanmar," April 25, 2021.

145. *Irrawaddy*, "Myanmar Regime Troops Detain Youths and Loot Shops in Night Raids," August 20, 2021.

146. *Irrawaddy*, "Myanmar Junta Kills Nearly 1,000 Civilians in Under 200 Day," August 17, 2021.

147. Naing Khit, "Myanmar's Military Chief Staged a Coup. But He Did Not Act Alone," *Irrawaddy*, August 13, 2021.

148. Ministry of Information, Constitution of the Republic of the Union of Myanmar, 2008, 3.

149. Hannah Beech, "Top Myanmar General Says Military Rule Will Continue into 2023," *New York Times*, August 1, 2021.

150. Ye Myo Hein, "Demystifying the Narratives on the Myanmar Military," *Irrawaddy*, August 13, 2021.

151. Hein.

152. Tom Allard, "ASEAN Appoints Brunei Diplomat as Envoy to Myanmar," *Reuters*, August 4, 2021.

153. *Kyodo News*, "ASEAN Envoy to Myanmar Says Military Agrees to Four-Month Ceasefire to Deliver Aid," September 6, 2021.

154. *Irrawaddy*, "Myanmar Junta Denies Accepting ASEAN Ceasefire Proposal," September 7, 2021.

155. *Irrawaddy*, "Head of Myanmar's Shadow Govt Says World Will Back Its Declaration of War Against Junta," September 7, 2021.

156. *Irrawaddy*, "Brother of Slain Myanmar Pastor Says Regime Fails to Take Accountability for Atrocities," September 23, 2021. Cung Biak Hum is a pastor at Thantlang Centenary Baptist Church, Chin State. He is also currently an active student at Myanmar Institute of Theology for Master Program.

157. Steve Warren, "Pastor Murdered by Soldiers While Trying to Save Burning Home in Myanmar," CBN News, September 22, 2021.

158. Naing Khit, "Diplomacy Is Wasted on Myanmar's Junta," *Irrawaddy*, September 22, 2021.

159. *Irrawaddy*, "UN Envoy Joins Her Predecessors in Myanmar's Graveyard of Diplomats," September 16, 2021.

160. "UN Envoy Joins."

Chapter Five

The Implications of Luther's Theology of Two Kingdoms in Dialogue with Engaged Religious Communities in Myanmar Today

Reinterpretation of the Myanmar Baptist Understanding of Church and State

The Myanmar Baptist understanding of the separation of church and state was not born on its own soil, but rather imported from the American Baptist Missionary Union. As such, it would be wise to briefly explore the genesis of the principle of the separation of church and state, and how it plays out today in the United States. Looking back at the relationship between church and state in the United States, one can see that the early Puritan settlers played an important role in framing the relationship between church and state as established in the American constitution, in which the 1879 Supreme Court evoked Thomas Jefferson's metaphor of "a wall of separation between church and state."[1] In 1947, in the *Everson v. Board of Education* case, the Supreme Court of the United States declared, "The First Amendment has erected a wall between church and state. That wall must be kept high and impregnable. We could not approve the slightest breach."[2] The First Amendment, passed by the Congress of the United States on September 25, 1789, reads, "Congress shall make no law respecting an establishment of religion, or prohibiting the free exercise thereof; or abridging the freedom of speech, or of the press; or the right of the people peaceably to assemble; and to petition the government for a redress of grievances."[3] It is understood that the modern phrase *separation of church and state* has evolved from this written document. It is also true that

160   *Chapter Five*

the early Puritan settlers brought their fear of losing religious freedom with the establishment of a state religion to America and transferred that fear to the framing of the constitution and therefore the government of the United States.

Roger Williams, a devout Puritan minister in colonial America, first called for a "wall of separation between church and state"[4] 150 years before Thomas Jefferson. The state of Massachusetts exiled Williams, seeing his view as very dangerous. Williams, therefore, left Massachusetts and founded Rhode Island, establishing a church there with his associate John Clarke in 1639. Williams described the church as a garden and the government as a wilderness, and said that Massachusetts had mixed the two, and in doing so corrupted the church.[5] His belief in both the purity of the Edenic garden of the church and the corrupt world of the state compelled Williams to call for a wall of separation, and he was convinced that any breach of the wall between church and state, any involvement either of a magistrate in churchly things or of the church in government, would bring the wilderness into the garden.[6] Williams further stated that the wall of separation came between the "garden" of religion and the "wilderness" of temporal government and it protected the garden from the wilderness, not the other way around.[7] It is believed that Thomas Jefferson accepted Williams's view, including this phrase in a letter to the Baptist church in Danbury, Connecticut, written on January 1, 1802:

> Believing with you that religion is a matter which lies solely between man and his God, that he owes account to none other for his faith or his worship, that the legislative powers of government reach actions only, and not opinions, I contemplate with sovereign reverence that act of the whole American people which declared that their legislature should "make no law respecting an establishment of religion, or prohibiting the free exercise thereof," thus building a wall of separation between church and State.[8]

Jefferson's letter articulates his belief that church and state should be kept strictly separate in public life. This group of Baptists in Danbury, Connecticut, had written a letter to Thomas Jefferson on October 7, 1801, signed by Nehemiah Dodge, Ephram Robbins, and Stephen S. Nelson on behalf of the Danbury Baptist Association, seeking his support for religious liberty in a predominantly Congregationalist community, stating their beliefs: "That religion is at all times and places a matter between God and individuals—That no man ought to suffer in name, person or effects on account of his religious opinions—That the legitimate power of civil government extends no further than to punish the man who works ill to his neighbor."[9] It is understandable that the Danbury Baptists were fearful that the government would someday establish a state religion. Jefferson was therefore sympathetic to their concerns. I believe that Jefferson's original intent was that church and state should stay out of each other's affairs completely. The foundation for the principle of separation between church and state is that the United States is individualistic and independent in its religious expression since there is no state religion. This independence of religion from the state has allowed the United States to be open to religious diversity, allowing people to believe what they want, albeit with the belief that religion is better than non-religion since religion has unique ethical teachings. Two separate studies from the Pew Global Attitudes Project and World Bank covering the period from 2008 to 2012 show that the higher a country's gross national income, the lesser people in that country will find religion to be important.[10] If this were the case, it would mean that the United States, with a gross national income of about $50,000, one of the highest in the world, would find religion to be less important. However, this is not true for the United States, but rather the opposite, giving birth to the term *American exceptionalism*,[11] which views the United States as a city built on a hill and a light to the nations across its borders. Not only do the American people find religion to be important, but "nine out of ten Americans identify with some religious group or tradition."[12] The notion of American exceptionalism in religion is attributed to cultural compatibility, a need for social identity, the independence of religion from the state, and the competitive religious environment.[13] The American culture is compatible with the American churches because both have emphasized individual initiative, freedom of choice, and self-governance.[14] Furthermore, America has a very competitive religious environment, since there is no state church, allowing churches to adapt easily to society.

Advocates of "separationism" believe that church and state will better achieve their ends if they remain independent of each other.[15] In other words, church and state should not interfere with each other's offices unnecessarily. However, the original intent of a wall of separation has been breached in modern history. Even Jefferson himself had no objection to the use of municipal buildings for worship by the different congregations in his village.[16] Furthermore, the case of *Engel v. Vitale* in New York State in 1962 addressed the daily reading of prayer by school teachers.[17] Similarly, in 1963, the case of *Abingdon School District v. Schempp* in Pennsylvania addressed the daily reading of Bible verses and reciting the Lord's Prayer in public schools.[18] By reading these prayers and Bible verses, the government was purposely promoting Christianity, which is against the Establishment Clause of the First Amendment. When government supports prayer and reading Bible verses in public schools, it is not only breaching the "Establishment Clause" of the First Amendment but also undermining people of other faiths and those without faith.

162   *Chapter Five*

Let us turn our attention to how Lutherans view the principle of separation of church and state in the United States. At the beginning of the twentieth century, American Lutherans, according to John R. Stumme, established themselves as strong separationists by supporting the American constitution.[19] They understood that they could practice their faith with full religious liberty without the unnecessary interference of the government.[20] This understanding is also affirmed by Lloyd Svendsbye when he says:

> American Lutheranism draws a strict line of separation between the sphere of the state and the sphere of the church. Neither was to interfere with the operation of the other, nor was either even to advise the other. A result of this view was that the church could not and did not function as the conscience of the state, nor did the church express responsibility for bearing a corporate witness to the state on major social issues. The Lutheran church, therefore, tended to accept without criticism what the state did.[21]

According to this view, the church has no role in politics at all. However, by the middle of the twentieth century in 1946, an American Lutheran theologian and historian, Conrad Bergendoff questioned the principle of the absolute separation of church and state and called for a "re-thinking of the relationship of the Lutheran Church to the community and state."[22] Negating the idea of mixing church and state business, David M. Whitford says, "If princes attempted to run states by the Gospel's call to turn the other cheek, mass exploitation and sin would result, and if pastors governed the church by the sword, the message of free grace would be hopelessly lost." Therefore, Whitford contends that secular authorities ought to devote themselves to the maintenance of law and order and leave the proclamation of the Word to the church, saying, "Pastors make poor kings, and kings make poor pastors."[23]

As an alternative to the absolute separation of church and state, as well as to the church's rule of the state or the state's rule of the church, Lutheran theologians such as George W. Forell, Herman A. Preus, and Jaroslav J. Pelikan proposed in 1953 the "interpenetration of church and state."[24] The Evangelical Lutheran Church in America, according to Stumme, maintains neither the absolute separation of church and state nor the mixing up of both but rather proposes going by the principle of "institutional separation and functional interaction" in church-state relations.[25] As such, Lutherans who believe in institutional separation and functional interaction reject both the absolute separation of church and state and the domination of either one by the other.[26] They have both practical and theological reasons for this position. Practically, the federal government invites religious agencies to participate more fully in the growing demands of health, education, and welfare; and theologically, Lutherans are revising their understanding of the two kingdoms

Implications of Luther's Theology of Two Kingdoms in Dialogue 163

or God's twofold rule of the world, as they want to return the church to a right understanding of the role of church and state in society according to Luther's original view.[27]

In an attempt to bring the church to a right understanding of its relationship to the state, ELCA Lutherans propose a threefold commitment: the integrity of church and state, the interaction of church and state, and religious freedom for all.[28] The integrity of church and state means that church and state must each be free to perform its own essential task under God's rule. In this respect, one should not confuse the office of the church with that of the state. Stumme clarifies the distinction between the office of the church and that of the state as follows:

> To guard against the dominance of one over the other and maintain the integrity of both, Lutherans propose the confusing of word and sword. The church may only propose, proclaim, and persuade, while the state may compel in earthly matters. The church has no divine authority to take up the sword to carry out its mission, and the state has no divine authority to preach the gospel or any other religious message. The church lives under the divine mandate not to invoke the state's coercive power to compel faith in God, and the state lives under the divine mandate not to coerce faith or disbelief.[29]

According to this view, the church as an institution should not use the sword or any coercive means in any aspect of its ministry both inside and outside the church. In 2020, the Evangelical Lutheran Church in America (ELCA) renewed their perspectives of God's two ways of governing as church and state. They recognized that God's rule is experienced in "two distinct but interconnected ways,"[30] which have been described as the "right" and the "left" hands of God. The "right" hand refers to God's governance of the world with his Word and Sacrament in our "inner" or personal relationship to God and fellow human beings, elaborating:

> Through the right hand, God acts upon the "inner" or personal dimensions of our lives through God's promise given in Word and Sacrament. God uses the Scriptures, prayers, sermons, worship, and human conscience to transform our relationship with God and thereby with each other. God's right hand conveys the tangible power of God's love and forgiveness to people of faith, which stirs us to forgive others, to express mutual love and care, and to strive for justice.[31]

The ELCA describes God's "left" hand as operating in the "outer" social, political, and economic world through human roles, structures, and institutions, to foster the well-being of people and the world.[32] They explain that God's two ways of governing are interconnected in five vital themes. First, God's law is God's will for human life to love God and our neighbors, which

164   *Chapter Five*

the Lutherans call the "theological use of the law."[33] Another law, which the
Lutherans call the "civil use of the law" includes coercive laws to protect
against criminality.[34] Second, God's rule in both hands is marked by equality.
Based on the doctrine of the "priesthood of all believers," all human beings
have sinned, and all are in equal need of redemption under God's right-hand
rule. Under God's left-hand rule, all people have fundamental dignity and
rights, for they are created in God's image.[35] Third, God's right-hand rule
inspires a powerful impulse of empathy to recognize and honor every human
being as a person with dignity and rights and helps us see even strangers as
neighbors.[36] Fourth, God has concern for justice in both ways of working. In
God's left-hand governance, earthly justice is fundamentally done to punish
the wicked for their wrong deeds and protect the upright for the welfare of
the people.[37] Fifth, God imparts purpose to the roles of worldly governance. If
government officials see their role in serving the public as a means primarily
for power and gain, it is the proper task of the church to declare that government, citizenship, and public service are gifts to be exercised with integrity
and respect for the well-being of human communities.[38]

When we turn to the relationship between church and state in Myanmar, a
different picture emerges with regard to the debate on church and state. The
Myanmar Baptist understanding of the principle of separation between church
and state came from both the church and the constitution of the government.
The last adopted 2008 constitution, which is the continuation of the 1974 constitution of the Union of Myanmar, is very controversial regarding church
and state. It contains the "Free Exercise Clause" of religion, which states
that every citizen is equally entitled to freedom of conscience and the right
to freely profess and practice religion, subject to public order and morality
or health.[39] However, the same constitution also includes the "Establishment
Clause," which stipulates that the Union recognizes the special position of
Buddhism as the faith professed by the great majority of the citizens of the
Union,[40] which sounds like Buddhism becoming the state religion. The constitution also states, perhaps for checks and balances, "The abuse of religion
for political purposes is forbidden. Moreover, any act which is intended or is
likely to promote feelings of hatred, enmity or discord between racial or religious communities or sects is contrary to this constitution. A law may be promulgated to punish such activity."[41] In spite of this legitimate stipulation, the
ultra-nationalist Buddhists and political opportunists manipulate and exploit
the state constitution and cause unnecessary violence between Buddhists and
non-Buddhists.

Some Baptists in Myanmar interpret the principle of separation of church
and state as justifying blind obedience to the oppressive rule of the state.
As a result, public engagement of the church has been called into question
many times, especially after the 1988 uprising, with a simple accusation

that the church has been quiet in the face of religious oppression, political repression, economic injustice, and ethnic persecution at the hands of the repressive military regime. This is a difficult question for the churches in Myanmar to immediately answer. Some of the majority Burman Buddhists fail to accept that ethnic minority Christians face double persecution under the totalitarian military regime on the basis of their ethnic identity and religion, whereas the majority Burman Buddhists face a single persecution, that is, political repression. Chin Baptist theologian Simon Pau Khan En admits that Myanmar churches do not engage with the sociopolitical situations of the country. He attributes the church in Myanmar's hesitation to engage with social and political issues under the military regime to three possible factors. First, the church was and is not bold enough to raise a prophetic voice against the military regime because of the minority inferiority complex of Christians, who form only about 6 percent of the entire population in a largely Buddhist country. Second, Christians in Myanmar overemphasize futuristic eschatology, which results in neglecting their present obligations in social and political engagement to make the world a better place. Criticizing this theological misconception, En states, "Christians in Myanmar are not prepared theologically to participate actively in the sociopolitical order of the country. Their eschatological expectation forces them to keep quiet and wait for the kingdom without meddling in the secular affairs of this world. They are happy to obey the government without any involvement." Third, the Baptist principle of separation of church and state has a significant influence upon the church as a whole, as Baptists represent the vast majority of the whole Christian population in the country.[42] Many Baptists interpret this principle to mean that the church should not meddle with the current sociopolitical situation in the country, and as a result they assume that the church should maintain neutrality and withhold itself from constructive engagement in public life, even in the face of sociopolitical issues that severely affect the entire country. It is understandable that ethnic minority Christians feel inferior because they are ethnically, religiously, and politically disempowered by their minority status. However, I do not believe that their futuristic eschatological expectation should prevent Christians in Myanmar from engaging in the secular affairs of the present world.

Another Chin theologian, Samuel Ngun Ling, also acknowledges the withdrawal of the church from public engagement in Myanmar, largely due to the principle of separation of church and state that the Baptists inherited from the Western missionaries. Ling contends that the churches should engage the public and lived experiences of the people without narrowly confining Christian spirituality to prayer in the church compound. In his view, "The church needs to play a prophetic role in all contexts and must be critically but

166   *Chapter Five*

non-violently responsive to whatever challenges might come to the mission and visions of the church."[43]

Lisu scholar, Oliver Byar Bowh Si offers another set of possible reasons for the silence of the Christian church under successive military dictatorships. First, people consider religion a private choice and believe that it has nothing to do with politics, which, I argue, is typical secular thinking. Second, churches prefer to stay separate from other social institutions due to fear that the military regime might jeopardize their existing institutions if they get involved in public affairs.[44] Bowh Si critiques the 2008 Myanmar constitution as extremely undemocratic, which guarantees a monopoly of political power to the military on the one hand, and, on the other hand, does not guarantee the rights and freedoms of the people of Myanmar.[45] Bowh Si is therefore more interested in a civil society where there is an opportunity for political dialogue between ethnic minority groups and the central government that can help bring an end to the current ethnic conflicts.[46] The silence of the church in the face of oppression by the military regime is discussed by yet another Chin scholar, Pum Za Mang. In Mang's view, the church in Myanmar has been silent in the face of political oppression, religious persecution, massive human rights violations, and ethnic cleansing by the military regime, intended to assimilate all ethnic minority groups into a homogenous Burman identity through a process called Burmanization. Mang's main interest is in pursuing a path to liberation from Burmanization through nonviolent resistance to the repressive state.[47]

In spite of different theological justifications for the rights of ethnic and religious minorities, each of the four scholars mentioned above recognizes religious persecution in Myanmar and at the same time calls for the public engagement of the church. However, they do not examine the pathways to religious freedom through the combined efforts of socially engaged Buddhist and Christian communities in Myanmar. Socially engaged religion rejects the idea of detaching from society in the face of suffering caused by natural disasters, social injustice, and political oppression, and calls people of faith to respond to those challenges through "people-power" such as public protests, ritual, and storytelling. As such, true religion always engages in society in order to alleviate suffering and transform humanity. Hence, the ideology of engaged religion supports peace, justice, and freedom, and denounces oppression in every aspect of life in society.

The Myanmar Baptists do not have any relationship with the Anabaptists. They do not share the Anabaptist goal of total withdrawal from human society and detachment from the daily struggles of the people. Therefore, some of the Myanmar Baptist understanding of a dichotomized separation between church and state is inconsistent with their predominantly Theravada Buddhist context, in which there is a reciprocal relationship between church and state.

As already discussed in chapter 1, there is no total separation of religion and politics in traditional Theravada Buddhism in Myanmar, but rather, a reciprocal or interdependent relationship between the two. As such, the monk serves as the intermediary between the ruler and the ruled, to protect the latter from the arbitrary and oppressive rule of the former. At the same time, the government must rule the country with Buddhist ethical principles of social justice and meet the basic needs of the people. If the government does not rule the people in accordance with Buddhist principles, what will the monks do? In such a situation, the monks will hold *Thapeik-hmaunk* (literally, "overturn the alms bowl") in public protest as a sign of refusing alms from the unjust rulers, blocking them from entering Nirvana. In this context, the only way for the unjust rulers to reenter Nirvana is to turn back to Buddhist principles in their governance to meet the needs of the people.

However, the traditional Buddhist principle of a reciprocal relationship between religion and politics (or between the sangha and the king) collapsed during the British colonial period as the British maintained religious neutrality, which was interpreted as strict noninterference by the government in religious matters.[48] The irony of the British colonial government's claim of "religious neutrality" or "non-interference," of course, was that in fact they did interfere with religious matters, showing a strong preference for Christians. As a result, British rule caused Buddhism to be in serious decline as the British government did not support the Buddhist ecclesiastical hierarchy, and the Burman kingship holding power over religious matters. Influenced by the Western ideals of the modern secular state, General Aung San, the founding father of Myanmar's independence, envisioned Myanmar as secular state, one that would embrace the country's reality of religious and ethnic diversity as strength. Unfortunately, Aung San's vision collapsed after his assassination, resulting in subsequent governments effectively treating Buddhism as a state religion.

However, unlike the preceding military regime, the NLD government is trying to celebrate the diversity of religions and cultures, and also to include different ethnic groups in the reform movement. The engagement of Buddhist and Christian communities with the democratization of the country and attempts to alleviate the suffering of the people in 1988, 1990, 2007, and 2021 have proved that religion plays an indispensable role in public life. Buddhist thought forms a clear basis for a theology of active resistance against an unjust government in the same way that both Luther and Bonhoeffer found such a basis in Christian theology. The idea of separationism between religion and politics is not only inconsistent but also paradoxical in the context of the Burman Buddhist majority. It forces the church to withdraw itself from engaging in public life. Religion and politics in Myanmar are interconnected and cannot be separated from one another.

168   *Chapter Five*

Suu Kyi has also affirmed the inseparable engagement between religion and politics, stating, "In Burma today, the large portion of monks and nuns see spiritual freedom and socio-political freedom as separate areas. But in truth, dharma and politics are rooted in the same issue—freedom."[49] Suu Kyi does not see religion and politics as separate. The time has come, therefore, for Myanmar Baptists to let go of the principle of total separation between religion and politics, and to instead opt for a model of institutional separation and functional interaction or two distinct but interconnected ways between religion and politics in Myanmar. This model will create space not only for the Burman Buddhist majority but also for people of minority faiths to act as a prophetic voice for social justice through engaged spirituality in society, which is currently rare in the Baptist Church in Myanmar.

THE LIMITS OF RELIGIOUS FREEDOM: INTERSECTION BETWEEN RELIGION AND POLITICS

On the morning of October 27, 2018, a gunman named Robert D. Bowers, aged forty-six, stormed into the Tree of Life Synagogue in Pittsburgh, Pennsylvania, where worshippers had gathered to celebrate their faith, and opened fire indiscriminately into the crowd, leaving eleven people dead and two wounded, along with four police officers who were injured in a shootout afterward.[50] His violent action turned a peaceful celebration into chaos. He was charged with twenty-nine criminal counts, which included obstructing the free exercise of religious beliefs and ethnic intimidation. According to the US Federal Bureau of Investigation, Robert Jones, a special agent in charge of investigating events that take place in Pittsburgh, Bowers gunned down congregants participating in a peaceful worship service, especially because of their faith. Before the gunman entered the Tree of Life Synagogue, he posted a message on social media, stating, "HIAS likes to bring invaders in that kill our people. I can't sit by and watch my people get slaughtered. Screw your optics. I'm going in."[51]

About four months later, on March 15, 2019, Brenton Tarrant, a white supremacist terrorist, attacked Muslim worshippers in two mosques, the Al Noor Mosque and Linwood Islamic Center, in Christchurch, New Zealand, leaving fifty-one people dead and wounding forty.[52] Before the attacks, Tarrant released a manifesto online entitled, "The Great Replacement,"[53] in which he interviewed himself about his motives for the attack, stating, "Was the attack anti-immigration in origin? Yes, beyond all doubt, anti-immigration, anti-ethnic replacement and anti-cultural replacement."[54] Tarrant's manifesto echoed the tiki torch–bearing white supremacists who had marched in

Implications of Luther's Theology of Two Kingdoms in Dialogue   169

Charlottesville, Virginia, on October 7, 2017, shouting, "You will not replace us!"[55] Mayor Mike Signer of Charlottesville asked white supremacists to go home on his twitter, saying, "Another despicable visit by neo-Nazi cowards. You're not welcome here."[56]

Janna Ezat, whose son, Hussein al-Umari, was killed in Christchurch forgave Tarrant at his trial, saying, "I weep every day for him and for my family's loss. I decided to forgive you, Mr. Tarrant, because I don't have hate, I don't have revenge. Hussein will never be here again, so I have only one choice: to forgive you." Unlike Ezat, who forgives Tarrant, Wasseim Sati Ali Daragmin addressed Tarrant directly in the court with a defiant statement that Tarrant had failed his mission, saying, "You think your actions have destroyed our community and shaken our faith, but you have not succeeded. You have made us come together with more determination and strength."[57] Tarrant faces a maximum possible sentence of life in prison without parole, a sentence never before imposed in New Zealand.[58]

Over two months later on May 28, 2019, the Western District Court in Yangon, Myanmar issued an arrest warrant for a heavyweight champion of hate-speech, notorious Myanmar hardline Buddhist monk, Wirathu, on a charge of sedition over defamatory remarks he made about the nation's civilian leader, Aung San Suu Kyi.[59] In one speech, Wirathu said that the civilian government was funded by foreigners and that a member of the government was "sleeping with a foreigner,"[60] which is believed to refer to Suu Kyi, as she was married to a British man who died of cancer on March 27, 1999, while Suu Kyi was under house arrest by the military regime. Wirathu has received massive support, not only from his own supporters but also from the military-backed political party, the USDP, for his offensive remarks against Muslims and the NLD government, frequently delivered in public. In January 2015, he called Yanghee Lee, the United Nations special rapporteur for human rights in Myanmar, a "whore." Wirathu has even told Buddhist women that it is better to marry dogs than Muslims.[61] He has referred to Muslims as "crazy dogs that are breeding so fast, stealing Buddhist women, raping them, and would like to occupy the country."[62] Despite dire warnings from both religious officials and the government, Wirathu has continued to broadcast hate speech against Muslims and criticize the NLD government for trying to change the constitution and minimize the representation of military appointees in parliament. He left his own monastery on May 28, 2019, and went into hiding. No one knew his whereabouts except a small handful of his supporters. On November 2, 2020, six days before the Myanmar general elections, Wirathu turned himself in at the Western District Chief's Office in Dagon Township, Yangon, after more than a year in hiding as a fugitive. He told his supporters, "The NLD government has sued me. It's an act of bullying and shaming a monk, a son of the Buddha."[63] Unquestionably, Wirathu

170   *Chapter Five*

believed that his surrender would gain support for the military's proxy party, the USDP, thereby defeating the NLD.

The emergence of the ultranationalist Buddhist organization Ma Ba Tha under Thein Sein's semi-civilian government administration, which influenced the government to enact controversial laws such as population control law, interfaith marriage law, monogamy law, and religious conversion law against people of non-Buddhist faiths, is a clear example of a harmful interplay of religion and politics in Myanmar. Thein Sein's administration intentionally failed to condemn those controversial laws. After the NLD came to power in 2016, the government's hands-off approach to Ma Ba Tha changed. The NLD government has declared Ma Ba Tha an unlawful group whose rhetoric is not in accordance with Buddhist teachings, recognizing only Ma Ha Na (the Sangha State Council) as legitimate.

About seven months later, on December 21, 2019, Junaid Hafeez, a university lecturer in Pakistan, was sentenced to death in the Punjab city of Multan for blasphemy. He was charged with insulting Islamic religious beliefs. For example, he claimed that the Quran was derived from Mesopotamian folk tales. He also kept material in his computer that included derogatory remarks about the prophet Muhammad.[64] According to Hafeez's father, conservative Islamic students did not like his son because of his liberal views. He was arrested in March 2013 for posting derogatory comments about the Prophet Muhammad on social media and spent more than six years in jail. Amnesty International called his death sentence "a gross miscarriage of justice" and described it as "extremely disappointing and surprising."[65] Insulting the Prophet Muhammad can result in a mandatory death penalty in Pakistan, where the population is about 95 percent Muslim. Hafeez's lawyers say he was framed by students from an extremist Islamic party because of his liberal and secular views about religion.[66] The Human Rights Commission of Pakistan (HRCP) has said that it is "dismayed by the verdict and the blasphemy laws are heavily misused."[67]

About five months after Hafeez's death sentence, police and National Guard troops dispersed peaceful protesters from Lafayette Square, next to the White House, with tear gas and smoke bombs on June 1, 2020. After dispersing protesters, President Donald Trump walked to St. John's Episcopal Church, held a Bible upside-down in front of the church without opening or reading from it and posed for photographs.[68] When a reporter asked Trump, "Is that your Bible?" Trump took a neutral position and replied, "It's a Bible."[69] President Donald Trump's visit to the church and a photo opportunity in front of the church without notifying the church shocked and outraged several religious leaders, including Republican senator Ben Sasse, who described it as a "photo op that treats the Word of God as a political prop."[70] The Catholic Archbishop of Washington, D.C., Wilton D. Gregory, calls Trump's visit to

Implications of Luther's Theology of Two Kingdoms in Dialogue 171

the church "baffling and reprehensible."[71] He continues, saying, "St. John Paul would not condone the use of tear gas and other deterrents to silence, scatter or intimidate protestors for a photo opportunity in front of a place of worship."[72] The Rev. Daryl Paul Lobban, a minister who is focused on social justice also said, "Churches have always been springboards for social action and social justice. There's a connection between a church building and uniting for justice. And now, after the visit from President Trump, there is energy to try and reclaim that space back."[73] Rev. Mariann Budde, the Episcopal bishop of Washington, DC, was also outraged by President Trump's visit to the church and said, "I am the bishop of the Episcopal Diocese of Washington and was not given a courtesy call that they would be clearing the area with tear gas so they could use one of our churches as a prop." She continues saying, "Everything he has said and done is to inflame violence. We need a moral leadership, and he's done everything to divide us." In a written document, Presiding Bishop Michael Curry, head of the Episcopal denomination, accused Trump of using "a church building and the Holy Bible for partisan political purposes."[74]

President Trump and his wife, Melania, had previously attended a church service at St. John's Episcopal Church on the morning of the inauguration day on January 20, 2017. President Trump failed to use the Bible appropriately. He may as well have posed with the Bible in one hand and a gun on the other. Holding the Holy Bible in public for a photo opportunity, in attempt to gain support from Christians, is not only inappropriate for the president but also completely violates the calling of his office. He deliberately used the Holy Bible for his personal political gain. In fact, President Trump is not the first American president to use religion as a steppingstone for political ends. Former president George W. Bush also breached the line between religion and politics by bringing a ritualized religious ethos in the White House. For instance, reading the Bible for personal devotion is not a problem, but "holding weekly Bible studies at the White House, attended by more than half of the staff and presented as if not compulsory, not quite *uncompulsory*, either was disconcerting to a non-Christian like me," says David Frum, an orthodox Jew who worked as a speechwriter for Bush in his early days of presidency.[75] The Bible should not be used as a weapon. Rather, it should be used to heal the wounds and comfort those who grieve.

On the other side of the globe on August 6, 2020, self-appointed evangelist David Lah was sentenced to three months in jail in Myanmar for defying the COVID-19 restrictions on social and religious gatherings issued by the Natural Disaster Management Law. Evidence of Lah's actions came from a video clip that went viral on social media of Lah at one of his religious gatherings, saying, "If you believe in Jesus Christ, you will be immune to the virus. It will never infect you. Those who are infected with the virus are

172   *Chapter Five*

human-oriented, denomination-oriented, not true believers in Jesus Christ. I guarantee in the name of Jesus that if you truly abide by the word of God, the virus will never harm you."[76] Another video clip showed Lah saying that the teachings of Buddhist monks are responsible for making people "sinful."[77] The backlash against David Lah extended not only to the Buddhist community but also to minority Christian communities in Myanmar, who make up about 6 percent of the population.

Days after he preached about the immunity of true believers of Jesus Christ to COVID-19, Lah himself was infected with the virus, along with several of his followers. At least twenty confirmed cases, including two deaths, have been linked to his religious gatherings. He had been charged with violating government orders aimed at curbing the spread of COVID-19. This story is horrifying, and a clear example of ignorance combined with manipulation. As the heat of public anger escalated, the Myanmar Council of Churches and the Catholic Bishops Conference Myanmar could not keep silent, issuing a joint statement on April 17, 2020, acknowledging that the aggressive preaching of an independent Christian preacher whose preaching had gone viral on social media had offended Buddhists, Muslims, Christians, and others. At the same time, they appealed to people of all faiths to come together to combat the common enemy, COVID-19, with common efforts instead of posting offensive comments on social media. They do not mention the name David Lah on the statement, calling him "an independent Christian preacher who does not represent any Christian churches and organizations in Myanmar."[78] Lah's supporters accused the government of violating religious freedom, suggesting that Lah was put in jail because of his Christian faith.

All these various stories, actions, and reactions from different parts of the globe show that the intersection of religion and politics is important both on a societal or government level and on an individual level. When addressing the repression of religious minorities in China, Iran, North Korea, and other countries around the world, former US president Barrack Obama made a connection between religious freedom and national security at the Annual National Prayer Breakfast on February 6, 2014, saying, "History shows that nations that uphold the rights of their people, including the freedom of religion, are ultimately more just and more peaceful and more successful. Nations that do not uphold these rights sow the bitter seeds of instability and violence and extremism. So, freedom of religion matters to our national security."[79] Religious freedom is a fundamental right of humankind, but it is not a license to hurt others who do not share the same faith. American political scientist Elizabeth Shakman Hurd introduces two faces of faith, making the distinction between bad and good forms of religion.[80] She borrowed the idea of two faces of faith from former prime minister of the United Kingdom Tony Blair, who says:

Implications of Luther's Theology of Two Kingdoms in Dialogue 173

> There are two faces of faith in our world today. One is seen not just in acts of religious extremism, but also in the desire of religious people to wear their faith as a badge of identity in opposition to those who are different. The other face is defined by extraordinary acts of sacrifice and compassion. For example, in caring for the sick, disabled or destitute. . . . All over the world, this battle between the two faces of faith is being played out.[81]

Harmful use of religion encourages extremism, which slips easily into violence.[82] On the other hand, peaceful use of religion contributes to the common good of humanity. Hurd's argument is that peaceful use of religion is to be restored and preserved, whereas harmful use of religion is to be reformed or disciplined with the help of the government and public authorities.

Donald E. Smith, professor emeritus of political science at the University of Pennsylvania, contends that there is a limited area in which the secular state can legitimately regulate the manifestation of religion, in the interest of public health, safety, or morals. Thus, he argues that the prohibition of human sacrifices should be justified even if a religion required such a sacrifice because taking human life is a crime under the law of the state.[83] John Murray Mitchell, a Scottish missionary to India, called the rite of *sati*, the burning of widows on the same funeral pyre as their dead husbands, the "inhuman rite."[84] When the British government in India was preparing to abolish the *sati*, which it did in 1829, the Brahmans vehemently opposed all interference, justifying it as a religious institution prescribed by the Veda, quoting "the precise passage enjoining that widows should consign themselves to the fire."[85] However, critical examination of the text in question reversed what the Brahmans affirmed. Horace Hayman Wilson, who worked under the British East India Company, used his extensive studies of Sanskrit and Hinduism to prove falsification of the text by the Brahmans, saying, "The Brahmans had actually falsified the text, and not merely mistranslated it; they had changed the words of the one book which they professed to receive with awful reverence as the eternal utterance of heaven."[86] This inhuman rite should be denounced as a clear example of deceptive manipulation of the text by an unscrupulous priesthood.

Similarly, female circumcision in Africa, referred to by its critics as "female genital mutilation," should also be abolished, even if religion and sociocultural practice might require such a practice.[87] Efua Dorkenoo, a Ghanaian-British activist against female genital mutilation, called the practice mutilation in medical terms rather than the religious concept of circumcision, which is performed to suppress and control the sexual behavior of girls and women.[88] Some advocates against female genital mutilation are accused of being Westernized Africans. Many refuse to condemn the practice under the guise of freedom of religious practice.[89] A critical examination of female

174 *Chapter Five*

genital mutilation is crucial in order to explore the consequences from different perspectives for the welfare of all human beings. In other words, what standards and criteria would be used to abolish female genital mutilation?

Critical assessment of the practice includes risk of infections such as tetanus, HIV/AIDS, and hepatitis B and C, as well as the risk of death due to excessive bleeding, since unsterilized instruments are often used, including knives, razor blades, scissors, thorns, and pieces of glass.[90] A growing number of children, resistant to the practice due to health risks and violation of their rights, run away from their families. Rosemary Mburu, a Kenyan gynecologist, has estimated that 15 percent of all circumcised females die of bleeding or infections.[91] For the rest of their lives, many women are afflicted by recurring infections, and some suffer complicated, often fatal, childbirths.[92] Nancy Bonvillain, a professor of anthropology, argues that women who are subjected to the procedure have reduced sexual desire, both because of the loss of part of their sexual organs and because of their fear of the pain involved with intercourse.[93] In 2008, the World Health Organization (WHO) issued a report calling national and international organizations to support specific actions directed toward eliminating female genital mutilation.[94] The report stated, "The African Union's *Solemn Declaration on Gender Equality in Africa*, and its Protocol to the African Charter on Human and Peoples' Rights on the Rights of Women in Africa, constitute a major contribution to the promotion of gender equality and the elimination of female genital mutilation."[95] Article 5 of the Universal Declaration of Human Rights cautions against female circumcision: "No one shall be subjected to torture or to cruel, inhuman, or degrading treatment or punishment."[96] Children should not be forced against their will to endure unnecessary pain in the name of religion and culture. Female genital mutilation, therefore, violates the rights of women and children to good health. It is, therefore, harmful to the well-being of humanity.

All these actions and reactions, both good and bad, are clear examples of the interplay and intersection of religion and politics in public life. Religion guides morality in public life. In other words, religion's moral teachings play a key role in measuring good governance for the well-being of humanity. Religious affiliation is a matter of personal choice. However, religious organizations are treated under the law no differently from voluntary, nonprofit societies; they are autonomous in their internal operation, entitled to government services, but also subject to the rule of public law.[97] Thus, the intervention of either side, religion or government, is required and even justified when one side misuses the other for its own ends. The government has no power over religion unless religious practices threaten public order, morality, or health. However, if religious practices or actions threaten public order and morality, the government has the right to intervene for the sake of humanity. Similarly, if the government manipulates religion to gain popular support for

Implications of Luther's Theology of Two Kingdoms in Dialogue   175

political ends, it is the responsibility of religious actors to speak up to prevent the government from crossing the line between religion and politics. Both religion and politics are sacred under God's rule. People who make either one ugly are dangerous extremists and self-seekers who bring conflicts, rather than solutions. Therefore, a right relationship between religion and politics allows each one to better serve humanity.

THE CALL FOR TRANSFORMATION IN MYANMAR SOCIETY

Transforming Ethnic Ethos

During his inaugural address on January 20, 2017, President Donald Trump laid out a vision for the United States that focused on benefiting American workers and families by choosing hardline rhetoric, instead of the inclusive language his predecessor used, and said, "From this day forward, it's going to be only America first. . . . We must protect our borders from the ravages of other countries making our products, stealing our companies and destroying our jobs."[98] Trump's vision of "America First"[99] has set America on a new trajectory, of turning away from the big heart the United States has shown in the past by sharing its resources with other nations. Furthermore, Trump makes stereotyped derogatory remarks about Mexican immigrants, saying, "They are bringing drugs. They are bringing crime. They're rapists," adding, "Some, I assume, are good people."[100] According to Trump's explanation, all violence in the United States seems to come from outside religions and countries.

The isolationist doctrine of America First, with its racist undertones, projects the fantasy of the nation-state with closed borders, detached from any moral responsibility to the burning world outside, believing in nothing other than its own identity and valuing nothing other than its own enjoyment.[101] On July 14, 2019, based on the Trump administration's plan to begin immigration raids in cities throughout the country, President Trump told four Democratic congresswomen of color—the US representative for New York's Fourteenth Congressional District Alexandria Ocasio-Cortez, the US representative for Minnesota's Fifth Congressional District Ilhan Omar, the US representative for Michigan's Twelfth Congressional District Rashida Tlaib, and the US representative for Massachusetts's Seventh Congressional District Ayanna S. Pressley—to go back to the country they came from, even though only Omar was born outside the country. He wrote on his twitter, stating, "So interesting to see progressive Democrat Congresswomen, who originally came from countries whose governments are a complete and total catastrophe, the worst, most corrupt and inept anywhere in the world." Trump

176   *Chapter Five*

added, "Why don't they go back and help fix the totally broken and crime infested places from which they came. Then come back and show us how it is done."[102] Even though Trump has repeatedly refused to back down from his toxic racist rhetoric against non-White and non-Christian women, saying, "I don't have a racist bone in my body,"[103] his cruel remarks are regarded as beyond the pale and his statement still affirms that he is a racist. Omar also responded to Trump, saying, "You are stoking white nationalism because you are angry that people like us are serving in Congress and fighting against your hate-filled agenda."[104] Again, during the first presidential debate on September 29, 2020, Trump refused to condemn white supremacy, and then responded to his opponent, Joseph R. Biden, who mentioned in particular the Proud Boys, a far-right, white extremist group that has endorsed violence, by saying "Proud Boys, stand back and stand by."[105] The Proud Boys, then, celebrated Trump's remark about them.

Racism in the name of national security, supremacy, purity, and so forth is nothing new to the world in which we all live. Myanmar is not an exception. Ethno-nationalism and religious extremism are on the rise. Different ethnic groups in Myanmar also have culturally stereotyped ideas about each other. Some stereotyped ideas and language are derogatory and racist, and have been displayed in society from streets to public institutions, public entertainments, and social media. Not only ethnic groups themselves but also Western Christian missionaries are responsible for such destructive stereotyped images as a tool of division rather than drawing together. For instance, Henry Park Cochrane, an American Baptist missionary to Myanmar, called the Chin people the "despised Chins, wild tribes in the northwestern hills."[106] Laura Carson, the first American woman Baptist missionary to the Chin people, who arrived in Chin State in 1899, also described the Chin Hills area as "beyond the pale of civilization;" the Chin people as "loathsome," and the nature of their mission as "loving the unlovely." Accordingly, the missionaries understood their mission as setting the people free by uprooting their culture, stating, "To these poor people we hope to introduce the elevating, uplifting influence of the Gospel of Christ and teach them the way of salvation."[107]

Burmans also refer to the Chin people as the "wild Chin" or "stinking Chin."[108] In response, the Chin's depiction of the Burmans also connotes rudeness, fickleness, deceit, and treachery.[109] Similarly, the Karen people view the Burmans as aggressive, arrogant, and somewhat immoral, while the Karen are pictured by the Burmans as docile, though stubborn when aroused, not overly bright, and good only for domestic service.[110] Francis Mason, who worked as a missionary among the Karen for over four decades (1830–1874), recorded how the Karen people experienced the Burman oppression before the British occupation and said, "Before the English took the country, the

Implications of Luther's Theology of Two Kingdoms in Dialogue   177

Karens had been often reduced to slavery by means of Burmese traders, who in the betel-nut season crowed into the jungles, and entrapped the Karens into debt by their tempting wares."[111] As a consequence, the Karen people had experienced a long history of oppression under the Burman authorities from generation to generation, and as a result they held aloof from the Burman. The cruelties they experienced under the Burman are still so bitter for the Karen people that Karen mothers still the cries of their children by telling them, "A Burman is coming."[112] It is also true that the Christian mission and the British rule immensely benefited the Karen people, with works affecting the education at mission schools, hospitals, and other social services, as San C. Po asserts:

> The educational, social, and spiritual progress of the Karens has been due to a great extent to the missionaries who have worked so faithfully with them. The Karens are not ashamed or afraid to proclaim that they owe what progress or advancement they have made to the missionaries whom they affectionately call their "Mother" under the protection of the British government whom they rightly call their "Father."[113]

It is, therefore, true and fair to conclude that under the British occupation's biased preference for Christians, there was less consciousness among Christians of their minority position during the British colonial period, which lasted from 1885 to 1948. At that time, the Christian churches enjoyed some status and prestige because of the identification of Christianity with the West and with modernization; Christians were particularly active in building schools and hospitals. However, it is equally true that there has been more Christian self-consciousness about their minority position in subsequent regimes when encouragement was given to a Buddhist resurgence as part of the effort of establishing national identity for Myanmar.

Even though the Burman and Shan people share the same religion, their different ethnicity still divides them. In a letter of the Executive Members of the Karen Central Organization of Burma to His Britannic Majesty's Secretary of State for Burma dated September 26, 1945, one day, when a Burman Buddhist monk was preaching to a crowd of Shan people about the abode of Spiritual Beings called in Burmese *Nat-Pye*, an old Shan among the crowd asked the monk whether there were any Burmans in *Nat-Pye*. The monk answered, "Certainly, the Burman would be there also." Then, the old Shan murmured, "Alack! *Nat-Pye* also will eventually be ruined by the Burman."[114] The Burmans are also falsely stereotyped as troublemakers. According to Cheery Zahau, a Chin human rights activist, the negative connotations of non-Burmans have been cultivated by official textbooks and in the classroom during her school life in Sagaing Division, Upper Myanmar.

178   *Chapter Five*

Those negative connotations include: "The Shan used a lot of drugs; the Karen were just separatists; the Chin were backward and uncivilized; the Kachin were savages living in a mountainous area."[115] Richard Cockett, a British historian, interviewed Zahau, who told him about those negative connotations of non-Burmans in school official textbooks. However, I personally have not experienced those kinds of formal negative connotations about any ethnic groups in the formal school textbooks throughout my entire life, only informal derogatory rhetoric in public space. Speaking the truth is important. However, false accusation erodes civility and creates unnecessary hostility. I think Zahau has gone too far and has exaggerated informal depictions of different ethnic groups in public space into formal instructions in public schools for her own ends. Approval from the Myanmar Department of Education would be required in order to officially prescribe those sensitive negative connotations in school textbooks. Therefore, I do not believe that the Myanmar Department of Education prescribed those negative connotations in school textbooks.

Apparently, in Myanmar, anyone with broken or halting Burmese is stereotyped as *Taing-Yintha* (non-Burman-speaking people), in opposition to the majority Burman-speaking people. *Taing-Yintha*, including Indian and Chinese immigrants, are often victims of ridicule and are categorized in Burmese social media and comedy with negative connotations. Nowadays, Indians are called *Kala* and the Chinese *Ta-yoke*. The use of the word *Kala* was very vague with no clear origin, as Thant Myint-U, a Burman historian, says, "All the many and varied visitors and immigrants—Bengali, Tamils, Singhalese, Afghans, Persians, Arabs, Armenians, Jews, Greeks, and Portuguese—were classified together under the single ethnic category of *kala*, an old word of no clear derivation. The newer *kala* from Europe were sometimes referred to as the *bayingyi kala*. *Bayingyi* was a Burmese corruption of the Arab *feringhi*."[116] Indeed, the Burman Buddhists classified all foreigners under a single category of *Kala*, and the Burman Buddhists who converted to Christianity were also labeled as followers of the religion of *Kala*. A Catholic missionary to Myanmar, Paul A. Bigandet, remarked on this in 1861, stating, "The few natives that became converts, joined with the Christians, and being merged into the community were called *Kalas*, because in the opinion of the Burman, they had embraced the religion of the *Kalas* and had become bona fide strangers having lost their own nationality."[117]

However, as time passed by, the use of the word *Kala* has changed. Nowadays, it refers exclusively to the Indians, regardless of religion. Myint-U also affirms this trajectory, saying, "The Indians are now called *Kala*, a word that took on increasingly negative connotations, while Europeans, on the other hand, are now referred to as *Bo*, which literally means a military officer but became a racial category (*bo-lo-pyaw*, to speak like a *bo*, means to speak English)."[118] Al Haj U Aye Lwin, one of the founding members of the Religions for Peace, also remarks, "Myanmar Muslims are often called *Kala*, a degrading and derogatory term that is loosely translated as "foreigners from India."[119] As far as my observation goes, the word *Kala* refers not only to Muslims but also to all Indians, regardless of religion. It is easy to see the negative stereotypes the Burman ascribe to *Taing-Yintha* in public space, from the street to entertainment on the stage. A popular Burmese entertainment called *A-Nyeint* embodies many derogatory stereotypes about *Taing-Yintha*, including Indians and Chinese, based on their skin color and faulty Burmese. The comedians make money by making their audience laugh several times with racist language about *Taing-Yintha*, thereby changing a happy entertainment into a source of resentment. The fault lies not only with the comedians but also with some people, themselves from *Taing-Yintha* groups, who are not aware of those derogatory languages and stereotypes. For instance, many Indians are still comfortable with calling themselves *Kala*, instead of Indians. The bottom line is that people need awareness, from a grassroot level to the top leadership levels, not to use such derogatory stereotypes about each other, since they do not bring different ethnic groups together but divide them further apart.

This does not mean that the majority Burmans are all bad people, or all non-Burman groups either. A popular Burmese saying, "One rotten fish fills the whole boat with foul smell," should not be interpreted with the reality of the whole people collectively. The good and bad that people do is based on personal morality. For instance, when violence between Buddhists and Muslims broke out in Lashio, northern Shan State, in 2013, a Buddhist abbot named U Ponnanda provided shelter for 1,200 Muslims in his monastery. As an engaged Buddhist monk, the abbot states his motives for sheltering them, saying, "I welcomed them on humanitarian grounds, and gave them food and shelter, feeling it was my duty as a Buddhist to protect those who were vulnerable. We were able to look after everyone, regardless of race and religion."[120] While some Burman-Buddhists conceive of nationalism and a nation in terms of race and religion, Aung San's concept of a nation is non-racial and non-religious. In 1946, Aung San stated his understanding of national identity in his speech, declaring:

A nation is a collective term applied to a people, irrespective of their ethnic origin, living in close contact with one another and having common interests and sharing joys and sorrows together for such historic periods as to have acquired a sense of oneness. Though religion, and language are important factors it is only their traditional desire and will to live in unity through weal and woe that binds the people together and makes them a nation and their spirit a patriotism.[121]

Aung San's nationalism finds unity in diversity and embraces diversity as strength. He further says that exclusionary nationalism can result in ugly consequences.[122] Unfortunately, Aung San's inclusive nationalism came to an end after his assassination. His daughter, Suu Kyi, emerged as an engaged Buddhist political leader in order to bring her father's vision back to life, particularly after the 1988 uprising, by pushing for the democratization of the country. However, her politics of ethnic and religious inclusion is viewed by many different peoples in many different ways. The ultranationalist Buddhists and the military generals in the country view her as a pro-Muslim, while Muslim extremists and some hardline ethnic groups see her as ruling like a tyrant over them.

As Myanmar was preparing for the general election to be held on November 8, 2020, the supporters of Chin National League for Democracy (CNLD) labeled the NLD as exclusively a political party of the Burman majority, showing they are ignoring facts they actually know about the existence of the NLD throughout the country, even in ethnic minority states. Because they consider the Burmans as their enemies, the supporters of the CNLD brand Chin supporters of the NLD as pro-Burman, willing to enslave themselves to the Burman majority. There is no doubt that racist rhetoric is on the rise in Myanmar. In the face of mounting white supremacy, Alana Lentin, associate professor of cultural and social analysis at Western Sydney University, presents three groups of people with regard to talking about race in the contemporary world. The first group is the "race realists," who are truly racists; the second group, the "race-critical antiracists," actively engage in fighting against racism. She argues that between these two groups, racist and race-critical antiracist, there is a third group of people who choose to be silent about race, believing that the best way to challenge racism is to refuse to speak about race. Lentin argues that racists are not created by race-critical antiracists, but rather, by the conditions established by racial rule over the course of modernity.[123] Lentin's argument about the situational demand to talk about race and in doing so to make it matter less in the future is consistent with Martin Luther King Jr.'s "Letter from a Birmingham Jail," written on April 16, 1963, as a response to eight white ministers from Alabama who had called King's movement "unwise and untimely," and "stirred up by outside agitators." King's letter shows that he is in Birmingham because injustice is there.[124] More importantly, King not only critiques the church for keeping silent in the face of injustice, but calls the church to repent for the silence of good people, saying, "We will have to repent in this generation not merely for the hateful words and actions of the bad people but for the appalling silence of the good people."[125] Religions exist not to destroy human life, but to value and enrich human life in society; as American historian Jon Pahl aptly states, "Religions exist to eliminate violence."[126] The mission of the church,

Implications of Luther's Theology of Two Kingdoms in Dialogue   181

especially, is to promote human dignity in the public sphere. Therefore, keeping silence in the face of dehumanizing forces can also be understood as supporting violence. It also can mean renouncing responsibility and accepting "blessed brutalities."[127]

As an ecumenical institution where people from different religious, ethnic, and cultural backgrounds come and study together to better serve our society, the Myanmar Institute of Theology (MIT) provides guidelines stating that each person has a responsibility to show love and respect for others' religious, ethnic, and cultural traditions. Regarding the conduct of everyone at the seminary, it is written in student handbook:

> MIT is comprised of different ethnic/language/religious groups and Christian denominations. Students should respect each other's culture, religion, tradition and doctrine. English and Burmese languages are encouraged to speak as common languages at MIT. The use of inclusive language is strongly encouraged. Physical violence, verbal violence, emotional and psychological violence, racist language, sexist language and sexual harassments that in any way demean another person's dignity are strictly prohibited. Any student who is found guilty of any of these offenses must accept the action taken by the school authority.[128]

In this way, MIT fights against any kind of violence and discrimination, and stands as an example of a Myanmar institution that embraces diversity as strength in order to build a better society beyond its wall. "Race realists" are occupied with narcissism and narrow identity politics. False stereotyping about different ethnic groups is disseminated by dangerous and aggressive people on social media, having a negative impact not only on the victims but also on the self-esteem of perpetrators themselves. People who want to build a better society and those who want to create chaos for their own gain and opportunity are totally different from one another. We are living in a time when people are crying for leadership that understands the sufferings of the people and heals those wounds instead of smearing them with salt. We need to see people as people, and stop stereotyping each other.

Transforming Religious Ethos

In 2003, General William Boykin of the United States Army, in his speeches to evangelical Christian groups, described the US battle with Muslim extremists as a fight against Satan, saying that militant Muslims sought to destroy America "because we're a Christian nation." Boykin recalled a Muslim fighter in Somalia who said that American forces would never capture him because Allah would give him protection. In his response to the Muslim fighter in Somalia, Boykin said, "I knew that my God was bigger than his.

182   *Chapter Five*

. . . I knew that my God was a real God and his was an idol. . . . The enemy is a spiritual enemy . . . called Satan."[129] US Senator Joseph Lieberman beautifully turned around the utter ignorance of Boykin's statement "my God was bigger than his God," with his eloquent remarks in October of 2003, at a conference of the Arab American Institute, in Washington, D.C., saying, "We meet here today not as Muslims or Christians or Jews, not as people of Arab or European descent or African or Asian descent. . . . We are children of the same God and the same father, Abraham. We are quite literally brothers and sisters."[130] I agree that America should send Lieberman's message to the world, which will cost them nothing.

Indeed, the core message of religion should be loving kindness, compassion, and peace to all living beings. Therefore, religion should not be politicized as a tool to create violence. During the missionary period in Myanmar, the Christian missionaries did many great things for the indigenous people, particularly in works affecting education, health care, and other social services. At the same time, some missionaries described people of other faiths as "heathen, superstitious," and "uncivilized people," claiming superiority over the native people.[131] For instance, in their visit to the Shwe Dagon Pagoda, Cochrane and his fellow missionaries stated, "We visited the most famous worship-place of Buddhists, the Shwe Dagon Pagoda, and for the first time saw heathenism as it is. But here we saw the yellow robed, blight of Asia, instead of light of Asia; graven image, superstitious worship of the common people."[132] Furthermore, despite the incredible respect the laity held for Buddhist monks in Myanmar, Helen G. Trager, an American visiting professor at the University of Rangoon (now the University of Yangon) disrespectfully accused the monks of "laziness, ignorance, idleness, pretentiousness, and lust for riches." She added that the writings of the Christian missionaries accused the Burman Buddhists of "dishonesty, falsehood, sensuality, love of pleasure, attachment to worldly objects, bloodthirstiness, cruelty, vindictiveness, treachery, deceit, and rapaciousness."[133]

As a response to the Burman Buddhists' resistance to Christianity, while affirming the superiority of Buddhism to other faiths, a Burman Buddhist scholar, Maung Htin Aung in his forward on Helen Trager's book *Burma through Alien Eyes: Missionary Views of the Burmese in the Nineteenth Century* taunted Adoniram Judson, the first American Baptist missionary to Myanmar who arrived in Myanmar in 1813, saying:

> Judson and his missionaries also felt frustrated because they found among the Burmese no religious vacuum which their religion could fill. Since the beginning of their history, the Burmese had professed Buddhism, one of the noblest faiths mankind has ever known; and the Burmese way of life itself had always been under the all-pervading influence of Buddhism. Judson made his first

Implications of Luther's Theology of Two Kingdoms in Dialogue   183

Burmese convert only after six years of valiant effort, and when war broke out in 1824, some eleven years after his arrival, the number of Burmese converts was only eighteen. As years passed and their endeavors among the Burmese continued to meet with failure, the missionaries were forced to seek converts in the remoter areas where Buddhism had not penetrated and where the pre-Buddhist religion of Animism still prevailed.[134]

There is no doubt that the Christian missionaries faced strong opposition from the Burman Buddhists in their effort to convert them to Christianity. The Buddhists also see people from Myanmar who have converted to Christianity as stooges of Western imperialism and followers of foreign religion who are unfaithful to the country. In fact, religion and nationalism are inseparable in Burman Buddhist thought. Religion cannot be forsaken without giving up nationality, and embracing the religion of another people is equivalent to becoming a member of the same social or political body.

Meanwhile, some of the missionaries, although not all, depicted the native people as irrational, uncivilized, weak, superstitious heathens who knew nothing about God, in contrast to the rational, civilized, strong Christians, who knew all about God. Accordingly, they sent people of other faiths into the Lake of Fire in Hell in their mission approach. Not seeing the revelation of God in other faiths in general, Buddhism in particular, the missionaries said to the Buddhists in Myanmar that their idols were silver and gold, the work of men's hands, and if they remained in Buddhism, they would go to hell, adding that if they would like to go into heaven, they must believe only in Christ. In this kind of conversation with the Buddhists, one of the aged Buddhists replied, "If what you say is true, then my ancestors have gone to hell. I want to go wherever they have gone. If they have gone to hell, I want to go there too. Our children may become Christians, but we are too old to change. We will die in Buddhism, as we have lived."[135] Instead of interpreting the Gospel in a new context, some of the missionaries attempted to uproot the religious and cultural values of the native people. The Burmese king once told Eugenio Kincaid, an American Baptist missionary to Myanmar, "One thing about your religion I do not like. It aims to destroy every other, and that is uncharitable. Your religion is good, but you allow not ours to be good."[136] Here one can clearly see that some of the Burman Buddhists appreciated the Christian faith and believed that the missionaries should learn from them how to give their appreciation to people of other faiths.

Christians should be aware of the fact that conversion from non-Christian religions to Christianity in the context of Myanmar has caused risk and suffering. It is an undeniable fact in Myanmar, both past and present, that new converts to Christianity were and are looked down on by their neighbors and relatives. Cochrane wrote about an old woman in a jungle-village who

184   *Chapter Five*

was ridiculed by her friends because of her conversion to Christianity during the missionary period, saying, "Oho! Grandma wants to go off with the preacher. She is becoming foolish in her old age." She gladly replied, "Oh, no! The preacher has told me how I may escape the penalty of hell, and I am so glad."[137] This is a clear example that new converts experienced expulsion from their family socially and they were labeled as stooges of foreign religion. Conversion in Myanmar, therefore, means a risk of life. Conversion, which makes the converts part of the community of their new church, is personal or individual. It turns the whole personality of a person, including his or her religious, social and cultural world, to Christ. Converts have to relocate themselves to a new religious, cultural, and social environment. At the same time, they must be aware of the fact that the Western expression of the Eastern people and religion during the missionary period should not be taken as absolutely true, because it is the Western depiction of the Eastern people. Dismissing Western superiority over Eastern people and religion, Mahatma Gandhi, in a 1938 conversation with some American missionaries who asked him the role of Christian mission in the new India that he was trying to build, replied, "To show appreciation of what India is and is doing. Until now they have come as teachers and preachers with queer notions about India and Indian great religions. We have been described as a nation of superstitious heathens, and knowing nothing, denying God."[138] Gandhi aptly pointed out the failure of Christian missionaries to recognize God's revelation and many good things in people of non-Christian faiths.

Myanmar is a religiously, ethnically, and culturally diverse society, with the overwhelming majority being Buddhists. After 2016, as the NLD government was trying to include different people in politics from various backgrounds, religions, and ethnicities, the hardline Buddhists are afraid of losing the Buddhist identity in a democratic society. That is why they are attacking not only the influence of the West but also people of non-Buddhist faiths, which is similar to the hermeneutic approach of Angarika Dharmapala (1864–1933), a Sri Lankan Buddhist writer and monk who was not only against the West but also against the ethnic and religious minorities, Tamil and Muslim, in Sri Lanka. R. S. Sugirtharajah, professor emeritus of biblical hermeneutics at the University of Birmingham, who analyzes the work and writings of Dharmapala in his book *The Bible and Asia: From the Pre-Christian Era to the Postcolonial Age*, writes:

Dharmapala's hermeneutics is a prime example of how natives themselves not only are quite capable of representing themselves but also are equally competent in producing racist, jingoistic, colonialist, nativist, and supremacist theologies. His vehement sentiments were directed not only toward the Christian West but also unleashed toward his own indigenous neighbors, in this case Tamils and

Implications of Luther's Theology of Two Kingdoms in Dialogue   185

Muslims. . . . His was a prime example of a colonial who, in the process of resisting, absorbs the colonial ideology and in turn recolonizes his own marginalized neighbors and becomes part of the colonial project and ideology. A mimetic resistance can end up not only mimicking the empire but becoming a menace to indigenous minorities.[139]

Dharmapala was a Sinhala nationalist who attempted to defeat colonialism and the Christian mission. He was educated in a Christian school where he was forced to attend church services and memorize texts from the Bible. He felt that the Christian mission school showed little respect for Buddhism. In other words, Dharmapala felt that the Christian mission claimed to preach the absolute truth, exclusive of Buddhism. For instance, Robert Spence Hardy, a Methodist minister, who worked in Sri Lanka for many years, attacked Buddhism by claiming that the Buddha's life was a myth, his teaching a mass of error, his code of morals imperfect, and his religion founded on principles that have no substantiality.[140] Being educated in such an exclusive atmosphere, Dharmapala reacted to the Christian teaching negatively and challenged Christian supremacy. His hermeneutic approach is what Sugirtharajah called a "tit-for-tat"[141] approach. He drew on the Christian Bible to attack Christian teaching. He exposed the gap between the ethical teaching of the Bible and the everyday lifestyle of missionaries and colonial government officials. For instance, he drew the contradiction between Christian love and the violent slaughter of animals. Dharmapala states that the Hebrew Scripture is a record of savage immorality; God has no compassion in his heart and loves bloodshed inspired by fanaticism, and monotheism is crude and unscientific.[142] He declared that if the Sermon on the Mount were removed from the Bible, biblical religion would be about "vengeance without any hope."[143]

Dharmapala claimed that the Sinhalese had lost their true identity and had become a hybrid race under the influences of foreign invaders.[144] However, while he may have been anticolonial in his resistance to British occupation and imperialist Christianity, he was equally colonial in defining a national identity that excluded Tamils and Muslims, introducing the notion of the Sinhalese as a superior race, a refined people, a unique race who have no slave blood in them, a pure and kind-hearted people with noble traditions, a noble literature and a noble religion.[145] To be specific, Dharmapala's hermeneutic approach is hostile to not only the West but also to the ethnic and religious minorities, Tamil and Muslim, in Sri Lanka.

Similarly, the ultranationalist Buddhists in Myanmar take advantage of their majority position to attack people of other faiths in the name of protecting race and religion. In fact, the world knows Buddhism as a peaceful religion. More specifically, some Buddhists who attended the Sixth Buddhist Council, held in Rangoon (now Yangon) from 1954 to 1956, accuse Christians

186   *Chapter Five*

of failing to bring peace to the world throughout its long history. Accordingly, they claim that Buddhism is the only religion capable of bringing peace to an entire world that has been failed by Christianity.[146] Suu Kyi also declares that Buddhists are generally more tolerant than Christians to people of other faiths, particularly to "spirit-worship"[147] in Myanmar. Nevertheless, the core message of Buddhism—loving-kindness, nonviolence, compassion, peace, and tolerance to all beings—has been tarnished by Ma Ba Tha and its supporters. However, one sign of hope is the fact that socially engaged Buddhists do not share the same view as the ultranationalist Buddhists. For instance, Ashin Sandartika publicly rejected Ma Ba Tha's movements and discriminatory politics in 2016, which supported the military-backed Union Solidarity and Development Party (USDP). Ashin Sandartika articulates an alternative philosophy of protecting Buddhism in a way that is tolerant of other religions, and he explicitly supports the National League for Democracy.[148] Furthermore, some monks who are recognized as engaged Buddhists have organized peace marches in Kachin State in 2012 to offer relief to victims of the conflict and to learn more about the experiences of the Kachin people.[149]

Socially engaged Buddhists in Myanmar are ashamed of Ma Ba Tha and see its movement as a false protection of race and religion. It is very common to hear socially engaged Buddhists say that it is not people of other faiths who make Buddhism ugly, but rather, Ma Ba Tha and its supporters themselves are responsible for the horrible image of Buddhism they show to the world. The ultranationalist Buddhists willfully ignore the peaceful aspects of their faith and claim violence as a sacred obligation in the name of protecting religion and race. Engaged Buddhists reject this view. They see violence as totally contrary to the teachings of Buddhism. Devoted Buddhist monks even use brass strainers to cleanse their drinking water, to avoid the possibility of killing insect life. According to Buddhist teaching, a good ruler vanquishes ill will with loving-kindness, wickedness with virtue, parsimony with liberality, and falsehood with truth.[150] Burmese Buddhists associate peace and security with coolness and shade, saying, "The shade of a tree is cool indeed; the shade of parents is cooler; the shade of teachers is cooler still; the shade of the ruler is yet more cool; but coolest of all is the shade of the Buddha's teachings." Therefore, to provide the people with the protective coolness of peace and security, rulers must observe the teachings of the Buddha.[151]

Alongside the ultra-nationalist Buddhists, some Pentecostal Christians also claim religious superiority and transmit hate speech against people of other faiths, categorizing them as "Hell-bound people." Samuel Ngun Ling accuses Western Christian missionaries of passing down false religious stereotypes in Myanmar, stating, "Missionaries passed down their stereotypical view of Buddhists to native Christians, regarding non-Christians as heathen, backward, uncivilized, uncultured, inferior and Hell-bound."[152] With their superiority mindset and triumphalism, some Pentecostal Christians in Myanmar still follow the legacy of the former Western missionaries, thinking of themselves as knowing all things about religious matters. Their approach to evangelizing people of other faiths is very exclusive and cynical, seeing them as those who will go into the lake of fire on Judgment Day. They do not have a desire to listen to the voices of people from other faiths and do not let them speak. In other words, there is no dialogue but only a monologue. Interpreting the religious values and beliefs of people from other faiths so negatively is a big hindrance to making the Gospel intelligible to them. It does not produce healthy conversation between the missionaries and the local people. Instead, it produces hostility and abhorrence between them.

Based on their own experiences under Burman domination for centuries of their history, Kachin scholar La Seng Dingrin argues that the Kachin people resist conversion to Buddhism for the natural reason that Buddhism is considered a religion of the Burmans, who have been their enemies for centuries. Dingrin suggests that one possible reason for the Kachin people to accept a new religion is the hope that Christianity will keep them safe from Burman aggression, during not only the colonial but also the postcolonial period.[153] Likewise, condemning U Nu's proposed government policy establishing Buddhism as the official state religion of Myanmar, Chin scholar, Lian H. Sakhong says, "The Chin never accepted Buddhism either as a culture or as a religion."[154] Categorizing one particular ethnic group with one particular religion undermines one's ethnic brothers and sisters who profess different faiths. This leaves little room for cooperation with people of different religions. One can easily imagine that when the state favors Buddhism it is very dangerous not to become a Buddhist. The truth is that the emergence of a popular religion professed by the overwhelming majority of people does not eradicate the minority religious groups.

History has proved that the majority communities are not the only provocateurs of religious conflict; sometimes minorities can even create problems for the majority. For instance, Indian scholar Santhosh J. Sahayadoss argues that the Hindu majority in India feels threatened when Christians claim that their intension is to Christianize the whole of India.[155] Similarly, the Buddhist majority in Myanmar also feels threatened when some Pentecostal Christians with exclusive views see them as those who will go into the lake of fire on Judgement Day and thereby declare their intention to Christianize the whole country. Hardline Chin Christians used religion as a stepping-stone for their political ends during the 2020 general elections. Some used social media, particularly Facebook, as a platform to disseminate ethnic and religious hate speech, not only against the Buddhist majority but also against Chin supporters of the National League for Democracy, branding the NLD as an exclusively Burman political party. They have posted images on Facebook of Chin

Christian Vice President Henry Van Thio and Chief minister of Chin State Lian Luai prostrating themselves before Buddhist monks when making donations, accusing them of worshipping the Buddhist monks and committing idolatry. They proclaim that the wrath of God will fall upon the Chin people collectively because of what Henry Van Thio and Lian Luai have done. In other words, they claim that Buddhists are not worshipping the true God, but rather, worshipping human-made idols.

As an academic and a religious actor, I can no longer keep silent when political opportunists are politicizing religion as a steppingstone for their political ends. Therefore, on August 22, 2020, and September 13, 2020, I posted on social media, asking hardline Chin Christians to stop attacking those who do not share the same faith, and to show respect to people of other faiths. I received many "likes," and many "angry emojis" as well. Some hardline Chin Christians do not respect the Buddhist culture and mode of reverence. They are totally unable to see the difference between worship and reverence. I remembered an old story about a young Christian boy respectfully going through the customary prostrations before a Buddhist monk and saying, "I do not *shikko* (worship) you as God, but I do not know of any other way to show my respect."[156] Some ignorant Chin Christians who have not spent even a single day at seminary for theological education attacked me by claiming that the Bible does not teach respect for people of other faiths. The truth is, however, that attacking people of other faiths does not make our religion superior; rather, it makes our religion ugly, dangerous, and destructive, creating unnecessary violence and hostility in society.

In order to reduce tensions between Buddhists and Christians in Myanmar, Karen scholar Saw Augurlion offers two different aspects of religion, the priestly and the prophetic. The priestly aspect of religion puts more emphasis on the extension of its own mission, that is, Christianization and Buddhinization, whereas the prophetic aspect puts more emphasis on addressing social issues and reforming social evils. Augurlion argues that the only way to reduce tensions between Buddhists and Christians in Myanmar is to look for points of agreement between the two faiths, with preference given to the prophetic aspect of religion.[157] While the Burman Buddhists have a dominant position in the state, the hardline ethnic Christians also attempt to protect their identity by strengthening their organizational ties and by emphasizing the priestly aspect of religion.[158] Augurlion argues that the priestly aspect of religion creates tension, and therefore emphasizes the prophetic aspect in the hopes of reducing religious conflict.

Looking at the overall picture of both religious tensions and interfaith activities, one can make an argument that religion can be a source for both violence and peace. This is a great opportunity for socially engaged religious actors to push for nonviolent activism and speak out against violence and hate

Implications of Luther's Theology of Two Kingdoms in Dialogue   189

speech in the name of religion. Aung San's inaugural address to the Buddhist monks at the AFPFL convention in January 1946, reminded the Buddhist monks of their calling to convey peace and loving-kindness to all peoples in Myanmar and beyond, stating:

> I would, therefore, like to address a special appeal to the Buddhist priesthood. Reverend Sangha, you are the custodians of a great religion. Please purify it and give it to the world. Your message to the peoples, not only of Burma but of the world, is that of love and brotherhood. Reverend Sangha, you have large and noble functions to perform in spreading peace and love in Burma and the world. Those are the high functions and high politics. Please take the message to the peoples, set their minds free from fear, bigotry, ignorance and superstition; teach them to build themselves a nobler, happier life. Those, and no less, are your tasks and your calling.[159]

Socially engaged Buddhist and Christian communities need to actively promote intrareligious and interreligious healing. The time has come for Myanmar Christians and Buddhists to share their faith without causing bad feelings in people who have a different faith. I am personally impressed by Suu Kyi's speech at a Christmas celebration at Vice President Henry Van Thio's residence in Nay Pyi Taw on December 21, 2019, highlighting Christians as peacemakers in the world and the paramount role of the government in bringing peace in the country, stating, "Christ as the Prince of peace brought peace to the world. The government in place of a king is called upon to bring peace to all ethnicities in Myanmar."[160] With this speech, Suu Kyi is calling Christians, with Christ as the Prince of peace, to support her leadership to end civil war and build a lasting peace. Therefore, as academic, religious and public leaders, what we can learn from our experiences is to leave behind our belligerent exclusiveness and false stereotyping and seek out the voices of the people around us in our own theological reflections and come to understand the radical inclusiveness of the claim that God's love is for all people, regardless of religion.

NOTES

1. Kenneth D. Wald and Allison Calhoun-Brown, *Religion and Politics in the United States*, 7th ed. (Lanham, MD: Rowman & Littlefield, 2014), 76.

2. Frank Swancara, *The Separation of Religion and Government: The First Amendment, Madison's Intent, and the McCollum Decision: A Study of Separatism in America* (New York: Truth Seeker Company, 1950), 183.

3. Swancara, 153.

190   *Chapter Five*

4. John M. Barry, *Roger Williams and the Creation of the American Soul: Church, State, and the Birth of Liberty* (New York: Penguin Group, 2012), 6.

5. Barry, 307–8.

6. Barry, 330.

7. Noah Feldman, *Divided by God: America's Church-State Problem and What We Should Do about It* (New York: Farrar, Straus and Giroux, 2005), 24.

8. Thomas Jefferson, "Letter to the Danbury Baptist Association," in *The American Republic: Primary Sources*, ed. Bruce Frohnen (Indianapolis, IN: Liberty Fund, 2002), 88.

9. Danbury Baptist Association, "Letter to Thomas Jefferson," in *The Sacred Rights of Conscience: Selected Readings on Religious Liberty and Church-State Relations in the American Founding*, ed. Daniel L. Dreisbach and Mark David Hall (Indianapolis, IN: Liberty Fund, 2009), 526.

10. Wald and Calhoun-Brown, *Religion and Politics in the United States*, 10. These data are available at www.pewglobal.org/category/datasets/. The 2010 per capita GNI was obtained from the World Bank (2012, 392–93) and is available at https://go.worldbank.org/0BP8VT4OE0.

11. Wald and Calhoun-Brown, 10.

12. Wald and Calhoun-Brown, 11.

13. Wald and Calhoun-Brown, 20.

14. Wald and Calhoun-Brown, 20.

15. Wald and Calhoun-Brown, 81.

16. Wald and Calhoun-Brown, 76.

17. Wald and Calhoun-Brown, 89. Steven Engel led a group of parents in New Hyde Park, New York State and brought lawsuit against school board President William Vitale, arguing that the daily reading of prayer by school teachers violated the Establishment Clause of the First Amendment of the constitution.

18. Wald and Calhoun-Brown, 89.

19. John R. Stumme, "A Lutheran Tradition on Church and State," in *Church and State: Lutheran Perspectives*, ed. John R. Stumme and Robert W. Tuttle (Minneapolis: Fortress Press, 2003), 52.

20. Stumme, 53.

21. Lloyd Svendsbye, "The History of a Developing Social Responsibility among Lutherans in America from 1930 to 1960, with Reference to the American Lutheran Church, the Augustana Lutheran Church, the Evangelical Lutheran Church, and the United Lutheran Church in America," (ThD diss., Union Theological Seminary, New York, 1967), 19–20.

22. Stumme, "A Lutheran Tradition on Church and State," 53.

23. David M. Whitford, "*Cura Religionis* or Two Kingdoms: The Late Luther on Religion and the State in the Lectures on Genesis," *The American Society of Church History* 73, no. 1 (2004): 52.

24. George W. Forell, Herman A. Preus, and Jaroslav J. Pelikan, "Toward a Lutheran View of Church and State," *Lutheran Quarterly*, no. 5 (August 1953): 287.

25. Stumme, "A Lutheran Tradition on Church and State," 51. Stumme states that although the phrase "institutional separation and functional interaction" first appeared

in the Lutheran Church in America in 1963, two members of the American Lutheran Church also served on the commission that produced the statement on church and state relations.

26. Stumme, 55.

27. Stumme, 55–56.

28. Stumme, 70.

29. Stumme, 58.

30. Evangelical Lutheran Church in America (ELCA), *A Social Message on Government and Civic Engagement in the United States: Discipleship in a Democracy*, June 24, 2020, 4.

31. ELCA, 5.

32. ELCA, 5.

33. ELCA, 6.

34. ELCA, 6.

35. ELCA, 6.

36. ELCA, 7.

37. ELCA, 7.

38. ELCA, 8.

39. Constitution of the Republic of the Union of Myanmar, 2008 (Yangon: Ministry of Information, 2008), 9.

40. Constitution of the Republic of the Union of Myanmar, 151.

41. Constitution of the Republic of the Union of Myanmar, 152.

42. Simon Pau Khan En, *Nat Worship: A Paradigm for Doing Contextual Theology in Myanmar* (Yangon: Myanmar Institute of Theology, 2012), 328.

43. Samuel Ngun Ling, *Christianity through Our Neighbors' Eyes: Rethinking the 200 Years Old American Baptist Missions in Myanmar* (Yangon: Judson Research Center, MIT, 2014), 148.

44. Oliver Byar Bowh Si, *God in Burma: Civil Society and Public Theology in Myanmar* (Las Vegas: Createspace Publishing, 2014), 67.

45. Bowh Si, 6.

46. Bowh Si, 18.

47. Pum Za Mang, "Separation of Church and State: A Case Study of Myanmar (Burma)," *Asia Journal of Theology* 25 (April 2011): 42–44. The term *Burmanization* means absorbing the non-Burman peoples (all ethnic minority groups) into one common Burman race, Burman religion (Buddhism), and Burman language. The term is given by critics of Myanmar governments since independence in 1948 because of its policy of transforming the Union of Myanmar into a virtual Burman nation-state.

48. Donald Eugene Smith, *Religion and Politics in Burma* (Princeton, NJ: Princeton University Press, 1965), 40.

49. Aung San Suu Kyi, *The Voice of Hope: Conversations with Alan Clements* (New York: Seven Stories Press, 2008), 32.

50. Campbell Robertson, Christopher Mele and Sabrina Tavernise, "11 Killed in Synagogue Massacre; Suspect Charged with 29 Counts," *New York Times*, October 27, 2018.

192 *Chapter Five*

51. Robertson et al., HIAS (Hebrew Immigrant Aid Society) is a Jewish nonprofit organization that provides humanitarian assistance to refugees.

52. Damien Cave, "New Zealand Massacre Sentencing: What to Expect," *New York Times*, August 23, 2020.

53. Nellie Bowles, "Replacement Theory, a Racist, Sexist Doctrine, Spreads in Far-Right Circles," *New York Times*, March 18, 2019. Behind the idea is a racist theory known as "the replacement theory," popularized by a French right-wing philosopher, Renaud Camus, which centers on the notion that white women are not having enough children and that falling birthrates will lead to white people around the world being replaced by nonwhite people.

54. Alana Lentin, *Why Race Still Matters* (Cambridge: Polity Press, 2020), 18.

55. Bowles, "Replacement Theory."

56. Matt Stevens, "White Nationalists Reappear in Charlottesville in Torch-Lit Protest," *New York Times*, October 8, 2017.

57. Emanuel Stoakes, "New Zealand Mosque Attack Victims Confront Gunman in Courtroom," *Washington Post*, August 24, 2020.

58. "Christchurch Shooting: Grief and Defiance as Victims Confront Gunman," BBC News, August 26, 2020, https://www.bbc.com/news/world-asia-53902158.

59. Zaw Naing Oo, "Arrest Warrant Issued for Myanmar Hardline Monk Wirathu," *Reuters*, May 29, 2019.

60. Hannah Beech and Saw Nang, "He Incited Massacre, but Insulting Aung San Suu Kyi was the Last Straw," *New York Times*, May 29, 2019.

61. Joe Freeman, "Myanmar Silences Radical Monk, but Legacy of Hatred Speaks for Itself," *Voice of America*, March 28, 2017.

62. Beech and Saw Nang, "He Incited Massacre."

63. Myo Min Soe, "Myanmar's Ultranationalist Monk U Wirathu Turns Himself in after a Year in Hiding," *Irrawaddy*, November 2, 2020. Wirathu said that the military representatives in parliament should be worshipped.

64. Ayesha Tanzeem, "Pakistani Scholar Sentenced to Death for Blasphemy," *Voice of America*, December 21, 2019.

65. "Junaid Hafeez: Academic Sentenced to Death for a Blasphemy in Pakistan," BBC News, December 21, 2019, https://www.bbc.com/news/world-asia-50878432.

66. *Independent*, "Outrage as Pakistan Sentences Academic to Death for Blasphemy," December 22, 2019.

67. Asad Hashim, "Pakistani Academic Junaid Hafeez Sentenced to Death for Blasphemy," *Aljazeera*, December 21, 2019, https://www.aljazeera.com/news/2019/12/21/pakistani-academic-junaid-hafeez-sentenced-to-death-for-blasphemy.

68. Ed Stetzer and Andrew Macdonald, "The Bible Is Not a Prop: In Fact, We Need It Right Now," *Christianity Today*, June 2, 2020. The killing of George Floyd by a white police officer, Derek Chauvin, in Minneapolis on May 25 sparked worldwide protests for racial equality, justice, and peace. Chauvin pinned Floyd's neck down with his knee for eight minutes and forty-six seconds, almost three minutes of which was after Floyd became nonresponsive.

Implications of Luther's Theology of Two Kingdoms in Dialogue   193

69. Zach Montague, "Holding It Aloft, He Incited a Backlash. What Does the Bible Mean to Trump?" *New York Times*, June 2, 2020. On the campaign trail in 2016, Trump told a crowd in Nevada that "nobody reads the Bible more than me."

70. Stetzer and Macdonald, "The Bible Is Not a Prop."

71. Michelle Boorstein and Rachel Weiner, "Historic D.C. Church Where Trump Stood with a Bible Becomes a Symbol for His Religious Foes," *Washington Post*, June 3, 2020.

72. "George Floyd Death: Archbishop Attacks Trump as US Protests Continue," BBC News, June 3, 2020, https://www.bbc.com/news/world-us-canada-52897303.

73. Boorstein and Weiner, "Historic D.C. Church Where Trump Stood."

74. Michelle Boorstein and Sarah Pulliam Bailey, "Episcopal Bishop on President Trump: Everything He Has Done and Said is to Inflame Violence," *Washington Post*, June 1, 2020.

75. David Frum, *The Right Man: The Surprise Presidency of George W. Bush* (Waterville, ME: Thorndike Press, 2003), 10. Also see Esther Kaplan, *With God on Their Side: How Christian Fundamentalists Trampled Science, Policy, and Democracy in George W. Bush's White House* (New York: The New Press, 2004), 5.

76. This short video clip was delivered by David Lah probably on April 1, 2020, defying the government's ban that took effect on March 13, 2020. It went viral on Facebook with tens of thousands of viewers, igniting mainline churches in Myanmar.

77. Pyae Sone Win, "Canadian Pastor Guilty of Defying Myanmar's Coronavirus Law," *Washington Post*, August 6, 2020.

78. The Myanmar Council of Churches and the Catholic Bishops Conference Myanmar issued this joint statement on April 17, 2020, signed by Archbishop Stephen Than Myint Oo, Cardinal Charles Maung Bo, Mahn Palmerston, Bishop John Saw Yaw Han, and Saw Shwe Lin.

79. Peter Baker, "Religious Freedom Is a Tenet of Foreign Policy, Obama Says," *New York Times*, February 6, 2014.

80. Elizabeth Shakman Hurd, *Beyond Religious Freedom: The New Global Politics of Religion* (Princeton, NJ: Princeton University Press, 2015), 22.

81. Tony Blair, "Taking Faith Seriously," *New Europe*, January 2, 2012.

82. Hurd, *Beyond Religious Freedom*, 23.

83. Donald Eugene Smith, "India as a Secular State," in *Secularism and Its Critics: Themes in Politics*, ed. Rajeev Bhargava (Oxford: Oxford University Press, 1998), 178–79.

84. John Murray Mitchell, *Hinduism Past and Present: With an Account of Recent Hindu Reformers and a Brief Comparison between Hinduism and Christianity* (London: The Religious Tract Society, 1897), 89.

85. Mitchell, 89.

86. Mitchell, 89. It has been calculated that from 1756 to 1829, when the *sati* was prohibited in British territory, no fewer than seventy thousand widows had thus been sacrificed.

87. Mary Nyangweso Wangila, *Female Circumcision: The Interplay of Religion, Culture, and Gender in Kenya* (Maryknoll, NY: Orbis Books, 2007), 8–46. This practice involves the pricking, piercing, burning, or excision, clitoridectomy, and/or the

194   *Chapter Five*

removal of part of or all tissues around a woman's reproductive organs, infibulation, and stitching together of the vulva in order to narrow the vaginal opening. This range of practice is commonly performed on girls between the ages of four and sixteen, among other reasons as an initiation rite into womanhood. The critics of female circumcision prefer the term *female genital mutilation* (FGM) to describe all forms of genital surgeries in the name of female circumcision insisting that any definitive and irremediable removal of a healthy organ or tissue is inherently mutilation. The term FGM is widely used by women's health and human rights activists, anti-circumcised organizations such as the Foundation for Women's Health Research and Development, the World Health Organization, the Inter-African Committee on Traditional Practice Affecting the Health of Women and Children, and the United Nations.

88. Efua Dorkenoo, *Cutting the Rose: Female Genital Mutilation: The Practice and Its Preservation* (London: Minority Rights Publications, 1994), 4.

89. Wangila, *Female Circumcision*, 9.

90. Wangila, 55–56.

91. Judy Mann, "Torturing Girls Is Not a Cultural Right," *Washington Post*, February 23, 1994. Also see Dorkenoo, *Cutting the Rose*, 15.

92. Dorkenoo, 15.

93. Nancy Bonvillain, *Men and Women: Cultural Constructs of Gender*, 2nd ed. (Upper-Saddle River, NJ: Prentice Hall, 1995), 232.

94. World Health Organization et al., *Eliminating Female Genital Mutilation: An Interagency Statement* (Geneva: World Health Organization, 2008).

95. World Health Organization et al., 1.

96. Universal Declaration of Human Rights, United Nations, 1948, https://www .ohchr.org/en/universal-declaration-of-human-rights.

97. Wald and Calhoun-Brown, *Religion and Politics in the United States*, 9.

98. David E. Sanger, "With Echoes of the 30's, Trump Resurrects a Hard-Line Vision of America First," *New York Times*, January 20, 2017.

99. O. Wesley Allen Jr., *Preaching in the Era of Trump* (Saint Louis: Chalice Press, 2017), 22. Allen, professor of Homiletics at Perkins School of Theology at Southern Methodist University and president of the Academy of Homiletics, argues that Trump's political campaign motto to "Make America Great Again" means to "Make America White Again." Allen, therefore, is opting to make the church great again by preaching respect for all human beings in the face of rising racism in the era of Trump.

100. Azam Ahmed, "And Now, What Mexico Thinks of Donald Trump," *New York Times*, July 2, 2015.

101. Saul Newman, *Political Theology: A Critical Introduction* (Cambridge, UK: Polity Press, 2019), 101.

102. Katie Rogers and Nicholas Fandos, "Trump Tells Congresswomen to Go Back to the Countries They Came From," *New York Times*, July 14, 2019.

103. Julie Hirschfeld Davis, "House Condemns Trump's Attack on Four Congresswomen as Racist," *New York Times*, July 16, 2019.

104. Rogers and Fandos, "Trump Tells Congresswomen to Go Back."

Implications of Luther's Theology of Two Kingdoms in Dialogue 195

105. Adam Nagourney, "Watch 4 Key Moments from Trump at the First 2020 Debate," *New York Times*, September 30, 2020.

106. Henry Park Cochrane, *Among the Burmans: A Record of Fifteen Years of Work and Its Fruitage* (New York: Fleming H. Revell Company, 1904), 62.

107. Laura E. Carson, *Pioneer Trails, Trials, and Triumphs* (New York: Baptist Board Education, 1927), 161–63.

108. F. K. Lehman, *The Structure of Chin Society: A Tribal People of Burma Adapted to a Non-Western Civilization* (Urbana: University of Illinois Press, 1963), 29.

109. Lehman, 29. Also see J. F. Embree and W. L. Thomas, Jr., *Ethnic Groups of Northern Southeast Asia* (New Haven, CT: Yale University Southeast Asia Studies, 1950), 15–16.

110. Fred R. von der Mehden, *Religion and Nationalism in Southeast Asia: Burma, Indonesia, the Philippines* (Madison: University of Wisconsin Press, 1968), 193.

111. Francis Mason, *Burmah, Its People and Natural Productions* (London: Trubner, 1860), 616.

112. Donald Mackenzie Smeaton, *The Loyal Karens of Burma* (London: Kegan Paul, Trench & Co, 1887), 151. This is typical in Myanmar. For instance, when I would cry during my childhood my mother used to whisper to me, saying, "A bad man" is coming who will beat a crying baby. Then, I stopped crying immediately so that I would not be beaten.

113. San C. Po, *Burma and the Karens* (Bangkok: White Lotus, 2001), 58.

114. Hugh Tinker, *Burma: The Struggle for Independence, 1944–1948, vol. 1, 1 January 1944 to 31 August 1946* (London: Her Majesty's Stationery Office, 1983), 492–93. This letter was signed by president of the Karen National Association, Saw Tha Din, general secretary of the Karen National Association Mahn Ba Kin, ex-member of the House of Representatives Saw Mya Thein, lecturer at Judson College Saw Johnson Kan Gyi, and vice president of Karen Social and Service Club Saw Ba U Gyi.

115. Richard Cockett, *Blood, Dreams and Gold: The Changing Face of Burma* (New Haven, CT: Yale University Press, 2015), 84.

116. Thant Myint-U, *The River of Lost Footsteps: A Personal History of Burma* (New York: Farrar, Straus and Giroux, 2006), 108.

117. Paul Ambrose Bigandet, *Outline of the History of the Catholic Burmese Mission from the Year 1720 to 1857* (Rangoon: Hanthawaddy Press, 1967), 4.

118. Thant Myint-U, *The Hidden History of Burma: Race, Capitalism, and the Crisis of Democracy in the 21st Century* (New York: W.W. Norton & Company, 2020), 19–20.

119. Regional Interfaith Network, "Seeking Peace for Myanmar along Interfaith Lines," *Regional Interfaith Dialogue, Connecting and Cooperating for Peace and Harmony in the Asia-Pacific Region*, August 11, 2014.

120. Htun Khaing, "The True Face of Buddhism," *Frontier Myanmar*, May 12, 2017.

121. Smith, *Religion and Politics in Burma*, 115–16.

196   *Chapter Five*

122. Josef Silverstein, *The Political Legacy of Aung San* (Ithaca, NY, Southeast Asia Program: Cornell University Press, 1993), 10.

123. Lentin, *Why Race Still Matters*, 171.

124. Martin Luther King Jr., *Why We Can't Wait* (New York: Harper & Row, 1964), 77–79.

125. King, 89.

126. Jon Pahl, *Empire of Sacrifice: The Religious Origins of American Violence* (New York: New York University Press, 2010), 20.

127. Pahl, 3.

128. Myanmar Institute of Theology, *Student Handbook*, 2020, 8.

129. Reuters, "Rumsfeld Praises Army General Who Ridicules Islam as Satan," *New York Times*, October 17, 2003.

130. Edward Wyatt, "Lieberman Heckled during Speech to Arab-American Group," *New York Times*, October 18, 2003.

131. Cochrane, *Among the Burmans*, 5, 27.

132. Cochrane, 128.

133. Helen G. Trager, *Burma through Alien Eyes: Missionary Views of the Burmese in the Nineteenth Century* (London: Asia Publishing House, 1966), 98.

134. Trager, xi.

135. Cochrane, *Among the Burmans*, 162–63.

136. Willis S. Webb, *Incidents and Trials in the Life of Rev. Eugenia Kincaid: The Hero Missionary to Burma, 1830–1863* (Fort Scott, KS: Monitor Publishing House and Book Bindery, 1890), 218.

137. Cochrane, *Among the Burmans*, 121.

138. Ninan Koshy, *A History of the Ecumenical Movement in Asia*, vol. 1 (Hong Kong: Christian Conference of Asia, 2004), 19–20.

139. R. S. Sugirtharajah, *The Bible and Asia: From the Pre-Christian Era to the Postcolonial Age* (Cambridge, MA: Harvard University Press, 2013), 150–51.

140. Robert Spence Hardy, *Christianity and Buddhism Compared* (Colombo, Sri Lanka: Wesleyan Mission Press, 1874), 82.

141. Sugirtharajah, *The Bible and Asia*, 148.

142. Anagarika Dharmapala, *Return to Righteousness: A Collection of Speeches, Essays and Letters of the Anagarika Dharmapala*, 2nd ed. Ananda Guruge (Colombo, Sri Lanka: The Government Press, 1991), 286, 3, 64.

143. Dharmapala, 286.

144. Dharmapala, 494.

145. Dharmapala, 515, 482, 479, 541.

146. Smith, *Religion and Politics in Burma*, 165. The Buddhists under the leadership of U Nu built *Kaba Aye Pagoda* (meaning world peace pagoda) in 1952 in preparation for the Sixth Buddhist Council, held from 1954 to 1956, with the principal purpose of bringing peace to the entire world.

147. Suu Kyi, *Freedom from Fear and Other Writings*, 61.

148. Benjamin Schonthal and Matthew J. Walton, "The New Buddhist Nationalisms? Symmetries and Specificities in Sri Lanka and Myanmar," *Contemporary Buddhism* 17, no. 1 (April 2016): 103.

149. Matthew J. Walton and Susan Hayward, *Contesting Buddhist Narratives: Democratization, Nationalism, and Communal Violence in Myanmar* (Honolulu: East-West Center, 2014), 12.

150. Suu Kyi, *Freedom from Fear and Other Writings*, 172.

151. Suu Kyi, 177.

152. Samuel Ngun Ling, "Interfaith Dialogue: Theological Explorations from Myanmar Context," in *Ecumenical Resources for Dialogue: Between Christians and Neighbors of Other Faiths in Myanmar*, ed. Samuel Ngun Ling (Yangon: Judson Research Center, Myanmar Institute of Theology, 2004), 27.

153. La Seng Dingrin, "Conversion to Mission Christianity among the Kachin of Upper Burma, 1877–1972," in *Asia in the Making of Christianity* (Leiden: Brill, 2013): 133–34.

154. Lian H. Sakhong, *In Defense of Identity: The Ethnic Nationalities' Struggle for Democracy, Human Rights, and Federalism in Burma* (Bangkok: Orchid Press, 2010), 47.

155. Santhosh J. Sahayadoss, *Martin Luther on Social and Political Issues: His Relevance for Church and Society in India* (Frankfurt: Peter Lang, 2006), 124.

156. Cochrane, *Among the Burmans*, 44. The Buddhist monk invited the young Christian boy whom he had known in the village. The monk was held in honor both by virtue of his office and his advanced age.

157. Saw Augurlion, *Christian Existence and Issues Related to Nationalism and Religious Identity in Post-colonial Myanmar* (Yangon, Myanmar: Judson Research Center, 2017), 202.

158. Augurlion, 201.

159. Maung Maung, *Aung San of Burma* (The Hague: Martinus Nyhoff, Southeast Asia Studies, Yale University, 1962), 127–28.

160. I watched a live stream of the Christmas celebration at Henry Van Thio's residence at Nay Pyi Taw on social media.

Conclusion

Religion by nature is peaceful. However, some people use religion as a pretext for violence, while others believe that religion exists to terminate violence and promote peace. The true fact is that people around the globe experience violence perpetrated in the name of religion. To speak about religion and violence, therefore, is to undertake a great personal risk. Even the university classroom or the seminary or the church is not entirely safe. Former British prime minister Tony Blair argues that religious extremism is an ever more dangerous phenomenon, which will fuel the twenty-first-century epic battles, and he calls on governments to switch tactics to combat religious extremism, stating, "The purpose should be to change the policy of governments; to start to treat this issue of religious extremism as an issue that is about religion as well as politics, to go to the roots of where a false view of religion is being promulgated and to make it a major item on the agenda of world leaders to combine effectively to combat it."[1] To this end, the government needs to instruct law enforcement to punish people who deliver hate speech or commit acts of violence. Anyone who violates the law should be punished, and the system must also be active in the community. Equally important is the role of religious leaders in combating religious violence since the government cannot transform society without the active participation of faithful citizens.

There are some differences between Luther's context and that of Myanmar. Luther lived in a predominantly Christian context, while Christians and other religious minorities in Myanmar live in a predominantly Buddhist context. In other words, Luther spoke from the context of the majority, while I speak from the minority context as a person who is oppressed politically, persecuted religiously, and discriminated against socially. Luther did not live in a religiously diverse society, with the exception of a few Jewish and Muslim communities. In contrast, Myanmar is a well-populated, religiously and ethnically diverse society. However, this does not mean that Luther's theology of God's two governances in the world is not applicable in the Buddhist context. It is applicable in a predominantly Buddhist context in Myanmar. First, according

200   *Conclusion*

to Luther's understanding of a dialectical relationship between religion and politics, no religion should ask secular authority to tell people what to believe. In other words, faith is a matter of one's own conscience and cannot be forced by anyone. Secular authority should not unnecessarily interfere in religious matters. It has no power over faith or conscience, although it does have power over men's bodies and property. Luther does not admit the interference of temporal authorities in religious matters to prescribe laws intended for the soul, and such laws would give the citizens the right to disobey and resist them. The interference of the military regime in religious matters in Myanmar especially by enacting "Religious Conversion Law" under the name of "Race and Religion Protection" is contrary to Luther's theology of God's two governances.

Second, there is the basis for a theology of resistance to repressive government in both Lutheranism and Buddhism in Myanmar. The burden of resistance was laid primarily on the "priests and preachers," in Luther's thought.[2] Similarly, in Buddhist thought, monks are responsible for protesting against repressive governments on behalf of the laity. The takeaway from both Luther and from engaged Buddhism is that the Myanmar Baptist understanding of the principle of separation of church and state is not effective in a predominantly Buddhist context, which expects a reciprocal relationship between religion and politics. The Myanmar Baptist understanding of the principle of separation between church and state causes the church to run away from tyranny and follow the state with blind obedience, while some Christians are satisfied with the status quo, wishing to let time pass before speaking. Absolute obedience to a coercive state is not a Christian choice; rather, it fits a typically secular understanding. The Lutheran model of institutional separation and functional interaction, establishing two distinct but interconnected systems for religion and politics, creates space for both religion and politics to give constructive advice and criticism to each other, when necessary, for the health of all human beings.

Third, there is a similarity between Luther's Germany and modern-day Myanmar, which is the outbreak of the peasants' war between the rulers and peasants in sixteenth-century Germany, echoed by the deep-seated ethnic conflicts between the Myanmar military and armed ethnic minority groups in the country. Unquestionably, Myanmar is notorious for the world's longest civil war, fought in the name of nationalism, regionalism, racism, religionism, revolution, evolution, devolution, resolution, and so forth. There is also no question that the Myanmar military regime has been ruining the country for decades for their own gain, consuming the country's resources foolishly and lavishly, at the expense of the ordinary soldiers and civilians. Unfortunately, the end result is the loss of precious human lives while the military officials feed their heavyweights lavishly. This is what Myint-U called a new

Conclusion 201

kind of capitalism: crony capitalism, ceasefire capitalism, army capitalism, elaborating:

> There were at least two paths to getting rich, very rich. The first was in the northern and eastern uplands, where men with guns were kingpins and their associates ran the rackets. Alongside drugs, timber, and jade came a host of other illicit and illegal operations. . . . Another way to make money was a relationship with a Burmese army officer, if possible, a very senior officer in an administrative position, ideally a minister or a regional commander. Some generals made money directly, through kickbacks. . . . Many more allowed their wives, children, and hangers-on to profit from their positions.[3]

Of course, a new kind of capitalism consumes the country's rich natural resources lavishly with zero desire to share with the poor. It is also true that civil war makes the top military leaders and their families rich, while ordinary soldiers are poor. In other words, the ordinary soldiers are fighting for the top generals in the name of nationalism. Tens of thousands of the soldiers lost their lives for the monetary gain of their superiors. Weapons have been misused to bring military officials incredible wealth. I am personally touched by the voice of an ordinary civilian named Kyaw Khine Win, who from painful experience expressed his critical feelings and his desire to see peace in the country to Suu Kyi, during her meeting with the public in Moe Nyein on January 9, 2020, stating:

> The round table peace talks between the two sides [the Myanmar military and the ethnic minority armed groups] ended with arguments about sharing natural resources and territories. The Myanmar armed forces do not represent the whole people of Myanmar collectively. Similarly, ethnic armed groups do not represent the whole ethnic people collectively. Both groups represent only their own small group and work for their own benefits. Those people who are under suffering are the ordinary civilians whose voices have not been heard yet in the round table peace talks.[4]

Surely, there are millions of people who have the same view as Kyaw Khine Win, whose voices are unheard, and who dare not speak up for fear of being threatened by both the military and the ethnic armed groups. I strongly believe that the voices of the civilians should also be taken seriously in order to build a lasting peace. As discussed in chapter 2, Luther critiques both the princes, for failing to rule the country with justice and meet the basic needs of the common people, and the peasants, for looting monasteries and churches, plundering castles, and leaving fields lying unattended. I believe Luther would also denounce the Myanmar military for seizing power from the legitimate government through a coup that involved detaining and killing

202 *Conclusion*

political leaders, activists, medics, journalists, artists, peaceful protestors, and innocent civilians, as well as burning homes and churches to ashes. There is a weakness in the Myanmar military regime that they are not aware of, allowing them to keep thinking of themselves as a legitimate government. This is a big problem.

Similar to Luther, Bonhoeffer writes from a context where Christianity is the dominant religion and is enmeshed with the Nazi government. Bonhoeffer, therefore, critiques not just the government but the church itself. Only the church in resistance (represented by Bonhoeffer's Confessing Church), distinct from the state, is the true church. The situation in Myanmar is different from Germany and is even more complex. Consequently, there are some differences between Bonhoeffer's theology and the Buddhist thought in the context of Myanmar. For instance, in Bonhoeffer's theology the government must protect all religions, whereas in traditional Buddhist thought the government gives special protection to Buddhism, which in practice results in the creation of first-class Buddhist citizens and second-class non-Buddhist citizens. Loyalty to Buddhism is linked with loyalty to the nation; as the common saying goes, "To be Burmese is to be a Buddhist."[5] In other words, minority religions have not been protected constitutionally or practically during the military regime. Bonhoeffer's engagement to defend the oppressed Jews and others during the Nazi's regime in Germany challenges the ultranationalist Buddhists in Myanmar for their intolerance and discrimination of people of other religions who are viewed as the "others." The ultranationalist Buddhists' view of loyalty to the nation with a particular religion—that is, Buddhism—leads to suspicion, intolerance, and discrimination of people who do not share the same religion. They willfully ignore the peaceful aspect of their faith, justifying violence against people of other faiths as a sacred obligation, while engaged Buddhists reject it.

Political crisis in contemporary Myanmar is almost the same as that of Bonhoeffer's time in Germany. Bonhoeffer lived in the time when German xenophobic nationalism was on the rise. Like Hitler's German churches, who saw the Russian communist movement spreading throughout Europe as a real threat to Germany, the ultranationalist Buddhists view democratization and modernization as a threat to the traditional Buddhist identity in Myanmar on the argument that Myanmar was founded as a Buddhist country. Bonhoeffer's relevance is continuously calling upon the ultranationalist Buddhists to embrace the politics of inclusiveness as Bonhoeffer reaches beyond Luther in order to protect the most vulnerable members of his society, breaking racial, religious, and cultural boundaries and embracing the politics of inclusiveness in his theology of empathic solidarity with the oppressed. Corruption, dictatorial oppression, racial discrimination, persecution of religious leaders and

Conclusion 203

political opponents, and the persecution of "non-Aryans" were the principal causes of the resistance movement.

In modern Myanmar, mainline denominations and Pentecostal churches have different ways of expressing their religious faith in public spaces; the former put greater emphasis on internal stability and social actions by helping those in need and participating in interfaith activities, while the latter put greater emphasis on religious revival through public preaching for soul-winning in the name of Jesus alone, occasionally referring to people of non-Christian faiths as "hell-bound people." The Catholic Church also engages actively in interfaith activities, particularly with the emergence of Cardinal Charles Bo as the first Burmese cardinal. The emergence of socially engaged interfaith activities in Myanmar is a positive sign that the church is showing its resistance as a tool in the fight against hate speech and contributes to constructive peacebuilding in society.

The application of Luther's theology of two kingdoms, in dialogue with socially engaged Buddhist and Christian communities in Myanmar today, will make a difference for the well-being of human beings in Myanmar. John Fea, an American historian, says, "History is the art of reconstructing the past."[6] In other words, history is composed of two things: facts, and interpretation of those facts to address the present challenges in a constructive way. We study the past to construct a better present and future. Our experiences teach us that a false faith, capable of violence and terrible things in society, has been displayed in public life not only by the ultranationalist Buddhists but also by some exclusive Christians in Myanmar. On the critical question of violence and nonviolence, Jesus's teaching of "love your enemies" (Matthew 5: 43–44) is the commandment from Jesus to opt for nonviolence to transform our enemy into a friend. Martin Luther King Jr., said that the Christian concept of "love your enemies" and the Gandhian concept of *satyagraha*, meaning "truth-force or love-force" became a driving force for him to transform an enemy into a friend.[7] King, as a "realistic pacifist," argues that the nonviolent approach does something to the hearts and souls of those committed to it.[8] Therefore, nonviolence became more than a theory; it became a commitment to a way of life for King.[9] Condemning Christian violence, Reinhold Niebuhr also says:

> Nothing is more futile and pathetic than the effort of some Christian theologians who find it necessary to become involved in the relativities of politics, in resistance to tyranny or in social conflict, to justify themselves by seeking to prove that Christ was also involved in some of these relativities, that he used whips to drive the money-changers out of the Temple, or that he came not to bring peace but a sword, or that he asked the disciples to sell a cloak and buy a sword.[10]

204 *Conclusion*

Although loving our enemies is not an easy task for human beings, Jesus really expects his followers to live this way. His command to love our enemies means turning violence into peace, and it unfolds that love is stronger than hatred. Ethnic armed groups and the People's Defense Force did not start the fighting against the Myanmar military. One can clearly see that after the military coup on February 1, 2021, it was the military who first created violence, by arresting and killing peaceful protesters and innocent civilians, including fighting against ethnic armed groups and People's Defense Force. They burned the houses of civilians and the Christian churches to ashes. As a result, thousands of people fled to refugee camps both inside and outside the country for their safety. In such a dangerous situation, ethnic armed groups and the People's Defense Force have no other option except to fight back against the military to protect themselves and other citizens under the leadership of a shadow government, the NUG, not under the leadership of the church.

Christian churches in Myanmar do not support violence, but rather, prefer peacebuilding through political dialogue for the common good. Katie Day, professor of church in society at Lutheran Theological Seminary in Philadelphia, and Sebastian Kim, professor of theology and public life at Fuller Theological Seminary, in their book *A Companion to Public Theology*, say, "Participation of the church in the public sphere is needed in fractious public spaces to engage with those within and outside its institutions on issues of common interest and for the common good."[11] Christian churches in Myanmar have protested against the Myanmar military, through nonviolent action, for seizing power illegally on February 1, 2021, from the democratically elected government, and have asked for justice as part of their functional role as a prophetic voice. They have also held vigils to restore democracy and peace to the country. Furthermore, they have been actively engaged in helping the victims of military violence by donating food, clothes, medicine, and money regardless of ethnic group and religion.

Similar to Jesus's teaching of "love your enemies," the teachings of the Buddha known as the Dharma do not support violence in the name of religion, but rather encourage all Buddhists to abide by the nonviolent Five Precepts, "not to take life, not to steal, not to commit adultery, not to tell lies, and not to take intoxicating drinks."[12] As discussed in chapter 4, Buddhist notions of good governance also support nonviolence in order to meet the needs of the people and rule the country with justice based on the "Ten Duties" of the ruler: liberality, morality, self-sacrifice, integrity, kindness, austerity, non-anger, nonviolence, forbearance, and non-opposition to the will of the people.[13] As a socially engaged Buddhist and a pragmatic pacifist, Suu Kyi always opts for nonviolent action in her political journey. She affirms nonviolence as the best approach for a long-term political movement

Conclusion 205

in Myanmar, and compares two persons, one with a gun in his hands, and the other without a gun, saying:

> There is a far difference in the attitude of a man with a gun in his hands and that of one without a gun in his hands. When a man does not have a gun in his hands—or a woman for the matter—he/she tries harder to use his/her mind in a sense of compassion and has intelligence to work out the solution. But if you put a gun into a person's hands, the gun is always there to use, so that the urge to exercise one's intelligence and compassion more becomes much less.[14]

In spite of the criticism she faces, Suu Kyi looks for the third way in bringing the two extreme groups to the round table to find the best solution for the conflict facing the status quo. She recognizes both groups as human beings who deserve to live as humans, although she might not like all things that both the military and ethnic armed groups have done. When Alan Clements asked about the military officials who ordered her house arrest, she responded:

> I liked most of them as human beings—I could never help seeing the human side of them, what is likeable. This is not to say I like what they did. There are lots of things that they did and they are doing which I do not like at all. You must not think that I was very angelic and never got angry. Of course, I get angry. But I never lost sight of the fact that they were human beings. And like all human beings, there's a side to them which must be likeable.[15]

For Suu Kyi, Jesus's command to love her once-enemies means to win their hearts through a nonviolent approach to them. She continues saying, "To forgive, I think, basically means the ability to see the person apart from the deed and to recognize that although he has done that deed, it does not mean that he is irredeemable."[16] Her politics seeks to liberate both the oppressed and the oppressors, like Nelson Mandela, who after his release from prison said, "When I walked out of prison, that was my mission, to liberate the oppressed and the oppressor both."[17] Myanmar needs leadership that celebrates the existing plurality and unifies the two extremes with socially engaged spirituality.

Socially engaged religion teaches that people of faith have a responsibility to address and reduce suffering in all of its forms, both physical and spiritual, including suffering resulting from social injustice, exploitation, oppression, false faith, and so forth. As such, true religion always engages with society to alleviate suffering and bring transformation. Hence, the ideology of engaged religion supports peace, justice, and freedom, and denounces oppression in every aspect of life in society. Socially engaged people of faith assume something inherently peaceful and benevolent about religion. Violence in the name of religion is a perversion of true faith. In other words, religious violence is

206   *Conclusion*

an obscenity, a deviation from the true character of religion. If we can wrestle more with this complexity in our teachings and our public spaces, our studies may be better able to overcome religious violence, which has been part of religion since its origin. There is no doubt that socially engaged Buddhists and Christians in Myanmar have common principles and goals to transform a violent society into a peaceful coexistent society through nonviolent action. Indeed, people do not lose hope, even amid suffering, that things will continue to move in the right direction, and they are resilient and supportive so that peace and justice will prevail in our land. Above all, socially engaged people of faith believe that dynamic transformation of society can happen in Myanmar, as the Buddhist belief *anicca* reminds us that nothing is permanent. Change is possible with the collective efforts of socially engaged people within the country.

NOTES

1. Toby Helm, "Extremist Religion Is at Root of 21st Century Wars, Says Tony Blair," *Guardian*, January 25, 2014.

2. Martin Luther, "Selected Psalms II," in *Luther's Works*, vol. 13, trans. C. M. Jacobs (Saint Louis: Concordia Publishing House, 1956), 49.

3. Thant Myint-U, *The Hidden History of Burma: Race, Capitalism, and the Crisis of Democracy in the 21st Century* (New York: W.W. Norton & Company, 2020), 52.

4. I watched a live stream on social media of Kyaw Khine Win asking ASSK in Moe Nyein on January 9, 2020, during her meeting with the public.

5. Aung San Suu Kyi, *Freedom from Fear and Other Writings* (New York: Penguin Books, 1995), 83.

6. John Fea, *Reflecting on the Importance of the Past: Why Study History?* (Grand Rapids, MI: Baker Academic, 2013), 3.

7. Martin Luther King Jr., *Strength to Love* (Philadelphia: Fortress Press, 1963), 151.

8. King, 152–53.

9. King, 152.

10. Reinhold Niebuhr, *Why the Christian Church Is Not Pacifist* (London: Student Christian Movement Press, 1940), 106.

11. Katie Day and Sebastian Kim, *A Companion to Public Theology* (Leiden: Brill, 2017), 2–19.

12. Suu Kyi, *Freedom from Fear and Other Writings*, 67.

13. Juliane Schober, "Buddhist Visions of Moral Authority and Modernity in Burma," in *Burma at the Turn of the 21st Century*, ed. Monique Skidmore (Honolulu: University of Hawaii Press, 2005), 125.

14. Burmalibrary, "Aung San Suu Kyi on Nonviolence," https://www.youtube.com /watch?v=j1ZlLd1fnxU, accessed November 19, 2022.

15. Aung San Suu Kyi, *The Voice of Hope: Conversations with Alan Clements* (New York: Seven Stories Press, 2008), 143. Suu Kyi said that her mother never

Conclusion 207

taught her to hate even those who killed her father. She never once heard her mother talk with hatred about the men who assassinated her father.

16. Suu Kyi, 180.

17. Nelson Mandela, *Long Walk to Freedom: The Autobiography of Nelson Mandela* (New York: Little, Brown and Company, 1994), 544.

List of Abbreviations

ABMA   All Burma Monks' Alliance
AMIRO   All Myanmar Islamic Religious Organization
ARSA   Arakan Rohingya Salvation Army
ASEAN   Association of Southeast Asian Nations
CDM   Civil Disobedience Movement
CDNH   Center for Diversity and National Harmony
CRPH   Committee Representing Pyidaungsu Hluttaw
ELCA   Evangelical Lutheran Church in America
IGE   Institute for Global Engagement
INGO   International Non-Governmental Organization
JRC   Judson Research Center
KIA   Kachin Independence Army
NCA   Nationwide Ceasefire Agreement
NLD   National League for Democracy
NUG   National Unity Government
OIC   Organization of Islamic Conference
PDF   People's Defense Force
PVO   People's Volunteer Organization
SAC   State Administration Council
SLORC   State Law and Order Restoration Council
SPDC   State Peace and Development Council
USDA   Union Solidarity and Development Association
USDP   Union Solidarity and Development Party

Bibliography

Ahmed, Azam. "And Now, What Mexico Thinks of Donald Trump." *New York Times*, July 2, 2015.

Allard, Tom. "ASEAN Appoints Brunei Diplomat as Envoy to Myanmar." *Reuters*, August 4, 2021.

Allen, O. Wesley Jr. *Preaching in the Era of Trump*. Saint Louis, MO: Chalice Press, 2017.

Althaus, Paul. *The Ethics of Martin Luther*. Translated by Robert C. Schultz. Philadelphia: Fortress Press, 1972.

Altmann, Walter. *Luther and Liberation: A Latin American Perspective*. Minneapolis: Fortress Press, 2015.

Anderson, Courtney. *To the Golden Shore: The Life of Adoniram Judson*. Grand Rapids, MI: Zondervan, 1976.

Annan, Kofi A. *Towards a Peaceful, Fair, and Prosperous Future for the People of Rakhine: Final Report of the Advisory Commission on Rakhine State*. Advisory Commission on Rakhine State, August 19, 2017. https://www.kofiannanfoundation .org/app/uploads/2017/08/FinalReport_Eng.pdf.

Aoley, P. V. "Sangha." *Encyclopedia of Hinduism*. Vol. 9. Edited by K. L. Seshagiri Rao and Kapil Kapoor. New Delhi: India Heritage Research Foundation in Association with Rupa & Co., 2011.

Appold, Kenneth G. *The Reformation: A Brief History*. Malden, MA: Wiley-Blackwell, 2011.

Armour, Rollin Stely. *Anabaptist Baptism: A Representative Study*. Scottdale, PA: Herald Press, 1966.

Augurlion, Saw. *Christian Existence and Issues Related to Nationalism and Religious Identity in Post-colonial Myanmar*. Yangon, Myanmar: Judson Research Center, 2017.

Augustine. *The City of God against the Pagans*. Translated by R. W. Dyson. Cambridge: Cambridge University Press, 1998.

Aung, Maung Htin. *A History of Burma*. New York: Columbia University Press, 1967.

———. *The Stricken Peacock: Anglo-Burmese Relations, 1752–1948*. The Hague: Martinus Nijhoff, 1965.

212   *Bibliography*

Aung, San Yamin. "Highlights of the U Ko Ni Murder Case." *Irrawaddy*, January 29, 2019.

———. "Interfaith Leaders Call on Individuals to Build Peace." *Irrawaddy*, September 19, 2016.

———. "Myanmar's Military and USDP Reject NLD Attempts to Limit the Armed Forces' Political Powers." *Irrawaddy*, February 27, 2020.

———. "Myanmar Opposition Party Demands Election Rerun with Military Involvement." *Irrawaddy*, November 11, 2020.

Ba, Vivian. "The Early Catholic Missionaries in Burma." Rangoon: The Guardian, 1962.

Bainton, Roland H. *Here I Stand: A Life of Martin Luther*. London: Hodder and Stoughton, 1951.

Bak, Janos. "The Peasant War in Germany by Friedrich Engels—125 Years After." In *The German Peasant War of 1525*. Edited by Janos Bak. London: Frank Cass, 1976.

Baker, Peter. "Religious Freedom Is a Tenet of Foreign Policy, Obama Says." *New York Times*, February 6, 2014.

Bangkok Post. "ASEAN Leaders Agree 5-Point Plan for Myanmar." April 25, 2021.

Bankier, David. "Nazi Party." *Encyclopedia of the Holocaust*. Vol. 3. Edited by Israel Gutman. New York: Macmillan Publishing Company, 1990.

Barry, John M. *Roger Williams and the Creation of the American Soul: Church, State, and the Birth of Liberty*. New York: Penguin Group, 2012.

Basham, A. L. "Asoka." *The Encyclopedia of Religion*. Vol. 1. Edited by Mircea Eliade. New York: Macmillan Publishing Company, 1987.

Beech, Hannah. "Top Myanmar General Says Military Rule Will Continue into 2023." *New York Times*, August 1, 2021.

Beech, Hannah, and Saw Nang. "He Incited Massacre, but Insulting Aung San Suu Kyi Was the Last Straw." *New York Times*, May 29, 2019.

Bethge, Eberhard. *Dietrich Bonhoeffer: A Biography*. Minneapolis: Fortress Press, 2000.

Bigandet, Paul Ambrose. *Outline of the History of the Catholic Burmese Mission from the Year 1720 to 1857*. Rangoon: Hanthawaddy Press, 1967.

Blair, Tony. "Taking Faith Seriously." *New Europe*, January 2, 2012.

Bonhoeffer, Dietrich. "Barcelona, Berlin, New York, 1928–1931." In *Dietrich Bonhoeffer Works*. Vol. 10. Translated by Douglas W. Stott. Edited by Clifford J. Green. Minneapolis: Fortress Press, 2008.

———. "Berlin, 1932–1933." In *Dietrich Bonhoeffer Works*. Vol. 12. Translated by Isabel Best and David Higgins. Edited by Larry L. Rasmussen. Minneapolis: Fortress Press, 2009.

———. "Conspiracy and Imprisonment, 1940–1945." In *Dietrich Bonhoeffer Works*. Vol. 16. Translated by Lisa E. Dahill. Edited by Mark S. Brocker. Minneapolis: Fortress Press, 2006.

———. *The Cost of Discipleship*. Translated by R. H. Fuller. New York: The Macmillan Comsany, 1949.

———. "Discipleship." *Dietrich Bonhoeffer Works*. Vol. 4. Translated by Barbara Green and Reinhard Krauss. Edited by Geffrey B. Kelly and John D. Godsey. Minneapolis: Fortress Press, 2001.

Bibliography

———. "Ecumenical, Academic, and Pastoral Works, 1931–1932." In *Dietrich Bonhoeffer Works*. Vol. 11. Translated by Anne Schmidt-Lange, Isabel Best, Nicolas Humphrey, and Marion Pauck. Edited by Victoria J. Barnett, Mark S. Brocker, and Michael B. Lukens. Minneapolis: Fortress Press, 2012.

———. "Ethics." In *Dietrich Bonhoeffer Works.* Vol. 6. Translated by Reinhard Krauss, Charles C. West, and Douglas W. Stott. Edited by Clifford J. Green. Minneapolis: Fortress Press, 2005.

———. *Gesammelte Schriften.* Band. 1. Translated by Eberhard Bethge. Munchen: Kaiser Verlag, 1958.

———. *Letters and Papers from Prison.* Translated by Eberhard Bethge. New York: The Macmillan Publishing, 1971.

———. "London, 1933–1935." In *Dietrich Bonhoeffer Works.* Vol. 13. Translated by Isabel Best. Edited by Keith Clements. Minneapolis: Fortress Press, 2007.

———. "Sanctorum Communio: A Theological Study of the Sociology of the Church." In *Dietrich Bonhoeffer Works*. Vol. 1. Translated by Reinhard Krauss and Nancy Lukens. Edited by Clifford J. Green. Minneapolis: Fortress Press, 1998.

———. *A Testament to Freedom: The Essential Writings of Dietrich Bonhoeffer.* Edited by Geffrey B. Kelly and F. Burton Nelson. New York: Harpers Collins Publishers, 1995.

———. "Theological Education Underground, 1937–1940." In *Dietrich Bonhoeffer Works*. Vol. 15. Translated by Victoria J. Barnett, Claudia D. Bergmann, Peter Frick, and Scott A. Moore. Edited by Victoria J. Barnett. Minneapolis: Fortress Press, 2012.

———. "The Young Bonhoeffer, 1918–1927." In *Dietrich Bonhoeffer Works*. Vol. 9. Translated by Mary C. Nebelsick. Edited by Paul Duane Matheny, Clifford J. Green, Marshall D. Johnson. Minneapolis: Fortress Press, 2003.

Bonvillain, Nancy. *Men and Women: Cultural Constructs of Gender*, 2nd ed. Upper Saddle River, NJ: Prentice Hall, 1995.

Boorstein, Michelle, and Rachel Weiner. "Historic D.C. Church Where Trump Stood with a Bible Becomes a Symbol for His Religious Foes." *Washington Post*, June 3, 2020.

Boorstein, Michelle, and Sarah Pulliam Bailey. "Episcopal Bishop on President Trump: Everything He Has Done and Said Is to Inflame Violence." *Washington Post*, June 1, 2020.

Bowh Si, Oliver Byar. *God in Burma: Civil Society and Public Theology in Myanmar*. Las Vegas: Createspace Publishing, 2014.

Bowles, Nellie. "Replacement Theory, a Racist, Sexist Doctrine, Spreads in Far-Right Circles." *New York Times*, March 18, 2019.

British Broadcasting Corporation. "Christchurch Shooting: Grief and Defiance as Victims Confront Gunman." August 26, 2020. https://www.bbc.com/news/world-asia-53902158

———."George Floyd Death: Archbishop Attacks Trump as US Protests Continue." June 3, 2020. https://www.bbc.com/news/world-us-canada-52897303.

———. "Junaid Hafeez: Academic Sentenced to Death for a Blasphemy in Pakistan." December 21, 2019. https://www.bbc.com/news/world-asia-50878432.

214   *Bibliography*

————. "Rohingya Crisis: Suu Kyi Says Fake News Helping Terrorists." September 6, 2017. https://www.bbc.com/news/world-asia-41170570.

————. "Rohingya Crisis: UN Sees Ethnic Cleansing in Myanmar." September 11, 2017. https://www.bbc.com/news/world-asia-41224108.

Burma Library. "Aung San Suu Kyi on Nonviolence." https://www.youtube.com/watch?v=j1ZlLd1fnxU. Accessed November 19, 2022.

Cady, John F. *A History of Modern Burma*. Ithaca, NY: Cornell University Press, 1960.

Carr, William. *A History of Germany, 1815–1945*. New York: St. Martin's Press, 1969.

Carson, Laura E. *Pioneer Trails, Trials, and Triumphs*. New York: Baptist Board Education, 1927.

Cave, Damien. "New Zealand Massacre Sentencing: What to Expect." *New York Times*, August 23, 2020.

CBS News. "European Leaders Condemn Coup as Myanmar's Military Seizes Power, Detains Aung San Suu Kyi." February 1, 2021. https://www.cbsnews.com/news/myanmar-coup-military-detains-aung-san-suu-kyi-latest-updates/.

Chain, Tun Aung. "The Christian-Buddhist Encounter in Myanmar." Paper presented at the Inauguration Ceremony of Judson Research Center at Myanmar Institute of Theology, Yangon, Myanmar, July 13, 2003.

Charney, Michael W. *A History of Modern Burma.* Cambridge: Cambridge University Press, 2009.

Cochrane, Henry Park. *Among the Burmans: A Record of Fifteen Years of Work and Its Fruitage.* New York: Fleming H. Revell Company, 1904.

Cockett, Richard. *Blood, Dreams and Gold: The Changing Face of Burma.* New Haven, CT: Yale University Press, 2015.

Constituent Assembly of Burma. *The Constitution of the Union of Burma.* Rangoon: Government Printing and Stationery, 1948.

Cook, Alistair D. B. "The Global and Regional Dynamics of Humanitarian Aid in Rakhine State." In *Islam and the State in Myanmar: Muslim-Buddhist Relations and the Politics of Belonging*, edited by Melissa Crouch. Oxford: Oxford University Press, 2016.

Cortright, David. *Peace: A History of Movements and Ideas.* Cambridge: Cambridge University Press, 2008.

Crossley, Robert N. *Luther and the Peasants' War: Luther's Actions and Reactions.* New York: Exposition Press, 1974.

Danbury Baptist Association. "Letter to Thomas Jefferson." In *The Sacred Rights of Conscience: Selected Readings on Religious Liberty and Church-State Relations in the American Founding*. Edited by Daniel L. Dreisbach and Mark David Hall. Indianapolis, IN: Liberty Fund, 2009.

Davis, Julie Hirschfeld. "House Condemns Trump's Attack on Four Congresswomen as Racist." *New York Times*, July 16, 2019.

Day, Katie, and Sebastian Kim. *A Companion to Public Theology*. Leiden: Brill, 2017.

DeJonge, Michael P. *Bonhoeffer's Reception of Luther*. Oxford: Oxford University Press, 2017.

Democratic Voice of Burma (DVB) in Burmese, November 2, 2016.

Dharmapala, Anagarika. *Return to Righteousness: A Collection of Speeches, Essays and Letters of the Anagarika Dharmapala*, 2nd ed. Edited by Ananda Guruge. Colombo, Sri Lanka: The Government Press, 1991.

Dingrin, La Seng. "Conversion to Mission Christianity among the Kachin of Upper Burma, 1877–1972." *Asia in the Making of Christianity.* Leiden: Brill (2013): 109–34.

Dorkenoo, Efua. *Cutting the Rose: Female Genital Mutilation: The Practice and Its Preservation.* London: Minority Rights Publications, 1994.

Eliot, Charles. *Hinduism and Buddhism: An Historical Sketch.* Vol. 3. London: Routledge & Kegan Paul Ltd., 1954.

Ellingsen, Mark. *Reclaiming Our Roots: An Inclusive Introduction to Church History*, Vol. 1. Harrisburg, PA: Trinity Press International, 1999.

Embree, J. F, and W. L. Thomas, Jr. *Ethnic Groups of Northern Southeast Asia.* New Haven: Yale University Southeast Asia Studies, 1950.

En, Simon Pau Khan. *Nat Worship: A Paradigm for Doing Contextual Theology in Myanmar.* Yangon: Myanmar Institute of Theology, 2012.

Encyclopedia of Hinduism. Vol. 9. (2011), s.v. "Sangha."

Ericksen, Robert P. *Theologians under Hitler*, DVD. A Film by Steven D. Martin, 2006.

Evangelical Lutheran Church in America. *A Social Message on Government and Civic Engagement in the United States: Discipleship in a Democracy.* June 24, 2020.

Fea, John. *Reflecting on the Importance of the Past: Why Study History?* Grand Rapids, MI: Baker Academic, 2013.

Feldman, Noah. *Divided by God: America's Church-State Problem and What We Should Do about It.* New York: Farrar, Straus and Giroux, 2005.

Fink, Christina. "The Moment of the Monks: Burma, 2007." In *Civil Resistance and Power Politics: The Experience of Non-violent Action from Gandhi to the Present.* Edited by Adam Roberts and Timothy Garton Ash. Oxford: Oxford University Press, 2009.

———. *Living Silence in Burma: Surviving under Military Rule.* London: Zed Books, 2009.

Fleming, Rachel. "Persecution and Coerced Conversion of Ethnic Chin Christians in Burma." Paper presented at the Second International Conference on Human Rights and Peace, and Conflict in Southeast Asia in Jakarta, Indonesia, October 17–18, 2012.

Forell, George W., Herman A. Preus, and Jaroslav J. Pelikan. "Toward a Lutheran View of Church and State." *Lutheran Quarterly*, no. 5 (August 1953): 287–90.

Foxeus, Niklas. "Contemporary Burmese Buddhism." In *The Oxford Handbook of Contemporary Buddhism.* Edited by Michael Jerryson. New York: Oxford University Press, 2016.

Fredholm, Michael. *Burma: Ethnicity and Insurgency.* London: Praeger, 1993.

Freeman, Joe. "Myanmar Silences Radical Monk, but Legacy of Hatred Speaks for Itself." *Voice of America*, March 28, 2017.

Frum, David. *The Right Man: The Surprise Presidency of George W. Bush.* Waterville, ME: Thorndike Press, 2003.

Fuller, Thomas. "Extremism Rises Among Myanmar Buddhists." *New York Times*, June 20, 2013.

Gerin, Roseanne. "Myanmar Top General Raises Questions with Visits to Mosques, Other Places of Worship." *Radio Free Asia*, September 23, 2019.

Goldman, Russel. "Myanmar's Coup and Violence, Explained." *New York Times*, May 29, 2021.

Gravers, Mikael. "Monks, Morality and Military: The Struggle for Moral Power in Burma—and Buddhism's Uneasy Relation with Lay Power." *Contemporary Buddhism* 13, no. 1 (May 2012): 1–33.

Gutman, Israel. "Arierparagraph." *Encyclopedia of the Holocaust*. Edited by Israel Gutman. New York: Macmillan Publishing Company, 1990.

Han, Naw Betty. "Interfaith Celebrations Aim to Unite Myanmar, NLD Says." *Myanmar Times*, October 18, 2017.

Hardy, Robert Spence. *Christianity and Buddhism Compared*. Colombo, Sri Lanka: Wesleyan Mission Press, 1874.

Hashim, Asad. "Pakistani Academic Junaid Hafeez Sentenced to Death for Blasphemy." *Aljazeera*, December 21, 2019, https://www.aljazeera.com/news/2019/12/21/pakistani-academic-junaid-hafeez-sentenced-to-death-for-blasphemy.

Hein, Ye Myo. "Demystifying the Narratives on the Myanmar Military." *Irrawaddy*, August 13, 2021.

Helm, Toby. "Extremist Religion Is at Root of 21st Century Wars, Says Tony Blair." *Guardian*, January 25, 2014.

Hertz, Karl H. *Two Kingdoms and One World*. Minneapolis: Augsburg Publishing House, 1976.

Hitler, Adolf. *My New Order*. Edited by Raoul de Roussy de Sales. New York: Reynal & Hitchcock, 1941.

Hoffmann, Peter. *German Resistance to Hitler*. Cambridge, MA: Harvard University Press, 1988.

Holloway, James Y. *Barth, Barmen and The Confessing Church Today: Katallagete*. Lewiston: The Edwin Mellen Press, 1995.

Htun, Htun. "Government Bans U Wirathu from Preaching Sermons." *Irrawaddy*, March 11, 2017.

Htun, Htun, and Pe Thet Htet Khin. "State Buddhist Authority Stands Its Ground." *Irrawaddy*, July 18, 2017.

Hubmaier, Balthasar. *Balthasar Hubmaier: Theologian of Anabaptism*. Translated by H. Wayne Pipkin and John H. Yoder. Scottdale, PA: Herald Press, 1989.

Human Rights Watch. *Crackdown: Repression of the 2007 Popular Protests in Burma*. New York: Human Rights Watch, December 6, 2007.

———. *The Resistance of the Monks: Buddhism and Activism in Burma*. New York: Human Rights Watch, September 22, 2009.

Hurd, Elizabeth Shakman. *Beyond Religious Freedom: The New Global Politics of Religion.* Princeton, NJ: Princeton University Press, 2015.

Hutterian Brethren. *The Chronicle of the Hutterian Brethren*. Vol. 1. Rifton, NY: Plough Publishing House, 1987.

Independent. "Outrage as Pakistan Sentences Academic to Death for Blasphemy." December 22, 2019.

International Crisis Group. "Myanmar's Military: Back to the Barracks?" April 22, 2014. https://www.crisisgroup.org/asia/south-east-asia/myanmar/myanmar-s -military-back-barracks.

Irrawaddy. "Brother of Slain Myanmar Pastor Says Regime Fails to Take Accountability for Atrocities." September 23, 2021.

———. "Head of Myanmar's Shadow Govt Says World Will Back Its Declaration of War Against Junta." September 7, 2021.

———. "In Myanmar, the NLD's Main Rival Finds It Hard to Accept Electoral Defeat." November 12, 2020.

———. "Ma Ba Tha's U Wirathu: Trump Similar to Me." November 18, 2016.

———. "Myanmar Junta Kills Nearly 1,000 Civilians in Under 200 Day." August 17, 2021.

———. "Myanmar Coup Highlights in 90 Days." May 1, 2021.

———. "Myanmar Junta Denies Accepting ASEAN Ceasefire Proposal." September 7, 2021.

———. "Myanmar President Reveals Details of His Arrest." October 14, 2021.

———. "Myanmar Regime Committed Almost 2,800 War Crimes in Last Six Months: NUG." June 13, 2022.

———. "Myanmar Regime Troops Detain Youths and Loot Shops in Night Raids." August 20, 2021.

———. "Religious Affairs Minister Says No Monk Is Above the Law." July 14, 2016.

———. "UN Envoy Joins Her Predecessors in Myanmar's Graveyard of Diplomats." September 16, 2021.

———. "World Buddhist Leaders Pen Letter to Burma." December 11, 2012.

Jefferson, Thomas. "Letter to the Danbury Baptist Association." In *The American Republic: Primary Sources.* Edited by Bruce Frohnen. Indianapolis, IN: Liberty Fund, 2002.

Kadoe, Naw Lily, and Fatimah Husein. "Ulama, State, and Politics in Myanmar." *Al Jamiah Journal of Islamic Studies* 53, no. 1 (2015): 131–58.

Kantarawaddy Times. "New Kayah State Party Officially Registered." Burma News International, August 14, 2017. https://www.bnionline.net/en/news/karenni-state/ item/3372-new-kayah-state-party-officially-registered.html.

Kaplan, Esther. *With God on Their Side: How Christian Fundamentalists Trampled Science, Policy, and Democracy in George W. Bush's White House.* New York: The New Press, 2004.

Karen News. "New United Karen Party's Registration Accepted by Union Election Commission." March 2, 2018. https://karennews.org/2018/03/new-united-karen -partys-registration-accepted-by-union-election-commission/.

Kelly, Geffrey B., et al. "As Hitler Manipulated the German Churches and Oppressed the Jews, Most Christians Remained Silent. Not Dietrich Bonhoeffer," *Christian History* 10, no. 4 (1991): 1–45.

Kha, May. "Monks Conference Calls for Harmony, Criticizes Interfaith Marriage Draft Law." *Irrawaddy*, June 17, 2013.

218   *Bibliography*

Khaing, Htun. "The True Face of Buddhism." *Frontier Myanmar*, May 12, 2017.
Khit, Naing. "Diplomacy Is Wasted on Myanmar's Junta." *Irrawaddy*, September 22, 2021.
———. "Myanmar's Military Chief Staged a Coup. But He Did Not Act Alone." *Irrawaddy*, August 13, 2021.
Kim, Hyuk. "A Complex Crisis: The Twisted Roots of Myanmar's Rohingya Conflict." *Global Asia* 12, no. 3 (September 2017): 266–78.
King, Jr,. Martin Luther. *Why We Can't Wait*. New York: Harper & Row, 1964.
———. *Strength to Love*. Philadelphia: Fortress Press, 1963.
King, Sallie B. *Socially Engaged Buddhism: Dimension of Asian Spirituality*. Honolulu: University of Hawai'i Press, 2009.
Kingston, Jeff. *The Politics of Religion, Nationalism, and Identity in Asia*. London: Rowman & Littlefield, 2019.
Klaassen, Walter. "Grebel, Conrad." In *The Oxford Encyclopedia of the Reformation*. Vol. 2. Edited by Hans J. Hillerbrand. New York: Oxford University Press, 1996.
Koshy, Ninan. *A History of the Ecumenical Movement in Asia*. Vol. I. Hong Kong: Christian Conference of Asia, 2004.
Kyaw, Nyi Nyi. "Islamophobia in Buddhist Myanmar: The 969 Movement and Anti-Muslim Violence." In *Islam and the State in Myanmar: Muslim-Buddhist Relations and the Politics of Belonging*, edited by Melissa Crouch. Oxford: Oxford University Press, 2016.
Kyodo News. "ASEAN Envoy to Myanmar Says Military Agrees to Four-Month Ceasefire to Deliver Aid." September 6, 2021.
Lall, Marie. *Understanding Reform in Myanmar: People and Society in the Wake of Military Rule*. London: Hurst & Company, 2016.
Lehman, F. K. *The Structure of Chin Society: A Tribal People of Burma Adapted to a Non-Western Civilization*. Urbana: University of Illinois Press, 1963.
Lentin, Alana. *Why Race Still Matters*. Cambridge: Polity Press, 2020.
Lindberg, Carter. *The European Reformations*. Oxford: Blackwell Publishing, 2010.
———. *The European Reformations Sourcebook*. Oxford: Blackwell Publishing, 2000.
Ling, Samuel Ngun. *Christianity through Our Neighbors' Eyes: Rethinking the 200 Years Old American Baptist Missions in Myanmar*. Yangon: Judson Research Center, MIT, 2014.
———. "Interfaith Dialogue: Theological Explorations from Myanmar Context." In *Ecumenical Resources for Dialogue: Between Christians and Neighbors of Other Faiths in Myanmar*. Edited by Samuel Ngun Ling. Yangon: Judson Research Center, Myanmar Institute of Theology, 2004.
Lintner, Bertil. "All Lies: Myanmar's Junta Clumsy Propaganda Has a Disturbing Familiar Ring." *Irrawaddy*, August 16, 2021.
———. *Burma in Revolt: Opium and Insurgency Since 1948*. Chiang Mai, Thailand: Silkworm Books, 1999.
———. *Outrage: Burma's Struggle for Democracy*. London: White Lotus, 1990.
———. "There Is a New Cold War in Asia." *Irrawaddy*, September 12, 2016.

Bibliography 219

Luther, Martin. "Admonition to Peace: A Reply to the Twelve Articles of the Peasants in Swabia." In *Luther's Works*. Vol. 46. Translated by Charles M. Jacobs. Edited by Robert C. Schultz. Philadelphia: Fortress Press, 1967.

———. "Against the Robbing and Murdering Hordes of Peasant." In *Luther's Works*. Vol. 46. Translated by Charles M. Jacobs. Edited by Robert C. Schultz. Philadelphia: Fortress Press, 1967.

———. "The Babylonian Captivity of the Church." *Luther's Works*. Vol. 36. Translated by A. T. W. Steinhauser. Edited by Abdel Ross Wentz. Philadelphia: Muhlenberg Press, 1959.

———. *Commentary on the Epistles to the Romans*. Translated by J. Theodore Mueller. Grand Rapids, MI: Zondervan Publishing House, 1954.

———. "Concerning Rebaptism." In *Luther's Works*. Vol. 40. Translated by Conrad Bergendoff. Edited by Conrad Bergendoff. Philadelphia: Fortress Press, 1958.

———. *D. Martin Luthers Werke: Kritische Gesamtausgabe,* 4. Band. Weimar: Germann Bohlaus Nachfolger, 1933.

———. *D. Martin Luthers Werke: Kritische Gesamtausgabe*, 5. Band. Weimar: Germann Bohlaus Nachfolger, 1934.

———. "The Freedom of a Christian." In *Luther's Works*. Vol. 31. Translated by W. A. Lambert. Edited by Harold J. Grimm. Philadelphia: Muhlenberg Press, 1957.

———. "Lectures on Genesis." In *Luther's Works*. Vol. 1. Translated by George V. Schick. Edited by Jaroslav Pelikan. Saint Louis: Concordia Publishing House, 1958.

———. "Lectures on Genesis." In *Luther's Works*. Vol. 2. Translated by George V. Schick. Edited by Jaroslav Pelikan. Saint Louis: Concordia Publishing House, 1960.

———. "Lectures on Genesis." In *Luther's Works*. Vol. 4. Translated by George V. Schick. Edited by Jaroslav Pelikan. St. Louis: Concordia, 1964.

———. "Lectures on Romans." In *Luther's Works*. Vol. 25. Translated by Jacob A.O. Preus. Edited by Hilton C. Oswald. Saint Louis: Concordia Publishing House, 1972.

———. "Luther at the Diet of Worms, 1521." In *Luther's Works*. Vol. 32. Translated by Roger A. Hornsby. Edited by George W. Forell. Philadelphia: Muhlenberg Press, 1958.

———. "Ninety-Five Theses or Disputation on the Power and Efficacy of Indulgences." In *Luther's Works*. Vol. 31. Translated by C. M. Jacobs. Edited by Harold J. Grimm. Philadelphia: Muhlenberg Press, 1957.

———. "An Open Letter on the Harsh Book of Peasants." In *Luther's Works*. Vol. 46. Translated by Charles M. Jacobs. Edited by Robert C. Schultz. Philadelphia: Fortress Press, 1967.

———. "Selected Psalms II." In *Luther's Works*. Vol. 13. Translated by C. M. Jacobs. Edited by Jaroslav Pelikan. Saint Louis: Concordia Publishing House, 1956.

———. "Sermons on the Gospel of St. John." In *Luther's Works*. Vol. 23. Translated by Martin H. Bertram. Edited by Jaroslav Pelikan. Saint Louis: Concordia Publishing House, 1959.

———. "Table Talk." In *Luther's Works*. Vol. 54. Translated by Theodore G. Tappert. Edited by Theodore G. Tappert. Philadelphia: Fortress Press, 1967.

———. "Temporal Authority: To What Extent It Should Be Obeyed." In *Luther's Works*. Vol. 45. Translated by J. J. Schindel. Edited by Walther I. Brandt. Philadelphia: Muhlenberg Press, 1962.

———. "A Treatise on the New Testament, That Is, the Holy Mass, 1520." In *Luther's Works*. Vol. 35. Translated by Jeremiah J. Schindel. Edited by E. Theodore Bachmann. Philadelphia: Muhlenberg, 1960.

———. "To the Christian Nobility of the German Nation Concerning the Reform of the Christian Estate." In *Luther's Works*. Vol. 44. Translated by Charles M. Jacobs. Edited by James Atkinson. Philadelphia: Fortress Press, 1966.

———. "Why the Books of the Pope and His Disciples Were Burned by Doctor Martin Luther." *Luther's Works*. Vol. 31. Translated by Lewis W. Spitz. Edited by Harold J. Grimm. Philadelphia: Muhlenberg, 1957.

Lwin, Ei Ei Toe. "NLD Considers Religious Harmony Law." *Myanmar Times*, May 20, 2016.

Lwin, Si Thu. "Interfaith Forum Denounces Violence." Translated by Kyaw Soe Htet. *Myanmar Times*, March 24, 2017.

Lwin, Thein Ko. "Inching toward Peace: State Counselor Calls for Peace Conference within Two Months." *New Light of Myanmar*, April 28, 2016.

———. "Religious Data from 2014 Census Released." *New Light of Myanmar*, July 22, 2016.

Mandela, Nelson. *Long Walk to Freedom: The Autobiography of Nelson Mandela*. New York: Little, Brown and Company, 1994.

Mang, Pum Za. "Separation of Church and State: A Case Study of Myanmar (Burma)." *Asia Journal of Theology* 25 (April 2011): 42–58.

Mang, Lun Min, and Ei Ei Toe Lwin. "Speech Highlights from Panglong Conference Opening Ceremony." *Myanmar Times*, September 1, 2016.

Mann, Judy. "Torturing Girls Is Not a Cultural Right." *Washington Post*, February 23, 1994.

Mann, Zarni. "Thousands Gather for Interfaith Rallies." *Irrawaddy*, October 11, 2017.

Mason, Francis. *Burmah, Its People and Natural Productions*. London: Trubner, 1860.

Maung, Maung. *Aung San of Burma*. The Hague: Martinus Nyhoff, Southeast Asia Studies, Yale University, 1962.

McCarthy, Stephen. "Overturning the Alms Bowl: The Price of Survival and the Consequences for Political Legitimacy in Burma." *Australian Journal of International Affairs* 62, no.3 (September 2008): 298–314.

McLeish, Alexander. *Christian Progress in Burma*. London: World Dominion Press, 1929.

Milbrandt, Jay. "Tracking Genocide: Persecution of the Karen in Burma." *Texas International Law Journal* 48, no. 1(September 2012): 63–101.

Min, Zaw. "Interfaith Friendship and Unity Group (Myanmar) and Religions for Peace—Myanmar Sign MOU." *New Light of Myanmar*, April 3, 2019.

Ministry of Foreign Affairs. "Religious Tolerance Recognized Hallmark of Myanmar Society." *New Light of Myanmar*, August 4, 2000.

Ministry of Information. Constitution of the Republic of the Union of Myanmar, 2008. Yangon: Ministry of Information, 2008.

Ministry of Religious Affairs. March 12, 2018.

Ministry of Religious Affairs. "Invitation to Submit Suggestions from the Public in Relation to the Draft Law on Religious Conversion." *New Light of Myanmar*, May 27, 2014.

Mitchell, John Murray. *Hinduism Past and Present: With an Account of Recent Hindu Reformers and a Brief Comparison between Hinduism and Christianity.* London: The Religious Tract Society, 1897.

Mizzima News. "Mon Unity Party Allowed to Be Registered as Official Political Party." July 15, 2019.

Moe, Kyaw Zwa. "What Another NLD Victory Means for Myanmar and the World." *Irrawaddy*, November 23, 2020.

Moe, Wai. "Aung San Suu Kyi's Security." *Irrawaddy*, December 23, 2004.

Moe, Wai, and Austin Ramzy. "Myanmar Sentences 3 to Prison for Depicting Buddha Wearing Headphones." *New York Times*, March 17, 2015.

Mon, Swe Lei. "New Kachin Party to Meet Public for First Time." *Myanmar Times*, July 26, 2019.

Mon, Ye. "Minister Promises Christians Removal of Dream-Inspired Stupa." *Myanmar Times*, September 8, 2015.

Montague, Zach. "Holding It Aloft, He Incited a Backlash. What Does the Bible Mean to Trump?" *New York Times*, June 2, 2020.

Morning Star News. "Christians in Burma Patiently Endure Building of Pagodas on Church Lands." May 3, 2016.

Muntzer, Thomas. "Sermon before the Princes." In *Spiritual and Anabaptist Writers.* Vol. 25. Edited by George Huntston Williams and Angel M. Mergal. Louisville, KY: Westminster John Knox Press, 1957.

Myanmar Catholic Dioceses. "A Brief History of Catholic Church in Myanmar." https//www. catholicchurchmyanmar.wordpress.com (accessed January 12, 2023).

Myanmar Council of Churches and the Catholic Bishops Conference Myanmar. April 17, 2020.

Myanmar Institute of Theology. *Student Handbook*, 2020.

Myanmar News Agency. "Clarification on Myanmar's Situation to UNSG's Special Envoy Mr. Ibrahim Agboola Gambari." *New Light of Myanmar*, November 7, 2007.

———. "Daw Suu Kyi Speaks on Unity: Virtuous Leaders Serve Public Interests with Genuine Affection: Chairman Bhamo Sayadaw." *New Light of Myanmar*, May 14, 2016.

———. "So-Called '88' Generation Student Group Agitating to Undermine Stability and Security of the State." *New Light of Myanmar*, August 25, 2007.

———. "So-Called '88' Generation Students and NLD Released Announcement the Protest was a Non-Violent One." *New Light of Myanmar*, September 7, 2007

———. "State Counsellor Daw Aung San Suu Kyi's Speech on the 2nd Anniversary of NLD Government." *New Light of Myanmar*, April 2, 2018.

———. "10 Muslims Killed in Bus Attack." *New Light of Myanmar*, June 5, 2012.

222 Bibliography

Myanmar Times. "Ceasefire Anniversary Prompts Calls for More Signatories." October 17, 2016.

Myint-U, Thant. *The Hidden History of Burma: Race, Capitalism, and the Crisis of Democracy in the 21st Century.* New York: W.W. Norton, 2020.

———. *The Making of Modern Burma.* Cambridge: Cambridge University Press, 2001.

———. *The River of Lost Footsteps: A Personal History of Burma.* New York: Farrar, Straus and Giroux, 2006.

Myint, Ni Ni. *Burma's Struggle against British Imperialism, 1885–1895.* Rangoon: The Universities Press, 1983.

Nachemson, Andrew. "Myanmar's Aggressive Nationalism in the Air Ahead of 2020 Elections." *Diplomat,* February 21, 2020.

Nagourney, Adam. "Watch 4 Key Moments from Trump at the First 2020 Debate." *New York Times,* September 30, 2020.

Nang, Saw. "Myanmar Gives Tourist Who Pulled Plug on Buddhist Chants 3 Months in Prison." *New York Times,* October 6, 2016.

Nation, Mark Thiessen, Anthony G. Siegrist, Daniel P. Umbel. *Bonhoeffer the Assassin? Challenging the Myth, Recovering His Call to Peacemaking.* Grand Rapids, MI: Baker Academic, 2013.

New Encyclopaedia Britannica. s.v. "History of Myanmar." 15th ed. (1993).

New Light of Myanmar. "No Rohingya Race in Myanmar, Says Deputy Minister." February 21, 2013.

———. "Only if Our Country Is at Peace Will We Be Able to Stand on an Equal Footing with Other Countries in Our Region and across the World." September 1, 2016.

Newman, Saul. *Political Theology: A Critical Introduction.* Cambridge, UK: Polity Press, 2019.

Nhat Hanh, Thich. *Going Home: Jesus and Buddha as Brothers.* New York: Berkeley, 1999.

———. *Living Buddha, Living Christ.* New York: Riverhead Books, 1995.

———. *The Miracle of Mindfulness: A Manual on Meditation.* Translated by Mobi Ho. Boston: Beacon Press, 1987.

———. *The Sutra on the Eight Realizations of the Great Beings.* Translated by Diem Thanh Truong and Carole Melkonian. Berkeley, CA: Parallax Press, 1987.

———. *Vietnam: Lotus in a Sea of Fire.* New York: Hill and Wang, 1967.

Niebuhr, Reinhold. *The Nature and Destiny of Man.* New York: Charles Scribner's Sons, 1943.

———. *Why the Christian Church Is Not Pacifist.* London: Student Christian Movement Press, 1940.

Nyein, Nyein. "NLD Reaches Out to Myanmar's Ethnic Parties Seeking Federal Union and End to Civil War." *Irrawaddy,* November 13, 2020.

Oo, Zaw Naing. "Arrest Warrant Issued for Myanmar Hardline Monk Wirathu." *Reuters,* May 29, 2019.

Oxford Dictionary of the Christian Church. s.v. "Zwingli, Ulrich." 3rd edition (2005).

Bibliography

Pahl, Jon. *Empire of Sacrifice: The Religious Origins of American Violence*. New York: New York University Press, 2010.

Paing, Tin Htet. "Nationalists Oppose NGO's Curriculum for Including Religious Education." *Irrawaddy*, March 7, 2017.

Pennington, Matthew. "Obama Orders U.S. Economic Sanctions on Myanmar Lifted." *Washington Post*, October 7, 2016.

Pipkin, H. Wayne. "Blaurock, George." In *The Oxford Encyclopedia of the Reformation*. Vol. 1. Edited by Hans J. Hillerbrand. New York: Oxford University Press, 1996.

Plate, Tom, and Jeffrey Cole. "Tom Plate and Jeffrey Cole Interview Lee Kuan Yew." *Asia Media*, UCLA Asia Institute, October 9, 2007.

Po, San C. *Burma and the Karens*. Bangkok: White Lotus, 2001.

Popham, Peter. "As Aung San Suu Kyi's Biographer, I Have to Say That the Only Good Thing She Can Do Now Is Resign." *Independent*, December 7, 2017.

———. "They Were Screaming: Die, die, die! The Dramatic Inside Story of Aung San Suu Kyi's Darkest Hour." *Independent*, October 16, 2011.

Price, James L. Jr. "Nicolaitans." *The HarperCollins Bible Dictionary*. Edited by Mark Allen Powell. New York: HarperCollins Publishers, 2011.

Pwint, Nan Lwin Hnin. "Myanmar Military, AA Swap Blame for Civilian Deaths in Chin State." *Irrawaddy*, January 14, 2020.

Queen, Christopher. "From Altruism to Activism." In *Action Dharma: New Studies in Engaged Buddhism*. Edited by Christopher Queen. Hoboken, NJ: Taylor and Francis, 2013.

Radio Free Asia. "Myanmar's Election Commission Approves 88 Generation Group's Bid to Form Political Party." August 24, 2018, https://www.rfa.org/english/news/myanmar/myanmars-election-commission-approves-88-generation-groups-bid-08242018161039.html.

Rahula, Walpola. *What the Buddha Taught*. Bedford, UK: Gordon Fraser, 1959.

Rajashekar, J. Paul William. "Faith Active in Love and Truth Realized in Love: A Comparative Study of the Ethics of Martin Luther and Mahatma Gandhi." PhD thesis, The Graduate College of the University of Iowa, July 1981.

Rasmussen, Larry L. *Dietrich Bonhoeffer: Reality and Resistance*. Louisville, KY: Westminster John Knox Press, 2005.

Regional Interfaith Network. "Seeking Peace for Myanmar along Interfaith Lines." *Regional Interfaith Dialogue, Connecting and Cooperating for Peace and Harmony in the Asia-Pacific Region*, August 11, 2014.

Religions for Peace. "Religions for Peace Second Advisory Forum in Myanmar Focuses on Religion in Nation-Building." May 7–8, 2019. https://www.rfp.org/religions-for-peace-convenes-second-advisory-forum-in-myanmar-focuses-on-religion-in-nation-building/.

The Republic of The Union of Myanmar. "President Signs State Counselor Bill into Law." April 6, 2016.

Reuters. "Rumsfeld Praises Army General Who Ridicules Islam as Satan." *New York Times*, October 17, 2003.

Riot Inquiry Committee. *Final Report*. Rangoon: Govt. Printing and Stationery, 1939.

Robertson, Campbell, Christopher Mele, and Sabrina Tavernise. "11 Killed in Synagogue Massacre; Suspect Charged with 29 Counts." *New York Times*, October 27, 2018.

Rogers, Benedict. *Burma: A Nation at the Crossroads*. London: Rider Books, 2012.

Rogers, Katie, and Nicholas Fandos. "Trump Tells Congresswomen to Go Back to the Countries They Came From." *New York Times*, July 14, 2019.

Roughneen, Simon. "Suu Kyi Says I Will Be Above the President." *Nikkei Asia*, November 5, 2015.

Saffin, Janelle. *Seeking Constitutional Settlement in Myanmar, Constitutionalism and Legal Change in Myanmar*. Edited by Andrew Harding. Oxford: Hart Publishing, 2017.

Sahayadoss, Santhosh J. *Martin Luther on Social and Political Issues: His Relevance for Church and Society in India*. Frankfurt: Peter Lang, 2006.

Sakhong, Lian H. *In Defense of Identity: The Ethnic Nationalities' Struggle for Democracy, Human Rights, and Federalism in Burma*. Bangkok: Orchid Press, 2010.

Sanger, David E. "With Echoes of the 30's, Trump Resurrects a Hard-Line Vision of America First." *New York Times*, January 20, 2017.

Saw, Khin Maung. "Islamization of Burma through Chittagonian Bengalis as Rohingya Refugees." Burma Library, September 20011. https://www.burmalibrary .org/docs21/Khin-Maung-Saw-NM-2011-09-Islamanisation_of_Burma_through _Chittagonian_Bengalis-en.pdf.

Say Pa, Anna May. "A Place at the Round Table: Equipping Burmese Women for Leadership." *MIT Journal of Theology* 5 (January 2004): 7–26.

Schlingensiepen, Ferdinand. *Dietrich Bonhoeffer: Martyr, Thinker, Man of Resistance*. New York: T & T Clark, 2010.

Schober, Juliane. "Buddhist Visions of Moral Authority and Modernity in Burma." In *Burma at the Turn of the 21st Century*. Edited by Monique Skidmore. Honolulu: University of Hawaii Press, 2005.

———. *Modern Buddhist Conjunctures in Myanmar: Cultural Narratives, Colonial Legacies, and Civil Society*. Honolulu: University of Hawai'i Press, 2011.

Schonthal, Benjamin, and Matthew J. Walton. "The New Buddhist Nationalisms? Symmetries and Specificities in Sri Lanka and Myanmar." *Contemporary Buddhism* 17, no. 1 (April 2016): 81–115.

Silverstein, Josef. *Burma: Military Rule and the Politics of Stagnation*. Ithica, NY: Cornell University Press, 1977.

———. *The Political Legacy of Aung San*. Ithaca, NY: Southeast Asia Program, Cornell University, 1993.

Smeaton, Donald Mackenzie. *The Loyal Karens of Burma*. London: Kegan Paul, Trench & Co., 1887.

Smith, Donald Eugene. "India as a Secular State." In *Secularism and Its Critics: Themes in Politics*. Edited by Rajeev Bhargava. Oxford: Oxford University Press, 1998.

———. *Religion and Politics in Burma*. Princeton, NJ: Princeton University Press, 1965.

Bibliography

Smith, Martin. *Burma: Insurgency and the Politics of Ethnicity.* London: Zeds Books Ltd, 1991.

Snyder, C. Arnold. "Swiss Anabaptism: The Beginnings, 1523–1525." In *A Companion to Anabaptism and Spiritualism, 1521–1700.* Edited by John D. Roth and James M. Stayer. Leiden: Boston, Brill, 2007.

Soe, Myo Min. "Myanmar's Ultranationalist Monk U Wirathu Turns Himself in after a Year in Hiding." *Irrawaddy*, November 2, 2020.

Soe, Zar Zar. "President U Htin Kyaw's Inaugural Address." *Myanmar Times*, March 31, 2016.

Spiro, Melford E. *Buddhism and Society: A Great Tradition and Its Burmese Vicissitudes.* Berkeley: University of California Press, 1982.

State Peace and Development Council. "Myanmar Ratifies and Promulgates Constitution." *New Light of Myanmar*, May 30, 2008.

Steinberg, David I. *Burma: The State of Myanmar.* Washington, DC: Georgetown University Press, 2001.

Stetzer, Ed, and Andrew Macdonald. "The Bible Is Not a Prop: In Fact, We Need It Right Now." *Christianity Today*, June 2, 2020.

Stevens, Matt. "White Nationalists Reappear in Charlottesville in Torch-Lit Protest." *New York Times*, October 8, 2017.

Stoakes, Emanuel. "New Zealand Mosque Attack Victims Confront Gunman in Courtroom." *Washington Post*, August 24, 2020.

Straits Times. "A Monk Gagged, but Can Hate Be Silenced?: The Nation." March 14, 2017.

Strong, John S. *The Legend of King Asoka: A Study and Translation of the Asokavadana.* Princeton, NJ: Princeton University Press, 1983.

Stumme, John R. "A Lutheran Tradition on Church and State." In *Church and State: Lutheran Perspectives.* Edited by John R. Stumme and Robert W. Tuttle. Minneapolis: Fortress Press, 2003.

Sugirtharajah, R.S. *The Bible and Asia: From the Pre-Christian Era to the Postcolonial Age.* Cambridge, MA: Harvard University Press, 2013.

Suu Kyi, Aung San. *Aung San of Burma: A Biographical Portrait by His Daughter.* Edinburgh: Kiscadale, 1991.

———. *Freedom from Fear and Other Writings.* New York: Penguin Books, 1995.

———. *Letters from Burma: With a New Introduction by Fergal Keane.* London: Penguin Books, 2010.

———. *The Voice of Hope: Conversations with Alan Clements.* New York: Seven Stories Press, 2008.

Svendsbye, Lloyd. "The History of a Developing Social Responsibility among Lutherans in America from 1930 to 1960, with Reference to the American Lutheran Church, the Augustana Lutheran Church, the Evangelical Lutheran Church, and the United Lutheran Church in America." ThD diss., Union Theological Seminary, New York, 1967.

Swancara, Frank. *The Separation of Religion and Government: The First Amendment, Madison's Intent, and the McCollum Decision: A Study of Separatism in America.* New York: Truth Seeker Company, 1950.

Tanzeem, Ayesha. "Pakistani Scholar Sentenced to Death for Blasphemy." *Voice of America*, December 21, 2019.

Tegenfeldt, Herman G. *Through Deep Waters*. Valley Forge, PA: Foreign Mission Society, 1968.

Tha, Kyaw Phyo, and San Yamin Aung. "State-Backed Monks' Council Decries Ma Ba Tha as Unlawful." *Irrawaddy*, July 13, 2016.

Thar, Nay. "Why Aung San Suu Kyi Did Not Sign the NCA." *Mizzima News*, December 8, 2015.

Thwe, Francis Khoo. "Archbishop of Yangon to Religious Leaders: Build Together a Myanmar of Peace and Justice." *Asia News*, October 3, 2013.

Tierney, Brian. *The Crisis of Church & State, 1050–1300: With Selected Documents*. Englewood Cliffs, NJ: Prentice-Hall, 1964.

Tinker, Hugh. *Burma: The Struggle for Independence, 1944–1948, Vol. 1, 1 January 1944 to 31 August 1946*. London: Her Majesty's Stationery Office, 1983.

Topich, William J., and Keith A. Leitich. *The History of Myanmar*. Santa Barbara, CA: Greenwood, 2013.

Trager, Frank N. "The Failure of U Nu and the Return of the Armed Forces in Burma." *Review Politics* 25, no. 3 (July 1963): 309–28.

Trager, Helen G. *Burma through Alien Eyes: Missionary Views of the Burmese in the Nineteen Century*. London: Asia Publishing House, 1966.

United Nations. Universal Declaration of Human Rights. Office of the High Commissioner, 1948. https://www.ohchr.org/en/universal-declaration-of-human -rights.

United States Commission on International Religious Freedom, *Annual Report 2021*. Washington, DC: USCIRF, 2021. https://www.uscirf.gov/publication/2021 -annual-report.

United States Senate. *Treaty of Peace with Germany*. Washington: Government Printing Office, 1919.

von der Mehden, Fred R. *Religion and Nationalism in Southeast Asia: Burma, Indonesia, The Philippines*. Madison: University of Wisconsin Press, 1968.

Wa, Maung Shwe. *Burma Baptist Chronicle*. Rangoon: Burma Baptist Convention, 1963.

Wald, Kenneth D., and Allison Calhoun-Brown. *Religion and Politics in the United States*, 7th ed. Lanham, MD: Rowman & Littlefield, 2014.

Walker, Tommy. "How Myanmar's Civil Disobedience Movement Is Pushing Back against the Coup." *Voice of America*, February 27, 2021.

Walton, Matthew J., and Susan Hayward. *Contesting Buddhist Narratives: Democratization, Nationalism, and Communal Violence in Myanmar*. Honolulu: East-West Center, 2014.

Wangila, Mary Nyangweso. *Female Circumcision: The Interplay of Religion, Culture, and Gender in Kenya*. Maryknoll, NY: Orbis Books, 2007.

Warren, Steve. "Pastor Murdered by Soldiers while Trying to Save Burning Home in Myanmar." CBN News, September 22, 2021.

Wayland, Francis. *A Memoir of the Life and Labors of the Rev. Adoniram Judson*. Vol. I. Boston: Phillips, Sampson, and Company, 1853.

Bibliography

Webb, Willis S. *Incidents and Trials in the Life of Rev. Eugenia Kincaid: The Hero Missionary to Burma, 1830–1863.* Fort Scott, KS: Monitor Publishing House and Book Bindery, 1890.

Weng, Lawi. "Thein Sein Says a Healthy Constitution Must be Amended." *Irrawaddy*, January 2, 2014.

Whitford, David M. *"Cura Religionis* or Two Kingdoms: The Late Luther on Religion and the State in the Lectures on Genesis." *American Society of Church History* 73, no. 1 (March 2004): 41–62.

William, Reggie L. *Bonhoeffer's Black Jesus: Harlem Resistance Theology and an Ethic of Resistance.* Waco, TX: Baylor University Press, 2014.

Win, Kanbawza. "Are Christians Persecuted in Burma?" *Asia Journal of Theology* 14, no. 1 (April 2000): 170–75.

———. "Colonialism, Nationalism and Christianity in Burma: A Burmese Perspective." *Asia Journal of Theology* 2, no. 2 (October 1988): 270–81.

Win, Pyae Sone. "Canadian Pastor Guilty of Defying Myanmar's Coronavirus Law." *Washington Post*, August 6, 2020.

Wink, Walter. *Jesus and Nonviolence: A Third Way.* Minneapolis: Fortress Press, 2003.

Wintle, Justin. *Perfect Hostage: A Life of Aung San Suu Kyi, Burma's Prisoner of Conscience.* New York: Skyhorse Publishing, 2007.

World Council of Churches. "Myanmar: Raiser Points Out Discrimination against Christian Minorities, Affirms Role of Interfaith Dialogue." WCC News, March 7, 2003. https://www.oikoumene.org/news/myanmar-raiser-points-out-discrimination -against-christian-minorities-affirms-role-of-interfaith-dialogue.

World Health Organization et al. *Eliminating Female Genital Mutilation: The Imperative.* Geneva: World Health Organization, 2008.

Wyatt, Edward. "Lieberman Heckled During Speech to Arab-American Group." *New York Times*, October 18, 2003.

Xinhua. "Myanmar Islamic Organization Condemns Extremist Terror attacks in Northern State." September 11, 2017.

Yegar, Moshe. *The Muslims of Burma: A Study of a Minority Group.* Wiesbaden: Otto Harrassowitz, 1972.

Zaw, Aung. "Burmese Monks in Revolt." *Irrawaddy*, September 11, 2007.

———. *The Face of Resistance: Aung San Suu Kyi and Burma's Fight for Freedom.* Chiang Mai, Thailand: Mekong Press, 2013.

———. "The Power Behind the Robe." *Irrawaddy*, September 12, 2017.

Zaw, Htet Naing. "Police: Loudspeakers Require Permission." *Irrawaddy*, October 4, 2016.

Zwingli, Huldrych. "Divine and Human Righteousness." In *Selected Writings of Huldrych Zwingli.* Vol. 2. Translated by H. Wayne Pipkin. Allison Park, PA: Pickwick Publications, 1984.

Zwingli, Ulrich. *Zwingli and Bullinger.* Vol. XXIV. Translated by G. W. Bromiley. Philadelphia: Westminster Press, 1953.

Index

AA. *See* Arakan Army
Abhiraja (Prince), 10, 50n20
Abingdon School District v. Schempp, 161
ABMA. *See* All Burma Monks' Alliance
The Abode of a Nat (Maung Htin Baw), 42, 56n153
Abwer, 106–7, 108, 113n110
Abyssinian Baptist Church, 95
Admonition to Peace (Luther), 70–71
Against the Robbing and Murdering Hordes of Peasants (Luther), 71–72
Alahaj Mofti Mohamad, 135–36
Albrecht of Brandenburg, 60
Alias Maung Sin, 56n154
All-Burma Congress of AFPFL, 14, 189
All-Burma Council of Young Monks Association, 42
All Burma Monks' Alliance (ABMA), 130
Allen, O. Wesley, Jr., 194n99
All Myanmar Islamic Religious Organization (AMIRO), 47
Althaus, Paul, 63, 97–98
Altmann, Walter, 72
America First, 175
American Baptist Missionary Union, 159

American Baptists, 9, 11–12, 23, 31–32, 160–61
American exceptionalism, 161
AMIRO. *See* All Myanmar Islamic Religious Organization
Anabaptism: branches of, 83n80; on circumcision, 75, 82n76; in Germany, 75–76; Hutterian Brethren in, 75, 83n80; on infant baptism, 74–75; Luther critique of, 74–79; Myanmar Baptists and, 166; *Schleitheim Articles* in, 75–76; as seditious, 79; Swiss, 74–75
Anawrahta (King), 8, 9–10, 11
Andrews, Tom, 149
Annan, Kofi, 44, 46
Appold, Kenneth, 61
Arakan Army (AA), 53n87
Arakan Rohingya Salvation Army (ARSA), 1–2, 44–45, 46–47, 139
Aris, 8, 9
ARSA. *See* Arakan Rohingya Salvation Army
"Aryan Paragraph," 89, 91–92, 109n21
Ar Yone Oo, 134–35
ASEAN. *See* Association of Southeast Asian Nations
Ashin Issariya, 135
Ashin Sandartika, 186

230 *Index*

Asoka (Emperor), 7
Association for the Protection of Race and Religion. *See* Ma Ba Tha
Association of Southeast Asian Nations (ASEAN), 146, 148
Attlee, Clement, 14
Augustine, 5n2, 63
Aung Gyi, 30
Aung Ko, 39
Aung Min, 24
Aung San, 12–13, 167; assassination of, 16–17; at Constituent Assembly (1947), 15–16; "Defense of Burma, January 30, 1945" by, 14; against discrimination, 14; on ethnic minorities, 14; at Executive Council meeting (1947), 16; inaugural address by, 189; inclusive nationalism of, 179–80; on racism, 15; Radio Address by, 15; U Saw against, 16–17, 52n63; secular nationalism of, 15
U Aung Than, 14
Aung Win Khaing, 43–44
Aung Win Zaw, 43–44
Aung Zaw, 124, 129–30
Aung Zeyya, 10–11, 51n26
U Aye Lwin, Al Haj, 48–49, 135, 179

The Babylonian Captivity of the Church (Luther), 65
Bagyidaw (King), 24–25
Band of German Maidens, 87
Ban Ki-Moon, 18
U Ba Pe, 14
baptism: adult, 75–77, 83n79; circumcision and, 75, 82n76; infant, 74–75, 76, 77–78; as inward transformation of outward expression, 76; orders of, 76. *See also* Anabaptism
Baptists, 4, 23–24, 29, 32. *See also* American Baptists; Myanmar Baptists
Barmen Confession of Faith, 89–90

Barth, Karl, 89–90
"Basic Questions of a Christian Ethics" (Bonhoeffer, D.), 104
U Ba Yin, 14
Beikthano, 8, 10
Bell, George Kennedy Allen, 105, 106, 107, 112n100
Bengali Muslims, 2
Ben-Menashe, Ari, 145
Bergendoff, Conrad, 162
Bethge, Eberhard, 103–4, 113n113
Bhaddanta Iddhibala, 135
Bhamo Sayadaw Bhaddanta Kumarabhivamsa, 134
Biden, Joseph R., 176
Bigandet, Paul Ambrose, 12, 178
Blackwood, Philip, 39
Blair, Tony, 172–73
Blaurock, George, 75, 83n79
Bo, Charles Maung, 133, 135, 172, 193n78, 203
Board of Censorship, 34
Bonfer, Peter, 11
Bonhoeffer, Dietrich, 3, 85; in *Abwer*, 106–7, 108; Abyssinian Baptist Church influencing, 95; in America, 95–96, 100, 111n73; arrest of, 113n110, 113n113; "Basic Questions of a Christian Ethics," 104; childhood of, 96; "Christ and Peace" by, 105; "Christology" by, 93–94; "The Church and the Jewish Question" by, 91–92, 98; on compulsory military service, 106; Confessing Church critiqued by, 99; conspiracy activities of, 96, 103, 107–8, 113n109, 113n113; *The Cost of Discipleship* by, 106; on discipleship, 99–100; on ethical principles, 101–2; at Friedrich Wilhelm University, 87; "The Fuhrer and the Individual in the Younger Generation" by, 96–97; Gandhi and, 105, 112n100; on grace, 99–100; against Hitler, 89;

Index

imprisonment of, 112n75; Luther's Two Kingdoms Theology received by, 90–95; on mandates, 90–91, 98; military training of, 104; "The Nature of the Church" by, 92–93; on order, estate, office, 91, 109n27; as pacifist, 103–5; political resistance of, 95–108; *Sanctorum Communio* by, 102–3; on Sermon on the Mount, 104; on *Stellvertretung*, 102; "The Theological Foundation of the Work of the World Alliance" by, 105; "Thy Kingdom Come" by, 91, 101; on unity of church and state, 94–95; "What is the Church?" by, 98; on WWI, 96

Bonhoeffer, Paula, 96
Bonhoeffer, Walter, 96
Boniface VIII (Pope), 59
Bonvillain, Nancy, 174
Border Guard Police, 1–2, 44–45
Bowers, Robert D., 168
Bowh Si, Oliver Byar, 166
Boykin, William, 181–82
de Britto, Philip, 22
"Brown Synod," 89, 109n20
Budde, Mariann, 171
Buddha Dhamma Parahita Foundation, 134
Buddha Sasana Council, 31
Buddha with headphones, 39
Buddhism, 3–4; Five Precepts of, 27; from India, 7–9; missionaries for, 7–8; Muslims and, 42–49; in Myanmar, 7–8; Sabbath in, 31; sermons broadcast for, 31, 40; as state religion, 28–30, 187. *See also* Burman Buddhists; engaged Buddhism; Ma Ba Tha; Mahayana Buddhists; Theravada Buddhism
Bund Deutscher Madel. See Band of German Maidens
Burgener, Christine S., 148, 149, 150
Burma Act of 1935, 13, 51n46
Burman Buddhists, 4–5, 9, 12, 21, 119

Burmanization, 12, 36, 166, 191n47
Burmans, 7, 8, 13; Mon influence on, 9–10; women, 9, 50n14
"Burma Proper," 13, 51n39
Burmese Baptist Convention, 29
Burmese Broadcasting Service, 31
Bush, George W., 171

Cady, John F., 47
Camus, Renaud, 192n53
Carson, Laura, 176
caste system, 8–9
Catholic Bishops Conference Myanmar, 172, 193n78
CDM. *See* Civil Disobedience Movement
Center for Diversity and National Harmony (CDNH), 133–34
Chan Htun, 17
Charles V (Emperor), 62, 68–69
Charlottesville, Virginia, 169
Chauvin, Derek, 192n68
Chin, 7, 12, 13, 29, 176
Chin Affairs Council, 29
"Chin Hills Regulation," 13
Chin Human Rights Organization, 35
Chin League for Democracy (CLD), 143
Chin National Democratic Party (CNDP), 143
Chin National League for Democracy (CNLD), 143, 180
Chin Progressive Party (CPP), 143
"Christ and Peace" (Bonhoeffer, D.), 105
Christchurch, New Zealand, 168–69
Christianity, 4; missions in Myanmar, 11–12, 22, 51n36; nationalization of, 31–32; Pali words prohibited for, 34, 41
Christian religious minorities: colonial rule and, 26–27; democratic government and, 28–31; military regime and, 33–37; monarchical period and, 21–26; NLD and, 37–41;

232 *Index*

persecution of, 21–41; socialist government and, 31–33

Christian Religious Organizations, 41, 56n152

Christians, 2–3, 5n2; double persecution of, 165–66; fight or flight by, 53n77

"Christology" (Bonhoeffer, D.), 93–94

"The Church and the Jewish Question" (Bonhoeffer, D.), 91–92, 98

circumcision, 75, 82n76

Civil Disobedience Movement (CDM), 144–45, 146, 149

Clarke, John, 160

CLD. *See* Chin League for Democracy

Clements, Alan, 120

CNDP. *See* Chin National Democratic Party

CNLD. *See* Chin National League for Democracy

Cochrane, Henry Park, 9, 176, 182, 183–84

Cockett, Richard, 178

Colman, James, 24

Committee Representing Pyidaungsu Hluttaw (CRPH), 145

Communism, 86

Concerning Rebaptism (Luther), 76

Confessing Church, 89, 99, 106, 107

Cook, Alistair D. B., 45

Cortright, David, 20

The Cost of Discipleship (Bonhoeffer, D.), 106

COVID-19 pandemic, 144, 146–47, 171–72, 193n76

CPP. *See* Chin Progressive Party

CRPH. *See* Committee Representing Pyidaungsu Hluttaw

Crystal Night, 88

Cung Biak Hum, 148–49, 158n156

Curry, Michael, 171

Cyprian of Carthage, 111n67

Danbury Baptist Association, 160

Daragmin, Wasseim Sati Ali, 169

"Defense of Burma, January 30, 1945" (Aung San), 14

DeJonge, Michael, 102

Depayin massacre, 120–21, 151nn25–26

U Dhammapiya, 133

Dharmapala, Angarika, 184–85

Dickens and Madson, 145

Diet of Worms (1521), 68–69

Dingrin, La Seng, 187

"Divine and Human Righteousness" (Zwingli), 74

Dodge, Nehemiah, 160

Dohnanyi, Hans von, 106, 113n110

Dorkenoo, Efua, 173

Duwa Lashi La, 148

Edict of Worms, 62

88-Generation Students Group, 129, 131, 143, 153n71

8888 Uprising. *See* Four Eights Uprising

ELCA. *See* Evangelical Lutheran Church in America

Eliot, Charles, 8

engaged Buddhism, 3; during 1988 uprising in Myanmar, 121–26; definition of, 115; during Four Eights Uprising in Myanmar, 121–26; *metta* in, 119, 135; Myanmar, British colonialism and, 118–19; in Myanmar society, 132–37; Nhat Hanh on, 116; U Ottama in, 118; practices of, 119; ten duties in, 115–16, 150n2; in Vietnam, 116–17. *See also* Hanh, Thich Nhat; Suu Kyi, Aung San

Engel v. Vitale, 161, 190n17

ethnic minority groups: conversion of, 12, 51n36; ethnic majority conflicts with, 12–21; grievances aired by, 18–19; merging parties of, 142–43; in Myanmar, 1–2, 12–13; Myanmar military against, 13; for NLD, 18; rights for, 14

Evangelical Lutheran Church in America (ELCA): five vital themes of, 163–64; on separatism, 162–64
Everson v. Board of Education, 159
Exsurge Domine, 65
Ezat, Janna, 169

female genital mutilation (FGM), 173–74, 193n87
First Amendment (US), 159–61
Fisher, Albert, 95
Floyd, George, 170–71, 192n68
Forell, George W., 162
Four Eights Uprising, 152n40; civilians killed in, 124; early origins of, 122; engaged Buddhism during, 121–26; outsiders unaware of, 125–26; Red Bridge Incident in, 122, 151n33; Saffron Revolution and, 131–32; students killed in, 122–23, 151n33; Suu Kyi on, 123
Frederick the Wise, 61–62
The Freedom of a Christian (Luther), 65
Frum, David, 171
Fugger family, 60
"The Fuhrer and the Individual in the Younger Generation" (Bonhoeffer, D.), 96–97
Fytche, Albert, 26

Gandhi (Mahatma), 105, 112n100, 184
Germany, 2–3; Anabaptism in, 75–76; "Brown Synod" in, 89, 109n20; compulsory military service in, 106; Peasants' War of 1524–1525 in, 69–73; Treaty of Versailles impacting, 85–86; xenophobic nationalism in, 85–86. *See also* Bonhoeffer, Dietrich; Hitler, Adolf; Luther, Martin; Nazi regime
Great Minster Church, 74
"The Great Replacement," 168, 192n53
Grebel, Conrad, 74–75, 83n79
Green, Clifford, 90
Gregory, Wilton D., 170–71

Hafeez, Junaid, 170
Haijtema, Klaas, 40
Hanh, Thich Nhat, 3; on compassion, 117–18, 150n10; on engaged Buddhism, 116; as mediator, 117; *The Miracle of Mindfulness* by, 117; in United States and Europe, 116; on Vietnam war, 116–17
Hanthar Myint, 136
Harakat al-Yaqin. *See* Arakan Rohingya Salvation Army
Hardy, Robert Spence, 185
Harlem Resistance, 95
Hassan Shah, 56n154
Hebrew Immigrant Aid Society (HIAS), 168, 192n51
Heckel, Theodor, 107
Hess, Johann, 78
HIAS. *See* Hebrew Immigrant Aid Society
Hindenburg, Paul von, 86
Hinduism, 4; in anti-Muslim riots, 42; caste system of, 8–9; in Myanmar, 7, 10–11
Hindu Religious Organizations, 41, 56n152
Hitler, Adolf: antisemitic beliefs of, 87–88; assassination plot against, 107–8, 113n110, 113n113; Bonhoeffer, D., political resistance against, 95–108; against Communism, 86; discriminatory policies against Jews by, 87; on "the Jewish question," 88; restrictions imposed by, 86–87; on Treaty of Versailles, 86. *See also* Nazi regime
Hitler Youth (*Hitlerjugend*), 87
Howe, Geoffrey, 124
HRCP. *See* Human Rights Commission of Pakistan
Htet Lin, 141
Htin Kyaw, 138
Htut Ko Ko Lwin, 39
Hubmaier, Balthasar, 76

234 *Index*

Human Rights Commission of Pakistan (HRCP), 170
human sacrifices, 173, 193n86
Hurd, Elizabeth Shakman, 172–73
Husein, Fatimah, 48
Hutter, Jacob, 83n80
Hutterian Brethren, 75, 83n80

Identity Cards of National Verification (ICNV), 46
IGE. *See* Institute for Global Engagement
India: Buddhism from, 7–9; Hinduism from, 10–11; *sati* in, 173, 193n86
indulgences, 60–61
INGO. *See* International Non-Governmental Organization
Institute for Global Engagement (IGE), 133
Interfaith Academic Conference on Security, Peace, and Coexistence, 133–34
International Non-Governmental Organization (INGO), 44
Islam, 4, 11. *See also* Islamophobia; Muslims
Islamic Religious Organizations, 41, 56n152
Islamophobia, 2; inter-communal violence between Buddhists and Muslims in Rakhine State and, 42–49; roots of, 42

Jefferson, Thomas: letter to Baptists by, 160–61; on separation between church and state, 159–60
Jews, 3; boycotting of, 87; discriminatory policies against, 87; Hitler blaming, 86; violence against, 88; yellow star for, 87–88, 109n15
Jones, Robert, 168
JRC. *See* Judson Research Center
Judson, Adoniram, 11–12, 23–26, 182–83
Judson, Ann, 11, 23

Judson Research Center (JRC), 50n6

KACC. *See* Khumi Affairs Coordination Council
Kachin, 7, 12, 13, 29
Kachin Baptist Convention, 34
"Kachin Hill Tribes Regulation," 13
Kachin Independence Army (KIA), 30
Kachin State Democracy Party (KSDP), 143
Kachin State People's Party (KSPP), 143
Kadoe, Lily, 48
Kala, 178–79
Karen, 7, 12, 13
Karen National Democratic Party (KNDP), 142–43
Karlstadt, 62
Kayah, 7
Kayah State Democratic Party, 142
Khin Maung Saw, 45
Khin Nyunt, 36
Khumi Affairs Coordination Council (KACC), 53n87
KIA. *See* Kachin Independence Army
Kincaid, Eugenio, 183
King, Martin Luther, Jr., 180
King, Sallie B., 115
Kingston, Jeff, 131
KNDP. *See* Karen National Democratic Party
Ko Hla Myo Aung, 40
Ko Ko Gyi, 143
Ko Ni, 43–44, 141–42
Kristallnacht. See Crystal Night
KSDP. *See* Kachin State Democracy Party
KSPP. *See* Kachin State People's Party
Kyaw Kyaw Win, 45
Kyaw Moe, 41, 56n152
U Kyaw Nyein, 14
Kyaw Soe Aung, 134
Kyi Lin, 43–44

Lah, David, 171–72, 193n76

Index 235

Lasserre, Jean, 104, 106
Lee, Yanghee, 169
Lee Kuan Yew, 129, 153n70
Leitich, Keith A., 153n68
Lentin, Alana, 180
Leo X (Pope), 60, 65
"Letter from a Birmingham Jail" (King, M.), 180
Lian Luai, 188
Lieberman, Joseph, 182
Lindberg, Carter, 79
Ling, Samuel Ngun, 165–66, 186–87
Lintner, Bertil, 11, 124
Linwood Islamic Center, 168
Lobban, Daryl Paul, 171
Lotzer, Sebastian, 70, 81n52
Luther, Martin, 2–3, 5n2; *Admonition to Peace* by, 70–71; *Against the Robbing and Murdering Hordes of Peasants* by, 71–72; Anabaptism critiqued by, 74–79; *The Babylonian Captivity of the Church* by, 65; on Book of Romans, 63; *Concerning Rebaptism* by, 76; at Diet of Worms, 68–69; earlier treatises of, 59–60; excommunication of, 65; *Exsurge Domine* burned by, 65; *The Freedom of a Christian* by, 65; on Genesis, 78, 83n95; as heretic, 62; on indulgences, 61; on "inner man" and "outer man," 65, 118, 151n13; as necessary evil between princes and peasants, 69–73; *An Open Letter on the Harsh Book against the Peasants* by, 72–73; on princes and religious matters, 62–63; resistance of, 63–69; on seditious heretics, 79; on spiritual government, 63, 67; *Table Talk* by, 78, 109n27; *Temporal Authority* by, 66–68; on temporal government, 63, 67; on theodicy of God, 99, 111n66; *To the Christian Nobility of the German Nation Concerning the Reform of the Christian Estate* by, 63–64; *A Treatise on the New*

Testament by, 76–77. *See also* Theology of Two Kingdoms
Lutherans, contemporary, 2–3; on separationism, 162–64, 190n25. *See also* Evangelical Lutheran Church in America

Ma Ba Tha, 1–2, 5n1, 37, 43, 55n139, 134, 186; banning of, 134, 154n92; establishment of, 132; NLD against, 170
Maha Dhamma Raja (King), 22
Ma Ha Na. *See* State Sangha Maha Nayaka Committee
Mahayana Buddhists, 8, 28
"Make America Great Again" motto, 175, 194n99
Mandalay, 27
Mang, Pum Za, 166, 191n47
Manohari (King), 9
Mantegazza, Gaetano, 9
Mantz, Felix, 74–75
Marks, John Ebenezer, 25
Mason, Francis, 176–77
Maung Byay, 24
Maung Htin Aung, 8–9, 27, 182–83
Maung Htin Baw, 42, 56nn153–54
Maung Maung, 16, 124, 138
Maung Maung Nyein Tun, 147
Maung Naw, 23, 24
Maung Pan Nyo, 56n154
Maung Pye, 24
Maung Tha Hla, 24
Mburu, Rosemary, 174
McLeish, Alexander, 23
Melanchthon, Philip, 62
Menius, Justus, 78–79, 84n102
metta, 119, 135
Metta Sutta, 130
MICC. *See* Myanmar International Convention Center
Mi Hkin-gyi, 50n14
military regime, 3, 18–19; Christian religious minorities and, 33–37; socialism and, 31–32

236   *Index*

Min Aung Hlaing, 18, 20, 137, 140, 142, 144, 146, 147–48
Mindon (King), 25
"Ministerial Burma," 13, 51n39
Ministry of Foreign Affairs, 33–35
Ministry of Religious Affairs, 28, 41
The Miracle of Mindfulness (Nhat Hanh), 117
mission schools, 26–27
MIT. *See* Myanmar Institute of Theology
Mitchell, John Murray, 173
Mon, 7, 8, 9–10, 11
Mon Unity Party, 143
"Moulvi-Yogi Aw-wada Sadan" (Shwe Hpi), 56n154
"Moulvi Yogi Sadan" (Maung Pan Nyo), 56n154
Moulvi-Yogi Sadan Vinnissaya Kyan (Alias Maung Sin), 56n154
Muller, Ludwig, 89
Muntzer, Thomas, 71–72
Muslims: Buddhists and, 42–49; in Myanmar, 7; in Pakistan, 170; riots against, 42; Rohingya, 45–46; Wirathu on, 169. *See also* Arakan Rohingya Salvation Army
Myanmar, 1; Anglo-Burmese wars in, 13, 23, 26; Baptists in, 4, 23–24, 29, 32; Board of Censorship in, 34; British colonial rule in, 11, 13, 26–27, 42, 45, 167; Buddhism as state religion in, 28–30; Buddhists in, 7–8; Burman Buddhists in, 4–5; call for transformation in, 175–89; capital moved in, 128, 153n68; "Caretaker Government" in, 147–48; cell phones in, 125, 132; Christianity introduced to, 11–12, 22–23, 51n36; Christians in, 4, 7; church building in, 34–35; civil war in, 12–13, 18; conflict between ethnic minorities and majority in, 12–21; constitution for, 15–17, 28, 29, 139–41, 156n113, 164, 166; as "country of particular concern," 33–34, 55n129; COVID-19 in, 144, 146–47, 171–72, 193n76; democratic government in, 28–31; demonetization in, 121, 125; diversity in, 2; "divide and rule" tactics in, 13; economic sanctions on, 20–21; education in, 35–36, 133–34; elections (1990) in, 126–28; elections (2015) in, 17–18, 37; elections (2020) in, 141–43, 144, 157n132; engaged Buddhism, British colonialism and, 118–19; engaged religious movement, society and, 132–37; English language in, 32; as ethnically and religiously pluralistic society, 7–49; ethnic cleansing in, 36, 46; ethnic groups in, 7; "Excluded Areas" in, 13, 51n46; foreigners expelled from, 32; "Frontier Areas" in, 15; Hinduism introduced to, 10–11; Hindus in, 7; India influence on, 7–8; Indian names in, 10–11, 50n21; innocent civilians killed in, 21, 53n87; interfaith forum in, 135–36; interfaith marriage in, 132–33; interfaith religious movements in, 4; International Day of Peace in, 134–35, 155n95; Islam introduced to, 11; *Kala* in, 178–79; military regime in, 33–37; "Ministerial Burma" in, 13, 15, 51n39; Ministry of Foreign Affairs in, 33–35; monarchical period in, 21–26; Monk uprising (1990) in, 126–28; Muslims in, 7, 14; natural resources in, 22, 31; pagodas in, 10–11, 34, 38, 41; politics of post 2015 elections in, 137–43; Protestant Churches in, 26, 32; racism in, 176–78; Red Bridge Incident in, 122, 151n33; religions in, 7; royal city in, 22–23, 24–25, 27; separation of church and state in, 164–68; social and religious engagement in, 3; socialist government in, 31–33; state of emergency in, 141, 156n121;

Index 237

students killed in, 122–23, 151n33; tea shops in, 122; transforming ethnic ethos in, 175–81; transforming religious ethos in, 181–89; Union of Myanmar, 12–14. *See also* Four Eights Uprising; Saffron Revolution; Spring Revolution (2021)

Myanmar Baptists, 4; Anabaptists and, 166; Burmese Baptist Convention for, 29; on separation of church and state, 159, 164; Theravada Buddhism and, 166–67

Myanmar Council of Churches, 29, 172, 193n78

Myanmar Institute of Theology (MIT), 181

Myanmar International Convention Center (MICC), 19

Myanmar military, 1–2, 4; against ethnic minority armed groups, 13; ministries controlled by, 47

Myanmar's Religion Act, 39, 55n147

Myconius, Friedrich, 78–79

Myint, Ni Ni, 11

Myint, Win, 140, 144, 145

Myint-U, Thant, 9, 25, 45, 50n20, 140, 178

Nagai, Makoto, 28

Nation, Mark Thiessen, 103

National Identity Card (NIC), 36

National League for Democracy (NLD), 1–2, 3, 17, 19, 20, 129, 131; Christian religious minorities and, 37–41; ethnic minority people for, 18; against Ma Ba Tha, 170; for Ma Ha Na, 170; Monk uprising (1990) and, 126–28; NCA endorsed by, 139; peacock for, 127, 152n60; policies of, 138; in 2015 general elections, 137; in 2020 general elections, 141–43, 144, 147, 157n132. *See also* Suu Kyi, Aung San

National Reconciliation and Peace Center (NRPC), 155n109

National Registration Card, 36

National Religious Minorities Alliance, 30

National Socialist German Student League, 87

Nationalsozialistische Deutsche Arbeiterpartei (NSDAP), 86, 108n3. *See also* Nazi regime

Nationalsozialistischer Deutscher Studentenbund. See National Socialist German Student League

National Unity Government (NUG), 145, 148, 149

National Verification Cards (NVC), 46

Nationwide Ceasefire Agreement (NCA), 2, 19–21, 139

Nat-Pye, 177, 195n114

Nat Shin Naung, 22

"The Nature of the Church" (Bonhoeffer, D.), 92–93

Nat worship, 10, 50n17

Nazi regime, 3, 86; on Aryans, 88, 89, 109n21; Barmen Confession of Faith against, 89–90; Bonhoeffer, D., political resistance against, 95–108; brown-shirted unit in, 87, 109n10; church controlled by, 89; Protestant churches and, 89; Roman Catholic Church and, 88–89; SA militia of, 87–88; violence of, 88; youth support of, 87. *See also* Hitler, Adolf

N' Ban La, 18–19

NCA. *See* Nationwide Ceasefire Agreement

Nelson, Stephen S., 160

Ne Win, 12, 30, 31, 122–23; against English language, 32; against ethnic minorities, 32–33; resignation of, 124

NIC. *See* National Identity Card

Nicolaitists, 61, 80n9

Niebuhr, Reinhold, 68, 100

Niemoller, Martin, 89

"1919 Act of Federated Shan States" (Myanmar), 13

238 *Index*

"1935 Burma Act" (Myanmar), 13
NLD. *See* National League for
Democracy
Al Noor Mosque, 168
NRPC. *See* National Reconciliation and
Peace Center
NSDAP. *See Nationalsozialistische
Deutsche Arbeiterpartei*
U Nu, 12, 28, 29–30, 31, 45, 187,
196n146
NUG. *See* National Unity Government
NVC. *See* National Verification Cards
Nyanissara, Ashin, 133
Nyan Win, 147
A-Nyeint, 179
Nyunt Shwe, 147

Obama, Barack, 20–21, 172
Ocasio-Cortez, Alexandria, 175
OIC. *See* Organization of Islamic
Conference
Omar, Ilhan, 175–76
On the Christian Baptism of Believers
(Hubmaier), 76
*An Open Letter on the Harsh Book
against the Peasants* (Luther), 72–73
Operation 7, 113n110
Organization of Islamic Conference
(OIC), 44
U Ottama, 118

Pacelli, Eugenio, 88
Pagan, 8, 9–10
pagodas, 10–11, 34, 38, 41
Pahl, Jon, 180–81
Pakistan, 170
Pali language, 10, 34, 41
Palmerston, Mahn, 172, 193n78
Panglong Agreement (1947), 12–13, 17,
21, 51n37
Panglong Conference, 4, 13, 15, 16,
52n58
Papen, Franz von, 88
Pastors' Emergency League, 89
patta nikkujjana kamma, 130, 154n79

Paya, 42, 56n154
PDF. *See* People's Defense Force
Peasants' War (1524–1525): background
history of, 69–70; Luther on, 70–73;
"Twelve Articles of the Peasants in
Swabia" in, 70–71, 81n52; unity
lacking in, 73
Pelikan, Jaroslav J., 162
People's Defense Force (PDF), 145
People's Party, 143
People's Volunteer Organization
(PVO), 17
Phone Maw, 122
Pius XI (Pope), 89
Po, San C., 177
Popham, Peter, 46
Pressley, Ayanna S., 175
Preus, Herman A., 162
Price, Jonathan, 24–25
Protestant churches, 32; missions of, 11;
in Myanmar, 26; Nazi regime and, 89
Proud Boys, 176
PVO. *See* People's Volunteer
Organization
Pyu, 10, 50n23

Raiser, Konrad, 36–37
Rajashekar, J. Paul William, 62–63
Rakhine State, 7; Advisory Commission
on, 44–46; ARSA on, 47; economic
struggle in, 48; education in, 48–49;
inter-communal violence between
Buddhists and Muslims in, 42–49;
international organizations in, 44;
Muslim community in, 45; residency
cards in, 46; Urdu in, 48–49
Rangoon Arts and Sciences
University, 122
Rangoon Institute of Technology
(RIT), 122
Red Bridge Incident, 122, 151n33
Reformation movement, 2, 61, 74,
82n71
Religions for Peace Myanmar (RfP-M),
133, 136–37

Index 239

Religious Conversion Law (2015), 43, 170, 200

religious minorities. *See* Christian religious minorities

replacement theory, 168–69, 192n53

Reublin, Wilhelm, 74–75, 76

RIT. *See* Rangoon Institute of Technology

Robbins, Ephram, 160

Rohingya, 45–46. *See also* Rakhine State

Roman Catholic Church, 2, 32; concubinage in, 61, 80n9; "courtship" model of, 22; indulgences in, 60–61; Luther on, 63–65; in Middle Ages, 59–60; missionaries for, 9, 11–12, 22–23; Nazi regime and, 88–89; simony in, 60

SAC. *See* State Administration Council

Saffron Revolution, 3; alms refused in, 130, 132, 154n79; Four Eights Uprising and, 131–32; issues in, 128–29; protesters detained in, 131, 154n83; Suu Kyi visited during, 130–31, 154n81

Sahayadoss, Santhosh J., 187

Sakhong, Lian H., 13, 187

Sanctorum Communio (Bonhoeffer, D.), 102–3

Sandar Win, 32

sangha, 21–22, 53n89

Sasse, Ben, 170

sati, 173, 193n86

Sattler, Michael, 75

U Saw, 14, 16–17, 52n63

Saw Augurlion, 188

Saw Christopher, 38–39

Saw Maung, 124–25, 126–27, 147

Saw Shwe Lin, 172, 193n78

Saw Tha Din, 194n114

Saw Yaw Han, John, 172, 193n78

Schappeler, Christoph, 70, 81n52

Schleitheim Articles, 75–76

Sein Lwin, 124

Senanayake, Dudley, 28

separation of church and state: in America, 159–64; American Baptists on, 160–61; Jefferson view on, 159–61; limits of religious freedom and, 168–75; Lutherans on, 162–64; in Myanmar, 164–68

Shan, 7, 13

Shin Arahan, 8, 9–10

U Shwe Baw, 14

Shwe Hpi, 42, 56n154

Shwe Ngong, 24

Siegrist, Anthony G., 103

Signer, Mike, 169

Silverstein, Joseph, 26

Simon Pau Khan En, 165

Sixth Buddhist Council, 185–86, 196n146

Sixth Great Buddhist Council, 28

SLORC. *See* State Law and Order Restoration Council

Smith, Donald E., 8, 26, 173

Smith, Martin, 152n40

socialism, 31–33

Soe Win, 39

SPDC. *See* State Peace and Development Council

Spiro, Melford E., 21–22

Spring Revolution (2021), 3; ASEAN and, 146; "Caretaker Government" and, 147–48; CDM in, 144–45, 149; electoral fraud claims in, 144; goal of, 149; NUG in, 145, 149; propaganda in, 145; protesters in, 144–45; SAC in, 144–45; as unique, 149; violence in, 144–45, 148–49

Stalsett, Gunnar, 136

State Administration Council (SAC), 144, 145

State Law and Order Restoration Council (SLORC), 3, 121, 125; Monk uprising (1990) and, 126–28; Order No. 1/90 by, 126–27

240

Index

State Peace and Development Council (SPDC), 34, 139, 153n72
State Religion Promotion Act (Myanmar), 31
State Religious Advisory Commission, 28–29
State Sangha Maha Nayaka Committee (Ma Ha Na), 39, 41, 55n144, 134, 170
Stellvertretung, 102
St. John's Episcopal Church, 170–71
Stumme, John R., 162, 190n25
stupa, 8, 38–39
Stylo, Saw, 38
Sugirtharajah, R. S., 184–85
Supayalat (Queen), 50n14
Suu Kyi, Aung San, 1–2, 3–4, 17, 43–44, 139, 140–41, 144–45, 180; attacks on, 120–21, 151nn25–26; on Christians, 189; criticism about, 46–47; on democracy, 142; against discrimination, 134; as engaged Buddhist, 119–21; on Four Eights Uprising, 123; house arrest of, 119–20, 126, 128, 130–31, 154n81; on meditation, 119; for multiparty democracy, 123; NLD led by, 37; pragmatic pacifism of, 20; presidency barred for, 137, 155n106; on religion and politics as inseparable, 167–68; on SLORC, 121, 151n29; as state counselor, 137–38; on tolerance of Buddhists, 186; at Twenty-First-Century Panglong Conference, 18–19; Wirathu on, 169
Svendsbye, Lloyd, 162
Swan Arr Shin militia, 129–30, 131, 153n72

Table Talk (Luther), 78, 109n27
Taing-Yintha, 178–79
Tarrant, Brenton, 168–69, 192n53
Tatmadaw, 18
Tegenfeldt, Herman G., 32–33
Temporal Authority (Luther), 66–68

Temporary Resident Card (TRC), 46
Ten Commandments, 27
Tetzel, John, 60–61
Thakin Ba Sein, 14
Thakin Chit, 14
Thakin Mya, 14
Thandar Shwe, 153n70
Than Htay, 144
Than Myint Oo, 172, 193n78
Than Shwe, 12, 127, 151n26, 153n70
Than Tun, 14
Thapeik-hmaunk, 167
Thein Sein, 13, 42–43, 44, 134, 142, 156n25, 156n113, 170
"The Theological Foundation of the Work of the World Alliance" (Bonhoeffer, D.), 105, 113n104
Theology of Two Kingdoms (Luther), 2–3, 4, 5n2; *The Babylonian Captivity of the Church* in, 65; Bonhoeffer, D., reception of, 90–95; *To the Christian Nobility of the German Nation Concerning the Reform of the Christian Estate* in, 63–64; *The Freedom of a Christian* in, 65; resistance and, 63–69; *Temporal Authority* in, 66–68
Theravada Buddhism, 8, 10–11, 41, 128; food offering in, 129–30; Myanmar Baptists and, 166–67. *See also* Saffron Revolution
Thibaw (King), 25, 26, 50n14, 50n20
Thida Htwe, 44
Thonze (Prince), 25
Thura Aung Ko, 136
U Thuzana, 38, 41
"Thy Kingdom Come" (Bonhoeffer, D.), 91, 101
Tierney, Brian, 59
Tin Aye, 141
Tin Oo, 120–21
U Tin Tut, 14
Tlaib, Rashida, 175
Topich, William J., 153n68

To the Christian Nobility of the German Nation Concerning the Reform of the Christian Estate (Luther), 63–64
Trager, Helen G., 182
TRC. *See* Temporary Resident Card
A Treatise on the New Testament (Luther), 76–77
Treaty of Versailles, 85–86
Tree of Life Synagogue, 168
Trump, Donald J., 37, 55n139, 170–71, 175–76, 193n69, 194n99
Tun Aung Chain, 8
Tun Kyi, 127
Tun Thein, 39
"Twelve Articles of the Peasants in Swabia," 70–71, 81n52
Twenty-First-Century Panglong Conference (2016), 17–19, 21, 139

ultranationalist Buddhists. *See* Ma Ba Tha
al-Umari, Hussein, 169
Umbel, Daniel P., 103
Unam Sanctam (Pope Boniface VIII), 59
Union Ceasefire Joint Monitoring Conference, 138
Union of Burma. *See* Myanmar
Union Solidarity and Development Association (USDA), 120–21, 129–30, 151nn25–26, 153n72
Union Solidarity and Development Party (USDP), 1, 17, 19, 37, 42–43, 134, 141–42, 186; electoral fraud claimed by, 144; in 2015 general elections, 137; in 2020 general elections, 147; for Wirathu, 169
"United States International Religious Freedom Act of 1998," 33
Universal Declaration of Human Rights, 174
Urdu, 48–49
US Commission on International Religious Freedom, 33–34, 55n129

USDA. *See* Union Solidarity and Development Association
USDP. *See* Union Solidarity and Development Party

Van Thio, Henry, 37, 188–89
VGastro Bar and Restaurant, 39
Vietnam, 116–17
Vishnu, 10

Ward or Village Tract Administration Law, 40, 56n150
Werner, Friedrich, 97
"What is the Church?" (Bonhoeffer), 98
Whitford, David M., 162
WHO. *See* World Health Organization
Williams, Reggie L., 95
Williams, Roger, 160
Wilson, Horace Hayman, 173
Win, Kanbawza, 36
Wink, Walter, 53n77
Wirathu, Ashin, 37, 55n139, 132; arrest warrant for, 169; banning of, 134; hate-speech of, 169; against Muslims, 43, 57n165; surrender of, 169–70, 192n63; on Suu Kyi, 169
World Council of Churches, 36
World Health Organization (WHO), 174, 193n87
World War I, 85–86, 96
The Worthy Ordinance for the Princely City of Wittenberg, 62
Wunna Maung Lwin, 148

Yanaung, 50n14
Yangon, 10–11, 27
Yegar, Moshe, 11, 42, 49
Ye Lwin, 39
Yusof, Erywan, 148

Zahau, Cheery, 177–78
Zahre Lian, 30
Zaw Min Tun, 137
Zaw Win, 40
zayat, 23–24, 54n94

Zeya Phyo, 43
Zwe Min Aung, 145

Zwilling, Gabriel, 62
Zwingli, Ulrich, 74–75, 82n71

About the Author

Pa Yaw is a lecturer in church history at Myanmar Institute of Theology, Insein, Yangon, Myanmar (Burma). He received a MATS (master of arts in theological studies) from Princeton Theological Seminary and a PhD from United Lutheran Seminary, Philadelphia. His interest in religion and politics in Myanmar comes from his own experiences of the social, political, and religious conflicts that have challenged modern Myanmar society and an aspiration to build a peaceful society through the common efforts of socially engaged people in Myanmar, which is characterized by ethnic diversity and religious pluralism. He is one of the contributors of *Baptist Beliefs and Practices* written in Burmese in 2013, published by the Myanmar Baptist Convention.